The Invisible Cage

Stanford Studies in Middle Eastern and Islamic Societies and Cultures

The Invisible Cage

SYRIAN MIGRANT WORKERS IN LEBANON

John Chalcraft

Stanford University Press
Stanford, California
2009

Stanford University Press

Stanford, California

©2009 by the Board of Trustees of the Leland Stanford Junior University. All rights reserved.

Printed in the United States of America on acid-free, archival-quality paper

Library of Congress Cataloging-in-Publication Data

Chalcraft, John T., 1970–
    The invisible cage : Syrian migrant workers in Lebanon / John Chalcraft.
        p. cm. — (Stanford studies in Middle Eastern and Islamic societies and cultures)
    Includes bibliographical references and index.
    ISBN 978-0-8047-5825-3 (cloth : alk. paper) — ISBN 978-0-8047-5826-0 (pbk. : alk. paper)
        1. Alien labor, Syrian — Lebanon — History. 2. Lebanon—Emigration and immigration—
History. 3. Syria—Emigration and immigration—History. I. Title. II. Series.
    HD8659.C48 2008
    331.6'2569105692—dc22

                                                                                    2008025748

Typeset by Publishers' Design and Production Services, Inc. in Minion.

To Radwan, his family, friends, and to all those Syrians
who have toiled in Lebanon

"What am I, a man or a resource?"

Ralph Ellison, *Invisible Man*

CONTENTS

LIST OF ILLUSTRATIONS

ACKNOWLEDGMENTS

IN WRITING this book I have incurred many debts. I owe the most profound gratitude to the trust of the many Syrians who had worked or were working in Lebanon and were willing to give up their time for interviews and discussion. I would like especially to mention Abd al-Qadir, Abed, Adib Mahrus, Armange, Hanna Awwad, Hanna Butros, Ibrahim, Jo Farah, Joseph, Nazir, Omar, Radwan, and Tony Elias. Their generosity, ambition, humor, courage, and endurance are humbling. Above all, I would like to pay tribute for their help on so many levels to Radwan, to whom this book is dedicated, his family, Abd al-Qadir, and Omar.

From start to finish, my other debts are heavy. I am grateful to Yasir Suleiman, who suggested the topic in early 2003. Talal al-Tahhan patiently helped and improved my grasp of Syrian colloquial. Kifah Hanna deserves special thanks for showing such generosity in taking me to her home village in Syria, introducing me to her family and friends, and then giving up much time in invaluable research assistance. I also thank Aziz and Laila for their wonderful hospitality and good company. Al-Hajj Ali and his extended family in Syria also deserve my gratitude for their wonderful hospitality and tolerance. Thanks are due to Khaled Malas for the significant research assistance he undertook. In Lebanon, I am particularly grateful to Samah Idriss and Kirsten Scheid, who welcomed me and proceeded to open their address books on my behalf. Thanks are due to Jihane Sfeir Khayat for introducing me to Abu Subhi in Ra's al-Nab'a and to his workers. Mona Harb gave me intellectual input and direction, and contacts in the early days of research. I am grateful to Rita Yazigi for her time and patience, for her witty insight into terrain about which I knew little, and for her help in the translation of some of the interviews. Issam Ayyad's small yet rich bookshop in Hamra, Beirut, his humor and courtesy, and his impromptu seminars on the history of the Left in Lebanon have left a lasting mark. Mas'ud Daher in Beirut and Abdallah Hanna in Damascus were both kind enough to welcome me into their homes and share their significant knowledge on the social history of the region. I thank Ghassan Ma'asri for translation of recorded interviews. I am also grateful to Trad Hamadeh for taking time to meet and help me in the southern suburbs of Beirut in a convivial café now destroyed. I also give a special mention to Jens Hanssen, long-standing inspiration and the ultimate source of many contacts in Beirut.

I am grateful indeed to Ralph Bodenstein, Christian Henderson, and Jim Quilty for their consideration, conversation, and insight, and for putting me up for several glorious months in the Peoples' Republic of Qasqas.

Numerous others helped out in ways large and small, both during fieldwork and writing up, and I thank them all: Mona Abdel Khalek, Abu Subhi, Diana Allen, Simon Assaf, Ali Atassi, Jihad Azour, Fahed Agha al-Barazi, Fadi Bardawil, Karim-Philipp Eid-Sabbagh, Emmanuel, Mona Fawwaz, Rania Ghosn, Carol Hakim, Trad Hamadeh, Sami Harb, Bernhard Hillenkamp, Thibaut Jaulin, Ray Jureidini, Ali Kadri, Hasan Karayem, Tarif Khalidi, Isam Khalifa, Tristan Khayat, Nadia Latif, Ziyad Majed, Fatima al-Mana', Franck Mermier, Yasser Munif, Omar Nashabe, Tony Naufal, Lin Noueihed, Yahya Sadowski, Fawwaz Traboulsi, Omar Traboulsi, Abeer Saksouk-Sasso, Reem Saleh, Maher al-Yamani, Michael Young, and Ahmad al-Za'atari. I thank with much appreciation those who engaged significantly with the argument of the book, in one or two cases perhaps without realizing it, or read and critiqued parts or all of the manuscript: As'ad Abu Khalil, Sharad Chari, Manu Goswami, Jens Hanssen, Laleh Khalili, Timothy Mitchell, Martha Mundy, and Yaseen Noorani. Barbara Drieskens deserves a special mention because the title of the book was, in significant measure, her idea. I am particularly grateful to the peer-reviewers at Stanford University Press: Ussama Makdisi and Elizabeth Picard were incredibly thorough and insightful, they saved me from many errors and ambiguities, and caused me to make some important changes to the argument. I am privileged to have mentors as brilliant, humane, and supportive as Michael Gilsenan and Zachary Lockman, whose intellectual influence continues to loom large, and who both helped out in numerous ways during this research.

The project could not have been undertaken without funding from the Carnegie Trust for Universities of Scotland, the British Academy, the Council for British Research on the Levant, and the Leverhulme Trust. Both the University of Edinburgh and the London School of Economics and Political Science were good enough to match buy-out funding with an equivalent period of Research Leave, an invaluable support. Stanford University Press, Kate Wahl, and the production team, especially Gail Farrar and Emily Smith, have been enormously efficient, accommodating, and friendly throughout the process of commissioning this manuscript and bringing it to press.

Finally, I thank Laleh Khalili, partner, lover, wife, and friend, source of intellectual inspiration, critical insight, ideas, contacts, and support in so many forms, through good times and bad. Thanks to Laleh, her generosity of spirit, and our joyous daughter May, not to mention Pablo who is soon to arrive in this world, life continues to be worth living and books worth writing.

The Invisible Cage

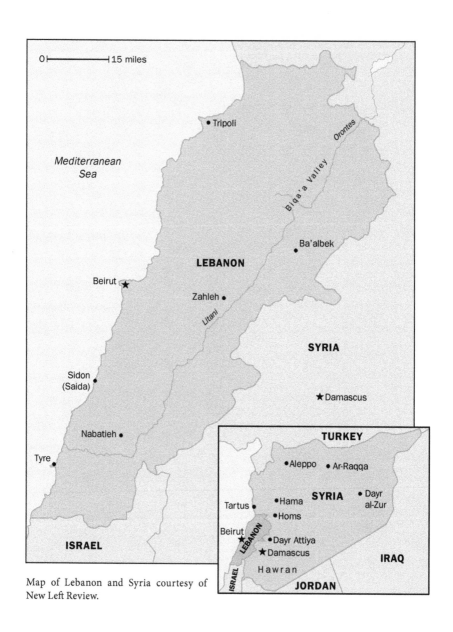

Map of Lebanon and Syria courtesy of
New Left Review.

INTRODUCTION

It is only because miners sweat their guts out that superior
persons can remain superior. . . . All of us really owe the
comparative decency of our lives to poor drudges underground.
—Orwell, ***Down the Mine***[1]

BETWEEN THE SIXTEENTH AND NINETEENTH CENTURIES, "labor shortage!" was
the constant lament of European colonists, slave-owners, colonial planters,
and mining operators.[2] Transnational and transregional laborers were usually
seized through military force, slavery, "coolie" labor, and indenture. From the
Cape of Good Hope to the Caribbean, from Shanghai to Peru, migrant workers were connected to processes of production and accumulation through directly exercised forms of overt physical and legal coercion. Many an astute
nineteenth-century thinker had not even considered the possibility that one
day perennial colonial labor shortage might turn to labor surplus.[3] Yet, as the
nineteenth century wore on, complaints about labor shortages were heard less
and less. Even indentured labor no longer seemed necessary to many, as persons prepared to sell long hours of hard, stigmatized, and disciplined labor for
low wages, or to work in crowded and competitive self-employment, started to
leave Ireland, southern and eastern Europe, Asia, Africa, and Latin America in
tens of millions.[4] The hundreds of thousands of Ottoman subjects—Lebanese
and Syrian—who left the eastern Mediterranean province of the *bilad ash-
sham* for the Americas, West Africa, and beyond between the 1870s and 1920s
were merely one group amid this more general mass migration. By the First
World War, the world had entered an epoch of seemingly limitless supplies of
international migrant "labor power."[5] In this new context, far from expending resources seizing slaves by force in the tropics, and then in maintaining
and controlling them, metropolitan receiving countries started to speak the
language of "overpopulation" and the "yellow peril." Governments began putting up barriers, developing guest-worker systems to prevent settlement, and,

ultimately, in the 1920s and 1930s, restricting entry altogether.[6] Thus the age, extending in various recognizable forms to the present, of so-called voluntary, spontaneous, self-initiated, and economic migration on a transnational scale, was born.[7]

Why were the whip of the slave master, property in the person, or the formally enforced rules and contracts of indenture no longer necessary in the mass production of menial labor involving long hours, low pay, hard work, obedience, stigma, and insecurity?[8] What was the nature of these forms of apparently "economic" force?[9] Why was it that what had once required coercion was now achieved through apparently voluntary effort, or via ostensibly economic and indirect means? How were legally free persons and their energies now bound to a migratory labor regime and structures of transnational accumulation? Through a detailed and as yet untold history of a prolonged case of circular labor migration between Syria and Lebanon, this book argues that existing answers to the question of "economic force" are unsatisfactory, and suggests an alternative.

Histories of migration drawing on theories of modernization and economic development, as well as migrant-centered, agency-recovering accounts inspired by cultural studies and postcolonialism, arguably efface the forms of power at work in the migratory labor regime. Accounts drawing on the Marxist tradition, furthermore, are problematic in their tendency to automate processes of labor subordination: Migrants are not simply human jetsam and flotsam—faceless stocks, pools, and reserves maintained or drained by the hydraulics of capitalism and imperialism. An important failing of existing approaches is that they only inadequately link agents to structures and vice versa, thereby missing and eviscerating the operations of the forms of agency-incorporating control and discipline in which I am interested. Strong forms of both agency *and* structural determination are heavily present throughout the history related in this book: the bold, masculinist and pan-Arabist claims of dignified workers engaged in remunerative labor, the acquisition of skills and the broadening of horizons, the personal satisfactions of providing for kith and kin against the odds, the harsh pressures of family expectations and cash and land hunger in villages on the Syrian plains, grinding exploitation and physical abuse at work, menial indignity and slum living in Lebanon, lives of poverty, the bitter frustrations of failed projects, and prolonged exilic rotation, violence, expulsion, and killing.

This history of an almost completely unknown but important case of migration and return combines the methods of ethnography and social history. Through a particular appropriation of the concepts of hegemony and elective affinities, it examines and explores the ways in which migrants are unfixed, made mobile, channeled, enmeshed, and subordinated within objectifying structures of accumulation by combinations of coercion and consent, repression and choice. Whereas the standard justification for the exploitation of migrant workers by host populations is that they "choose to come here," in what ways are these choices, which are undoubtedly made at some level, embedded in structures that distinguish them from empowerment? I argue that while forms of direct and unmediated discipline disappeared from the world of migrant labor, in their place came the direct and indirect discipline of a constructed "labour market," comprised less of the benign forces of the "invisible hand" and more of the ensnaring operations of an invisible cage.

STORIES ABOUT MIGRANTS

Existing scholarship on migration, whether based on conventional economics, Marxism, modernization theory, economic sociology, or cultural studies, has done remarkably little to explore the particular work of hegemonic incorporation in which I am interested. In conventional economics, migrants motivated by rational calculations as to individual material gain (based on Smith's natural human "propensity to truck and barter") flow from labor-abundant, capital-poor areas to labor-scarce, capital-rich regions in accordance with the operations of supply and demand. Migratory processes are seen to be rooted in specialization, the deepening division of labor, and the development of cash exchange; they contribute through factor mobility to wealth creation. Free movement is expected to equilibrate wages and profit rates in the long term and diminish macroeconomic and demographic imbalances. Migrants' position in host societies is largely determined by their own choices, market advantages, and skill endowments.[10]

In this view, migratory processes and social relations more generally are constructed out of the rational choices of exchanging acquisitive individuals who are, in principle, equally potent. As such, inequality, coercion, politics, alienation, and structural power tend to disappear from view, and the multiply determined and purposeful social subject is reduced to a *homo economicus*. This approach misses what Francis Wilson called "the importance of the distribution of power in moulding the forces THAT shape even a micro-economic structure and determine the range of choices within it."[11] Social relations are transformed into relations between quantities and objects—Marx's commodity fetishism. Conventional economics ultimately comprise a powerful ratification of economic inequality and of what Friedrich Engels saw as the "domination over men *by virtue of*, and *through the intermediary of*, the domination over things."[12] The language of choice and exchange is better seen therefore as part of the unfinished and unstably "fixed" hegemonic apparatus of the market economy, rather than an analytical tool for actually understanding the hegemonic incorporation of migrant subjects.

The depoliticizing, uncritical, and technocratic stance of conventional economics has long been opposed by research inspired by Marxism. Here, the circulation and exploitation of migrant workers is understood in terms of the development of capitalism, imperialism, and neo-colonialism.[13] Marx ridiculed Adam Smith's rosy account of labor market formation in which "the idyllic reigns from time immemorial." In place of exchange and specialization, Marx spoke of conquest, enslavement, murder, plunder, and force, which, during the prehistory of capital, divorced direct producers from control over means of production, shattered feudal bonds of protection, and left immediate producers with no way to live except by selling their labor power to capitalists controlling the means of production, a sale often involving migration.[14] Once capitalism was established, its fundamental secular tendencies—a shift in the organic composition of capital reducing both the share of variable capital (wages), and the number of surplus hours extracted per unit of capital, reductions that imply a declining rate of profit and employment—create a floating population, an industrial reserve army forced to migrate in search of increasingly elusive wage labor.[15] A related reading links mass migration to capitalism's tendency to undergo crises of overaccumulation, boom and bust, and its fundamental instability and constant restructuring, forcing masses of people to move in search of employment.[16] Other Marxist accounts understand migration less in terms of the operations of "pure" capitalism, but in terms of how capitalism, linked to imperialism, distorted development in the colonial and Third World by imperial policy and surplus extraction, preventing normal capitalist development and forcing those unable to find a living to migrate to the world of advanced capitalism.[17] A variation of this account understands circulatory migrant labor as a subsidy to advanced capitalism, in which social costs of reproduction are defrayed in preserved-dissolved forms of precapitalist domestic community in the sending areas.[18]

These profoundly structuralist readings are problematic because they automate mechanisms of circulation and subordination. The question of how purposeful and acculturated subjects are articulated to objectifying structures is sidelined. Migrants are discharged and absorbed as jetsam and flotsam according to the hydraulics of capitalism, class, reification, and commodity fetishism. In this schema, the discussion of the unfinished cultural and political work of relations of subordination and domination, the qualities of migrants—their ideas, projects, purposes, subjectivities, moral economies, household dynamics, and political statuses and relationships—become epiphenomenal. If conventional economics stresses only choice, structuralist Marxism sharply underplays the decisions and initiative of migrants themselves. There is no sense that subjectivity and politics operate substantively to constitute multiple forms of accumulation. What matters are the laws of capital accumulation, the actions of capitalists and imperialists, or the actions of those who set out as an organized working class to overthrow those capitalists. Other forms of agency become residual, obstructive, unscientific, and backward. Ultimately, in much Marxism, the problem is that there is no subject left to hegemonize.

A homologous problem appears in migration studies inspired by linear and teleological forms of modernization theory. Adam Smith linked the free movement of factors of production (including labor) to a secular shift from societies that were poor, rude, barbarous, and miserable to those that were wealthy, flourishing, and civilized. The languages of modernization and Orientalism alike have depicted both migrants and sending societies as mired in tradition, backwardness, overpopulation, and stagnation, and described migrant journeys and transitions to a usually Western modernity embodying a better life—advanced, rational, mobile, and free.[19] In this context, the key task for migrants is assimilation into host societies, conceived problematically as relatively homogeneous and internally harmonious.[20] In these accounts, in which dominant values and overly linear historical trajectories are both assumed and naturalized, the problem of hegemonic incorporation disappears from view. Where subject positions, social structures, and the direction of historical change is given in advance, there is little room for considering the complex processes that construct dominant order and link active and diverse subjects to them.

Economic sociology eschewed the historical metanarratives and political commitments of Marxism and modernization theory alike, and sought to modify the disembedded economism of conventional economics. Economic sociologists have explored, ostensibly in a value-free mode, the importance of social context by adopting Max Weber's notion of socially oriented economic action, and appropriating the Hungarian economist Karl Polanyi's concept of embeddedness.[21] Core-periphery linkages (transportation, media, recruitment agencies) are said to help account for why migrant flows are strongly associated with structures established during a bygone age of colonial rule. Social networks play an important role in structuring, sustaining, and even initiating migrant flows. Social capital, not just individual market advantage, plays an equally decisive role in upward mobility, entrepreneurship, and success in the receiving country. The structure and nature of the job market, such as in the formation of a "secondary sector" for migrants, is also seen to be important.[22]

Nonetheless, issues of hegemony, and power relations more broadly, remain curiously absent and undertheorized in the economic sociology of migration. Although some attention is paid to racial prejudice, political indifference or even hostility, colonialism, and imperialism either barely exist, or are considered an irrelevant artifact of some distant past. This lens is partly allowed to stand unchallenged by a relentless Westcentrism or a focus on the interests of host societies. Piore's seminal book, for example, fails even to mention the global South in the list of phenomena explicitly excluded from his theory. Piore identified the central problem in migration processes not as the exploitation of cheap labor, nor as the subordination or racialization of those struggling to reestablish structures of community and identification. Instead, according to Piore, the so-called immigrant problem is the fact that conflicts develop between native labor and immigrants once the latter, usually after settlement processes are well developed, start to seek out the jobs that natives want.[23] For Piore, the key problem with migration, in other words, is that at some point, settled or second-generation migrants want to escape the world of menial, humiliating, and dirty labor, which conflicts with the interests not only of native labor but also of industrial society at large. Industrial society is seen to require a "secondary labor market" as a matter of demand-side necessity, conceived in homogenizing and objectivist terms. The problem turns out to be one of assimilation read in terms of the host society's "interests."

Moreover, for all the emphasis on social context, contemporary global migration is mostly conceived of by economic sociologists as spontaneous or voluntary, as if there was no larger economic power structure within which transnational migration, and the choices that are undoubtedly made by migrants at the immediate and apparent level, is embedded. There is no sense of how choice can be part of a larger hegemony. Also, entrepreneurship, in Schumpeterian mode, is often seen as the golden achievement of those migrants ready to manipulate social networks and exploit forms of social capital. There appears to be no critical awareness here of how the model of the subject as entrepreneur is complicit with the ideal capitalist subject, manipulating relations of production and commodities in order to turn money into more money according to Marx's famous formula, M-C-M'. In many ways, "the economy" retains its objectivity, autonomy, and naturalized status in much economic sociology, in spite of the aspiration to embeddedness and social context. The active cultural and political work of hegemonic incorporation is thus rendered invisible as a serious problem. Indicative is how the virtually unlimited global supply of migrants is noted but generally passed over in silence in Piore's account.[24]

Cultural and postcolonial studies, eschewing the positivism and empiricism of conventional economics and economic sociology, and skeptical of the grand narratives of Marxism and modernization theory alike, opened new areas of inquiry in migration studies. Migrants were read in antifoundational and sometimes celebratory mode as hybrids, agents, and boundary-crossers. Cultural historians and others aimed to recover agency, voice, subjectivity, identity, and "positionality," thereby elucidating and interpreting the more pluralized and multiply-situated experiences of subaltern migrants.[25] Khater's important and richly historical work on Lebanese return migrants, for example, set out to capture "the humanity of the people involved," and how rather than moving "from one pre-established historical evolutionary step to the next, these emigrants shaped their own world in a myriad of ways."[26] In place of strong causal models, cultural studies preferred expression, voice, representation, interpretation, and identity.[27] In place of grand macrological abstraction were the micrological, "the everyday," and the subjective. Migrant identities were made complicated in these forms of rewriting. Transmigrants, for example, were neither those assimilating to a dominant culture nor those involved in rotational migration, but those with social networks and forms of home and identity located in more than one national culture.[28] Instead of migrants as mutes or proletarians tossed passively on the currents of history, one found active subjects deploying strategies, which were in turn embedded in and informed by social meaning, local communities, honor codes, gender, sexuality, consumption patterns, household structures, and so on.

The interpretive and sometimes celebratory recovery of agency, however, tends to omit, underplay, or place on one side the objectifying structures of military, political, or economic power and related forms of alienation and oppression. The discovery of the migrant subaltern as agent and dignified social subject making choices and struggling among circumstances is too easily conflated with the idea of the subaltern as fundamentally empowered, integrated, and in charge of his or her destiny.[29] Khater's work, for example, includes little sense of how the creative mixing and matching of tradition and modernity by return migrants reproduced civilizational hierarchies or new categories of national exclusion back home on Mt. Lebanon. The assault on determinism and teleology, and an expressive and individualized approach to culture, too easily morphs into the dissolution of social power *tout court*. It is as if the sinking of the ship of Marxism dragged the problem of economic power down with it.[30] The problem of how purposeful subjects are instrumentalized in the construction of political economy and of objectifying and radically unequal structures of accumulation is lost from view. The notion of hegemonic incorporation becomes elusive at best and meaningless at worst.

More fruitful, arguably, than the standard works in conventional economics, Marxism, modernization theory, economic sociology, and cultural studies are those approaches that take seriously structure and agency on the one hand and political economy and culture on the other. A number of studies assume that unfinished processes of accumulation and exploitation are important, but neither shape from the outside, nor simply constrain, cultural meanings and social and political relations, but work *through* them. In Gonzalez and Fernandez's work, for example, the Bracero Program of 1942–1964, in which millions of male Mexicans worked as farmhand guest-workers in southern United States, was gendered from top to bottom. It was designed for men who could both handle "man's work" and who were attached to families in Mexico and hence would return without "problems." Likewise, the more recent *maquila* programs, developed to provide labor to Export Processing Zones, were designed for women, who were thought to be cheaper and more submissive than men in this kind of work.[31] To give another example, Catherine

Choy links race, nationality, gender, and class in the making of international Filipino professional nurse migration to the United States from the late 1960s.[32] In her work, the culture of migration, the practices of recruiters, the forms of exploitation, the Americanized hospital training system in the Philippines that prepares Filipino women to work in the United States, and the racialization of social hierarchy that did not end in 1946 but continues to shape practice are all important. Such approaches, in which accumulation is combined and uneven, and the economy and migratory processes an ongoing construction, seem to agree with Geoff Eley's important claim that "between [objectivist] social history and [subjectivist] cultural history, there is really no need to choose."[33] This is because political economy often works through culture and social relations. My own approach links structures and agents, meaning and political economy, and coercion and consent via a particular version of the notion of hegemony.

HEGEMONY AND ELECTIVE AFFINITIES

Since the writings of Antonio Gramsci, the concept of hegemony has long served historians and theorists seeking to escape forms of materialism and determinism in the Marxian tradition. The notion of hegemony points in diverse ways to the notion that systems of domination derive their power not from simple repression but from channeling and harnessing the agency of their subjects. Scholars of migration (as opposed to those of multiculturalism and social diversity), however, have not made much of the concept, perhaps surprisingly, given the numerous accounts that challenge the simple notion of voluntary migration. A particular appropriation of the notion, however, can shed light on the topic of "voluntary" or "economic" migration, in which choices are undoubtedly made by purposeful subjects. The great advantage here of the notion of hegemony over that of ideology is that it takes purposeful subjects seriously and assumes that they are not simply dupes suffering from false consciousness or from what Marx called the "idiocy of rural life."[34] Hegemony opens up a space between conventional economics and cultural studies on the one side, in which choices are either disembedded from structure, depoliticized, and/or equated with empowerment, and Marxism on the other side, in which precious few historically significant choices are actually made by migrants.

Gramsci understood hegemony above all as the moral and intellectual leadership of a fundamental class (either the bourgeoisie or the proletariat) over subaltern social groups.[35] The use of hegemony here is somewhat different. Whereas capitalism has arguably always been far too differentiating, acculturated, and combined and uneven, especially when considered transnationally, to generate fundamental classes burdened in advance with different versions of social leadership and emancipation, surplus-generating processes of accumulation based on the labor of diverse social subjects are nonetheless a structural feature of order.[36] My interest, therefore, is not in understanding how subaltern social groups accept the hegemony of a given fundamental social class, but instead in how the diverse subjectivities of purposeful and acculturated social subjects are connected to and work to reinforce objective (transnational) structures of accumulation and power.

Hegemony in the formulation adopted here, perhaps surprisingly, is not about popular consent to dominant arrangements. Subaltern groups, by virtue of their powerlessness, are rarely asked whether they agree to dominant structures. Where agreement is thought to exist, it may be simply expedient, it may be temporary, it may be feigned, it may miss the point, it may be irrelevant, or it may suddenly change. The essence of hegemony is the existence of situations in which subaltern subjects agree to something much narrower and more localized or completely different to the totality of dominant structures, but thereby unwittingly reinforce those structures. In other words, even strong areas of *doxa* or agreed common sense—that which goes without saying—are not always necessary for effective hegemony. Hegemonic structures, instead, are effective through their ability to incorporate, harness, and subordinate the activities, energies, and choices of diverse social subjects, positions, purposes, projects, and ideas. The forms of economic power and discipline under investigation here are hegemonic in this sense. Migrant energies are harnessed to surplus-generating processes through combinations of coercion and consent, repression and choice, and both control over persons through the ownership of things, and the acquisition of things through the control over persons. Hegemony invites us to think of the economy neither as a domain of choice nor a self-generating system of laws, but as an unfinished structure of power.

The notion of "elective affinities" sheds much light on the intended meaning here. An apparent contradiction in terms, the fundamental idea concerns how choices (forms of election) forge "affinities," or strong, durable, structural relationships, and that this process involves unintended consequences and forms of oppression. In the eighteenth century, chemical meaning of elective affinities (*Wahlverwandtschaft*), substances *a*, *b*, and *c*, for example, might have an affinity to combine with substance *A*. Such combinations might take place, but the combination *Ab* had the ability to displace the combination *Ac* and *Aa* to displace both *Ac* and *Ab*. In Goethe's novel of the same name, the would-be adulterous passions of a husband (Eduard) and his wife (Charlotte) for Ottilie and the Captain, respectively, who come to stay—initially "only for a short while"[37]—draws the four in unintended ways into powerful structural relationships, while Eduard and Charlotte's passions remain unrequited. The new combinations have the power to break up existing weaker links, such as those linking Eduard and Charlotte. As Eduard put it, "The affinities become interesting only when they bring about divorces." Indeed, a divorced or escaped element must "go off and drift around again in the void," going through "a very hard time before it again finds refuge."[38]

In Max Weber's famous formulation, various elements of Calvinism—the idea of a vocation and a calling in one's work; the notion that through thriftiness, continuous enterprise, and hard work one could show one's devotion to God; and the idea that success in this world might be an indicator of salvation in the next—worked in the construction of the cosmos of modern capitalism through the promotion of rational and continuous enterprise based on hard work, saving, and reinvestment. Yet, the activities of purposeful subjects worked in the constitution of a powerful structure in unintended and oppressive ways. For as Weber wrote, the care for external goods was supposed to lie on the shoulders of the saint like a light cloak, but fate decreed that it become an iron cage—inasmuch as materialism and consumerism became dominant forms within capitalist civilization. The notion of a calling in one's work, moreover, became unnecessary as capitalism's subjects became "specialists without spirit and sensualists without heart," and now "[prowl] about in our lives like the ghost of dead religious beliefs." Profit for its own sake, not salvation or godly devotion, became the meaning and goal of economic action.[39] In these unintended ways, forms of subjectivity were displaced and alienated.

The important point is that unintended consequences and forms of displacement are involved in all these accounts of elective affinity. This displacement operates to disrupt the identity of purpose and subjectivity on the one hand, with the objective, mediating power structure so produced on the other. This is arguably the essence of hegemony and the reason why its operations are oppressive. The idea is one in which diverse subjectivities, motivations, goals, projects, ideas, and purposes are linked through unintended consequences to deepen and extend particular objectifying structures. These structures capture, harness, and control the energies of social subjects, while dispensing with, displacing, repressing, or transforming their motivations, goals, and projects. Precisely because hegemonic objectifying structures are capable of harnessing diverse subjectivities and social interests (not just Ac, for example, but Aa), new or dominant combinations displace and repress older or weaker ones. In this version of hegemony, power operates less through forging consent, *doxa*, common sense, or offering the concepts within which controversies are couched, or through preconstituting, in some mysterious way, social subjects in their entirety. Rather, power operates through capturing and ensnaring bodies, their energies, and activities, and thus transforming subjectivity into objective structure, purpose into instrumentality, and ends into means. Hegemony's "trick" is not to predetermine the subjective content of the choices that are made. Choices are made out of diverse materials and capacities that are put together in ways that are not all controlled in advance by the system. Hegemony works to harness and channel and turn to advantage those choices that actually are made.[40] Such alchemy, involving the "crystallization of social relations," helps to account in turn for the power of structures of capital accumulation.[41] Such power is established not through capitalism's ability to dupe in any simple way, or align all subjectivities, or to create a shared common sense, or because of the overweening class power of capitalists and imperialists, but through its ability to combine and harness diverse subjectivities and purposes, including even those of salvationist religion. It is hardly surprising, then, in view of these multiple displacements, that the hegemonic capitalist system—where true capitalist believers are much thinner on the ground than is generally admitted—contains many antagonistic subjectivities. Such antagonism does not stem in Eurocentric mode from the French revolutionary tradition of the logic of democratic equivalence, but from the forms of recombination and repression unleashed within the system more generally. In the case of migrants, arguably, the meanings of exile are grounded in these multiple displacements and unintended consequences.

Unintended consequences such as these are possible because it is always an abstraction to conceive of workers as either merely a cost of production in a labor market based on exchange, as in conventional economics, or as so many quotients of labor power, conceived as a commodity distinctive from its bearer, contracted out, and set in motion as "living labor," as in Marxian economics. In reality, employers always hire persons, who, unlike other production inputs, costs and commodities, are multiply determined social subjects capable of interpreting their own condition and of purposeful action beyond the narrow concerns of the enterprise or the labor market, or the supposed rules of "the economy" in general. The notion of labor power as a commodity contracted out by a bearer is an artifact of the economic imagination and contractarian theory guiding practice.[42] It is a too often reified form of commodity fetishism, and forms of powerful justification for a mode of subordination. In actual practice, employers and customers deal with persons at all points in relations of production and exchange, persons who are always bound up with their supposed labor power at some integral level. Employers purchase the ability to command the mind, body, and capacities of a person for a period—a combination of direct and indirect control. As Bridget Anderson has argued, both the premodern personalistic idiom of power and the materialist idiom of power under capitalism are at work in the employment of migrant domestic workers: "The employer of the migrant domestic worker exercises both forms of power."[43] Through these forms of power, the "very lifeblood" of workers is coined into dollars and cents.[44] As Claus Offe put it, the "labour market cannot function without a *coercive* implementation of the fiction that labour power *is* a commodity."[45] In many ways it is with the implementation of this command structure in the migratory labor regime that this book is concerned, as the form of command involved is highly varied across time and space. Through the labor market, actual persons are sutured to a system of control and order that did not and does not define the limits of their subjectivity.

Thus, the proposition that this book seeks to work through is this: Forms of hegemonic control are crucial in understanding "voluntary" and "economic" international labor migration, but significant light can be shed on these forms of control by looking beyond the automatic hydraulics of capital and class, the sledgehammer of imperialism, and faceless flows of labor power, and thinking in terms of unfinished, acculturated, subtle, and ensnaring operations of hegemonic incorporation.

SOCIAL HISTORY AND ETHNOGRAPHY

To make the necessary connections between subjectivity and social structure, my research, undertaken during the eventful years (2003–2007) surrounding the Syrian military withdrawal from Lebanon in April 2005, involved much tacking back and forth between the methods of ethnography and those of social history. On the one side, I sought out small groups of informants among Syrian workers, with whom trust was variably but increasingly established, and with whom I conducted repeat interviews and conversations in both Lebanon and Syria over three to four years. It is arguably only through close, qualitative understandings of popular subjectivities that the elective and hegemonic aspects of the migratory regime could be understood. My research tended to sacrifice the representativeness of the sample in favor of the depth and quality of the qualitative material. Whether this was the right choice is for the reader to decide, but some sort of choice had to be made here, given finite resources. Inevitably, such a choice will shed light on some features but not on others. I took a dim view of the existing survey and questionnaire work that had already been done, as it seemed to indicate patently unlikely results, such as in a country of tension, massacre, and mass eviction, the notion that Syrian workers were happy in Lebanon and had no problems there. I did, however, search for all available documents, statistics, reports, and publications in order to get a sense of social and economic structures, while mining the press from the 1940s onward for (geo)political shifts, and the vitally important opinions and social interests of the literate and the wealthy in Lebanon, who played important roles in transforming conditions on the ground for Syrian workers. This material was supplemented with interviews with a variety of journalists, officials, intellectuals, and others in Lebanon and Syria. This was particularly useful for the recovery of important transcripts unavailable in the press for one reason or another. For the pre-1945 period, and for much else besides, I made use of secondary and published material on Syria and Lebanon, and on migration and labor in general.

COMPARATIVE HISTORY

The first major wave of "voluntary" outmigration from the eastern Mediterranean began in the late nineteenth century. Migration started relatively late from the Ottoman Empire, which avoided slavery and indenture because of its relative economic independence within the world system until the late nineteenth century. Outmigrants particularly came from Mt. Lebanon, which was increasingly linked to the world economy through the production of raw and spun silk for the Lyon silk industry. Mt. Lebanon at that time was part of a special semiautonomous region—the *mutasarrifiyya*—within the Ottoman Empire, created with French "protection" after the conflicts of 1860. Especially following the downturn in the fortunes of the silk industry in the 1890s, outmigrants from Mt. Lebanon came to number more than 10,000 a year. By the early 1900s, the area of outmigration had expanded to include the hills of the Anti-Lebanon (the Qalamoun in particular), where the cash economy had spread—an area located in what was to become the Syrian Arab Republic in 1946. After the First World War and the break up of the Ottoman Empire, the colonial powers divided the northern part of the *bilad ash-sham* into the Mandates of Lebanon and Syria. During the interwar period, migrants departed for West Africa and beyond in increasing numbers from the south of Lebanon, and for Haifa in Palestine from the fertile Syrian plain southwest of Damascus, the Hawran. With national independence (Lebanon in 1943 and Syria in 1946) and the further spread of the cash economy, areas of outmigration were extended in the 1950s and 1960s to include the grain-producing plains of Syria, and the Akkar region of northern Lebanon. For the first time, in tens and then hundreds of thousands, Syrians went to neighboring Lebanon, which rapidly became a regional, financial, and commercial hub. As elsewhere in the global South, regional centers of accumulation such as the Gulf countries—Argentina, Malaysia, and the Ivory Coast—were attracting international labor migrants for the first time in large numbers from countries near and far. Syrian migration to Lebanon, in a prolonged cycle of migration and return, although interrupted by political crises, has endured to the present, while areas of outmigration in Syria came to include the eastern steppes and the desert by the 1980s. In the early 2000s, Syrian workers comprised between 20 and 40 percent of the total Lebanese workforce, they were worth up to $1 billion annually to their Lebanese employers, and their remittances made up as much as 8 percent of the Syrian GDP.[46]

Syrians in Lebanon, by conventional understandings, were "voluntary" migrants in the modern sense. Their migration was certainly different in some important sense to slavery, whereby laborers were procured by force, natally dishonored, and became alienable property in law.[47] Like other "economic" migrants, Syrians were not refugees—persons expelled directly or indirectly from their countries of origin because of threats to the life and liberty of their person through political persecution and war.[48] In contrast, Syrians were "voluntary" labor migrants because they departed at least nominally according to their own volition, albeit within a determinate structure, they were legally free to change employers, and a distinction could be made between their person and their labor power, the latter supposedly becoming a saleable commodity that bearers dispose of freely. Like other labor migrants, they were often (but not always)[49] young males from the countryside, although increasingly female since the 1960s, and the great majority set out as individuals aiming to better their condition, usually with the object of earning cash in order to return home with increased resources for families, smallholdings, and small businesses.[50] As elsewhere, settlement processes began, usually against the initial intentions of migrants, but like other modern migrations, Syrian migration to Lebanon did not follow the familiar premodern pattern whereby whole communities, peoples, or societies moved together from one location to another more or less definitively.[51] Syrians moved initially as individuals, a pattern widely noted in other cases. As the British Consul in China stated in 1868, "The principal object of this emigration is not so much colonization as the supply of labor."[52] Syrians, like other modern labor migrants from Asia, Africa, and Latin America, were not colonists. According to Glenn, "Migrants are recruited by receiving countries strictly to fill labor needs, not to become permanent members of the society."[53] They moved, "unassisted . . . by . . . armies of *conquistadores*, tradesmen and missionaries,"[54] into already structured communities as "guests and aliens." They were located at or near the bottom of racial and civilizational hierarchies; the non-Europeans among them usually did not "become white" (as many southern and eastern Europeans did) and were often excluded from host nation membership as "aliens ineligible for citizenship"; and they were regarded as unskilled and unqualified, taking on menial, low-paid, insecure, stigmatized, and often dangerous, dirty, or exhausting labour.[55]

Like other "voluntary" and "economic" migrants, Syrians did not originate from pristine, untouched, traditional, premodern, and/or precapitalist regions. Sending areas were becoming involved in the institutions and forces of capitalist modernity—what Janet Abu Lughod strikingly called the "world power system of economic dependence."[56] "Contrary to popular stereotypes," wrote Hondagneu-Sotelo, "migration originates not in stagnating, 'backward' societies, but in those societies undergoing rapid-paced urbanization and industrialization," especially those in which "rural subsistence economies" are being undermined.[57] By the same token, "where the world market had not yet penetrated," noted Zolberg, "the mobilization of manpower required coercion, especially when it entailed long-distance relocation."[58] Sassen distinguished at least four phases of incorporation over the last two centuries: (1) migration from the immediate peripheries of Ireland, Poland, Italy, and Belgium; (2) migration from the expanded periphery, including all of eastern and southern Europe; (3) migration from an even more expanded periphery, including China, Mexico, and North Africa in the later nineteenth century; and (4) during the post-1945 decades, new migration from the Caribbean Basin and a growing number of countries in South America, Africa, and Asia.[59] Syrian outmigration—first overseas and then to neighboring countries—fits Sassen's third and fourth phases without any striking particularity.[60]

CIRCULAR MIGRATION

The case of Syrians in Lebanon involves a prolonged pattern of circular migration involving mostly male, menial labor. Patterns of settlement and community formation in Lebanon were slow, repeatedly truncated, or broken up, and migrants tended to return to Syria on a regular basis and often retired there. Migrants tended to "live in the country of destination only while employed." There was an ongoing basic separation between reproduction and maintenance of the workforce on the one side, and its daily renewal and employment on the other.[61] Although women did migrate to Lebanon to work in agriculture, domestic labor, tourism, and entertainment, sometimes independently and sometimes as subordinate family members, they nonetheless were relatively few in number. And although numerous wealthy, bourgeois Syrians also visited Lebanon on business, and moved there on a permanent basis in large numbers in the 1960s, when fleeing Arab socialism and Ba'thism, the great majority of Syrian migrants were rotating, menial workers who generally took unskilled, low-paying, dead-end jobs, connoting "inferior social status and involving hard or unpleasant working conditions and considerable insecurity."[62] This situation endures to the present and even expanded in the 1990s, while the Lebanese practice of hiring Syrian female domestics largely ceased in the late 1970s and 1980s.

Some might like to see such migratory patterns, along with the pattern of permanent rupture and assimilation, as leftovers from a backward past and hardly worth studying. Certainly it has been suggested in rather overreaching fashion that the idea of migrants as transients who move for work and eventually return is a conception anchored in "earlier historical moments."[63] Many have turned to the study of female, professional, and/or skilled migration, in particular noting that since the 1960s such forms of migration, especially to the United States, have become far more common than before. Certainly debates in migration policy and public perceptions shifted their attention during the 1970s and 1980s from single, male migrants and issues of labor competition and control, to issues of minority youth, birthrates, education, multiculturalism, and controversies over benefits and "welfare mothers."[64] The old lament that insufficient attention was paid to return migration is no longer warranted, as the topic has received significant research for over two decades.[65]

However, part of the reason for studying the case of Syria and Lebanon is to insist that unskilled, circular migration, whether male or female, is not a form that is simply anchored in earlier historical moments—a rather teleological conception at best, and in this case a rather severe arrogation of world historical time to a particular set of developments in certain countries such as the United States. It is simply not the case, in spite of the undoubted novelty and utility of the idea, that world migration is now dominated by transmigrants who "forge and sustain multi-stranded social relations that link together their societies of origin and settlement" and are "at home in both societies."[66] Leaving aside the fact that return migrants also "forge and sustain multi-stranded social relations" linking sending and receiving countries, and the complications of the notion of being "at home," and an identity-based desire to explore one's roots linked to tourism and the reactivation of certain family ties can hardly equate to being "at home" in the sending country of one's ancestors, global capital accumulation is far more combined and uneven than the idea of transmigratory centrality would suggest, whether in the United States or elsewhere. And just because female and skilled migration has become more common in many parts of the globe, this does not mean that other kinds of migration have come to a halt, or that female migration is not menial, or that circular and unskilled migration becomes unworthy of attention, or that it cannot increase again, even if made illegal by border controls, which in many countries have been increasingly tight since the 1970s. As Sassen has insisted, "Both backward and very modern and highly dynamic growth sectors ... generate a vast array of such [menial] low-wage jobs [taken by migrants]."[67] And it was not only "early capitalism" that provided few guarantees that sick, disabled, elderly, unemployed workers would be cared for, encouraging return migration to the sending-country village where such services could be obtained.[68] German capitalism in the 1960s, hardly "early capitalism," severely restricted migrant rights.[69] In Lebanon, furthermore, contemporary capitalism has not extended these social benefits to migrants (rather, it has withdrawn them), likewise in the United States and elsewhere the trend in a context of neoliberal policy has been to strip such benefits away, reinforcing the pressure on migrants to return.[70] Illegality itself has often functioned as a mechanism that generates insecure menial workers through criminalization who, lacking papers, have difficulty settling and therefore cannot access the social benefits associated with legal status.[71] The increased use of deportation, militarized border enforcement, and so on, also can reinforce circular patterns. Few would disagree that menial labor—insecure, stigmatized, low-skill, and poorly paid work—continues to play a crucial role in the lives of migrants, from Buenos Aires to Beirut.[72]

In fact, far from being an outlying case, it is arguable, particularly when the lens is widened to include South-South migration, that circular, menial labor migration is one the more common migratory experiences of the last 150 years. Mexican migration to the United States has been circular and unskilled, notwithstanding important patterns of settlement, for much of its existence.[73] Even those who live and work for many years in California often maintain the dream of returning to Mexico and buying a ranch or small business.[74] Apartheid South Africa institutionalized a system of return migration during much of the twentieth century. A Transvaal Local Government Commission of 1921 reported: "The native should be allowed to enter the urban areas, which are essentially the white man's creation, when he is willing to enter and to minister to the needs of the white man, and should depart therefrom when he ceases so to minister."[75] In both pre-1914 and post-1945 Europe, circular patterns were dominant for long periods.[76] Of the 8 million Italians who left their country between 1945 and 1983, for example, 5 million returned.[77] In the 2000s, patterns of migration from Eastern Europe stemming from recent European Union enlargement have often been circular. In South-South migration, circular and short-term migration is particularly marked, as Parnwell's survey argues.[78] Of the millions of migrants working in the Persian Gulf and other oil-rich countries, return and unsettlement is overwhelmingly dominant.[79] Circular patterns are common also in southeast Asia, particularly Malaysia,[80] Latin America, the Caribbean, and sub-Saharan Africa.[81] In China, the tens and even hundreds of millions of people involved in (admitted domestic) rural-urban migration includes much circular migration. Sassen has pointed out that "we are seeing generally more and more circular migration in the Mediterranean but also in the Americas."[82] Whatever the long-term consequences of migratory departure, as Castles and Kosack stated, "few migrants actually intend to remain away from their country of origin forever when they first depart, and there is no way of knowing in advance whether an individual will settle permanently or not."[83] With regard to these features, Syrian migration to Lebanon can hardly be seen as a hangover from a backward past, nor as the vanguard of a future world of migration. It is in many ways a familiar pattern of migration under conditions of combined and uneven global capitalism, and it provides a rich basis for comparison to other cases.

PROLONGED UNSETTLEMENT

Nonetheless, migration from Syria to Lebanon has some distinctive features. First, unsettled circulation between Syria and Lebanon, ongoing since the 1950s, has in some senses been remarkably prolonged. As has been noted, guest-worker programs break down and "transitory migration movements seem inevitably to generate permanent migrant communities."[84] Moreover, unlike the Gulf countries, where workers have often been housed in compounds, segregated from the citizenry, contracted by large companies, and sent home at the end of contracts, in Lebanon, conditions for settlement were apparently more propitious, because of the existence of numerous small and non-oligopolistic industries, based on unstable, uncertain, and variable demand, that employed Syrians all over town and country, and were not prepared to foot transportation or housing costs, and in fact preferred migrants to be able to move around and change employers.[85] Under these nonsegregated conditions of work and residence, it is reasonable to argue, as Piore does, that settlement is more likely. Furthermore, unlike many countries around the world, Lebanon has never actively pursued policies to prevent settlement or encourage return. In Kuwait, for example, the basis of migration policy since the 1970s, where nonintegration was viewed as the basis for social stability, has arguably been "to maintain the transient character of labor immigration in order to ensure that the migrants did not settle down permanently in the country."[86] In South Africa, from the 1880s onward, a specific set of policies such as pass laws and the compound system were partly responsible for the fact that "the oscillation of workers backward and forward did not gradually diminish as elsewhere."[87] Far from implementing a system of pass laws, Lebanon has never required that Syrians return after completion of a contract, as Singapore, Malaysia, Japan, and Hong Kong do, for example, nor has it ever stipulated that migrants cannot be pregnant on arrival (as is the case, for example, in Singapore and Malaysia).[88] No sterilization programs or antisettlement measures of any kind have ever been sanctioned by the Lebanese government. Indeed, it is perfectly legal for Syrians to bring their wives and children to Lebanon as they please. Finally, one might think that cultural commonalities, ties of history, language, custom, and even actual family would further encourage settlement, where the border was an artificial colonial creation of the 1920s. It would seem, then, that there would need to be some explanation for why Syrian migrants spawned no second generation in Lebanon, even after around half a century of mass migration.

Of course, much work has shown how ineffective government restrictions are on settlement patterns. Indeed, restriction can provoke settlement, as in the often-cited case of border controls in Europe in the 1970s, which induced migrants to make a final decision to stay in the receiving country because of the difficulty of reentry. Such migrants often brought their families in accelerated fashion before it was too late. Restriction, in short, forced migrants to choose one country or the other, and the so-called dull compulsion of economic forces often meant they chose the receiving country. The open border between Syria and Lebanon does, in fact, seem to have played a role in prolonging the pattern of temporary migration and return, because workers did not have to choose between the two countries. As has been noted, return flows are usually relatively high when migration is "unimpeded by political controls."[89] But this is not the main reason for prolonged circulation, as I will argue. Syrians responded to social needs in unplanned and unintended fashion to form embryonic communities in Lebanon over time, notwithstanding the open border. However, these emerging communities were thwarted and truncated, partly by recurrent hostility and violence, but above all by high social costs (rents, utilities, health, education, transportation, and food) in Lebanon, where there was virtually no government or nongovernmental social assistance. However, in Syria, Ba'thist redistributive measures had long subsidized costs, especially in agriculture, making a return viable. Syria was distinctive for not having been levered by debt into structural adjustment, and for this reason village communities continued to be viable, and no mega-slums filled with dispossessed small-holders and agricultural laborers encircled Damascus or Aleppo. Migration from Syria to Lebanon, therefore, was distinctive not because it involved the circulation of menial labor, but because this circulation was strikingly prolonged.

A second distinctive feature of Syrian migration to Lebanon is that feminization was relatively slow compared to, for example, Mexican migration to the United States. Women did migrate, but in relatively small numbers. Their numbers even shrunk during the 1970s and 1980s when they were no longer sought after for domestic work in Lebanon. It is important not to link this automatically to some form of essential and timeless Arab patriarchy.

The Arab world, as elsewhere, has seen how patriarchy has been both pressured and reinforced by patterns of outmigration, not to mention fractured by issues of region, class, geography, sect, and so on. Moreover, female outmigration should not automatically be seen as a form of women's emancipation, as patriarchy often works through the wage labor relation, as reflected in indices such as wage rates.[90] That Alawi women worked in fewer numbers in Lebanese households under highly exploitative conditions after the 1970s can hardly be seen as a major social regression. Of greatest importance, female outmigration from Syria was most crucially limited because the Syrian countryside and its domestic communities of production have never been devastated by structural adjustment, nor has Syria housed Export Processing Zones "schooling" women in wage labor, consumption, and migration. Part of the feminization of migrant flows from Mexico, it has been argued, had to do with the economic crisis of the 1980s, which "propelled married women with small children into the labor force," whereas Mexican women in the labor force in the 1960s and 1970s were more likely to be single.[91] Syria never borrowed heavily from international financial institutions, it did not suffer a debt crisis such as Mexico's, and it has never submitted to International Monetary Fund–sponsored structural adjustment programs.[92] On the contrary, a state supportive of agriculture has ensured that domestic communities of production based on much unpaid female domestic labor remain in some sense viable in Syria.

Third, Lebanon is practically unique in that the poorer, sending country had a major and sometimes heavy-handed military presence (during 1976 to 2005) in the richer, receiving country. Military service in Lebanon acted as a contracting mechanism, in that conscripts worked in Lebanon either during their military service, or returned to do so after they had established contacts in Lebanon through military service. Others were contracted by officers, who sometimes muscled in with their labor crews on particular projects. On the other hand, many workers wanted to have nothing to do with the army, partly because of a standard fear of the intelligence services, but also because they did not want to be associated with the Syrian army in the eyes of the Lebanese. They wanted "to stay after the Syrian army had left," as it was often put. Moreover, it is too much to ascribe to the army the main reason for the continuance of the open border in the 1990s and 2000s. If this is true, then why did the open border both pre- and postdate the military presence? Also, the role of the army changed over time. During the early 1990s, it underpinned the pax Syriana and the menial labor regime. By the late 1990s and early 2000s, it was one of the main factors provoking hostility to Syria and Syrian workers in Lebanon, especially where Syrian intervention became more flagrant and invasive, over constitutional amendments, electoral laws, and the like. Overall, as we shall see, the army did little systematically or progressively to protect or enhance the position of Syrian workers in Lebanon. It was instead an important element in the reproduction of insecurity, menial labor, and prolonged unsettlement.

A final distinctive feature, and that most interesting for my purposes, was that, in a post-1970s world, where border restrictions have tended to intensify, Lebanon's borders generally remained open in regard to Syrians—notwithstanding forms of expulsion from particular areas during the civil war, and the mass flight of Syrians from Lebanon in the face of popular hostility in early 2005, and under Israeli bombardment in the summer of 2006. This remarkable state of affairs flowed from two distinct political settlements: the Christian-dominated "merchant republic" of the 1950s and 1960s, and the pax Syriana of the 1990s and early 2000s. This unusually "free labor market" was further characterized by the fact that Syrians were not contracted to work in Lebanon, in the main, through monopolistic or large employment agencies, or exploitative contractors. Migration worked through social networks of kith and kin. Migrants were not bound to particular employers through contracts or mechanisms such as passport removal, and the costs and inconvenience of traveling to Lebanon were very low. In other words, these distinctively "free market" aspects of Syrian migration to Lebanon, and the fact that they were unraveled at particular moments, offer a chance to explore over several decades their construction as distinctively hegemonic forms of control.

The chapters that follow trace a detailed history in broadly chronological fashion. Chapter 1 deals with the period of outmigration from the region before the Second World War. The remaining four chapters discuss migration from Syria to Lebanon during the 50 years since. Following the logic of elective affinities, Chapters 2 and 4, which cover the merchant republic of the 1950s and 1960s and the pax Syriana of the 1990s, respectively, are mainly concerned with how migrants as social subjects were bound through forms of "election" to the structures of the migratory regime. Chapters 3 and 5, examining the civil war of 1975–1990 and the break up of the pax Syriana since the late 1990s, respectively, focus on structures, or forms of fraught "affinity," involving unintended consequences, exploitation, hostility, violence, and unsettlement.

1 BY GOD, MY BROTHER, COME BACK TO US

INTRODUCTION

Slavery and indentured labor on capitalist lines were largely unknown in the Ottoman Empire before the nineteenth century. European colonists could neither hunt for slaves nor build slave plantations in Ottoman domains, owing to the relative military and political autonomy from Europe of this powerful land-based empire. The institutions of Ottoman slavery, moreover, were not so much about profit-making enterprises oriented to production, but above all about military and administrative recruitment whereby young, often Balkan, Christians were seized, schooled, and converted to Islam, often becoming loyal Sultan's servants exercising power at the heart of government. The transregional movement of labor "against community" was not a mass phenomenon. Where it occurred, it was usually a relatively local move for harvest, an unusual corvée for the purposes of the army or urban provisioning, or the particular travel of an individual. Other migrants moved within whole communities (whether as nomads, pilgrims, or persecuted groups), or moved between communally based institutions (such as guilds) in the different cities of the maghrib (North Africa), the *mashriq* (the Levant) and the Mediterranean. All this started to change in the nineteenth century with Ottoman incorporation into a world economy based on London, as market relations and liberal imperialism articulated diverse regions and communities. Apparently "voluntary" labor migrants started to leave the *bilad ash-sham* (Syria) on the eastern Mediterranean in their hundreds of thousands, particularly from the 1890s onward.

Even though very few migrants moved from what became Syria to work in what became Lebanon, the history of economic and "voluntary" labor migration in the *bilad ash-sham* clearly began two or three generations before national independence and the cycle of migration and return on which this book focuses. This chapter examines this important historical background on the basis of mostly secondary sources in order to argue against the conventional view that these migrations involved either the modernization and assimilation of backward groups, the forceful eviction of vast masses of proletarians, or the empowered and hybridizing choices of subaltern agents. Outmigrants were instead gradually unfixed, entangled, and displaced within the cosmos of modern, transnational capitalism through combinations of coercion and consent, repression and choice. They became increasingly stitched into circuits of economic power, and enmeshed in new structures of direct and indirect control, less through the sledgehammer of class power, and the delusions of false consciousness, and more through subtler but more powerful mechanisms involving elective affinities and processes of hegemonic incorporation.

SELLING LABOR OVERSEAS

There is no disagreement in the historiography that outmigration from the *bilad ash-sham* increased during the last quarter of the nineteenth century in a way unprecedented in centuries. Himadeh estimated that 120,000 persons departed between 1860 and 1900; Moussali estimated that 700,000 left between 1860 and 1932.[1] Khater judged that as many as one-third to one-half of the rural population of Mt. Lebanon migrated to the United States between 1870 and 1920.[2] The British consul wrote in 1902 that "emigration is always on the increase and has now extended from the Lebanon and Anti-Lebanon to all districts of Syria."[3] Widmer, writing in the 1930s, claimed, "There is hardly a village in the Lebanon or in all Syria that has not contributed a portion of its population to swell the number of emigrants."[4] In the 1930s, it was said that no village in Lebanon counted less than one-third of its population abroad, and that it was hard to find a Christian family in Damascus without at least one migrant.[5] Thoumin wrote of the mountain in the 1930s that "the case of a family composed of a father, a mother and six children, of which four are in America, and of which the parents themselves spent 10 or 15 years abroad is quite frequent." Thoumin also listed the Christian villages of the Qalamoun (in the Anti-Lebanon of Syria), which counted many migrants abroad as residents.

Likewise, the 1,000 Christians of Homs counted 1,700 more of their community in the Americas. The Muslim populations of the Qalamoun showed a lower but still significant rate of outmigration. For example, in Yabroud, there were 4,000 Muslims present, and a further 1,000 abroad. Thoumin, even more strikingly, wrote that in the Syrian "countryside—except the Ghouta—it is rare to encounter a group of four or five Muslims without one of them proposing to speak to you in Spanish or Portuguese." Particular Syrian villages were linked to particular destinations: Nebek to Florida, Yabroud and Kara to Argentina and Brazil, Dayr Attiya to Argentina, and Dayr al-Qamar (in the Shuf, Lebanon) to Senegal.[6] In 1924, remittances from migrants abroad to Lebanon and Syria were estimated at $19 million a year, whereas the total commodity export from these countries was only $17 million a year.[7] In other words, persons had become Syria and Lebanon's most valuable export over half a century.

As contemporaries noted, this form of migration was distinctive, and in certain respects new. It neither involved the decisive resettlement of whole communities, nor groups of persons fleeing political persecution or war, nor the institutions of slavery, nor small numbers of the wealthy or connected taking up official positions or living in small merchant communities in distant lands. The Phoenicians had established colonies around the Mediterranean in ancient times; the Turkmen had come as a people to northern Syria on the eve of the Ottoman conquest in the early sixteenth century; Kurds from Anatolia had settled in northern Syria in the eighteenth century; and Druze communities had emigrated from the Aleppo region in the nineteenth century following disturbances. There were also migrations of merchants in small numbers from Syria to Egypt, Livorno, Marseille, and Manchester from the seventeenth to the early nineteenth century.[8] During the last quarter of the nineteenth century, Circassians had immigrated into the *bilad ash-sham* in numbers, and, more dramatically, during and after World War I, around 150,000 Armenian refugees arrived in Beirut, Aleppo, and Alexandretta, escaping persecution on a genocidal scale.[9] Instead, however, of what Widmer called "age-old" migrations of peoples, the later nineteenth century witnessed "individual emigration on a large scale." Young persons, mostly but not always men, usually aged 20 to 45, set out to look for work overseas on a temporary basis, often with the expectation of return, in order to make money and improve circumstances at home.[10]

New forms of economic migration built on, extended, and commodified existing and sometimes preexisting patterns involving regional and local movements for various kinds of economic purposes. The most important of these migrations in the rural world involved cultivators from the slopes and mountain villages of the Lebanon and Anti-Lebanon working at harvest time in the grain-producing plains on the fringes of the eastern desert, in the more intensively cultivated coastal plains, and in the gardens and orchards surrounding cities and towns.[11] The harvest in the high and relatively cold plateau and villages of the Qalamoun, on the eastern slopes of the Anti-Lebanon, for example, did not begin until the second half of July. Men and women from these villages therefore descended to work in harvesting in the plains in June and early July.[12] For example, in an area known as "la noukra" between Jabal Druze and Mt. Hermon, a rich-soil, rain-fed plain, the harvest began in mid-June and workers came down from the Qalamoun. Some came alone, others brought their families. Once the harvest in the Hawran was completed, these families returned to the Qalamoun to the harvest there.[13] Similarly, around 2,000 Turkish and Kurdish agricultural laborers descended from Turkey to the harvest in the plains around Aleppo in the 1930s.[14] From the late nineteenth century, landowners growing potatoes, beans, and cereals on Mt. Lebanon (especially Ehden) started to purchase land and grow olives on the coastal plain, particularly at Zgorta. After the June harvest on the mountain, cars would be hired to move furniture and everything else to Zgorta for the olive harvest in October.[15]

Migrations also stemmed from slack periods in grain-producing regions. Unlike the more intensive labor in orchards and gardens in the Ghouta around Damascus, for example, grain and cereal production involved a downtime, allowing artisanal employment in place or outmigration.[16] Some worked as manual laborers outside the village—in porterage, for example.[17] Some peasants, at least in the 1930s, hired themselves, with oxen and plows, to be paid by the day or for a specific area, bringing their food with them.[18] Others moved in search of wild products, such as sumac in mountains for tanneries, or liquorice roots in the plains.[19] The greatest demand was in labor-intensive harvesting, especially in olives, figs, and citrus on the coastal plain, and the grain and cereal harvests in plains such as the Hawran and Amouk. In the 'Ajlun district, south of the Hawran, field crop-based villages such as Hawwara drew migrants at harvest time from Golan and Palestine, while hiring camels and labor from semi-nomadic bedouin.[20]

Even leaving aside the seasonal movement of predominantly desert-based tribes, there were extensive movements of nomadic and semi-nomadic populations within the more settled areas. For example, nomads tending goats in summer pastures in the Biqa' journeyed down the Litani river with tens of thousands of goats to winter in south Lebanon, selling manure to Tyre-based merchants, who stored the product on the beach before distributing it by lorry and boat.[21] In another case, nomadic groups raising sheep around water sources in the Qalamoun in the summer descended at the first frosts east and north toward the desert, negotiating protection from the more desert-based bedouin tribal confederations for the winter.[22] Other semi-nomadic groups on Mt. Lebanon or in the Biqa' made for the coast or headed down the Orontes valley toward the plain of Homs.[23] For the harvest in the Syrian plains near the desert, in the 1930s nomads of various kinds were "a major labour reserve."[24]

Thus, local and regional migration for economic purposes by a wide variety of groups was not simply a matter of overseas migration, nor solely an invention of the late nineteenth century. The use of cash was not completely new. Sometimes harvesting teams were assembled under contractors or heads of households who were paid cash, which was then often distributed to workers as wages.[25] Nonetheless, these kinds of regional migrations remained circumscribed, limited, and "only slightly remunerated."[26] Harvest work in labor-intensive olive- and fig-picking on the coastal plain did not necessarily involve cash payment. Fig- and olive-pickers were often paid between one-sixth and one-twelfth of the quantities harvested. For such painstaking work, paying in kind assured effective harvest.[27] New forms of cash-based and international labor migration, therefore, greatly enlarged and commodified preexisting and emerging patterns of regional migration.

UNEVEN INCORPORATION

Migration did not stem automatically from world economic incorporation, even allowing for the unevenness of the latter. Local dynamics associated with geography, economic practice, communal forms, and political arrangements mediated relations between macrological processes and migrant flows. The first and most significant wave of migrants came from among the Christian communities of Mt. Lebanon. These groups were not from a stagnant region, but from one outstandingly integrated into the transnational cash economy, especially through the production of silk cocoons and threads for sale to Lyon. The trade took off during the 1860s during the sericulture blight in Europe. The Druze communities of the Mountain, on the other hand, who were far less integrated into this cash economy, more economically independent, but by no means wealthy, were far less involved in early outmigration.[28] Migrants clearly did not simply drain out of the poorest areas. Indeed, outmigrants from the relatively poor, rain-fed, grain-producing plains to the east and north of the Lebanon and Anti-Lebanon ranges, and from the Biqa' valley, the Hawran, and Akkar in the north, were relatively few before World War II.[29] This unevenness, however, had much less to do with some absolute lack of world economic integration, and much more to do with the specific arrangements that developed or reproduced themselves in different regions.

COMMUNAL ARRANGEMENTS

In some cases, even as late as the 1940s, villages in Syria based on communal ownership continued to exist, and exhibited a very low degree of market dependency. In such areas, the "peasant" was said to be "almost self-sufficient": "He produces enough to meet most of his wants and buys very little from the market."[30] This structure existed in villages where land was owned collectively (musha')—a widespread form of tenure in the grain-producing plains of Amouk, Ghab, Biqa', and Hawran, and on the western fringes of the desert, away from intensively cultivated gardens and orchards close to towns, fruit plantations, and coastal or mountainous regions such as anti-Lebanon and Jabal Alawi. Communal ownership meant that families cultivated particular parcels of land collectively owned by the village. Land parcels were periodically reallocated in accordance with numbers of males available for cultivation. In such villages, direct production was carried out by those who had a key bundle of right of access, usufruct, and control over the land. Weulersse called this "the absolute identification of use and ownership" which "automatically prohibits all foreign interference, while the practice of periodic redistribution by head maintains equality and social peace." He noted that "sufficiently numerous" villages of this type exist in Syria, and gives the example of Saglaya close to Aleppo.[31] Such villages had no internal mechanism for evicting laborers. The absence of rival and exclusive property rights, and the fact that direct producers were also the collective owners of the means of production, meant that men had access to land (and hence access to means of production and subsistence in accordance with their numbers), even with the growth (within limits) of the population. These arrangements had no means of producing the category "labor-power" or conceiving of it as a commodity. Where seasonal labor was required, laborers would not be hired, either internally or externally; instead, cultivators would be assisted by other families from the quarter or village.[32]

An attenuated version of communal ownership—dubbed "communal tenure" by Weulersse—also discouraged outmigration. In villages based on communal tenure, control over land assets was consolidated most commonly by the arrival of an outsider or notable, whether through violent seizure, purchase, debt dispossession, or in exchange for protection against exterior menaces (such as that from bedouin) or for local arbitration, particularly in open country where urban justice was inaccessible. This process reached back in particular to the mid-nineteenth century, having been encouraged by new Ottoman Land Codes.[33] First, Article 8 of the 1858 Land Law prohibited collective ownership: "In no case can the total lands of a village or canton be conceded as a block to the inhabitants as a group." Land, with demarcated boundaries, now had to belong definitively to a single individual, and often this turned out to be a notable, "with or without the agreement of the peasants."[34] Such land was registered with the state, and henceforth state powers guaranteed its existence as something recognizable as private property. Weulersse gives the example of the village of Tell Selhab in the Alawi part of the Ghab plain, where half the village lands were now in the hands of a village proprietor. Weulersse rightly points out that this seizure of land, against which villagers sometimes struggled, worked toward the separation of the direct producers from ownership of their means of subsistence—a key precondition for the production of labor as a commodity. This process now had the backing of a state that appears to have been trying to extract revenues more effectively as part of a self-strengthening drive in the face of European colonialism. Nonetheless, in many cases the structure of the domain was not modified. The practice of redistribution continued and ownership rights were partly theoretical; the only real change was that a number of *fellahin* who had been owners with effective usufruct rights now became more like tenants under greater control of the landowner.[35]

PROPERTY RIGHTS, CASH, AND RENT LEASING

In other cases, communal ownership and communal tenure had been more definitively broken up. Villages with larger land-holdings, increasingly exclusive property rights based on an end to redistribution and irrevocable partition, and a more extensive use of cash came into existence. This was often a slow and piecemeal process that often began with a local notable gaining stronger control over the lots closest to the village, especially the more intensively cultivated and valuable gardens, olive trees, and vines. The process was partly reversible, as when these villages began cultivating previously uncultivated land, on a *musha'* basis, and the new land was subject to redistribution. At this point, the process begins again. Weulersse gave the example of Maallaka in the Biqa' valley and Tel Aran near Aleppo as villages of this kind.[36] Under such circumstances, larger and more consolidated estates came into being. In some cases, large estate formation involved eviction and dispossession, a technique used by landowners to raise the rate of exploitation and increase levels of feudal obligation for those left behind or threatened, and a factor in new forms of forced migration.[37] In other cases, especially between the wars, estate formation involved the more widespread use of rent leasing land to newly subordinated tenants, as landowners began to see this as the most profitable way to exploit their domains. The pressing need for cash on the part of rent-leasing tenants paved the way for outmigration of certain family members in search of cash. Such forces were intensified because, only now, in these kinds of domains, with the establishment of rival and exclusive property rights to land, could division of the land through inheritance on Qur'anic grounds take place. This process led to "a true pulverization of property"[38] and the effective dispossession of new family members from access to adequate means of subsistence, forcing them to turn to other sources of subsistence. One way to acquire such means of subsistence, in which property rights were more secure, was to turn to the cash economy, a process that could pave the way for cash-hungry outmigration. Finally, the entrenchment of property rights implied the enclosure of common land, cutting off noncash means of subsistence, implying a parallel eviction into the cash economy.[39] Forms of enclosure were linked not only to the power of the propertied but also that of the state, especially under the French Mandate. Under the Mandate, for example, common grazing rights—the means of independent subsistence for many cultivators—were seen by officials as a menace. Hence, "goats have always been a menace to the natural growth of forests in this country and since under the Turkish regime no regulations were enforced preventing goats from entering the forests, the new growth was destroyed by them in extensive areas."[40] This vision of a *mise en valeur* of a natural resource, in this case the forests, based on market economy tied to state power, worked against forms of economy not based on rival and exclusive property rights and cash payments, reducing independent means of subsistence for direct producers. Meanwhile, Mandate policy worked to entrench property rights in land and "give a legal footing to lands that had been acquired by seizure and pillage."[41] Property rights, cash economy, state enforcement, and the discourse of conventional economics advanced together. Mundy and Saumarez Smith note that "from the 1920s people began to move not into but out of the ['Ajlun] region for work—for seasonal work to the ports and fields of Palestine and then, slowly, to the growing towns of Transjordan for study or work in the army and trade."[42]

SHARECROPPING AND DEBT

On the other hand, where large estates reincorporated tenants as indebted sharecroppers, outmigration was heavily restricted. Sharecropping meant that a peasant family worked a small plot on a landed estate and handed over some proportion of the harvest to the landowner while cultivating the rest on their own account for their own consumption. Arrangements varied according to the division of the crop at harvest, but also by the extent to which the sharecropper provided seed, livestock, and tools, and according to what kinds of dues, taxes, and forms of forced labor were imposed.[43] After decades of world economic incorporation, the landowner's portion was often a cash crop, regularly an inedible one, whereas the peasant's plot produced more diversified food crops mostly for home consumption. Under these conditions, the marketing of the cash crop was the affair of the landowner, his deputies, and city merchants, and had little to do with the peasant family producing for subsistence, whose trips to the market were far more infrequent. Such families lived on locally produced bread, burghul, and milk, in houses built by villagers from local materials. They had little furniture, cotton rolls served as bedding, clothes were made in the household, and the baskets and pots for storing food and items such as drinking flasks were made either in the household or the village. The key purchases in this context were limited to imported fabric used to make clothes and bedding.[44]

For sharecroppers, the pressures of the cash economy were indirect but acute. Where landowners' rate of profit was in direct proportion to the area devoted to the cash crop, subsistence plots accorded to peasants came under pressure. The resultant land poverty, in addition to harvest fluctuations caused by fickle weather patterns, the attendant lack of food security and reserves, the need in many sharecropping contracts to provide seed and livestock, the very oppressive and increasingly bureaucratic and cash-based taxation (often levied before harvest), the need to pay out for major social occasions such as weddings, and the local political clout of landowners and merchants, levered peasant families into heavy indebtedness to local moneylenders, merchants, or the local landowner, who were often the same person.[45] Notables borrowed from banks at low interest, new credit facilities that peasants had no ability to access, and then made loans at usurious rates of 30 to 40 percent or more.[46] Heavy debtors were not permitted to abscond, and so became *de facto* peons. Therefore, the growth of sharecropping in a context of growing cash economy worked to *fix* certain kinds of cultivators to the land and forestall the possibility of outmigration. Sharecroppers found themselves trapped in both direct and indirect control, suffering "all the ills of servitude, but without the relative security that this might offer."[47] The binding of sharecroppers to particular "lords"—part and parcel of world economic incorporation—helps explain why outmigration from the grain-producing plains of Syria was so limited until the 1950s and 1960s.

PEASANT PROPRIETORS, CASH, AND SILK

Collective ownership, collective tenure, and sharecropping were the dominant relations of production in the interior grain-producing and rain-fed plains in the 1930s. What appeared to many French observers as archaism, and to modernizers and developmentalist Marxists as undifferentiated backwardness, had already been through a series of transformations pressuring noncash means of existence and creating sharecroppers tied by debt. Land parcels largely owned and exploited by individual families were more common in irrigated regions and the coastal zones, where vines, olives, figs, oranges, and lemons were intensively cultivated; in orchards and gardens close to towns; and in the mountains of Lebanon and Anti-Lebanon where water, political refuge, and security were available. In these areas, collective rights were often only exercised with regard to the general distribution of water; in other domains, "the proprietor [was] sovereign." In these areas, the use of cash, the division of labor, and specialization were more developed. Large estates growing olives, vines, and oranges were said to be "less miserable," since these crops required a "minimum of consenting collaboration" between the *agha* and cultivator, as the latter held a valuable crop in his hands. "Hence the master is interested in having good tenants and keeping them, which implies on his part certain accommodations."[48] More strikingly, a particular kind of contract—the *mugharisa*—worked to give formerly landless tenants the chance to acquire land. This co-planting contract was based on the fact that olives and vines needed to be grown for some years prior to giving any yield. Here, sharecropping did not work because there was no crop to share for a number of seasons. Hence, peasant families were drawn to cultivate by the promise that "in exchange for their five to seven year labor investment, peasants would acquire one quarter of the new ... land" brought under cultivation.[49] In some instances, the cultivator merely acquired rights to the trees and not the soil. In this case, when the trees disappeared, the rights did also, leaving the cultivator utterly dependent on the original landowner. But many peasants acquired rights to the soil—rights that were increasingly recognized and registered with the state. Here, peasants became owner-proprietors producing not just for their own subsistence, but for the cash economy, engaged in buying and selling themselves. These patterns particularly emerged in intensively cultivated regions of Mt. Lebanon, the Lattakia coast, and the Orontes valley (near Antakya). For some French observers, this meant a veritable "social emancipation," a profound economic change, and the emergence of a class of peasant proprietors.[50]

These factors formed the background to the ways in which cultivators in Mt. Lebanon responded to new demands for silk worm and thread production for French industry from the 1860s onward. World markets were clearly not simply superimposed by force on a stagnant agrarian "Orient," but linkages, at some levels, were actively forged by existing partially local dynamics. On Mt. Lebanon, silk had become by the 1900s an "essential cash crop on which Lebanese peasants depended for their survival."[51] More and more of the land was devoted to the cash production of silk, less and less to the production of diversified food for home consumption. Increased purchasing power, the use of cash, and the reduction of alternative noncash means of existence, debt, and attempts to escape it levered cultivators into the cash economy through combinations of coercion and consent. In Mt. Lebanon in the late nineteenth century Khater speaks not of "unbridled consumerism" but a shift from matters of survival to a "quest for some modicum of luxury"—meaning purchases of coffee, rice, and sugar.[52] "Sugar was among the most luxurious and novel" of the new products. Historically, diets had been sweetened by grape or carob molasses, honey, figs, and so on—local products acquired without cash. But the consumption of sugar produced on plantations in the Caribbean and elsewhere increased during the later nineteenth and earlier twentieth century.[53] Rice, which had been very expensive, came to be in widespread use. And coffee, which had previously been the drink of the *shuyukh*, was now the drink of choice.[54]

At stake in these processes were violence, hierarchy, and new consumption choices, which were only made, as Mintz puts it, "within a range of possibilities laid down by forces over those who were, supposedly, freely choosing exercised no control at all."[55] On the global level, the cheap prices of sugar, rice, and coffee owed much to colonial production based on plantation slavery, indenture, cheap colonial labor, and racial hierarchy.[56] European merchant trade in the Levant on terms favorable to Europeans owed much to the changing balance of military power between the Ottomans and the European empires. Enlisting British support to put down Mehmet Ali, provincial governor of Egypt (1805–1848), the Ottomans signed commercial treaties with Britain and later others, abolishing Ottoman monopolies and giving European merchants favorable tariffs. French merchants gained a particular priority in the Levant when Mt. Lebanon was given a special partially autonomous status as a *mutasarrifiyya* under some measure of French control and protection after the rebellion, civil strife, and sectarian killings of 1860.

On the local level, increased silk production was not simply a disembedded, atomized, and voluntaristic choice, or a matter of increasing the value of one's land through growing mulberry trees and raising silk worms. It also involved patriarchal control, the disciplines of debt, and various kinds of labor repression and violence. The growth of market economy was associated with indebtedness. This was partly because the more prices were set by the market, the more exceptionally good harvests were incapable of drawing peasants out of debt because in such cases of abundance, prices fell. Certainly, Weulersse associated growing indebtedness with "richer" regions, close to cities, where debt contracts were more rigorously enforced and cash production more common.[57]

Silk thread, moreover, was produced in part on the broken backs of orphans and unmarried daughters. On Mt. Lebanon, "men, whose identity and honor were tightly linked to tilling a plot of land, were hesitant to be seen in a factory." This attitude "severely limited the supply of male labor available to factory owners," who constantly complained about this.[58] Those clinging to economic independence refused to descend into the factories: "Only those few who did not own even a small piece of land accepted factory work, and they did so reluctantly. Yet even they were uncooperative in following the dictates of the foreman as well as an artificial work schedule, and they generally voted against becoming proletarian by staying home."[59] Peasants revealed their reluctance by disappearing even after European factory owners had trained them and given them cash advances for their labor.

Therefore, French factory owners began filling their factories with girls from orphanages, the only social group sufficiently weak and powerless to be set upon by the disciplines of commodification.[60] But, faced with land hunger, debt, and taxation, and looking for a way to avoid the slide into "landless laboring," "those men who were most in need of cash sent their daughters to work in the proliferating silk factories." As Khater puts it, women's honor was sacrificed to safeguard the fathers'.[61] As one French report put it, "It is difficult to give a complete picture of the miserable aspects of the lives of women employed in spinning silk, of the horrible deformations of their hands, of the bad state of health amongst many of them, and of the repulsive odors which attach to their clothes." Outside the factory, moreover, women were tainted socially and lost their marriage chances if they worked through years of marriageable age.[62] The forms of agency that women then acquired, what Khater calls the "power of independent and individualized decision making" were unsurprisingly "not necessarily . . . [viewed] as liberating."[63] Within the factories, the hierarchical logics of patriarchy, now reconstituted, operated to control the female labor force, supervised and disciplined by men.[64]

These processes meant a higher standard of consumption for some, but created new kinds of dependency highly relevant to cash-hunger and outmigration. Once ensnared within the global market, the very instability and rapid fluctuations of that market had a dramatic impact. The opening of the Suez Canal in 1869, and increasingly cheap silk production in China and Japan formed the background to French merchants' switching to the Far East for their silk supplies. By the 1890s, Lebanese silk was in a slump from which it never recovered. Khater argues that with stagnating silk prices, "the elevated expectations of peasants (and not their poverty) propelled many of them to leave the mountain and to emigrate to the Americas."[65] Cultivators and workers had become increasingly linked to a market system with endemic instabilities of its own. Khater aptly writes that "peasants stepped further into the market economy, added more debts, and became more vulnerable to the changing fortunes of the silk market."[66] Families who had become heavily dependent on cash incomes generated through the silk industry now had to consider how to prevent a slide into landlessness and dishonor. Given the striking coincidence of the slump of the 1890s with the emergence of outmigration on a mass scale from the *bilad ash-sham*, it seems reasonable to see the slump as a crucial mechanism shaking loose the population of Mt. Lebanon. This time, the gendered dynamics of social reproduction meant that it was mostly young men, not unmarried girls, who were to take on the main burden of departing from the domestic community of production to earn cash. Previously established patterns of migration were insufficiently lucrative, and outmigrants increasingly looked overseas. As Hourani has noted, the bulk of the migrants from the 1850s to the early 1900s were young men from Christian mountain villages.[67] As Widmer puts it, most went to better their economic conditions, but many were "forced to go by their inability to gain an adequate livelihood for themselves and their families."[68]

CONSCRIPTION

In certain areas, conscription also put a squeeze on access to noncash means of existence and intensified the search for cash. Although too little is known about the impact of conscription on the peasantry in the late Ottoman Empire, it has tended to be treated as a cause of outmigration because cultivators were psychologically averse and entirely unaccustomed to military service. While there is no reason to doubt that such factors mattered, it also seems fair to point out that conscription struck at the ability of peasant communities to materially reproduce themselves. This is because conscription seized and threatened to seize able-bodied young men who would otherwise be earning cash or working in domestic production and who were crucial for the status, standard of living, and income of the families concerned. As the Ottomans faced European power and nationalist secession, and appropriated the European conscript-army model, conscription levels were raised. From 1895 in particular, the Ottomans pushed a military recruitment campaign deeper into the settled countryside of the province of Syria. "The programme," writes Akarlı, "created a commotion among the Syrian peasants, who were unaccustomed to and uninterested in military service of any kind. Emigration began to appear as an attractive idea." This especially affected Muslims in districts adjacent to Mt. Lebanon. By 1906–07, the Ottoman authorities were frustrated at their inability to contain the "escape" of enlistable peasants from the provinces of Syria and Beirut.[69] However, Mt. Lebanon was exempt from compulsory Ottoman military service from 1860 onward. Christians in Syria were exempt only until 1909, when conscription became "very burdensome" due to the Balkan wars.[70] Certainly Ottoman border regimes did not present a significant barrier to outmigrants. Whereas conscription played a role in prompting outmigration, it did so partly through the very mechanisms of increasing actual or feared cash-hunger. Had conscription been accompanied by real benefits, it may well have been viewed in a completely different light.

DEMOGRAPHY

Debates have long raged over the importance of population pressure in migration. Whereas demographers have often maintained that population growth puts pressure on resources and land, Marxists have equally consistently maintained that the structure of resources and the relevant mode of production puts pressure on population and defines its movements. Against the first position, whether in the *bilad ash-sham* or elsewhere, there is no simple correlation between population growth and the changing rate of outmigration. Population growth did not peak during 1900 to 1914, when migration appears to have done so, nor did it suddenly end when migration almost ceased in the 1930s. The population was not rising only in areas that sent migrants, and receiving areas occasionally had a higher rate of population growth and higher population density (a result not just of net immigration) than sending areas. And some migrants came from areas where the population was not growing. Certainly population growth and/or imbalance cannot be seen as a sufficient or even a necessary condition for labor migration. Widmer, writing in the 1930s, rightly argued that population growth could be only of secondary importance, and the main causes of migration from Syria and Lebanon were political and economic.[71] Nonetheless, some argue that the growth of population exerted an "intense pressure" on resources and thus was an important feature of migration. On the one hand, land prices were driven skyward "beyond the reach of our average peasant," and on the other hand, the subdivision of land through inheritance made plots unsustainable.[72] It is not clear, however, that a doubling in population would increase the price of land, all other things being equal. For this to happen, the land has to be for sale in the first place, which was a production of state policy and market economy, not of population. Likewise, subdivision required the prior establishment and practice of exclusive and rival property rights, and the application of inheritance law to them, a process that took place in many ways on the Mountain through the nineteenth century, as noted earlier.

It is extremely difficult, moreover, to specify the meaning and details of the highly abstract notion of population pressure and to link it to forms of migrant agency. The argument here is that since population growth contributed to the squeeze on access to alternative means of existence, and to cash-hunger, then it must have played some role in outmigration. However, the political, institutional, and economic advent of market economy, in the ways described earlier, and the way these forms worked themselves out in particular locations, was responsible for ensuring that population pressure *translated into* cash and subsistence hunger and therefore pressure to outmigrate. Hence, demography was secondary to the power structures of market economy in determining the basis of economic migration.[73]

EDUCATION AND THE PRESS

Numerous accounts of migration from the Levant as from the rest of the world have stressed growing awareness and the spread of education, literacy, and the press as part and parcel of outmigration because it communicated opportunities to potential outmigrants, opened their eyes to worlds beyond their own relatively closed and "traditional" vistas, and made them think in larger terms about possibilities for livelihoods in particular and life in general. This kind of approach involves the problematic assumption that information, education, and the press are neutral processes that merely raise awareness about the true state of the world outside and reality in general. In serving such an enlightening function, these institutions thus become essential components of civilization and modernization, or, in anticolonial mode, the coming to consciousness of the new nation. Since the writings of Antonio Gramsci, at least, it has been harder to view the institutions of civil society, intimately linked to hegemony, leadership, and relations of coercion, in this rather naïve light. In the study of the nineteenth-century *mashriq*, Ussama Makdisi has pioneered a more critical approach to such matters with his study of the ways in which missionaries, Ottoman and European schools, the press, and the spread of literacy, linked to Ottoman state building and European imperialism, worked to build up new ways of seeing the world, in particular a "culture of sectarianism" in Mt. Lebanon, Beirut, and beyond.[74] Such a method can be fruitfully applied to the study of outmigration, which was neither a simple matter of growing "awareness," nor, in the more Marxian version, a question of the "propaganda" of the steamship companies falsely speaking of lands of milk and honey overseas in order to boost ticket sales. In combination with power relations, new forms of education, the press, and literacy worked to construct the world and the self in new ways in terms of categories related to colonial discourse and modernist value. One might hypothesize here that far from enlightening the simple peasants of the Mountain, these discourses worked to insert them within an emerging, global, civilizational hierarchy; normalized certain courses of action and thought; and played a role in creating sites of value and desire in the colonial centers overseas.

The emerging languages of *mise en valeur* (valorization or profit-making) and economic thinking worked to specify and construct the related categories of "manpower" and "labor." This category was to be rigorously applied to migrants, not simply as a purely cultural or individual matter but also because this category was increasingly written into state policy, structures of accumulation, and new forms of control and servitude. Where the goal was to develop and exploit the "natural resources" of Syria and Lebanon—their soil, water, minerals, fisheries, forests, livestock, summer resorts,[75] and the labor supply—those who worked for human needs or for use-value rather than profit were increasingly seen as ignorant and backward. Speaking of the peasant, an authoritative voice tied to languages of economic thinking in the 1930s claimed, "He is ignorant and works not for profit but for mere subsistence."[76] The expansion of money for its own sake, the transformation of money (M) into more money (M') via the commodity form (C) was now deemed more rational than the search for use-value regarding particular, definable, and vital needs.

Far from being simply enlightened by new forms of education, it seems reasonable to hypothesize that most migrants were enlightened as to their own relative lack of education and therefore status and opportunity. Although there were numerous educated persons among the migrants, according to Widmer, the largest group was from "the lower strata of society, consisting mainly of laborers."[77] In this sense, migrants were made to appear and see themselves as backward and underdeveloped.

MIGRATION AGAINST COMMUNITY

Mass industrial employment was unavailable in the towns and cities of the *mashriq*, where conditions for the industrial production of manufactured tradable goods were hostile, and opportunities for accumulation existed in nonindustrial investments in land, commerce, and physical infrastructure. Indeed, in all of Syria and Palestine, before 1914, there were fewer than 100 factories employing more than 50 workers each.[78] New and restructured crafts and service work in the towns involved crowded and competitive forms of self-employment and waged-labor with limited capacity to absorb those moving off the land.[79] State employment was a possibility only for a very few. Local employment opportunities, therefore, did not keep pace with growing pressures for cash, the undermining of older livelihoods, and the attrition of independent access to noncash means of subsistence.

Nonetheless, rural-urban migration in search of work was on the increase from the late nineteenth century onward. Workers came from nearby regions to Damascus, Aleppo, and, to a lesser extent, Homs to work temporarily (usually for 1 to 3 months), especially in construction. These migrations became increasingly permanent during the French Mandate. Construction workers from Dayr Attiya, in the Qalamoun, specializing in clay work usually for waterproofing (*tayyana*), formed one such group.[80] Infrastructural investment, especially in the port cities, created slots for manual and "dirty" labor of various kinds. Villagers temporarily left the Hawran, especially with the arrival of the railway connection in the 1890s, to work on railway and harbor construction, and as porters in the rapidly expanding port of Haifa, which, rather than Damascus or more distant Beirut, seems to have been the main destination for such workers, who lived on the Tel al-Amal (Hill of Work) on the eastern entrance to the town. As porters in Haifa in the 1930s, these workers would certainly have been witness to the labor mobilization and strikes of that period, although their role in this has not been researched.[81] Hawranis did work in small numbers in Beirut, however, and others came from the countryside around Homs. For example, in 2004, I interviewed an octogenarian, Elias (b. 1923), from *wadi al-nasara* in the Homs region, who had worked on earthworks overseen by the British army for the Tapline oil pipeline in Beirut in the early 1940s. At Syrian Lira (SL) ½ to 1 per day, and staying four to a room, Elias had worked for six months and then for three months among about 100 mostly Lebanese workers.[82] Although the evidence is thin, menial work in workshops in Beirut does not seem to have involved sufficient advantages by comparison with similar work in Syria to sustain significant migration from the State of Syria to Lebanon under the Mandate. Jubran Hilal (1908–1990), a Christian trade unionist from Ma'lula in the Qalamoun, worked as a baker's boy in Bab Tuma, Damascus, in his teens. His memoirs afford a tantalizingly brief mention of how he set off on foot to Beirut in the mid-1920s and worked in a bakery there for six months before making a permanent return. He writes that he sought to escape oppressive hours and working conditions but once in Beirut he started to miss Damascus too much.[83]

Cash, on the other hand, was to be found, and rumored to be found, in greater quantities in overseas colonial centers, heavily implicated in the plunder and profit associated with colonialism. Under these circumstances, and with the development of a transport infrastructure of railways and steamships, which both undergirded and served as a by-product of world economic incorporation, and with generally open borders in the Americas, increasing numbers of peasant-workers set out overseas. Once a few demonstrated their financial success on return, and social networks of various kinds were established, cultivators under pressure from socioeconomic circumstances at home started to travel in numbers.

Colonial economies were undergoing major shifts that created demands for menial, waged-labor. In the United States, for example, independent Euroamerican artisan-farmers and homesteaders who had seized and taken advantage of "open resources" through the mass dispossession and genocide of settler colonialism were increasingly drawn into the market economy through debts, mortgages, state policies, the division of labor in farming and manufacture, the railroads, and new forms of accumulation and consumption. Independent craftsmen, homesteading, and household putting out systems were put under pressure and displaced by cash-based industrial expansion and infrastructure building during the second half of the nineteenth century.[84] These shifts created demands for primary sector waged jobs, which were more secure, better remunerated, protected, and unionized, on the one hand, and secondary sector, menial, dirty, poorly paid, and dangerous jobs on the other hand, in the railroads, mines, plantations, canneries, logging camps, and so on. Whereas former homesteaders and new waves of European immigrants tended to fill the primary sector jobs of the labor aristocracy, those at the bottom of racial and civilizational hierarchies—colonial migrants from Asia and Latin America, and ex-slaves from the southern states—often filled degrading, secondary sector jobs. Coercion, politics, culture, and economic factors were all at play in the production of this segmented labor market, which can hardly be explained by *either* dual labor market theory alone *or* simple racism. Economic structures and racial hierarchy—"socially constructed processes which define group identities and interests"—appear to have grown together and "co-produced" each other in powerful ways.[85] And the segmented labor market was not merely a reflection of factors on the demand side, as is often assumed or argued. The *supply* of impoverished and unorganized colonial workers on a significant scale fed back to encourage patterns of accumulation that involved menial, dangerous, unstable, and poorly remunerated labor.

In keeping with the semicivilized status widely accorded Levantines, *turcos*, Arabians and Syrians, as migrants from the Ottoman *bilad ash-sham* were known in different parts of the Americas. Such migrants neither worked in the relatively stable, primary sector jobs of the white labor aristocracy, nor, commonly, in the back-breaking, dangerous, and filthy "coolie" labor of the plantations and railroads. Instead, many Syrians, perhaps a majority of all those who went to the Americas, started work in peddling. In Mexico, for example, Syrians and Lebanese worked in peddling while Chinese and Japanese were engaged in manual labor building railways.[86] Rural households, no longer able to provide for all their needs independently, were increasingly eager to buy from itinerant peddlers, particularly when more established retail outlets were distant in areas where demand was limited, fluctuating, and fragmented into multiple locations, and before the advent of automobiles. It was this "slot" that Lebanese and Syrians, willing to lug their wares long distances in heat and cold, in search of cash, made their own. From Buenos Aires to Boston, recently arrived Syrians were to be found selling door-to-door fancy goods, household items, hardware, lace, buttons, trinkets, and, coining Orientalist biblical exoticism into cash, crosses from the "Holy Land."[87]

Departing migrants were torn from familiar structures of value, community, and recognition and had to endure what the History Task Force call the "pain and sacrifice of dismantling the networks of kinship and sociability that give life meaning."[88] In some senses, migrants underwent dismemberment—in the figurative sense of breaking limb from limb and in a literal sense of the migrant ceasing to be a clearly defined member of a known community. Dismemberment occurred as the constituent elements of personhood were dragged around, "shoved about, used indiscriminately, or even left unused"[89] by the alienation on the international labor market of the commodity labor-power to which bearers were inextricably attached. The intimate and daily pressures on communities, families, women, and children left behind, moreover, were formidable. A vivid glimpse of such strains is afforded by a letter written by a resident of the village of Dayr Attiya in the Qalamoun to his brother in Brazil in April 1933:

> By God, my brother, come back to us! Stop everything and come back to us, even if you are poor and have nothing. Come back to us hungry or naked, God will take care of everything. Come back to us to see your parents and family weighed down with calamities, and whose backs are bent with misfortune, and who unceasingly mourn their bad luck by day and night. It makes no difference to us if you bring with you thousands in gold, or you return as you left, empty-handed. Only one thing concerns us: to see you among us soon.[90]

This excerpt offers a fleeting glimpse into the intimate worlds of communities torn asunder by migration. The repeated emphasis on the fact that even without funds, the migrant should return is a powerful indication that the search for much-needed cash was precisely the *raison d'etre* of the migration. Nonetheless, the writer attempts to override this original rationale by making an urgent appeal to filial duty and the ties of family now clearly jeopardized as a result of cash-migration. The implication of the reference to "bent backs" and "calamities," and the exhortations to return, even penniless, is that the family is in dire material need of assistance and an extra pair of hands at home, and not necessarily remittances, which may have been uncertain or nonexistent, especially given the writer's apparent uncertainty about the economic status of his brother.[91]

In fact, immediate riches in the Americas were unlikely. Social and economic conditions abroad were tough.[92] A measure of such pressures is that in spite of the shame, women who joined their men overseas also went out to work in the streets because of the pressing need for cash.[93] Moreover, migrants now encountered a structured assault on their identities and sense of self. These were colonial migrants, entering previously structured communities, and unassisted, in Bauman's striking phrase, by "armies of *conquistadores*, tradesmen and missionaries."[94] Khater writes that the dominant culture in the United States was "not particularly hospitable," where migrants were faced with various kinds of civilizing mission and blunt racism and reaction.[95] Mostly, Khater argues, migrants could achieve "financial success" in the United States only if they could successfully not appear "different." This struggle over migrants' "Otherness" touched "almost every aspect of their lives." "Their clothes, language and accent, food, and social habits became measures of their Otherness."[96] In other words, the confrontation with this dominant, colonial, and Orientalist discourse was a profoundly intimate affair. Syrians "found themselves caught in the midst of the artificial construct of 'East' and 'West.' Were they of the 'traditional' (read: backward) 'East' or of the 'modern West'? Were they on the side of science or enlightenment or that of superstition and ignorance?"[97]

In this harsh context, it is not at all surprising that, in nostalgic mode, migrants conceiving themselves to be in exile, hankered after the homeland in an "East" conceived as spiritual, warm, pastoral, idyllic, and communal, in contrast to the cold, alienated, and modern West.[98] Nonetheless, those who did return found that migration was, in Stuart Hall's terms, a "one way trip." As has been written regarding other return migrants, "eager homecomers . . . anxious to pick up the threads of a cherished way of life . . . [found] themselves strangers and intruders in their own land."[99] These multiple forms of alienation set the stage for the long, arduous, and often unfinished task of renovating and rebuilding means of production and independent existence and forging new forms of identification and community.

RENOVATION

At no point were those who set out overseas to earn cash in return for labor or services fully proletarianized or completely commodified. Although exposed to the rigors and disciplines of commodification, rent from their communities and inserted elsewhere as aliens and inferiors, they were only ever, in Polanyi's language, "fictitious commodities." They were not the beggars of Marx's primitive accumulation, spewed forth by absolute dispossession and utterly subordinated to the demands of capital. Instead, potential migrants were, first of all, reproduced by the institutions and dynamics of sexual reproduction. That is, in Polanyi's terms, unlike other commodities, such as bales of cotton, they were not produced for the market, but by nonmarket-strategic processes, gendered dynamics, marriage patterns, and unpaid, and therefore uncommodified and unproletarianized, female labor. Moreover, male migrants played a specific, gendered role, that of breadwinner, and were linked thereby to domestic communities of production and reproduction. Migrants aimed to earn the wherewithal to establish such domestic communities more securely through either obtaining a home, marrying well, multiplying their offspring, acquiring independent noncash access to the means of subsistence (that is, land for subsistence farming, the unpaid labor of women and children), or independent control over means of production linked to markets (that is, small businesses, land for cash crop production, and so on). In this way, usually young migrants neither planned to nor actually did work out their years selling their labor for cash. They sweated in order to escape and become their own boss as quickly as possible, or, at the very least so that during unemployment and eventual retirement they could draw on their domestic communities for material and social security, and live, in some sense, "at home." Migrants, then, carried on a continuous struggle to recuperate the wherewithal to acquire use-values and the means of a more independent existence.[100]

"Syrians" who migrated were usually linked to domestic communities of production on departure. It was not the landless, proletarianized, and most impoverished who departed, not least because they lacked the resources to absent themselves from the domestic community and pay for the ticket overseas.[101] Instead, it was often those aiming to prevent a *slide into* landlessness, and struggling to regain elements of independence in changing times, that motivated persons to undertake the risks and uncertainties of migration. Absolute numbers of landless agricultural laborers living by cash alone in the *bilad ash-sham* were quite low. In the 1940s, Weulersse wrote that the agricultural worker, the *ajir*, was an exception. The *ajir*, it was said, appears only as a temporary assistant in small property, or in the service of petit bourgeois in town or small notables of the village, and even then many such workers were not paid—but lodged and fed. The status was temporary because those aiming to marry had to establish themselves as sharecroppers.[102] One estimate for "floating laborers" in 1924 was as high as 92,700, but the source gives no indication of whether such workers were entirely severed from alternative means of subsistence and permanently dependent on cash. Indeed, given that the same source suggested that in the 1920s and 1930s the employment of daily paid laborers was "little resorted to except in the immediate vicinity of towns," it would appear that such a "floating" population was only temporarily so.[103] In short, those who left were not the vast masses of dispossessed proletarians envisaged in Marx's primitive accumulation, but those based in heavily pressured and changing domestic communities.[104]

Only a few lived out their lives solitarily hauling household goods and knocking on doors across rural areas in the Americas. Syrians who stayed in the *mahjar* found ways to "invent home" and to protect themselves against the rigors of commodification and proletarianization. Some saved enough to rent a stall in urban markets; some settled as shopkeepers; others expanded further to become wholesalers, and still others acquired sufficient capital to become manufacturers of textiles and other goods.[105] Migrants generated their own needs: Workshops or shops were established producing or importing Lebanese or Syrian cuisine. By the early 1900s, the numbers of women departing the *bilad ash-sham* drastically increased as men abroad acquired the means to marry them in the *mahjar*. These marriages brought a second generation into being. As numbers grew, and a sense of community developed, organizations, clubs, and churches were established. In time, political disputes imported from Lebanon and Syria were joined.[106] A full-length monograph published in Arabic in Havana, Cuba, in the 1930s, aiming to acquaint Arabs in the Americas with the noble cause of Arab nationalism, and French atrocities in putting down the Syrian Great Revolt of 1925–1927, is a striking example of the political and cultural extension of community in the *mahjar* over time.[107] As settlement and community building went ahead in foreign lands, however, and as second generations grew up entirely outside of their parents' birthplaces, material, familial, linguistic, and cultural links to domestic communities in the Levant were progressively severed, at least until the later twentieth century, when "transmigrants" started to discover their roots and to reactivate linkages long broken up.

Those who returned to Lebanon and Syria did not (re)enter the ranks of waged-labor. As Khater showed, and in contrast to earlier scholarship assuming that migrants journeyed to America to assimilate and become American, many migrants intended to return, and did so, even if, and sometimes especially because, they had been financially successful and thus acquired the resources to make a successful return.[108] Many returnees no longer plowed but owned larger tracts, bought education for their children, owned bigger houses, and wore expensive clothing and gold watches to display their success.[109] Local consumption patterns changed. In the Anti-Lebanon, by the 1930s, small villages that had been self-sufficient around 1900, now in receipt of significant remittances, were said to maintain a continuous commerce with the big towns. Thoumin wrote that "thirty years ago, the voyage of an inhabitant of Yabroud to Damascus marked a noteworthy event," and on return the villager would make customary visits. After 1929, a bus, "often full" goes every day to Damascus and returns in the afternoon. Women would go to the Hamidiyya market to buy fabrics, printed cottons, artificial silk, shoes, aluminium pots, glass cupboards, French hats, sewing machines, and even phonographs.[110]

UNINTENDED CONSEQUENCES

While migrants were exposed and exposed themselves to the rigors of commodification and proletarianization, their constant aim was to escape this condition. Such a goal might take years or even a lifetime to achieve, but many did so, albeit in greatly varying degrees. Under existing circumstances, most migrants clearly felt that the securest way to improve their conditions was not to unionize, confront capital and the state head-on, and nail their colors to the uncertain fortunes of the socialist revolution, but to save up, maintain linkages to domestic communities of production, sacrifice themselves while pining their hopes on their children, and/or create new forms of access to means of production. For those with family responsibilities and very little material room to maneuver, and who were faced in any case with exclusion and stigma in regard to existing labor movements, national and civilizational categories, such "conservative" patterns made sense. These did not stem from nostalgia, petty bourgeois backsliding, or false consciousness, as many Marxists claimed. Such ways of living, however, were based on individuals and families and were not antisystemic. New access to means of production often involved the production of commodities for the market and was easily developed to include the capitalist exploitation of labor. Remittances and earnings drew more migrants and their families, and sending areas further into the cash economy and consumer culture. Such patterns meant a higher standard of living for some, but tied Lebanon and Syria more firmly into the world power system of economic dependence. These patterns generated surpluses for those controlling global financial, commercial, and industrial circuits, and transferred power into the hands of those in the colonial centers who made key decisions over the allocation of economic resources.

These patterns further devalued and undermined the old established ways of making a living, intensified cash hunger, and worked to entrench rival and exclusive property rights that destroyed access to common lands and rights and noncash forms of independent subsistence. Cash economy in the Levant and in the transnational world more generally often meant debt servitude without security, patriarchy without protection, colonial violence without justice, and civilizational hierarchy without meaningful civilization. Direct and exposed forms of hierarchy and subordination did not disappear, contrary to the claims of many strands of modernism. Instead, market economy added the "control over things" (that is, commodities, land, natural resources, and so on) to the arsenal of means of control over persons, which included a remaking of languages and practices of civilization, race, and gender.

Migration, with all its social miseries and forms of commodification and communal dismemberment, seemed only to pave the way for more migration. The offspring of return migrants, whether newly educated or not, were unlikely, under polarizing conditions, to find adequate employment in the sending countries. Economic dependency, moreover, now linked whole economies and societies to the vagaries, instability, and perpetual flux and creative-destruction of the global economy. Finally, the civilizational hierarchy already established by the mid-nineteenth century remained remarkably stable. The Beiruti thinkers of the *nahda* in the 1860s conceived of Arabs and Syrians as semi-civilized, below civilized Europeans but above barbarians from Africa. It is remarkable to observe how little this hierarchy was changed by decades of outmigration and effort. In many ways, migrants further appropriated civilizational hierarchies as their own and brought them back to sending countries. The Lebanese were still conceived as semi-civilized in the years following World War II, hence their categorization as "white" by South African apartheid, while Egyptians, for example, were categorized as "black."[111]

WORLD ECONOMIC DISARTICULATION

The global system of productive power established on a world scale through European colonialism, liberal capitalism, and, in a subordinate sense, by transnational labor migrants, in the nineteenth century entered a profound crisis and in various crucial ways broke up during the first half of the twentieth century. World economic incorporation had accompanied unprecedented transnational labor flows on a global scale, and the crisis and break up of the system accompanied the dismantling and attrition of such movements, which had been drastically reduced by the Second World War.

From the later nineteenth century onward, countries in the Americas were raising barriers. Mexico's immigration and naturalization law of 1886 "deprived women who married foreigners of their Mexican nationality." In 1890, 1894, and 1915, Uruguay repeatedly prohibited Asian and African immigration, with varying degrees of success. Cuba's Spanish rulers banned the Ottoman influx in 1891. Haiti closed its doors on all Syro-Lebanese in 1903.[112] Britain, France, and Germany all began to restrict immigration in the late nineteenth century.[113] The United States, after successive waves of agitation, closed its doors to Chinese, Japanese, and various other Asian migrants from the 1880s onward. Most other immigrants were heavily restricted by the closures of the early 1920s.

The First World War temporarily put a stop to the vast bulk of migrant flows. The Bolshevik Revolution of 1917 delinked in significant respects the vast territories and populations of the new Soviet Union from the world economy. After the Great War, London no longer had the imperial clout or will to underpin and enforce a liberal world economy. The United States scaled back the imperialism and jingoism of the 1890s and 1900s, and although hardly passive in its own hemisphere, remained in isolationist mode, at least compared to the post-1945 period, with regard to the world economy at large. Tariff barriers were raised and protective measures were enacted almost universally. The rise of fascism in Europe and imperialism in Japan involved, *inter alia*, a drive for economic autarchy. The world economy of the later nineteenth century was breaking up.

The worldwide depression of the 1930s meant that for many migrants, including Syrians and Lebanese, "the attraction of the prospect of better living

conditions" elsewhere had "entirely disappeared."[114] Meanwhile, economic collapse, the horrors of the First and Second World Wars, imperial weakness, and
the rise of anticolonial nationalism delivered a series of blows to the much-
vaunted superiority of Western civilization. "Throughout, the political and
moral standing of the European West appears to be in decline."[115] Remittances
to the *bilad ash-sham* almost entirely ceased in the 1930s, either because of
restrictions on the outflow of foreign exchange, or depression-linked poverty
among migrants, or because links to local communities were diminishing in
any case as the first generation grew old, and the second generation no longer looked on the "old country" as home.[116] As international labor migration
and remittances *inter alia* dried up, Syria was confronted, like many other
countries of the world, "with the necessity of becoming self-sufficient and of
developing a system of autarchy which will enable the country to furnish the
means of existence for its population."[117]

CONCLUSION

The half century or so before World War I witnessed the birth of circuits of
transnational labor migration on a mass scale, whether in the Ottoman *bilad ash-sham* or the wider world. Migrants descended from Mt. Lebanon, the
Anti-Lebanon, and beyond into a stratified global labor market and transnational cash economy, and were subjected to the rigors of commodification
and civilizational hierarchy, because of immense pressures on their modes of
social reproduction, the growing need for cash, new consumption patterns,
and the attrition of alternative noncash means of existence. Against the in-
nocence of modernization theory regarding power relations and colonialism,
the "economism" of Marxism, the objectivism of social and economic history, and the voluntarism of agency-centered approaches, I have argued that
these social and economic pressures involved and were driven forward by
various combinations of coercion and consent, involving military, political,
economic, and cultural power, and were linked to forces from both within and
without the region. Colonial military power, imperial "protection," unequal
commercial treaties, French Mandatory state power, Ottoman state-building,
conscription, taxes, notable and landlord control and violence, and new forms
of gendered and debt servitude, as well as the sale of cash crops, diligent attempts to build up stock, and new consumption patterns all combined to produce a hierarchical market economy, which intensified the pressure on the
rural population to depart the domestic community to obtain cash. Although

the choices of migrants came to be at stake, no individual migrant or group chose the terms on which their battle for cash and livelihoods would be joined. Migrants negotiated within a new and changing structure, the product of this vast orchestration of complex forces.[118]

Colonial labor migrants were not colonizers. They were not surrounded by their own armies, missionaries, and traders, and, in search of cash, they often left their families at home. Such migration involved the radical dislocation of existing structures of identification, value, understanding, aesthetics, and community. Migrants were inserted into communities that not only saw them as civilizationally, racially, and culturally inferior but also as mere resources, as manpower, or as commodities only temporarily present within a host community whose identity and history lay elsewhere. Indeed, many migrants, seen in Orientalist terms, were not thought to possess a recognizable history at all. Faced with this onslaught, migrants aimed to put back material and affective structures together in new and meaningful ways—to, in Martin Heidegger's phrase, "world the earth." They did so not by engaging in an impractical socialist assault on the edifice of global capitalism. At least among the first generation, political and ideological struggle was often deferred. Rather, migrants improved their lives by saving up, starting families, opening small businesses, or buying land back in the sending countries through which they could acquire independent means of subsistence.

Migrants aimed to recuperate their economic independence and reestablish some sense of belonging, but even though individuals and families often raised their local status and standards of consumption, migrant agency was articulated to a transnational system of surplus-generation, colonial power, and civilizational hierarchy that was not dismantled, and was more likely entrenched and extended by migrant circulation. These processes only paved the way for more migration in the future. It was the rejection of migrants by receiving countries, and the erection of restrictions and barriers, not the movement of migrants, that played a role in the break up and subsequent crisis of liberal capitalist economy in the first half of the twentieth century.

This economic crisis, the fall of the Ottoman Empire and the colonial partition, the shattering effects of two world wars, European imperial overstretch and weakness, the example of the Soviet Union, the rise of the United States, the emergence of new social groups in the colonized world, the attrition of older structures of authority and reciprocity at the hands of local state-building, colonial rule, cash economy, and popular protest, and the rise of anticolonial nationalism, which incorporated such protests and new political ideologies, all contributed to the emergence of Lebanon and Syria as independent nation-states during and immediately after the Second World War. In the years that followed, for a variety of reasons, migration once again was on the rise. The Lebanese started to reenter on new terms the wealthy states of the global North. But for the first time, Syrians started to look closer to home for places to earn much-needed cash. In the 1940s and 1950s, Lebanon became for the first time a migrant destination, and a new pattern of "South-South" regional labor migration was born.

2 WE WERE LIKE GHOSTS, UNSEEN

INTRODUCTION

After the Second World War, an economic system with a global design was reestablished, but this time under the hegemony of the United States, not Britain, and truncated by the Soviet Union and its sphere of influence. During the period of British dominance, migration had predominantly involved movement to the imperial centers and their settler colonies. In the age of nominally independent nation-states, however, new migratory flows across national boundaries arose within the global South as new forms of accumulation, regional intermediation, state intervention, and dependent development created sharp divergences in the formerly colonized world. Lebanon became a regional hub and major labor-receiver for the first time during these decades. In this it was comparable to Argentina in Latin America, the Ivory Coast in West Africa, and, later, Malaysia in southeast Asia. Oil wealth and export industry also played important roles in these processes in countries as diverse as Saudi Arabia and Venezuela, in the case of the former, or South Korea and Mexico, regarding the latter.[1] These kinds of South-South migration flows have received far too little attention in a historiography dominated by the study of South-North migration. Certainly the case of the whole generation of Syrian workers who migrated to Lebanon in the 1950s and 1960s remains almost invisible in the historiography. As we shall see, however, this was a mass migration of menial labor on which the Lebanese economy was built and on which the Syrian economy came to rely.

This chapter intends to recover some aspects of the history of this almost completely unknown but important wave of economic migration. An important aim is to emphasize the combinations of structure and agency, coercion and consent that unfixed, structured, and drew labor from Syria to Lebanon. This involves a specific history that pays due attention to the projects, purposes, and goals of migrants themselves, without ignoring the ways in which such migrants became entangled in forms of social power over which they had no control.

OUTMIGRATION TO LEBANON

Emigration from Syria slowed with the closure of borders overseas, the global economic crisis of the 1930s, and World War II. Economic growth in the years immediately following 1945 also kept rates of outmigration down.[2] Over the next 20 years, however, for a variety of reasons, Syrian nationals set out to work and study in countries near and far in increasing numbers. Degree holders, technicians, and students went to Europe and the United States, while businessmen, merchants, skilled workers, and landholders formed the majority of those moving, usually on a temporary basis, to the Gulf and other states in the Arab world.[3] Professionals migrated in numbers. Between 1956 and 1969, for example, Syria reportedly lost 2,769 doctors and 3,049 engineers— more than half the total of engineers and doctors graduating in this period.[4] This movement of persons was one way in which Syria became tied to the transnational economy during the years after independence. By the late 1970s, indeed, total remittances to Syria were estimated at $750 million a year[5]—a significant proportion of Syria's GDP.[6]

Whereas the skilled and the wealthy moved to many countries, including Lebanon, the great majority of unskilled, rural, and relatively poor international migrants set off in growing numbers to nearby Lebanon, which was becoming a regional mercantile and financial hub.[7] "An important emigration from rural areas appeared for the first time in Syria: unskilled, mostly male manpower left the country to obtain employment in Lebanon in the agricultural and industrial sectors, in construction and public works."[8] Meyer's study of the Euphrates Valley found that migrants to neighboring Arab countries had lower literacy rates and generally smaller land-holdings than those moving to Kuwait and Saudi Arabia.[9] The available statistics regarding Lebanon indicate upward movement from the late 1940s onward. In 1950, remittances from Syrian labor in Lebanon were estimated at LL3 million/ $950,000 annually.[10] By October 1951, the Lebanese Ministry of Labor and Social Affairs was lodging complaints about "serious" competition from Syrian labor in Lebanon.[11] In 1952, 10,000 Syrians were said to be working in Lebanon 240 days a year.[12] In 1958, 60,000 Syrian workers were reportedly in Lebanon.[13] A 1961 estimate put the total at only 50,000.[14]

The major increase seems to have come during the 1960s, when numbers apparently doubled and doubled again, making this cycle of migration and return a genuinely mass phenomenon. Certainly the 1960s, or the years after 1958, are identified by most observers as decisive.[15] From the late 1950s until the early 1970s, numbers of entries and exits by Syrians, counted by General Security at the border, showed a sharply upward trend, apart from a likely war-related stagger in 1967. Hence, during the five-year period from 1959 to 1963, entries of Syrians averaged 244,461 a year. The average number of annual entries during the next five years, 1964 to 1968, almost tripled to 682,848. And during the peak years of 1969 to 1973, the number increased significantly again to 1,033,383.[16]

As for numbers of immigrants actually working in Lebanon in 1964, the Lebanese Ministry of Labor estimated there to be 145,000 Syrians.[17] Estimates from 1968,[18] and 1970[19] indicated a dramatic rise to totals of 270,000 and 279,541, respectively. If these figures are even approximately correct, and I have been able to discover little about how precisely they were derived, then Syrians had quickly come to make up a highly significant proportion of the Lebanese workforce, estimated in 1970 at only 572,000 resident Lebanese.[20] For every two working Lebanese there was one Syrian worker. Indeed, more than one-seventh of the Syrian workforce was now apparently working in Lebanon.[21] Syrian labor had become "very useful for the Lebanese economy,"[22] and the two countries were deeply interdependent.

UNFIXING SHARECROPPERS

Just as in Lebanon, where new sending regions—such as Akkar in the North, the South, and the Biqa' Valley[23]—emerged, new areas of Syria were now involved in international labor migration. Outmigration expanded initially (until the mid-1960s) to include the grain-producing plains and poorer mountainous regions of Homs and Tartous, Jabal Alawi, Hawran, and Jabal Druze—all relatively close to Lebanon and with family and other connections across the recently drawn border. Syrians from the Hawran started to arrive as workers in the port of Beirut from the 1930s, but only appeared there in numbers[24] after Haifa was closed through the establishment of the state of Israel and the mass expulsion of most Palestinian and non-Jewish Arabs from within its borders.[25] Especially after labor struggles in the port, Hawranis quickly became a well-known group of Syrians in Lebanon.[26] Most Syrians in the growing belt of shantytowns surrounding Beirut in the 1950s and 1960s were from southern Syria or Jabal Alawi. Syrians from Jabal Druze joined their co-religionists in the Druze *bidonville* of Wata Mussaitbé and the Shuf.[27] Alawi maids, often from Jabal Alawi and the Homs region, descended to Tripoli to work for Sunni merchant families and from there to many parts of Lebanon. Whereas sharecroppers had been fixed in place as debt peons before independence,[28] in the 1950s and 1960s, global and cash economy, land reform and state intervention, property rights, cash hunger, the destruction of alternative means of subsistence, land poverty, and rising consumption patterns and aspirations worked to unfix the sharecroppers, farmers, and laborers of the grain-producing plains.[29]

LAND OWNERSHIP

Land reform played an important role in these unfixing processes, above all because it resulted in the growth of landownership among small-scale cultivators. As previously discussed, sharecroppers were in many ways tied to their location by debt and feudal obligation. Consumption was limited and market dependency was low—threads, fabrics, aluminium pots and pans, and perhaps kerosene stoves and fuel were the main household items purchased with cash. Landowners took violent sanction against those who overstepped their proper place in the consumption hierarchy. Sharecroppers' lack of resources also diminished their ability to migrate abroad.[30] Before 1958, 1.1 percent of all landowners controlled more than one-third of Syria's cultivated land.[31] One of the consequences, however, of the redistribution associated with the land reforms of 1958 and 1963, products of Ba'thist, anticolonial nationalism, was an enormous increase in property ownership. Batatu noted that the number of landholders in Syria increased from 292,273 in 1958 to 468,539 in 1970–71.[32]

New land parcels were rarely enough, especially for the sons of the male family heads in whose name the land was individually registered, particularly if they wanted to start their own families. Numerous families holding fewer than two hectares (about 5 acres), especially in years of drought or bad harvest, were unable to make a sustainable income.[33] Those looking to defray debts or to supplement inadequate incomes were forced onto the market. Batatu writes that crop failure and drought were the "fundamental sources of their [Syrian peasants'] economic insecurity and of the anguish and privations that intermittently mar their life."[34] Abu-Aianah also stresses that in the context of outmigration, much of the countryside depended on rain that was "unreliable from year to year."[35] Certainly the drought of the last three years of the 1950s drove many "to seek food and work in the cities or in the Lebanon."[36] But natural and climactic factors were only part of the story, given that property allocation remained profoundly unequal, increasingly individuated, and exclusive.[37] In fact, circuits of ownership and control, which determined who had sufficient and who had insufficient land to cope during periods of drought and crop failure, were just as fundamental as climate to such anguish and privation. Repeated (and predictable) natural crises, in combination with land poverty and debt, worked to lever peasants into the cash economy. Subsistence crises among sharecroppers drove them further into webs of obligation and dependency vis-à-vis local landowners and usurers. On the other hand, similar crises of debt and subsistence in a context of small ownership were far more likely to provoke outmigration in order to prevent the slide into landlessness among families who had the resources to afford to send one member abroad or lose labor services for a temporary period.[38] But with small ownership came two further factors, more usually associated with consent than coercion, and downplayed by many Marxian understandings of migration.

First, small landowners, as owners of the land and its product, had a greater incentive to improve their holdings and their stock. Here, such owners were not simply forced onto the market by the need to defray taxes or debts, but had new reasons—namely, secure access to the fruits of their labor—to develop their activities and take their produce to the market. There was less room for the attitude struck by an Alawi peasant in the mid-nineteenth century, when replying to a question about the scarcity of fruit trees: "Why should I plant a tree? I shall not be allowed to eat of its fruit."[39] Ownership called for agency of a certain kind, that of those who increase their stock and productive output. Such cultivators were not forced to buy and sell by increased taxes levied by imperialists seeking to expel them into the cash economy. Instead, the Syrian Ba'th presided over land redistribution, a reduced tax burden, and subsidies to agriculture in the 1960s and later.[40] Land reform intertwined with political projects, a concern for social justice, and economic attempts to develop the internal market.[41] The control of resources afforded by ownership gave rise to a form of migration unthinkable under sharecropping arrangements, whereby sons or fathers moved to earn cash to buy more land, or more seed, tools, livestock, machines, or irrigation facilities on existing lands. As Meyer found in the Euphrates Valley, "land-owners in particular and to a lesser degree also the beneficiaries of the Agrarian Reform are overrepresented among the migrants."[42]

SUGAR, PRIMUS STOVES, AND EDUCATION

Second, in part as a consequence of the spread of landownership, small cultivators were able to develop previously unknown consumption patterns and aspirations. With the ascendancy of the Ba'th party, the diminishing influence of the old "feudal" landowners, usurers, and merchants,[43] and the age of Nasserism and Arab nationalism, "sons of the nation" were seen as having the right to new consumption patterns and heightened status. The modest luxuries increasingly common on Mt. Lebanon decades before, such as sugar, tea, coffee, and tobacco, as well as household goods such as primus stoves, were now more widespread in the interior plains of Syria.

Such changes are glimpsed in Sweet's 1950s doctoral research on Tell Toqaan, a village living primarily by sheep and goat raising, gardening, farming, and local artisanal production situated between Aleppo and Hama.[44] Economic self-sufficiency was eroded as cotton became valuable as a cash crop in the 1950s. Tractors and trucks appeared, alongside migratory seasonal labor at harvest time, and a year-round "availability" of landless men.[45] Threshing machines were now purchased for SL60/ $15 from Aleppo.[46] Sweet's informants said on the one hand that times had improved with the attrition of Ottoman and tribal oppression, and the technology, economy, literacy, food, crops, and tools brought by the French and by independence. On the other hand, there were losses: Wedding pageantry was diminished, there were no more purebred mares, the excitement of the departure of the village camel caravan to Aleppo was no more, and, more important for the argument here, the cattle herd and rich grazing zone was gone[47]—a factor contributing to market dependency. Tel Toqaan, indeed, was said to have become a "money village."[48] Tea and coffee were purchased, along with the Swedish- or German-made primus stoves "found in all households."[49] New inequalities meant that only the rich could now afford to put on feasts for births, circumcisions, and bridal homecomings.[50] The relatively wealthy also displayed their status with city-made shoes, shoehorns, and watches, whereas ordinary folk acquired matches, cigarette lighters, flashlights, primus stoves, kerosene lamps, and rubber boots. All such purchases meant "an increasing dependence on a world market."[51] These new patterns of consumption and production both expressed choices *and* entangled villagers within new expectations and patterns of hierarchy and dependency. Many were thus produced as land-poor and cash-hungry, and in search of opportunities outside the village as a matter of survival, higher consumption, and status.

I interviewed a certain Abu Yusuf (1960–), from the countryside around Homs, whose childhood and family history was marked by the transformations associated with land reform. His father was born in 1918 and had worked as a sharecropper for one of the "feudalists" (*iqta'iyyin*) near Homs. In those days, Abu Yusuf insisted, one lived by "eating and drinking, nothing more." For those working on the estates of Al-Barazi, he said, "everything was forbidden, even education." Abu Yusuf's family, however, acquired 10 dunums (just under 2½ acres) in 1959 because of the land reform, which represented a "salvation from feudalism."[52] The family set aside 2 or 3 dunums for the growth of tobacco as a cash crop, harvested in August, which they sold not to merchants but to the state, albeit for what he said were low prices. There was some tobacco left over for consumption. Indeed, Abu Yusuf joked that his father had been smoking for 60 years and was still in fine health. But the family also grew a greater variety of crops on the land remaining, which made them "more wealthy," presumably in terms of use-values. The family's new status as small landowners enabled new ambitions and consumption patterns, but these accompanied their own forms of land- and cash-hunger and discipline. Certainly 2½ acres could not support the whole family, which now bought tea, rice, sugar, and salt from local shopkeepers on credit, with debts to be paid after the tobacco harvest. But the harvest proceeds were inadequate, and the family got into debt. Moreover, the eldest of the nine brothers went to university in order to get a family member into a profession. During the long years of secondary and further education, he contributed little to the family income, and the other siblings had to leave school to earn cash to help defray his expenses, including books and travel costs. Abu Yusuf thus went as a boy to Lebanon to work in the orange harvest, first in the school holidays in the early 1970s, saving up what he said was good money. He returned with the equivalent of $68 in 1971, $100 in 1972, and $136 in 1973. He saved intensively, he said, never visiting the casino or smoking, because although young, he felt very responsible to his family and their need for money and he was honored by the gratitude accorded him by his father.[53]

Abu Yusuf's story exemplifies some of the combinations of coercion and consent driving family members to migrate in search of cash. In this case, the break up of so-called feudal control and obligation, small land ownership, land hunger, new consumption patterns (such as rice and sugar), new aspirations (such as education for the eldest son), and attendant debts and obligations were the various forces evicting Abu Yusuf from the domestic community and driving him to seek temporary work in Lebanon, contributing to the family income, forgoing educational opportunities, but taking his place as a loyal son and brother. Collective associations were developed by peasants in the Hawran to facilitate the purchase of necessary items and avoid the slide into debt,[54] but these associations could not compete with the opportunities for hard cash presented by outmigration. Meyer argues that remittances were mainly used "to cover the general *living costs* of the household members and to pay *debts*."[55]

STORIES OF POVERTY AND AMBITION

Similar combinations of poverty and aspiration are vividly present in Tony Elias's (1954–) recounting of his early days in Lebanon in the late 1960s. Tony Elias was from a poor family in *wadi al-nasara* between Homs and Tartus that acquired some land, possibly through land reform, in the late 1960s. "My parents, and people generally in this village," Tony related, "had no money." The olive trees on the family's land were too young to produce anything until the mid-1970s. Hence, in the late 1960s, his father worked in manual agricultural labor but year-round work was unobtainable. His mother did agricultural labor on her brother's land for wages paid in olive oil. "He gave her around half a tin [per day] of the green olives, just half a tin I swear. I can still see it, half a tin, enough for one meal, poor thing."[56] It was said by others in the village that Tony's mother had been dispossessed of her land by her brother—a glimpse of how gender was intimately involved in unequal resource distribution.

Tony left for Beirut 1969 and started running deliveries by bicycle for a supermarket. "I was very happy to cycle around the streets. I was only fifteen and I was happy that I was riding a bicycle. I would think that if only the kids from the village could see me. I loved to ride between the cars, especially because I was from the village, and here we do not have that much. It was as if I was in a different world: a large world with beautiful people and cars. I would stand in the street for an hour to watch the cars. It was a wonder. . . . It was nice. Lebanon is beautiful. You know even right now if my situation was different I would go."

Tony Elias's nostalgia for Lebanon, conveyed to me in his home village in the summer of 2004, should be seen in the light of his subsequent history. Poor health forced him to return more or less permanently in the early 1990s, and so he was denied the chance to earn money and increase his status, and had to work in Syria for many years in a dull administrative post. His intense recollection of boyhood wonder, slipping occasionally into the present tense, then, was the memory of a man who had not become tired of years of living in Lebanon with its multiple stigmas, expenses, disappointments, hopes, and dangers, but who longed from afar for an ambition denied. Although this nostalgia accounts for the emphasis Tony placed on those boyhood scenes, there is no reason to believe that they never took place at all. There is nothing surprising in a boy from the countryside marveling at the "large" and wealthy world of Beirut, which in 1969 was at the height of the pre-war boom. Indeed, if Tony had not been ambitious, there would be no basis for a subsequent nostalgia stemming from disappointment. It seems reasonable to suggest, then, that Tony's dreams and aspirations were combined with the heavy pressures of economic coercion, in which Tony's mother was paid—even on her own brother's land—in starvation rations for a day's labor. These elements of coercion and consent, rather than being contradictory, were more likely part and parcel of the same reality—not least because Tony's wonder at the city was probably reinforced by his humble origins and lack of economic independence at home.

Hanna Awwad (1933–) first went to Lebanon in 1950 from a Christian village in *wadi al-nasara*. From the age of 11 to 17 he worked in Syria, without wages, for 10 or 11 months a year in what he regarded as dead-end and not very respectable tasks of pasturing livestock, farming, and ploughing on the 30 dunums (about 6½ acres) or so owned by the family.[57] "I left school and went . . . to Lebanon. . . . Because we had no money to go to school. There was no money in general. We lived in relative poverty. We used to work in farming, ploughing our lands in the old way using cows. I left the farm and went to Lebanon." At that time, he continued, "Everybody went to Lebanon, I mean men older than us. They went there to work and they made good money. They started buying nice clothes and so on. We saw them doing that and we decided to go to Lebanon and do the same. We emigrated . . . to Lebanon in order to achieve something in our life. We wanted to work, save money and build a house." Hanna Awwad went on: "In this part of the world, they say that a man without a house to reside in has nothing. If you do not have a house to live in, where would you live? Out in the street? This is absolutely unacceptable. . . . If a man wants to get married, if they have a baby where shall they stay? Stay in the street!! . . . This house will gather the whole family together . . . through it a man establishes something for his family." Hanna remarked, "By achieving that [the higher income and household], we had the ambition to start some sort of [technical or liberal] profession for our children if we can."[58]

Hanna's recounting touched on a number of important themes: land shortage and attendant poverty, lack of schooling, dead-end work in the village; the ambition to find something better, and the need to do so in order start an independent family and a household. There was also the knowledge that good money was to be earned in Lebanon, signaled by their compatriots who returned in "nice clothes," and who, by doing so, showed the feasibility of the process. Such clothes were powerful symbols—not of fashion or lifestyle consumerism—but of a move off the farm and to cleaner, higher-status work, which could ensure the children a future. Noteworthy also is the lack of emphasis on the kind of work that Hanna Awwad was to pursue. The important thing was not the profession that Hanna Awwad would have, or the quality of work he would find. Rather, the goal was to acquire money, to become better, to build a home in Syria, and to pave the way for his children's education and entry into the professions.

Hanna Butros (c1945–) was also from a village in *wadi al-nasara*. He went to Lebanon looking for work for the first time in 1958. He already had a male relative there who, expressing vividly the negative connotations associated with farm work, told him "What do you want to stay here [in Syria] for? To chase the cows and the cattle?"[59] Hanna Butros described his memories of his first trip to Beirut: "Very good memories. They cannot be erased. . . . We were in poverty over here, there was no work. I went there and found a job, which made me very happy. . . . We started going to places. Pardon me, but we didn't know what the cinema was. We had no cinema back in those days. Over there we had the money to go to the cinema and to go out on trips. We visited the Cedars. We visited different places and looked at the world."[60] In Hamra, Beirut, "you could not tell night from day. Anytime you went, you found people and you found the shops open. It was the most beautiful life and the most refined."[61] Hanna Butros continued, "By comparison, here, we were nothing—nothing at all! We were a dot, zero, considering how Lebanon was at that time. I used to come back [to Syria in the 1960s] wearing a suit [laughs]. I would find my friends here in a mess, grazing the cows, without even a pound to buy a packet of cigarettes, and . . . going to school wearing trousers with patches [laughs]. So when I came here wearing a suit, they would say, 'It seems like yesterday that he left for Beirut and now he's a kid wearing a suit.' All the boys wanted to go to Beirut [laughs]."

Hanna Butros's images and stories powerfully evoke the contrasts between poverty, "chasing cows," "mess," and "trousers with patches" in the Syrian countryside and employment, the cinema, the Cedars, shops, fine clothes, going out, beauty and refinement in the Lebanese city. In his story, the superiority of the latter life was self-evident: "All the boys" from the village, as he put it, on seeing his suit, wanted to copy what Hanna had done. It is too crude, however, to see Hanna's tale as simply supporting the "bright lights" theory of labor migration. On the one hand, Hanna's attitudes very much formed part and parcel of the warp and weft of social expectations (now backed by migrant cash), which formed a cultural structure within which others had to labor. In other words, notions of bright lights are not simply "found" but made, circulated, reinforced, recognized, and so on in ways that brought pressures to bear on new generations of migrants and structured their trajectories. On the other hand, and above all, political economy underpinned the story at all points: Life in the village *was* relatively poverty-stricken and land-hungry. Work *was* egregiously limited in Syria. And much higher incomes *were* to be found in Lebanon. Just as behind the dull pressure of economic compulsion one finds dreams and ambition, behind aspirations stand the dull pressures of economic compulsion. These two figures were part of the same historically constituted reality, and reinforced rather than contradicted one another.

EARNING POWER IN LEBANON

Income mattered enormously in the motivations of individual migrants, and the ability of migrants to raise greatly their earning power by going to Lebanon is unquestionable. Nonetheless, it is not always helpful to speak simply of income differentials between Lebanon and Syria. Much depends on the ways in which the labor market is constructed. Rarely did Syrians do the same work in Syria as they did in Lebanon, so income differentials in similar professions is not always a relevant measure.[62] Moreover, many Syrians were not earning cash at all in Syria, as they were attached to the family economy. Further, jobs with higher incomes in Syria were not open to certain kinds of migrants. Those from poor rural families, with little education, certain accents and manners, lacking connections, and so on, often had no realistic access to higher-status jobs in Syrian towns, so the income level of such jobs was largely immaterial.

The same strictures applied to jobs in Lebanon: Certain kinds of jobs were inaccessible for Syrians, and others wide open, regardless of income levels in other professions, as we shall see. Given the segmented and historically constructed dynamics of the "labor market," differential earning power cannot easily be read off global statistics, even supposing such statistics existed. One can, however, make some sense of what earning power was possible, and what these quantities meant to migrants.

From the limited data available, it seems that in the 1950s Syrian men could expect to earn the equivalent of $0.64 to $1.91 a day in Lebanon.[63] In 1952, the Lebanese daily, *Le Jour*, reported that Syrian workers earned an average of LL2.5/ $0.78 daily.[64] Joseph worked among his fellows "non-stop until we could barely stand" as an assistant in a sandwich shop in Hamra, Beirut, for LL2/ $0.64 a day in the mid-1950s.[65] Joseph said this was a good wage, similar to that of a government employee in Syria during the same years. Hanna Butros was paid LL3/ $0.96 per day as a teenager working in a paint factory in Beirut in the late 1950s.[66] In March 1958, the Lebanese daily, *Makhbar Sahaf*, reported that Syrians earned LL5/ $1.59 per day.[67] Hanna Awwad said that he earned LL5–6/ $1.59–1.91 per day working as groundsman and ball-boy in a French-owned tennis club in 1950. All such wages were significantly higher than the SL0.5–1/ $0.16–0.32 per day, reported by Elias, for manual labor on earthworks near the coastal town of Chekka in the early 1940s. As such, these wages, especially at the higher end, represented significant earning power. As Hanna Awwad declared of his wage: "Perfect for me, as before we went to Beirut, we had nothing. Everything became better when we started working there. . . . We were able to buy stuff and to save [about half the earnings] as well."[68] According to 'Aziz, a retired teacher present at this interview, Hanna's earnings were indeed "very good compared to the salaries of educated people [such as teachers and civil servants] in Syria at the same exact era." Hanna Awwad agreed: "Oh yes, we were doing very well in Lebanon. In Syria I had no chance to find a proper job as I am not educated at all."

In the 1960s and 1970s, wages for Syrians in Lebanon seem to have risen quite significantly. Reports from this period usually fall within the range of LL5–20/ $1.59–8.70 a day.[69] Tony Elias was earning LL5/ $1.59 a day as a painter in the late 1960s and early 1970s.[70] Abed was earning LL5/ $1.59 a day in his first job as assistant to a skilled plasterer in the mid-1960s.[71] Hanna Butros was paid L9/ $2.87 a day by late 1960s. An estimate of the average daily wage in Lebanon in 1973 was LL10/ $4.37.[72] Joseph, working in a responsible and trusted position on the till in a well-to-do restaurant called "American Dream" in upscale Hamra in Lebanon's capital, was earning, including tips, as much as LL13–20/ $5.68–8.73 a day in the early 1970s.[73]

DEMOGRAPHY

The foregoing sheds some light on the meaning of the highly elusive and abstract notion of population pressure, often deployed in explanations of migration. Demographic pressures cannot be ascertained by crude measures of density or by problematic notions of what is or is not a "normal" rate of growth or family size. This is because population pressures must be seen in relation to the existence or absence of resources. Crude measures absurdly suggest that crowded places such as New York City, for example, are prime sites for outmigration. Nonetheless, even if this point is accepted, such pressures can only in a grossly generalized and misleading way be specified through an abstract macrological measurement balancing aggregate resources against aggregate population such as those so effectively criticized by Timothy Mitchell in the case of Egypt.[74] Such measurements tell us little about who migrated from where and precisely why. Population pressures emerge as selective according to how resources are monopolized and denied. Institutions such as state-enforced private property rights, *and* social positions, inequality, and identity (most prominently gender) play a crucial role. Selective pressures are brought to bear where certain male junior siblings are excluded from education and land, for example. Commonly, males are earmarked for the role of migrant breadwinner, and females for the role of child-bearer and homemaker.

In this context, it seems reasonable to suggest that population growth in rural Syria, partly occasioned by reproductive strategies and values—but also by the fact that Ba'thist policies after 1963, particularly because of the provision of public services and food subsidies, involving the "drastic and rapid reduction of crude death rates" in Syria[75]—contributed to the land-hunger of and cash pressures on particular groups, acting as a spur to migration. Migratory pressures, then, were heavily mediated through political, economic, and social arrangements. Unsurprisingly, therefore, demography did not provide a sufficient condition for outmigration. Between 1936 and 1947, for example, Syria's population reportedly increased by 50 percent (from 2 to 3 million), but outmigration increased little during these years. Moreover, whereas the Syrian population continued to grow at similar rates during the 1950s and 1960s, migration was far higher during the 1960s.[76]

INTERNAL MIGRATION

Lebanon was by no means the only destination for relatively poor and un-educated rural inhabitants searching for cash, livelihood, and independence. Many migrants moved to Syrian cities, Damascus above all, but also Aleppo, Homs, Hama, and new cities such as Al-Thawra on the Euphrates. In 1970, Damascus, with a quarter of its population born elsewhere, was overwhelmingly the most important destination, accounting for nearly a quarter of all internal migration in Syria in 1970.[77] In 1970, Damascus City and Governorate had a net positive balance of +175,542 persons.[78] There was also work to be had in Aleppo, particularly in textile workshops and factories, whose industrialists received some tariff and other kinds of protection from the government after the break up of the Customs Union with Lebanon in 1950. Cultivators from the plains of Idlib and Armenaz went to work there,[79] as did artisans from the villages around Idlib and Deret Azzé, whose livelihoods had come under immense pressure or been ruined because of competition from both imports and protected industry in Aleppo. "Some [such workers] emerge," it was said, "and succeed in establishing small factories for mechanised weaving."[80] Such artisans-cum-proletarians described a strikingly common migrant journey from self-employment through wage-labor back to self-employment. Peasants from "well beyond" the western plateau also moved in smaller numbers to become manual laborers in regional towns—Afrine, Azaz, and Membij—in the Aleppo region.[81] The population of al-Thawra, a new city in al-Raqqa Governorate and a product of statist developmentalism astride the new Euphrates Dam in the North, increased during this period from 20,000 to 120,000.[82] As Abu-Aianah notes, "The entire [Syrian] countryside pushes out its population, except for the countryside of al-Raqqa and that of Damascus which depend on irrigated agriculture and have good transport facilities, and are close to work opportunities in the capital."[83] Rural-urban migration was said to be bolstered by the fact that some would get a taste for the pleasures of the city on military service.[84] For the better off, with the expansion of education, the city was the place to send offspring aspiring to join the liberal professions.[85]

Other major destinations for cultivators from the plains searching for revenue for a decent life for the family[86] were in the countryside. First, the increased demand for wheat during the Second World War, and for cotton during the Korean war in the 1950s contributed to the "boom" of the 1950s. This was accompanied by mechanization, the appearance of tractors and harvesters, an increase in the cultivated area, new kinds of entrepreneurship undertaken by merchants and capitalists, and cash-crop production (especially cotton and wheat) in the northern plains of Syria,[87] as well as the development of the al-Jazira region north of the Euphrates.[88] Al-Hasaka Governorate in the far northeast, bordering the Tigris, was a net-receiving region in 1970 because of these developments.[89] On these plantations, jobs for migrants included sharecropping, rent-leasing (whereby land plots were leased to families of cultivators in return for cash payments), wage-labor, tractor-driving, mechanical work, irrigation maintenance, and so on.[90] Entrepreneurs in the Al-Jazirah region considered local labor unsuited for work due to their lack of experience in intensive agriculture. Hence, they recruited in the region of Aleppo, where workers had more experience in market gardening and cotton plantation. Therefore, peasants from Jabal Baricha, Sfiré, Kurd Dagh, Jabal Armenaz, and Jabal 'Ala moved, some temporarily during the summer, and others permanently, to the Euphrates Valley and Khabour.[91] Migrant tractor drivers and mechanics, strikingly enough, came from as far away as the poor region of Akkar in northern Lebanon.[92]

From a family of cultivators in the Idlib region, Abed (1934–) returned from military service in 1960. His mother had long since passed away, his father's second wife had just died, and his younger brother was on military service. After some sort of unspoken dispute with his family, Abed left for al-Raqqa to try to make a better living.[93] "I left on my own. . . . I took my own path." Armed with his experience in agriculture, he went to al-Raqqa where there was land, irrigation, and the possibility of growing cotton. "I went to rent a piece of land to plant cotton in which I had experience." But, Abed went on, "I didn't like the quality of life over there, it was harsh. . . . For such a project to get going one needs to be married, the wife is important in such a case. This is because there is no baker in that place, so the wife must bake the bread. She does the *saj*, the cooking, the washing and in her free time will help in the land. [Without such help] it was hard." Without the crucial support of a wife in social reproduction as well as farming, Abed was unable to make this life work. He returned to his home region after just a few months, setting up his own place and working in a stone quarry making mosaic tiles. However, Abed continued, "I worked for two years and then a friend told me that work in Lebanon pays better so I left and took my brother's job for three months as he had to leave [Lebanon] at that point."[93] In this case an internal migrant became an international migrant when internal projects did not work out because of the absence of family support in al-Raqqa, and when better paying work in Lebanon became possible through social networks.

Land reclamation schemes also involved migration across northern Syria. The statist development of 43,000 hectares (over 100,000 acres), for example, on the plain of Ghab on the middle Orontes from 1952 to 1967 for growing cash crops (wheat, cotton, sugar beets), involved the permanent resettlement of over 100,000 poor Alawi sharecroppers and landless cultivators from nearby Jabal Alawi, Jabal Zawiyya, and Salamiye. Small land plots were distributed to peasant families who, in return, were expected to cultivate cash-crops under official direction.[94] Development projects sometimes induced migration abroad. Meyer has shown how the conversion of the irrigation system in the middle Euphrates Valley, for example, meant that "farmers were not able to cultivate their fields during the execution of the scheme for . . . up to several years," inducing a search for work abroad.[95]

Finally, one of the most important single internal migrations in Syria during these years was a mass expulsion and had little to do with the duller disciplines of markets. Al-Qunaitra in the southwest shows up in the official statistics in 1970 as the most significant area of outmigration by a factor of three, with a negative balance of –106,571 persons.[96] Israel was victorious in the six-day war of 1967 and occupied the Golan Heights, largely destroying the town of al-Qunaitra, with a population of 60,000. The Israelis then engaged in familiar practices of clearance, depopulation, and paramilitary settlement, displacing and expelling about 100,000 Syrians from the area of occupation, and establishing an impermeable border, in the process. Most of these involuntary migrants went to Damascus.[97]

The Syrian defeat had another indirect consequence for migration. The length of compulsory national military service—already a reason to avoid Syria for a migrant like Joseph[98]—was increased from 18 months to 2½ years, and conditions were toughened.[99] Conscription pressures were exerted just when young men were hoping to head to Lebanon to earn much-needed cash. Further, whereas migrants to the Gulf required a passport, which was very difficult to obtain without doing military service, migrants could go to Lebanon without a passport, and hence could leave without having completed their military service.[100] Migrants could therefore go to Lebanon from their early teens, whereas international labor migration to the Gulf was blocked until migrants were in their early to mid-20s. On the other hand, the Lebanese authorities handed over absconders as a matter of routine, and call-ups were issued to migrants at their residences and/or workplaces in Lebanon—so Lebanon was no haven from the reach of the Syrian military.

PROXIMITY, TRANSPORT, AND SOCIAL NETWORKS

Migrants to Lebanon did not tend to acquire work through major contractors or contracting agencies, whose services were not required, whether for transport, work/residence permits, visas, accommodation, or placements. Contractors, or even smugglers, therefore, had no basis for interposing themselves between employers and migrants. Transport was cheap and easy, primarily because of the expanding network of paved roads, and work/residence permits and visas were mostly nonexistent. For various reasons, the Syro-Lebanese border was basically open. These factors account very much for why Lebanon was such a popular destination for international migrants from Syria with limited resources. Accommodation and work, moreover, were often found through social networks of friends and relatives. Numerous families had branches in both Lebanon and Syria.[101] The Mandatory border had only been drawn in 1920 by the French, and the same border became international only in 1946 with the independence of Syria. In this context, workers did not have to plan, save up, or mobilize significant resources before departing for Lebanon. As Hanna Awwad put it in representative fashion, "There was no plan. . . . If you have two pounds you can get to Beirut. I have a brother who lives there. He went there years before me. I knew that I would stay with him. . . . He helped us to find jobs and start working."[102] These sentiments were typical. The great majority of migrants had a story of a cousin, brother, father, neighbor, or friend who recommended them for a job, or gave them a place to live. Once in Lebanon, newly arrived migrants could link friends or relatives to jobs and housing. These networks were passive most of the time, but activated and highly efficient at salient moments. They also expanded very rapidly, given an individual's range of contacts and family members.

A rather different, "social network" facilitating recruitment also became far more significant with the momentous changes in Syria in the early 1960s. The rise of the Ba'th Party, the United Arab Republic of Syria and Egypt 1958–1961, the land reforms of 1959 and 1963, and, above all, the Ba'thist seizure of power in 1963 confronted Syria's landowners and bourgeoisie with what many of them saw as a "vindictive land grab"[103] and "doctrinaire take-over of the national production and trade by the state."[104] Only in 1963, indeed, was the hold of the notables, whose power reached back to the eighteenth century in many cases, finally prized from the levers of state power in Syria. No longer were such families routinely able to list off relatives who were prime ministers and chiefs of staff. Instead, those of more humble origins, intellectuals, junior officers, trade unionists, civil servants, lawyers, journalists, provincial farmers, and even former peasants, ascended as never before to important decision-making positions in Syrian politics. These groups brought with them stronger notions of the meaning of national independence on the international scene and were determined to use the state for national development, industrialization, education, and social justice.

Similar political and sociological developments in Iraq and Egypt, and the lack of business opportunities in Jordan, made Lebanon an attractive destination for many of the old "feudalists" (iqta'iyyin), as they were popularly known. Many such families had members, houses, business contacts, and friends in Beirut, a mercantile and financial hub and a safe-haven for capital because of the liberal currency and capital regime, banking secrecy, and light taxes. As Rania Ghosn argues, wealthy Syrians were able to reconstruct an already familiar—through visits, shopping trips, and the like—social space in Beirut. Even poorer members of such families could, through contacts and family names, raise the capital and other kinds of powers and resources necessary to do business.[105] This was a migratory experience utterly different from that of ordinary people from the countryside. Wealthy Syrians quickly acquired Lebanese citizenship, and acceded to command posts within the Lebanese economy. A number of them, in a familiar pattern associated with wealthy "exile" groups, were to become avid supporters of isolationist trends in Lebanese nationalism in the 1970s.

The families that moved had been employers in Syria, and often became employers in industry and construction in Lebanon. In some cases, they brought with them Syrian workers, or sought them out as a "known quantity" once in Lebanon. In other cases, Syrian workers searched out their compatriots for employment. Certainly those I interviewed knew about these families and the major role they played and were occasionally employed by them. Hanna Awwad, for example, worked in tiling for the Malas family in 1963 and later for the Bobais and Hanunu families.[106]

These political changes in Syria, and the flight of the bourgeois elements to Lebanon also altered the economic balance between the two countries. On the one hand, Syria was plunged into something of an economic crisis by the flight of capital. It was estimated by Syrian officials that more than $200 million was smuggled to Lebanon and Switzerland during 1959 to 1964. This sum represented more than one-sixth of the entire Syrian 1965 GDP, which stood at $1.12 billion.[107] Such a capital flight diminished employment opportunities for rural-urban migrants and others in Syria. On the other hand, the vast sums brought into the Lebanese economy contributed to the boom of the mid-1960s. Here, the dynamic interrelations between processes of accumulation and dependent development, and hence between forces of eviction and attraction in international migration, are vividly apparent.

Once the number of Syrians working in Lebanon reached tens of thousands, and especially after their number increased to six figures, the opportunity to work in "booming" Lebanon probably became open through contacts to Syrians all over Syria, and not just to those in the areas bordering Lebanon who had originally had family or contacts in Lebanon. The case of Abed, noted earlier, is a good example of an early migrant from the Aleppo region who, via the information of a friend and a job provided by his brother, decided to make this long-distance move. Moreover, the families that came from Aleppo, such as Kekhya and Hanunu, may well have been important in initiating new flows of migrants from northern Syria. New roads, in turn, cut journey times from the Aleppo region. It seems to agree with the empirical evidence, in any case, to date the arrival of increasing numbers of Syrians from the northern parts of Syria to the mid-1960s, rather than before. Hamidé, for example, does not mention outmigration to Lebanon in his 1959 survey of migration in and from the Aleppo region in the north.[108] Indicative of new trends was the departure to Lebanon during the construction boom in the early 1970s of al-Hajj Ali (1946/7–), from a landless Syrian Kurdish family of agricultural laborers in the Aleppo region.[109] We will hear much of his progeny in subsequent chapters. Certainly by 1970, mention is made of workers from the Aleppo region in the shantytowns of Beirut.[110] A 1972 article stated that Syrian peasants searching for manual labor came from all over: the Hawran, the Euphrates region in the northeast, the Aleppo plain, the countryside of Ladhiqiyya, and the lowlands of Homs.[111]

OPEN BORDERS

The open border between the two "brotherly" countries of the historic *bilad ash-sham* was at least as important as geographic proximity, social networks, and transport infrastructure in shaping the direction taken by cash-hungry migrants. As we have seen, the Israeli border, based on a virulent mixture of Zionism, nationalism, and settler colonialism, drawn in 1948–49, and redrawn to encompass the Golan Heights in 1967, formed an impenetrable barrier for Syrian migrants. The Lebanese border, in complete contrast, was probably one of the more permeable national borders in the world, at least with respect to Syrian nationals.

Under the mandate there were no barriers to the movement of goods and persons between the State of Syria and "Grand Liban." For economic and social reasons, however, as we have seen, very few Syrians moved for temporary employment to Grand Liban. From independence until March 1950, the two countries, their common interests directed by the *Conseil Supérieur des Intérêts Communs*, established in 1944, were united in a customs union allowing goods and persons the freedom of movement. Regarding the small number of Syrians appearing for work in Lebanon at that time, the Lebanese authorities proposed to treat them no differently than Lebanese nationals. For example, Gabriel Murr announced in June 1947 with regard to labor on the Tapline oil pipe, "We are going to accept Syrian labour power on the building sites and installations of the company on the same conditions as the Lebanese employees and workers."[112] Clearly such a policy was in line with the employers' interests in cheap labor. At some point during these early years, the basic understanding that each of the two countries ought to treat migrants from the other equally was established. This principle put in its first formal appearance in a 1949 agreement signed by the two foreign ministries regarding Lebanese and Syrian seamen working in their neighbor's country. It was reported that "the agreement granted Syrian seamen in Lebanon the same rights which Lebanese [seamen] enjoy in Syria on the basis of reciprocal treatment."[113] In practice this meant an almost complete absence of special regulation.

After the first blush of independence, relations between Lebanon and Syria started to cool with disputes over the price of Syrian wheat, which Lebanon relied on, the fact that Syria's balance of payment problems were worsened by Lebanese reexport to Syria, and the matter of some Syrian capital flight to Beirut. The proposed Syrian development of Lattakia port, furthermore, was resented by the Lebanese as a rival to Beirut.[114] But the real problem was more systematically oriented to the divergent interests of dominant groups in the two countries. President Bishara al-Khoury and his New Phoenician associates, including Michel Chiha, were dismantling wartime controls, aiming to build a laissez-faire economy for finance, regional trade, and tourism.

As Gates argues, the financial and mercantile elite in Lebanon had no aim to develop economic productive forces based on industry, agriculture, or technical or structural change. In this context there was no developmentalist policy to devalue the currency and thereby make exports cheaper and consumer imports expensive. On the contrary, Lebanon's policy-makers took "extraordinary measures" to keep the currency strong to facilitate entrepot trade and domestic consumption.[115] In this context, they signed an agreement with France, tying the Lebanese lira into the franc zone in order to maintain its strength and international credibility.[116] Syria, on the other hand, with a more significant agricultural base and war-boosted industrial interests in textiles, sugar, and glass, increasingly aimed, in a more developmentalist fashion, to procure for the country agricultural and industrial equipment, protect agriculture and industry against foreign competition, and encourage exports.[117] This implied a customs policy of protection, and independence from the French franc, the oscillations of which had caused considerable hardship in the 1930s.[118] The Lebanese agreement to join the franc zone, then, marked a significant divergence. In the context of relations soured by conjunctural factors, therefore, and above all because of increasingly opposed economic policies, the break up of the customs union came amid border closures and recriminations in March 1950.

Apart from the temporary border closure, the trickle of Syrians of humble origins going to Lebanon to find work was not significantly affected by these events. In the negotiations following the break-up of the union, Beirut sought a return to the "free movement of goods, people, and capital."[119] Such demands made sense in terms of Lebanon's laissez-faire orientation, and more important were the outgrowth of the interests of the mercantile-financial bourgeoisie, seeking to support their business in real estate, tourism, and so on.[120] Syria agreed to Lebanon's demands for an open border, except regarding the movement of capital,[121] which Syria sought to keep within the country. In other words, the basically unregulated movement of Syrian workers continued across the border. Indeed, the newly established Ministry of Social Affairs in Lebanon announced on July 11, 1950, that it was not necessary for Syrians seeking to work in Lebanon to obtain a work permit (*ijazat 'amal*) and that Syrians were to be treated exactly like Lebanese.[122]

In formal terms, this situation continued only until March 5, 1953, when the two countries signed the major economic agreement officially governing, with later amendments, bilateral economic relations until the early 1990s. The body of the agreement says nothing about migrant workers, but an addendum in the form of an exchange of letters stipulated that "Syrians moving to Lebanon must obtain a permit" from special offices. The letters note that, in response to Lebanese pressure, such permits will be made widely available, particularly for those coming from districts adjacent to the Lebanese border.[123] It would appear from this that the Lebanese were more interested than the Syrians in maintaining an open border. In practice, it would seem that the formal requirement that Syrian workers obtain a permit was waived in any case regarding temporary and seasonal workers, a category into which the vast majority of rural Syrians fell. Even where the formal requirement remained, the regulation seems to have been easily and routinely evaded by the overwhelming majority of Syrian workers entering Lebanon. Hence, it was reported in the 1960s and 1970s that Syrian entry to Lebanon "does not require an authorization from either government, and is achieved by the simple presentation of the identity card."[124] Workers agreed: No permits were necessary, and at most identity cards were required. Joseph entered and left Lebanon using only his identity card, for instance, until the civil war.[125] Adib Mahrus, furthermore, who worked in construction in Lebanon from the 1970s, insisted that the borders had always been open: "From the 1970s. From the time of Camille Chamoun, the time of Chehab, from the time of Frangieh . . . the borders have always been open."[126]

The open border stemmed from the interests and ideas of dominant groups in the two countries. Elites were largely serene in the face of the movement of large numbers of Syrian workers. Financial and mercantile interests in Lebanon did not employ Syrians in numbers, but they upheld a laissez-faire economic vision that assumed the free movement of persons, and believed that Syrian cheap labor complemented Lebanon's wealthy and labor-scarce service economy. Syrians, who stayed temporarily, had no legal status as residents, kept their heads down, worked hard, ignored politics, and left their families and armaments at home—unlike the Palestinians—were not seen as a threat to Christian dominance or the delicate sectarian balance. Indeed, it seemed natural that the apparently booming economy of the "Switzerland of the East" should employ workers as "muscles" from poorer neighboring countries, especially when it was widely held that insufficient numbers of Lebanese were available to do manual, low-paid, or menial jobs. The developing study of "manpower" assured the educated classes that Syria was "favored" with the availability of cheap and abundant labor-power, enhanced by "remarkable displacement of peasants towards the urban centres," which, fortunately, meant "a very strong [downward] pressure on wages." The resulting low level of wages was said to compensate for the lack of quality in the Syrian worker, who, at least, was "skillful and persevering, hard-working, enduring, attentive, enthusiastic . . . [and] always desirous of perfecting himself."[127] There were further political and economic benefits to the presence of Syrian workers. This reserve army of cheap labor brought downward pressure to bear on wages and conditions among the Lebanese workforce, which, particularly after 1958, was becoming increasingly organized and assertive, and, in a country where high politics was dominated by the political bosses (zu'ama'), was threatening to engage in politics itself. Some pictured a Lebanon with a Maronite core enjoying not only a fertile, agricultural hinterland in the Shi'a regions in the Biqa' and the South, but a useful reserve army of labor from relatively poor, adjacent Syria. Lebanese employers in construction, tourism, industry, and agriculture, moreover, did have a direct interest in cheap labor. When regulation loomed, formal representations were made. For example, the Beirut Chamber of Commerce and Industry expressed its opposition in an August 1974 memorandum to the Labor Minister (Amil Ruhana Saqr) to proposed restrictions on work permits granted to Syrian workers in Lebanon.[128]

Pressure for restriction was occasional and relatively weak. Legal circles, for example, complained about the fact that so many Syrians worked without permits. In February 1966, Lebanese officials argued that the murky status of Syrians could cause legal problems in court cases with Syrian involvement.[129] Or, it was occasionally proposed that Syrian workers in Lebanon be taxed. In August 1968, for example, in the context of bilateral wrangling over trade, political asylum and Lebanese press campaigns against Damascus, the issue was raised by the Minister of Economy.[130] But Lebanon was under no fiscal strain during these years, and such an impractical and potentially delicate question (in regard to relations with the Syrian government) had little impact on policy-makers. Finally, there was some limited pressure from the labor movement for protection against unfair labor competition.[131] Such pressures, felt sporadically throughout the period, at best persuaded the Ministry of Social Affairs to debate the issue, call for action, and even propose restrictions on permits and on certain occupations. But the rest of the government remained largely unmoved, and even when restrictions were announced by the Ministry, enforcement mechanisms were lacking, employers and workers were evasive, and in practice Syrian workers appeared to have experienced little or no state-based restrictions on their employment in Lebanon.

The situation was totally different with respect to the Palestinians, over 100,000 of whom appeared after the catastrophic mass expulsion from their homeland in Mandate Palestine (*al-nakba*) during 1948–49. Palestinians living in the camps were employed in work similar to that of the Syrians. In the 1970s, for example, most were employed in "lower-paid jobs" in agriculture, industry, building, trades, services, and transport—most on a daily basis as agricultural laborers and unskilled manual workers, and at low-grade service jobs.[132] Nonetheless, almost from the outset, Palestinians were regarded as more controversial. Unlike the Syrians, the Palestinians had not come voluntarily, and in practice they had no home to go back to. Lebanon therefore had to accommodate them in some way—an accommodation that embroiled Lebanon in the Arab/Israeli conflict, and might involve an unwanted and bloody confrontation with Lebanon's powerful and militarized southern neighbor. Debates about labor competition were heavily colored by these concerns, and hence tended to focus on Palestinians rather than Syrians.[133] Edouard Saab, for example, writing in *Le Jour*, on May 24, 1952, claimed that "we have more to fear from the competition of Palestinian refugees [than of Syrian workers]"[134] In 1953, the Ministry of Social Affairs blamed outmigration on Palestinian competition.[135] These debates were laced from an early stage with dark mutterings about the supposedly nefarious doings of Palestinians. At one point, for example, rumors circulated that Lebanese workers had been fired by certain foreign shipping companies in order to make way for Palestinian labor that was in fact spying for Israel. "Where is the Ministry of Labor?" one newspaper demanded, "Where is the Ministry for Social Affairs, [the] protection of the worker and the Lebanese employee?"[136] Controversy over migrants was therefore colored by larger strategic concerns, and while these only became more acute over time with regard to the Palestinians, for the time being, Syrians were seen in an altogether more positive light.

The Syrian authorities saw little harm and some benefit in the growing cycle of temporary outmigration and return from the countryside. Rural migrants kept out of politics, in the main, and brought remittances home to Syria. Syria's transformation into a net importer of food during the 1970s intensified the state's interest in acquiring foreign exchange via remittances to pay for these imports.[137] Committed Arab nationalists, moreover, increasingly appearing among the ranks of policy-makers in Syria from the late 1950s onward, started to see intra-Arab labor migration as a welcome step toward Arab unity. In 1956, a Council of Arab Experts in Bhamdoun put down a timetable for complete Arab economic unity, stipulating freedom of movement of capital and persons, and freedom of work and employment across the Arab world. The scheme stayed on paper for the most part, but exemplified a growing current connecting the movement of labor to pan-Arabism.[138] This was an issue that was embraced by the Left in both countries. The unions welcomed the formation of the United Arab Republic in early 1958.[139] For example, on November 4, 1971, the construction workers' unions from Syria and Lebanon met and agreed to consider a proposal wherein Arab workers in both countries could be considered not as foreigners but accorded rights and legal status in both countries according to equal treatment.[140]

AN INTEREST IN COMMON

Labor migration between the two countries, at least until the 1970s, for divergent reasons, was an interest held quietly in common. The open border for workers was a token, as was repeated in diplomatic forums, of the cooperative, brotherly, natural, and historical links between Syria and Lebanon.[141] When the countries met to discuss economic issues, the question of Syrian workers in Lebanon was rarely controversial enough even to appear on the agenda.[142] Disputes over the labor supply were limited, short-lived, or linked to other issues. For example, in September 1959, Syria retaliated against a Lebanese refusal to allow Syrians to travel by Beirut airport without a Syrian exit visa by raising the exit tax and imposing security validation for Syrians coming to Lebanon. As a result, 700 Syrians were turned back at the border.[143] The Syrians correctly understood this restriction to be harmful to Lebanese interests, and the dispute was quickly resolved. Conversely, for instance, when Hafez al-Asad acceded to the presidency in 1970, and "abolished the formalities to which Syrians coming to Lebanon had been subject," the Lebanese saw this as a positive sign of good relations with Syria.[144]

   Officials of the two countries, on the other hand, clashed more seriously over other commercial, political, and strategic issues: the relative share of the customs duties on commodities imported into the Arab world through Beirut, the price of Syrian wheat, water rights on the Orontes River, political and press freedoms in Lebanon, and political asylum for Syrian dissidents in Lebanon, which Syria believed gave unnecessary support to "troublemakers" and opponents of the government.[145] Finally, and particularly after the defeat of 1967, Syria considered Lebanon's nonconfrontational stance vis-à-vis Israel an abdication of weighty pan-Arab responsibilities, and a Syrian national security problem to boot, as Lebanon sat astride the Biqa' Valley, a passageway through which Israeli tanks could invade Syria.[146] In comparison with these key areas of conflict, occasional disputes over labor migrants were insignificant.

JOBS IN LEBANON

The open border institutionalized the opportunity for Syrians to migrate to Lebanon. By the Second World War, Lebanon was already relatively wealthy in GDP terms in comparison to Syria. Across the Ottoman Empire in the nineteenth century, the economic center of gravity had shifted from the interior to the coastal ports, which became centers of finance, commerce, and communications. Beirut had become the major port on the eastern Mediterranean during these years. Mt. Lebanon and the coastal plain were relatively wealthy because of small landownership and the use of cash, and had been integrated early to global markets through the production of silk. Outmigration had brought tens of millions of dollars of remittances into what became Lebanon. Wages for day labor and prices were already higher in Lebanon than in Syria during the interwar period.

After independence, Lebanon quickly became a major regional financial center. International banking confidence in Lebanon improved with the break-up of the customs union because this removed threats of Syrian restrictive pressures and meant the rise of an unregulated economy, a strong lira, and a stable macroeconomic and political environment. Lebanese western orientation in foreign policy, and the fact that Lebanon's government was supported against a Nasserist, leftist, and radical nationalist challenge by the United States Marines in 1958, increased the confidence of regional investors in Lebanon. All of these factors, both political and economic, drew mostly financial and commercial capital to Lebanon as a safe haven.[147] From the late 1950s to the early 1970s, the Syrian pound slipped by about 40 percent against the Lebanese currency—hardly a startling plunge, but enough to increase the value of Syrian migrant workers' remittances by a corresponding proportion.

Wealthy bankers and merchants bought real estate and commissioned the construction of imposing offices and apartment buildings, ate out at restaurants, and hired chauffeurs, concierges, cleaners, maids, gardeners, cooks, and others in petty-service trades, such as mechanics.[148] Their capital was also invested in construction, real estate, and tourism, along with hotels, sports clubs, cinemas, nightclubs, restaurants, and the like. In the late 1960s and early 1970s, as confidence returned after the Intrabank crash of 1966, construction boomed as never before. In 1972, the built area of Beirut was twice the size it had been in 1968.[149] Many of the wealthy Syrian families entering Lebanon in the 1960s got involved in construction. One interviewee reckoned that 50 percent of the construction in Beirut by the 1960s was undertaken by Syrian businessmen—often employing their compatriots.[150]

In urban areas, hotels, tourism, small retail, service work, and especially construction accounted for the bulk of Syrian employment.[151] It was reported in 1972 that Syrians comprised at least 90 percent of manual laborers in construction and around 70 percent of more skilled labor. They had also moved into related trades, such as painting, carpentry, metalwork, pouring concrete, plastering, whitewashing, electricity and plumbing, making glass, aluminium, and so on.[152] Many worked in tourism and entertainment. Hanna Awwad, for example, worked in the early 1950s as a groundsman and ball-boy in a tennis club in Beirut serving rich bourgeoise students and the "many aristocratic families who came from Iraq, Syria, Saudi Arabia, etc."[153] Syrians worked in industry, and more generally made up the "unskilled labour of the capital."[154] A survey conducted by the *Centre de Protection Maternelle et Infantile* in the early 1970s of 1,516 heads of households living in the shantytown of Karantina at the northeastern entrance to Beirut shows that most (107) of the 179 non-Kurdish Syrians were construction workers. The rest were grocers (20), traders (12), chauffeurs (10), bakers (8), carpenters (5), secondhand clothes dealers (5), butchers (4), cooks (4), and tailors (4).[155]

After construction, the major employer of Syrians in Lebanon was agriculture. But whereas the construction boom played an important role in drawing in cheap labor from Syria, in agriculture the same role was played by an ongoing economic *crisis*. As the Beirut Chamber of Commerce and Industry consistently pointed out in the 1950s, the strong currency, the lack of tariff protection or subsidy, and the absence of policies oriented to agricultural (or industrial) development worked against the interests of farmers (and industrialists),[156] in spite of the fact that these sectors still accounted for almost a third of Lebanon's total national income in 1956.[157] Pressures were particularly acute in agriculture. In 1974, the many farmers earning the equivalent of around LL3/ $1.31 per day were at the "lowest rung of Lebanese society." Holdings were often minutely divided, with around 80 percent of cultivators holding less than one hectare (2½ acres). Farmers, who had no insurance against natural disasters and drought, or protection against foreign competition, faced high input costs because of oligarchical control over input imports, and put their produce onto an unstable market through exploitative middlemen who took substantial profits. Rents were high, especially on irrigated land, and the absence of agricultural credit meant usury was still common at rates of 3 to 10 percent per month.[158] Cultivation was stigmatized to boot: "The idea that agriculture is the domain of the ignorant and illiterate is anchored in the minds of many people."[159]

These pressures turned the Lebanese countryside into a major eviction mechanism. Absolute numbers of Lebanese working in agriculture fell steadily, in spite of a growing population. In 1970, the agricultural labor force had fallen to 127,000.[160] Only 14 years previously, according to one study, the agricultural labor force stood at 219,330 people,[161] and in 1948, almost half the Lebanese workforce was agricultural. Beirut's population included 291,730 internal migrants in 1970, over 30 percent of the city's population.[162] These processes drew in cheaper Syrian migrants, often Alawis, to work the land, now acting as a supplementary income to urban and overseas Lebanese landowners, merchants, professionals, and small-business owners, who ceased to work on the land but rarely sold it, prizing their apple orchards and citrus plantations, for example, as a connection to home and community, while seeking out cheap manual labor, and paying for it with urban or overseas earnings.[163] Agricultural crisis, rather than boom, drew in migrants, forging in the process economic hierarchies on a transnational scale.

Analogous processes were at work in the urban setting. Overseas, the Lebanese needed trusted employees to oversee and run the daily operations of the businesses they left at home. Henri Allam, for example, the Lebanese manager of American Dream in Hamra, left Joseph in charge of his restaurant during ever longer trips abroad in the 1960s. In a variation on this theme, Syrian Kurds came to inhabit the Jewish quarter of Wadi Abu Jamil near the Grand Serail as space opened up in the wake of outmigration by Jews in particular after 1967.[164] In other cases, the line of causation was reversed. Instead of outmigrants drawing in the labor of inmigrants, inmigrants provided a resource that the Lebanese could use to accumulate wealth or acquire higher status and move to better neighborhoods or overseas. For example, a government survey of 1963 showed that out of the 13,419 persons living in the shantytown of Karantina, 8,010 were Lebanese (and Armenian) and 5,409 were foreigners (mostly Syrian). By 1971, these proportions had reversed, and of 12,663 inhabitants, only 3,713 were Lebanese and Armenian and 8,950 were foreigners (again, mostly Syrian).[165] Incoming Syrians rented rooms and shacks from their former owners, their Lebanese and Armenian occupiers, who through such rental income acquired the wherewithal to move out.[166]

Overall, accumulation and migration were intertwined in transnational chains reaching up from poverty and toward wealth. This point draws attention to often occluded links between outmigration and inmigration. The idea is also to emphasize the rather counterintuitive notion that pull-factors can stem from economic crisis as well as from economic boom. Indeed, the Lebanese countryside, where costs were high, may have been worse off in terms of popular purchasing power than the Syrian countryside, where costs were low and labor-repressive agriculture, usury, and impoverished sharecropping were actually breaking up.

THE DIVISION OF LABOR

The key urban occupation for most Syrian migrants was heavy work in construction, and in rural areas, agriculture. Smaller proportions worked in petty service, manufacturing, and retail trades, or acquired jobs in the more skilled building trades such as painting and decorating. In Meyer's study, less than 8 percent of outmigrants from the Euphrates Valley working abroad "were employed in a higher position than that of an unskilled worker."[167] Why did Syrians get these jobs and not the Lebanese? The conventional explanation is that the relatively better-off and more educated Lebanese were unavailable in sufficient numbers to fill all such manual occupations, and were unwilling to take such low-paid and stigmatized jobs, and Syrian occupational qualifications were generally of a "relatively low standard."[168] The first part of the explanation is both overly generalized and misleading, as far more Lebanese were uneducated or worked in manual occupations than is generally appreciated. The second part captures an element of truth, but raises further questions as to how such jobs came to be both low-paid and stigmatized, and as to the structural elements that worked to define certain jobs in these ways.

Lebanese workers were, to a surprising extent, poor, uneducated, and engaged in unskilled or semi-skilled labor themselves. The IRFED report of 1960–61 claimed that fully 49 percent of the Lebanese population were either poor (40 percent) or destitute (9 percent).[169] As for education, in 1972, the Central Statistical Directorate estimated that fully *80 percent* of the Lebanese workforce had only a primary education, less than a primary education, or no education at all.[170] Large numbers of Lebanese, moreover, were engaged in low-paid, manual, and unskilled work. The 1942 census, for example, counted just over 1 million Lebanese, with 301,906 declaring an occupation. Of these, 134,168 were categorized as "laborers" and 17,871 as "servants." Hence, roughly half the economically active population of Lebanon were accounted for by laborers and servants.[171] During the 1950s, a small number of relatively large economic establishments provided figures to the Ministry of Labor and Social Affairs (founded May 1951) regarding their Lebanese workforce. Of the 36,984 persons reported, well over one-third (16,013 persons) were unskilled.[172] Or, of the total number in work in Lebanon in November 1970 (538,410), 183,720 were "non-agricultural workers and laborers," a significant 34 percent of the in-work labor force.[173] The statistics also show that there were 26,250 day workers in agriculture, meaning that there were 209,970 workers and laborers in Lebanon in 1970, about 39 percent of those in work.[174] The same statistics also list "day workers" by sector, clearly distinguishing them from "salaried/permanent" workers. Day workers were largely those working in casual, insecure, or temporary kinds of labor, hired by the day. Such workers come to more than one-fifth of the total.[175]

These figures suggest that perhaps one-third of the Lebanese labor force, even in the "miracle" economy, was basically poor, uneducated, and engaged in casual, unskilled, or semi-skilled labor.[176] Certainly Lebanese rural-urban migrants, arriving from poor areas in the South, the North, and the Biqa', lived in numbers alongside Syrians, Kurds, and others in the shantytowns around Beirut. The IRFED report of 1960 described Karantina as "a heterogeneous mass of refugees and provincial immigrants, of which 40% are Armenians, 30% rurals from South Lebanon and 30% Syrians."[177] A significant sector of the Lebanese workforce, therefore, was potentially in competition with incoming Syrians.[178] It is highly misleading to imagine, along with the comfortable vision—backed by conventional economics—of certain Lebanese elites during these years, that Syria supplied a manpower which the "Switzerland of the East" simply lacked.

Nor was it generally the case that Syrian workers brought with them the skills that were lacking in Lebanon. It is true that certain Syrian towns and villages were renowned for their expertise in particular building trades. To pick two examples, workers from the villages of the Qalamoun specialized in work in clay (al-tin); those from Tel Aran near Aleppo worked in gypsum (al-jibs). These skills were used in varying degrees in Lebanon. But most Syrian migrants were ex-cultivators, in many ways similar in background to Lebanese migrants departing the land. Moreover, whatever the particular specialty of departing Syrians, once in Lebanon they were often bent to work long hours in unskilled, low-paid, heavy, manual, and repetitive tasks in harvesting, pouring concrete, fetching and carrying, excavation, and the like—tasks that bore little specific relation to the skills they may or may not have acquired in Syria. Abed (1934–), for example, had worked in agriculture, tile-making, and quarrying in Syria in the early 1960s before moving to Lebanon to become assistant to a skilled plasterer in 1963. In terms of skills, Abed, like many others, had to start all over again once he arrived in Lebanon.[179]

Instead, the employment of Syrians over Lebanese had to do primarily with political economy, and secondarily with social networks and attributions of collective identity. By political economy, I mean that Syrians were employed because they could be paid less and were more manipulatable than their Lebanese counterparts. Their lower wages were partly determined by the fact that their social reproduction (involving costs of upbringing, food, housing, land, utilities, health, and education for themselves and their families) took place in cheaper Syria. Hence, a given wage, all other things being equal, purchased relatively more use-values in social reproduction in Syria than in Lebanon, and was thus worth more to Syrians than to Lebanese.[180] Syrians in Lebanon were mostly male, tended to lived 5 or 6 to a room, and left their families at home in Syria.[181] In the shantytowns surrounding Beirut, they lived in miserable dwellings made of old wooden boxes, tarred cartons, and sheet metal.[182] Social costs were kept to a minimum in Lebanon and defrayed in cheaper Syria. For this reason, Syrians could be induced to work for lower wages than Lebanese.

Also important, however, was that during the very years (1958 onward) when Syrians were starting to arrive in large numbers, and before their sectoral distribution was institutionalized, the Lebanese labor movement found its voice and recorded significant gains, making unorganized, low-paid, and malleable Syrian labor more attractive to employers by comparison. On the one hand, un-unionized Syrians could be and were expected to be more docile on the job than Lebanese, to follow orders, not to demand days off or pay rises, and to work longer hours and take fewer breaks. On the other hand, after 1963, because of the gains of the labor movement under President Fuad Chehab (who served from 1958 to 1964), Lebanese employees had to be registered in the newly created national Social Security system, protecting workers against sickness, job loss, retirement, accidents, and so on. Employers had to defray roughly one-third of the costs of this scheme, and complained bitterly. Those employing Syrians took on no such costs, nor even the bureaucracy of work contracts. Workers were hired and fired on the spot. Legal issues were minimal, and even accident insurance was optional. These political and economic factors were arguably the most important elements determining the division of labor; they defined the meaning of the term *lack* in regard to local labor scarcity, which was not simply *discovered* in an inert socioeconomic structure determined by the forces of supply and demand, but *made* out of a combination of interests and struggles.

Social networks and attributions of collective identity also played a role in the national and confessional division of labor. Networks linked Syrian workers to Syrian entrepreneurs in construction. Porterage was dominated by Syrian Kurds, at least in Karantina, a situation perpetuated by their informal recruitment networks. Workers in the port of Beirut in the late 1940s and 1950s were mostly from the Hawran, a situation that endured over time. Social networks linked Alawis to agricultural labor. The ranks of ambulant sellers (newspaper sellers, lottery ticket sellers, and chewing gum vendors) in Karantina were dominated mostly by Shi'a Lebanese migrants from the southern towns of Nabatiye, Marjayoun, Bint Jubail, and Sur.[183]

Attributions of collective identity summarized, stabilized, and reproduced occupational specializations. Syrians came to be known for their stamina, manipulability, and ability to engage in hard work, and were thus sought after by employers for particular kinds of labor, whereas Lebanese were rejected. Syrian Alawi men were sought out in agriculture, but Alawi women—"stout" and "brown"—worked from their early teens as domestic maids in wealthy households.[184] Alawis were expected to fill these lowly roles, supposedly appropriate to their disposition. In this context, it was considered more fitting and natural for a poor Lebanese to work in petty self-employment in services, such as in newspaper selling, than to engage in heavy, manual labor.

CONFLICT AND COOPERATION

Although the labor market was segmented by social networks and collective identity (in addition to geography and occupation), competition between Syrians and Lebanese existed where the former were employed because they were cheaper and more manipulable, features constituted in part by attributions of identity itself. Many Lebanese workers, especially in the more skilled construction trades, petty services, and retail, lost out to Syrian workers, their conditions, wages, and jobs coming under pressure in the face of cheap competition. There was also resentment at the presence of Syrian "scab labor" undermining labor solidarity and powers of institutional disruption, some "wildcat" fighting between workers, and a limited measure of union activism, none of which made a significant impact on the existing order. Neither elites nor the *status quo* in Syro-Lebanese relations were favorable to regulation. Conservative Christian leaderships were unlikely to side with impoverished Lebanese workers, traditionally organized by Leftists opposed to Maronite sectarian preponderance.[185] Many on the Lebanese Left, moreover, saw in labor migration progressive pan-Arabism, and so did not wholeheartedly support the Lebanese workers' demands.[186]

Antagonism between Lebanese and Syrian workers, nonetheless, was sporadically present. Indeed, the oldest living memory I came across in an interview was of fighting between Lebanese and Syrian workers. Elias, encountered in Chapter 1, who worked temporarily on earthworks near Chekka in the 1940s, recalled one such fight. Elias had hidden behind a rock following an attack, and started throwing stones at his Lebanese aggressors, demanding that each come and face him, one by one. His antagonists somehow discovered that Elias was a Christian, not an Alawi, as they had thought. At this, they invited him to dinner to make amends. The story was related to the English "doctor" and the assembled company of friends and family as a tale of manly challenge and riposte, and likely aimed to demonstrate the honor, solidarity, and hospitality of the Christians as compared to Alawis. A middle-aged schoolteacher, smallholder and former Ba'thist present at the interview, suggested afterwards that the fight was actually because Elias represented scab labor to the Lebanese.[187] It does not seem too far-fetched to imagine that both sect and labor issues were at play in these and other forms of conflict and cooperation during the 1940s.

In the aftermath of the break-up of the customs union, before new arrangements were institutionalized, sections of the labor movement seized the chance to demand the protection of Lebanese workers. In June 1950, workers' syndicates requested an end to the engagement of foreign labor in industry.[188] In the same year, the taxi drivers' syndicate denounced competition from foreigners working in public vehicles.[189] These demands were aimed at Syrians, not just Palestinians, and bore fruit immediately as the Justice Minister announced that he would consider a law forbidding Syrians to work in Lebanon.[190] The newly formed Ministry of Labor and Social Affairs was sympathetic to Lebanese workers' plight, moreover, and announced in October 1951:

> In view of the competition of Syrian labour which has taken on a serious character, Social Affairs demand from the government the prevention of the clandestine entry of Syrians, to search for Syrians without permits in the markets

and the factories, and to impose on them a renewable permit to stay of two weeks, and to deport all Syrians without a residence or work permit.[191]

On 4 December 1951, the same Ministry ruled that unskilled foreigners working in hotels, restaurants, and clubs would not have their permits renewed.[192] There is no evidence that this ruling was ever effectively enforced, however. And Beirut continued in representations to Syria to propose entirely unrestricted and open borders, and no trace of this labor struggle exists in either Lebanese legislation or the key bilateral agreement signed with Syria in 1953.

A glimpse of labor antagonism and how subsequent diplomacy shaped policy is afforded by an incident in early June 1951, when an "intense battle" was reported between Syrian workers from the Hawran and Lebanese workers in the Port of Beirut.[193] The battle appears to have led to the precipitate deportation of these Syrian workers, along with their families, and the hasty claim by the head of police that the reason for the deportation was that these Hawranis had illegally entered the Palestinian refugee camps.[194] The Syrian government took the incident extremely seriously and closed the border on June 7–8, 1951, in retaliation.[195] The Lebanese government tried to make amends, announcing on June 10 that the eviction from the port was simply because the Syrians were not allowed into customs zones in the Port of Beirut. The head of police was said to have bungled the explanation of the decision.[196] The Lebanese went on to apologize to the Syrians for the incident and affirmed its "eagerness that Syrian workers in Lebanon enjoy the same freedoms and labour rights as Lebanese workers in Syria."[197] In this way, the Lebanese government restored confidence with the Syrians that it was committed to the open border. Incidents such as these indicate both that labor antagonism existed on the ground, and that political sensitivities in bilateral relations worked against Lebanese interventionism.[198] The issue of restrictions on Syrian workers remained a matter of occasional debate and some ineffective measures in the next two decades, but the situation on the ground was never significantly transformed.[199]

In the early 2000s, Syrians who remembered working in Lebanon in the 1950s and 1960s told a story of better days of tolerance and good relations between Syrians, Lebanese, and the various communitarian groupings. Joseph, for example, maintained that sectarianism and discrimination only really mattered after the mid-1970s. Things were different in the 1950s and 1960s, he said. These were the best years of his life. He obtained his first job via a Christian, and he lived in a room with fellow Syrian Christians in Hamra, a mixed neighborhood. He had friendly non-Christian neighbors, and both Syrian and Lebanese friends. His first job in a sandwich shop involved working for a Lebanese Sunni Muslim, who treated him well, like one of his own. "He knew my name was . . . [Joseph] but that did not repulse him." He secured a better job as a waiter in Uncle Sam, a restaurant in Hamra, via a Druze Lebanese customer who he had befriended at the sandwich shop. There, most of his fellow workers were Lebanese. "There was no discrimination. Eid al-Adha would pass and we would not know. Ramadan would pass and even though the Muslims would be fasting, we would not know. We could not tell a Muslim from a Christian. It was a good environment in Lebanon."[200]

Abed told a similar story, telling me that Lebanon "used to be different from now. . . . You could go out till morning and nobody would interfere in your life. I used to go out to Jounieh, Broumana, take the Telefrik to Harissa [all Christian places and sites] and [even] when they knew I was Syrian they would welcome me. Usually they wouldn't even ask. The sectarianism of today did not exist then. Now it is much different." It is true, moreover, that Abed, a Sunni Muslim, took his first job in Lebanon with a Maronite Lebanese skilled plasterer.[201] Hanna Butros said that before the civil war "you would not tell a Muslim from a Christian. People were living together." The clashes of 1958, for example, were simply to do with political projects of leaders, not chauvinism among the people.[202]

Tony Elias—an orthodox Christian—explained that he worked under master painters from a great variety of backgrounds during 1970–74 in Lebanon: "The master would . . . normally be a Lebanese or a Syrian, from all the provinces. Or from Egypt or Jordan, or whoever, even Lebanese. There were Christians, Druze, Shi'a—a variety." And among the workers there were "Christians with us, as well as Muslims and Druze." Tony insisted that during these years the relations between these sects were "good" with "no problems at all." Moreover, "the Syrian would work in a Lebanese house, whether the owners were Christian or Muslim, they would not ask him about his faith. . . . Why would he ask? He cared about his business. If you have a project and you need workers, you would not care whether they were Christian or Muslim because you would worry about your project and your [material] benefit only." He told a story about how all the different confessions would break bread together:

> You know what I would do, when I was sixteen years old after I had been there for a year: the master would call me and ask me what I would want to eat for lunch. I would say a can of sardines, for example, and he would ask all the

other workers as well and write the orders down, a can of tuna, a kilogram of
tomatoes, mortadella and so on. Then I would go to the shop and buy their
orders with cola drinks and put them all in a bag. We would sit all together
on the ground. . . . We would put the food on the floor and eat. There were
Muslims and Christians, and there was one from Hama, these are normally
sectarianist Sunnis: his name was Mustafa. He was a good boy. We lived with
him as if we were one. We did not consider that we were different. We would
all sit on the floor, put our food on top of a bag, and we would all eat from each
other's food or have a taste. Some men brought with them food from their
wives' cooking at home and they would share it with the rest of us. We shared
olives and everything.

Tony Elias insisted that this was quite normal in those days. Hanna Awwad
reckoned, in a more sober mode, that there had always been discrimination
between sects, religions, and Lebanese and Syrians, but admitted that things
got worse from 1975.[203]

In part, these stories were the nostalgia of looking back on days of youth
and personal mobility made rosy by the passage of time. They were about what
was important in migrants' own telling of their history. They were also surely
colored by the contrast with the subsequent and bloody history of civil war.
They also owed something to the attempt to convey to their English interviewer that tensions between Syria and Lebanon were not inherent and natural
to the people of the historic *bilad ash-sham* or Arabs in general, but a product
of politics, lies, and misunderstandings. The details of these stories, nonetheless, caution against any reading of these years implying that conflict between
incoming Syrians and existing Lebanese was endemic or inevitable. They are
consonant with a pattern of occasional conflict and co-existence that was char-
acteristic of those decades, but was to change radically as Lebanon descended
into civil war and underwent Syrian military intervention.

LIKE SUGAR IN TEA

Compared with what was to come, in the 1950s and 1960s Syrian workers remained relatively invisible to ministers, political bosses, officials, technical
intelligentsia, political movements, the media, and so on. Syrians were neither
counted, registered, taxed, nor valued in economic studies. They were not politically or collectively organized, they laid claim to no great public, cultural
recognition, and their presence was not connected prominently to any major

controversy. One indication of their relative invisibility comes from a two-volume reference work on Lebanese-Syrian relations. This work records 5,337 "events" in relations between the two countries from 1943 to 1985. Only 17 such "events" relate directly to Syrian workers.[204] Even when General Security announced that there were more than a quarter of a million Syrian workers in Lebanon, silence and disinterest followed. One of the few articles on the topic put it this way: "Quarter of a million Syrian workers melt away every evening like sugar in tea," a striking enough metaphor for the practically invisible footprint that Syrians seemed to leave in a polity and society that derived great benefit from their "muscles" but seemed to ignore everything else about them.

The author of this article was an intellectual who, unusually enough, had worked "as one of them" for "not less than three years." He wrote, "In spite of the great crowds of us in the workshops and factories and farms, and in spite of tiring and productive effort that we exerted without counting up the hours of labour, we were like ghosts, unseen: perhaps we were never even there."[205] Here, effort and productivity are contrasted with invisibility and a striking absence of recognition. The only time that "we suddenly found ourselves in the spotlight," the writer noted, was when the security forces showed up to search the Khabayni Café or the Café of the Syrians for a fugitive or for explosives. At these times Syrians were ordered into waiting lorries into which they then crowded without demur. "To where? Nobody asked." This rough treatment "was the only type of 'interest' to which we were subject at any point," a fact that for the writer highlighted the absence of any kind of protection, social security, collective organization, or even labor office dealing with Syrian workers' affairs in Lebanon.[206]

CONCLUSION

This chapter has recovered some aspects of the rather invisible history of migration from Syria to Lebanon during the 1950s and 1960s when it became a mass phenomenon for the first time. I have traced how a new migration flow, stemming primarily from Syria's grain-producing plains, came into being, first from the regions bordering Lebanon, and increasingly from points further North and East. I have argued that this migrant flow was driven above all by cash-hunger and new aspirations in Syria, and by increased earning power in Lebanon, and was shaped by transport, geography, social networks, and, most important, the open border. Outmigration was neither a crisis-driven flood of human jetsam and flotsam driven by desperation and the whip of hunger, but nor was it an upwardly mobile journey for youthful entrepreneurs seeking to maximize their wealth through endless accumulation and aspirations of an individualistic life of consumption.

Outmigration was embedded within the projects of those who undertook it. The household economy linked to gendered practices operated powerfully to designate men as breadwinners, and hence outmigrants, and women as carriers of the burden of household social reproduction and farm and craft labor. Male migrants, linked to family and other social relationships, had certain kinds of projects and hopes—to make something of their lives, to buy a house, land, a small business, better clothes, and so on. They aimed to convert cash into use-value. Such projects were also shaped and made urgent by social expectations.

The whole cycle of migration and return was constructed within a dominant political economy that drove cash-hungry and land-poor Syrians from the land and employed them in Lebanon where they were cheaper and more manipulable than their Lebanese counterparts. This political economy was linked to the common interests of powerful groups in Syria and Lebanon, which for various often divergent reasons saw this migration flow in a positive light. Lebanese elites justified their stance with regard to the economics of laissez-faire, based on the idea that the two countries had complementary economies: Syria supplying the labor and Lebanon supplying the capital. It was this dominant political economy, along with its powerful economic vision and common interest within bilateral relations, that ensured above all that Syrian workers were relatively invisible and uncontroversial. The tangle of interests and different yet congruent visions from both above and below were not basically in conflict when it came to the movement of Syrian workers across the border. The sorts of antagonisms that the system did involve, such as protests from the Lebanese labor movement, were insufficient to provoke larger conflict or transformation. What appeared to Lebanese elites as laissez-faire, of course, was in fact a particular project of ownership and control, the product of dominant interests and visions, secured through channeling, harnessing, and activating the interests and decisions of different social actors. The stability of the overall pattern was the result of a complex and partly conjunctural alignment of forces and interests. The hegemony that this system represented was not one based on a single fundamental class, but on a number of powerful sets of interests that, for conjunctural reasons, found themselves generally aligned. These alignments were to shift dramatically in coming decades and transform the migration cycle in significant ways.

The foregoing suggests that migrants are best understood neither in Marxian mode as proletarians, nor with conventional economics as simply units of price in a market. Nor has it been particularly helpful to think in terms of petty bourgeoisie, working-class, or peasantry. It seems instead that the unit of analysis at the level of the individual migrant refers to persons with names, purposes, and stories, who are thrown into multiply determined social situations as subjects of and subject to different elements of social power. The full implications of Syrian workers' unintended entanglement in forms of social power over which they had no control will only become clear in the following chapters.

3 IN THE NAME OF THE MARTYRS

> *What are these castles except that which our hands made, built*
> *on the skulls of our martyrs, and mixed with the sweat of our*
> *workers?*
>
> **—League of Syrian Workers, 1979**

INTRODUCTION

In the 1970s and 1980s, Syrian migrants, many of whom had set out to Lebanon with such high hopes in the 1950s and 1960s, found themselves entangled in unintended ways in economic crisis, violence, eviction, and killings, as the political and economic settlement underpinning of the Christian-led "merchant republic" broke up, and Lebanon suffered 15 years of civil war. Many workers and their families returned to Syria, and tentative processes of settlement were definitively broken up. The political underpinnings of the free market in Syrian labor were dramatically exposed where, in Christian areas at least, that free market was definitively unmade. This chapter will trace how Syrian workers, so long accepted in Lebanon as useful and hard-working resources, came to be seen as the enemy in Christian areas, and how older Lebanese understandings about the positive role of foreign labor in general were seriously challenged during the economic crisis of the 1980s. Paradoxically enough, even amid the tensions and crises of the civil war, the late 1970s also witnessed the most significant period of collective action by Syrian workers in Lebanon from independence to the present. This chapter examines these strikes and protests, understanding them above all in terms of political conjuncture. I will explain the dynamics of return and unsettlement during these years, paying attention to the salience— even amid violence and economic crisis—of gendered roles and family ties.

MIGRATION DURING THE WAR

In spite of limited data, it is possible to make some educated guesses about the broad trajectories of migration and return from Syria during the 1970s and 1980s. The claim that Syrians simply left Lebanon in 1975 and did not return until the early 1990s is misleading. Bourgey maintained, somewhat more plausibly, that after 1975 only "a major part" of the Syrian workforce returned to Syria, as they "did not want any longer to work in Lebanon in the regions controlled by militias hostile to the government in Damascus."[1] My own research suggests that more Syrian workers stayed during 1975–1982 than is usually supposed. One of the few estimates of numbers during this period was given in the Damascene weekly *Al-Ishtiraki*, at 30,000 in mid-1980.[2] This is not an insignificant figure, measured against a resident Lebanese workforce estimated to number 550,000 persons in 1985.[3] The League of Syrian Workers in Lebanon (established in 1977) maintained, in 1981, probably with some exaggeration, that Lebanon was still heavily dependent on Syrian labor, with many important sectors depending "completely or partly on Syrian labour." The League claimed that Syrians made up 90 percent of bakers, 80 percent of the manual labor in the cultural and press sectors, 75 percent of construction workers, and 50 percent of workers in agriculture, services, and ports and shipping, not to mention workers in glass and plastic industries and in spinning and weaving. The League pointed out that there were Syrian workers in Sidon, 'Aley, Shtura, Ba'albek, Shweifet, and Tripoli.[4]

Further, only about half my interviewees, admittedly a sample too small to be seen as representative, left the country for a significant period during 1975–1982, while the other half stayed. Some interviewees even went to Lebanon for the first time during this period. Salim al-Dahash (1961–), for example, a Sunni Arab from a small village in the Aleppo region first came to Lebanon to work in construction in 1979, in spite of the war and atrocities, about which he said he was unafraid. He maintained that "Lebanon had a positive image in spite of the war," and he did not want to go to the Gulf which, he had been led to believe at school, was still in the pockets of the feudal lords (*bekawat*) who looked down on the poor.[5] Others returned to Lebanon during this first period (1975–1982) of the war. Tony Elias, for example, left Lebanon in 1974 to do his military service in Syria, proceeded to work in Libya until 1979, and then returned straight to Lebanon, to work in Hamra, Beirut, as a self-employed painter. Tony far preferred Lebanon to Libya. He maintained that the latter was uncivilized, a condition symbolized by the ubiquitous *jallabiyya*, associated by Tony with bedouin and a lack of education. More important, perhaps, he was unable to save money in Libya, as everything he earned was used up in transport and other costs. He went straight to Lebanon on his return.

Abed stuck out conditions in Lebanon for the entire war. He had wanted to go the Gulf in 1974, even before the war in Lebanon. But, as he said, "it took them too much time to send me the visa, and then I got an offer to work for 500 Riyals [per month]. I didn't accept that offer as I was making LL300 [$131 per month] here [in Lebanon] and that made more than 500 Riyals." In other words, Abed ran up against the formalities associated with migration to the Gulf as well as poor earning incentives. His own estimate of Syrian workers' movements was that "between 1976 and 1982 the number of Syrians in this area [al-Zarif, Beirut] did not change. They only left from the other areas. But I would assume that the percentage [of those Syrians who quit Lebanon altogether] was 50 percent."

The overwhelming majority of Syrian workers, whatever their sect, however, left the Christian areas of Lebanon during 1975–1976, when identity card killings began at the hands of the Kataeb and other Christian militias. Large numbers of Syrians were seen fleeing northward out of Tripoli in September 1975 and eastward toward Damascus in October.[6] Certainly the thousands of Syrians living in the slum areas of Maslakh, Karantina, and in and around the Palestinian camps of Dubayya, Jisr al-Basha, and so on were forced out during the first eight months of 1976. In addition, the League of Syrian Workers in Lebanon claimed in 1979 that as many as 3,000 Syrian workers had to leave the Port area during the 3 to 4 years after the outbreak of the war.[7] Abed reckoned that "95 percent of those [Syrian workers] who were in the Christian areas left . . . [as] there was killing, for no reason, just because they were holding a Syrian [identity] card. . . . They left the Eastern areas and came to West Beirut, to the Muslim areas. They came to Hamra, Mazra'a, Museitbeh [etc.]." Indeed, by 1978, the Christian area of Mt. Lebanon was increasingly autonomous in socioeconomic terms.[8] Nonetheless, some of my interviewees worked in Christian sectors for one reason or another until 1982.

The Israeli invasion of 1982, the economic crisis of 1983 onward, and the bitter rounds of fighting throughout the country, however, seem to have driven the last remaining Syrians from Christian areas, and the majority of Syrians to depart Lebanon altogether as the 1980s went on. Winckler estimated that numbers working in Lebanon fell once again during the second half of the 1980s.[9] Abed reckoned that only about 3 percent stayed on and of those who left, most did not return again until the 1990s. Certainly, Tony Elias departed with the Israeli invasion and did not return until the early 1990s. Nonetheless, a number of informants stayed, including Abed himself. Adib Mahrus continued to work in Lebanon throughout the war, even maintaining that plenty of work remained.[10] Both men found construction work during the periods of reconstruction and relative calm that punctuated the war. Salim al-Dahash also stayed throughout the war, having found secure work as a concierge. Indeed, it was said that Palestinian concierges were increasingly being replaced by Syrians. The former had been perceived as reliable on account of their higher levels of education, but were starting to become increasingly undesirable as they were drawn into the conflict, especially after the "war of the camps" (principally involving the Amal-led seige of the Palestinian camps) in the mid-1980s.[11] Older and more trusted construction workers were selected by building contractors and entrepreneurs to staff newly constructed buildings. This is what happened to Adib Mahrus, who morphed from construction worker, to site guard, and then to concierge by the early 1990s.

Notwithstanding cultural reservations, transport costs, and burdensome formalities, many of the Syrians who left Lebanon, or who departed from Syria for the first time, sought employment in the Gulf, especially during the oil boom of 1973–1981. Winckler noted that during the second half of the 1970s, "many peasants in such rain-fed regions as the Hawran and Jabal Druze were . . . tempted to seek their fortunes in the Gulf." But opportunities there dwindled with the fall in oil prices after 1981.[12] Nonetheless, in the late 1980s, there were still around 200,000 Syrians, comprising the great bulk of Syria's regional migrants, in oil-exporting countries.[13] During the 1970s and 1980s, moreover, deteriorating relations between Syria and Iraq and Jordan "disrupted" the flow of migrants there.[14]

ASIANS AND ALAWIS

The departure of Syrian workers from the Christian areas of Lebanon, alongside the continuing and perhaps surprising strength of the Lebanese economy until about 1983, was probably the single-most important of the pull factors in the arrival of Asian labor in Lebanon from the mid-1970s onward. As was reported in 1984, "Pakistani, Bangladeshi, . . . Ethiopian, Egyptian, Filipino, Sri Lankan, Indian, Thai and Korean workers" had appeared in numbers in "bakeries, factories, construction sites, households, agriculture, restaurants and even in hospitals, where they work as registered nurses and nurses' aides."[15] Asian labor in Lebanon was negligible before 1975, but in 1982, Asians took over a quarter of foreign work permits.[16] Demand for non-Syrian foreign labor started to rise significantly in 1977, when about 8,000 permits were granted or renewed, peaked in 1983, when 45,000 permits were issued, and started to diminish with the economic crisis, with the lowest numbers of permits being issued in 1986.[17] Such workers, unlike Syrians, could not quit their jobs or change employers when they had signed contracts, which many employers considered advantageous. Owing to lower social costs in countries such as Sri Lanka, moreover, they could be paid even less than Syrians. Contracting agencies were on hand to deal with bureaucratic and legal issues. And it was also said that Asian workers' lack of education and Arabic language left them unable to claim even the most basic of human rights, while their trustworthiness and good manners enabled "inhuman" exploitation.[18] For those running households, Asians were a welcome alternative to Syrian Alawi maids, who were no longer considered suitable for such demeaning work given the fact that the Alawi sect was widely believed to dominate the Syrian government, and hence the employment of Alawis might lead to political difficulties, especially after the Syrian army had entered Lebanon in June 1976.[19]

PRESSURES TO MIGRATE

It would be correct to assume that those ready to take their chances in war-torn Lebanon were under significant pressure to depart Syria. In terms familiar from previous decades, land poverty, cash-hunger, debt, rising consumption aspirations, and social expectations—combined with population growth, recurring drought, and irregular rainfall—were still basic to these pressures. Where the sons of land-poor cultivators sought to marry and start independent households, they had few alternatives but to migrate to earn the necessary cash. Such persons continued to reach their early teens in large numbers, as Syria's population more than doubled from around 6.3 million in 1970 to about 13.8 million in 1994.[20]

There were new pressures associated with the 1970s and 1980s. With al-Asad's cautious rapprochement with elements of the Syrian urban bourgeoisie after 1973, Batatu argues, the fortunes of capitalized middle-size and larger farmers and *mustathmirs*—capitalist leaseholders—waxed, "even as the position of the small-scale landholding peasants became less secure."[21] Investors were encouraged after 1973: Fruit and vegetables were exempted from price controls, there was no "de facto limit on leaseholdings," and "powerful elements in the state apparatus who benefited from their operations . . . connived at their leasing of plots owned by the state or by tribal chieftains, or by the poorer peasantry."[22] This channel for private investment was deliberately left open by the government "attempting to attract the new fortunes accumulated after 1973 and during the 1980s by Syrians working in the Gulf."[23] These policies increased economic inequality in the countryside. New patterns of commercial exploitation may have been linked to the depletion through overuse of subterranean water in some areas, greater reliance on machines, soil degradation, and the higher cost of food.[24] The state continued to allow meat, poultry, and eggs to be marketed through middlemen,[25] which pushed up prices. Meyer also points to the "increasing *salinity* in the soil of the fields especially in the Lower Euphrates valley."[26] These factors all put pressure on livelihoods, intensified land-hunger, or diminished the local demand for labor while increasing the pressure to earn cash. A powerful indicator of how food security and self-sufficient peasant cultivation was diminishing came during the 1970s, when Syria became a net food importer for the first time.[27] Where domestic communities were increasingly buying their food from the market, cash-pressures were increased. The "sharp swing in world grain prices" in the 1970s increased such pressures, and not only at the level of domestic communities but also from the point of view of the state, whose financial burden was increased.[28] This development put a premium on migrant remittances, both for cash-poor families on the one hand, and, on the other, the state seeking to earn hard currency for macroeconomic and regime stability.

In certain areas, development-related displacement played a role. Rabo noted in the 1980s that "seasonal migration abroad is now essential" for many of the 64,000 individuals who had earlier been forced to leave the inundated zone of Euphrates Dam west of Raqqa and work the land further into the eastern steppe where rains were more uncertain and land less fertile.[29]

The development of the cash economy diminished access to alternative means of existence and social security provided by local communal and informal mechanisms. As a villager and large landholder from the village 25 miles east of Raqqa studied by Rabo reported in the 1980s, "The former tribal life was better than this. Things were run on the tribal principle and nobody used to eat [out of house and home] another man close to him. Now the power is in the hands of the state—the party. It rules the world. Today if you have no money no one cares about you."[30] These sentiments were widespread and unlikely to be solely about nostalgia. They referred to new elements in the social structure: Client relations with the ruling party were increasingly important regarding access to material resources, property rights were more rival and exclusive than before, market relations were more developed, self-interest was increasingly calculated in monetary terms, and the challenge of work and wages disrupted and transformed—and often rewrote—codes of honor and status.[31] In this context, incomes, productivity levels, and the pressure to earn cash increased, and access to alternative and noncash means of subsistence diminished. Where new needs for cash could not be fulfilled locally, then outmigration became an alternative and in many ways a necessity.

The cash economy now encapsulated the furthest corners of the Syrian countryside. Whereas before 1945 the Qalamoun and the Ghoutas had been most affected, and in the 1950s and 1960s the grain-producing plains transformed, the pastoral nomad economy of the eastern steppe was similarly enframed and unfixed. In the 1970s and 1980s, poorer nomadic families in the desert (badiyya) were driven into wage labor in greater numbers. Those families living in extreme poverty—owning, say, two dozen sheep, a few goats, and chickens—supplemented family incomes with the casual laboring of men, women, and children. Such individuals worked from ragged tents pitched near Palmyra or Syria's phosphate workings, in construction in Syrian cities, or as migrant laborers in Jordan, Iraq, and Lebanon. As in other cases, where men had to leave a relatively independent communal economy for the first time, there was a considerable issue of honor involved in working for someone else. It was said that the Bani Sakhr tribesmen were "too proud" to engage in wage labor on a short-term basis. The 'Anazah, it was said, "disdain the idea of looking after other people's sheep." Similar issues had dogged the expansion of the cash economy, from Mt. Lebanon to the eastern steppe. And, as elsewhere, independent means of subsistence were tenaciously defended. As Norman Lewis puts it, "The tribal people of the badiyah do everything they can to supplement what they get from their sheep [but few give up, in spite of outmigration]. Nearly all of them regard their flocks as their basic asset, to be nurtured and increased."

Such groups also "insist" that the badiya is theirs and not the government's, staking further claim to their basic means of livelihood.[32] The "preservation-dissolution" of precapitalist forms is by no means simply a matter of the interests of capital, but it is also a matter of the determination of those affected to hold on to their independence, and to resist and negotiate new realities in ways that make sense in terms of previous ways of life. Renovation was as important as preservation. As elsewhere, forms of independence are undermined, or forced to take new forms by the expansion of the cash economy and its associated power structures and discourses. By the 1980s, for example, semi-nomadic sheep herders in northern Syria were dependent on diesel for their trucks and were therefore "sensitive to prices in diesel," tying them to market economy on a transnational basis.[33] By the late 1980s, then, in association with the spread of the cash, and the partial, but not complete, destruction of independent circuits of production and exchange, it is fair to say that outmigration affected every part of Syria.

On the more positive side, although this phenomenon has been little discussed, the division of rural labor in cultivated regions was redistributed in a kind of silent revolution by statist development and infrastructural work, especially with regard to the provision of electricity and water. In 1970, most cultivators "fell asleep and woke with the sun." By 1992, however, "thanks largely to the building of the Euphrates dam, no fewer than 7,630 villages [95 percent of all villages] . . . had been electrified. The government met the costs of the infrastructure and the price of electricity to farmers was subsidized."[34] Farm irrigation, some labor-saving machinery, and the provision of household water, heating, and lighting cut out untold hours of particular kinds of unwaged domestic labor and drudgery, the burden of which had chiefly fallen on women and children. Gathering fuel (wood, manure, scraps, etc.) for cooking and for heating in the winters—especially in northern Syria where it was particularly cold—along with bringing in household water could easily mean two or more hours of labor a day, depending on the local situation. The labor input was drastically reduced where electricity and piped water appeared. The introduction of piped farm irrigation also had a tremendous, if uneven, impact. In the 1960s, for example, Al-Hajj Ali and his family had laboriously used a rope and bucket to irrigate the fields in his small village on the eastern plain of Aleppo. By the 1990s, the Hajj was using a pump powered by cheap electricity (at $15 every two months) with low-maintenance, cheap, and durable pipes that drip-fed individual plants.[35] The family labor input to this new irrigation was minimal.

Rural women were not at all suddenly transformed into leisured housewives. As Rabo's research on the Euphrates Valley from the 1980s shows, women continued to do "all the back-breaking, tedious, recurrent tasks inside and outside the house," and in the process bore "the main burden of the social reproduction of labour."[36] Indeed, and as we have seen in the case of Abed in the last chapter, men could only "establish themselves economically through access to, or partial control over, a woman's labour."[37] But these changes may have played a role in the shifting division of labor in the household economy.

Women were made available for doing farm work previously done by men, or for working for cash on the fields of neighbors and relatives, and engaging more frequently in international labor migration. And where women were doing farmwork, or where older tasks were cut out, the labor of men was also made available for economic migration. Electrification and piped water may have been one of the factors in the long-term process of the feminization of farmwork, and may have thereby contributed to female outmigration and more permanent and extensive forms of male migration. Outmigration and agricultural intensification further contributed to feminization in the 1990s.[38]

Rising expectations also played a role. Just as in the 1950s and 1960s, it would be an exaggeration to depict the Syrian countryside as wracked by crisis, evicting desperate economic refugees willy-nilly toward cities and foreign lands. In fact, there was protection against price fluctuations via official procurement prices for the major cereals—wheat, barley, and lentils—as well as for cotton, tobacco, and sugar beet. The way prices were set involved a net subsidy to farmers. Seeds, fertilizers, and pesticides were also often provided by the state on concessionary terms.[39] Indeed, according to Rabo, the rural inhabitants were eager to demand and embrace "electricity, . . . running water, better roads, more rural schools and higher crop yields." These changes, combined with the welfare aspirations of the state and its "rhetoric of development," brought "increasing expectations" as to living standards.[40] Whereas those who came of age in the 1950s and 1960s were apt to see tea, sugar, coffee, and tobacco as luxuries, those coming of age in the 1970s and 1980s, whose memories of the age of the feudalists were dim, wanted more. Migrants could dream of success abroad. Migration to the Gulf could enable a good marriage, an independent household, the funds to buy land or a small business, and even the purchase of a car. Meanwhile, however, even the cost of the sum of money given to the bride's family at marriage, the *mahr*, had increased, according to some, to SL5,000–6,000/ $1,359–1,630 by the end of the 1970s.[41] Rising costs increased the pressures, as did the heavy discipline of social expectations among local communities. As Rabo put it, "Relatives and friends . . . expect hard evidence of the migrant's new material wealth each time he returns home."[42] In this context, Rabo's informants noted that working in the Gulf involved severe hardships: the heat, the cost of living, social isolation, and bad treatment. "But they all say it is worthwhile since the pay is good. Migration is strictly for work, and many people say they work more or less day and night." "The move is never permanent, even though some have worked more or less continuously for the past decade."[43] In these ways, whole regions became heavily dependent on outmigration. In the village studied by Rabo, one-quarter of male heads of household had migrated, as had many unmarried men "who migrate more often than the older men." Destinations depended on where the jobs were, legal and political issues, and the existence of networks. Migrants from this village worked nearby in al-Raqqa, in construction in the Damascus region, and in Jordan.[44] In 1980 remittances from all migrants abroad were officially estimated at $773.5 million per year.[45]

FORCES OF ATTRACTION

One clear indication that labor was not simply evicted from Syria, but owed its mobility also to migrant decisions and the forces of attraction abroad, is that the Syrian countryside seems to have suffered a scarcity of labor in the 1980s. Rising wage rates for agricultural workers during these years were said to be related to the exodus of adult males.[46] In 1977, it was said that an unskilled construction worker in Saudi Arabia could earn five times the wage of his counterpart in Damascus.[47] But what could possibly be attractive about going to war-torn Lebanon?

First, the Lebanese economy remained surprisingly resilient until around 1983. Income per capita was higher in nominal dollar terms in 1982 than it had been in 1974.[48] The Lebanese pound maintained its relative strength until 1984.[49] Gulf money still found its way to Lebanon. The economic activity supported by the Palestine Liberation Organization (PLO) alone contributed a significant proportion of the Lebanese GDP.[50] Remittances continued to flow back to Lebanon. Indeed, remittances accounted for over 50 percent of the GDP in 1981 and 1982. Remittances in 1971 had been worth $273 million; in 1975 they had increased to $515 million. But by 1981, these figures had ballooned to $1,920 million. Such remittances compensated for a fall in economic activity and the growing trade deficit.[51] There was also a lucrative war economy based on guns, drugs, and racketeering of various kinds. In this context, although data are strictly limited, there is no evidence that earning differentials between Syria and Lebanon were significantly reduced. Adib Mahrus earned LL3 a day in heavy lifting and carrying in construction when he first arrived in 1974. After one or two years, he began earning LL3–7/ $1.31–3.06 a day. By the late 1970s, "Once I got more skilled in the work and worked with the *ustadh* [a civil engineer and building entrepreneur] I could get LL10/ $4.37 or LL11/ $4.80 or LL15/ $6.55 per day."[52] In short, at least until 1983, the Lebanese economy continued to operate as a significant force of attraction. Moreover, wartime physical destruction effectively paved the way in calm periods for much labor-intensive work in clearing and reconstruction.

The second attraction for going to war-torn Lebanon was that wartime conditions withdrew Lebanese labor in large numbers from sectors, which consequently demanded Syrians and others. First, and least important, some were fired. The political economy inducing the hiring of non-Lebanese was actually intensified during the war. As was occasionally remarked, the absence and incapacity of the state in enforcing hiring and firing laws enabled many employers to fire their Lebanese workers and replace them with foreigners who would work in harsh conditions and for low wages.[53] Second, other young male Lebanese left the workforce because they enrolled in significant numbers in the militias. This created demand for foreign labor, especially in crafts and craft-like occupations.[54]

Finally, and most important, many Lebanese left the country. Before 1975, there were perhaps 50,000 to 80,000 Lebanese in Gulf countries. By 1982, there were estimated to be 250,000.[55] A village such as Bishmizzine sent migrants to as many as 40 different countries worldwide. As one inhabitant put it, "We have been afflicted with too many advantages, but the worst of them is migration."[56] The exodus included degree holders as well as skilled, semi-skilled, and unskilled workers.[57] One example of a migrant from a family of poor peasants in the South (outside Sidon) was the future billionaire and several times Prime Minister Rafiq al-Hariri.[58] These outmigrations created gaps and demands for labor in many sectors, particularly, according to Isma'il, regarding crafts and manual labor in agriculture, industry, and services.[59] In a continuation of pre-war patterns, outmigration from the countryside was particularly significant. The agricultural population fell from 487,000 in 1970 to 297,000 in 1987. Meanwhile, in spite of the war, the Lebanese population reportedly increased. Likewise, the agricultural labor force fell from 127,000 persons in 1970 to 88,000 in 1987 due to migration to cities and overseas.[60] Such movements, especially combined with remittances, created demand for Syrian migrant workers.

After 1983, the economy began a steep decline: The currency began a long and precipitous descent,[61] and budget and trade deficits, debt, unemployment, and inflation intensified.[62] In 1985, real income was said to be at 60 percent of the 1974 level.[63] The economic downturn in the Gulf reduced employment and remittances drastically and diminished the flow of political money from the Gulf.[64] The Palestinian economy was lost with the exodus of the PLO in

1982. Israeli occupation crippled the economy of the South, sending Lebanese migrants to northern Israel.[65] From 1984 to 1987, it was said that middle-class society in Lebanon was "shattered."[66] Reportedly, 330,000 Lebanese left during 1983–84 alone.[67] By 1987, economists wrote that Lebanon had entered the "nightmare land and vicious circle of widespread poverty and deprivation, social unrest . . . , [and] hyperinflation."[68]

YOUR ENEMY IS THE SYRIAN

It was no economic crisis that caused Syrians to flee Christian areas during 1975–76. This movement was an expulsion, based on coercion and various political, economic, and social measures, which both directly and indirectly forced Syrians to leave or flee for fear of life, liberty, and security areas dominated by the Christian militias—Mt. Lebanon, the northern coastal plain, and the eastern districts of Beirut.[69] The Syrians were not simply fleeing the destruction and killing found in any war zone. Rather, they were targeted by the Christian militias, and conceived of as a party to the conflict, as the pattern of escape to non-Christian–dominated areas shows. In a stunning reversal of the laissez-faire attitude to Syrian workers adopted by the Christian-dominated Lebanese elite in the 1950s and 1960s, Syrians were seized and executed on sight in numbers by Christian militias from 1975 onward. As Hanna Butros told me, with a chuckle, "They [the Kataeb] would capture one [of us Christian Syrians] and say, 'Even if Jesus was Syrian we will slaughter him.' That was the war."[70] The Syrians—whether Christian or Muslim—had lost their status as those who "melted away like sugar in tea," and become "the enemy." They were drawn into a civil war not of their own making. Syrian workers were identified with, and to some extent identified themselves with, an oppositional bloc of forces, the leftist, Ba'thist, pan-Arabist, Palestinian, and Muslim opposition to the Maronite-dominated, conservative, Lebanese elites.

This was no bourgeois attempt to remove surplus labor in the context of an economic crisis, for there was no such crisis. In fact, since 1973, Lebanese financial and mercantile elites were well placed to reap the benefits of the oil boom. And it was by no means clear in 1975 that Asian labor would provide a cheap and convenient alternative and that employers were not actively seeking them out. Nor was anti-Syrian militancy a response to the emergence of an assertive, visible, and politicized second generation making new claims and seeking to move into sectors coveted by native labor.[71] No such generation had come into existence, and labor activism postdated the outbreak of the civil war. Nor were Syrians being attacked in revenge for the alleged and real atrocities committed by the Syrian army in Lebanon, for the simple reason that the Syrian army did not intervene until June 1976, by which time most Syrian workers had been forced out of Christian areas. As Abed put it, "They [the Christians] say the Syrian army mistreated them, but they [the Kataeb] did that [identity card killings] first."[72] Even when the Syrians did intervene, they did so in order to prevent the total defeat of the Maronite militias, not to slaughter them.[73] Nor, finally, was this simple sectarianism, inasmuch as both Christian (even Maronite) and Muslim Syrians were targeted.

The hegemony of Lebanese Christian and conservative Sunni financial and mercantile elites, and the "clientelist structures of the prewar Lebanese state,"[74] were starting seriously to break up by the early 1970s. The radical blasts of pan-Arabism, Ba'thism, and Nasserism sweeping the region since at least 1956 eroded the symbolic legitimacy of the U.S.-supported, isolationist, conservative, and sectarian power elite, especially among the majority non-Maronite population. In addition, for all the achievements of Chehabist reform from 1958 to 1964, Lebanon arguably failed to build a state for all its citizens when this was at least a distant possibility in the 1960s.[75] The sharp social and economic inequalities exposed by the Mission-IRFED report of 1961 were only partially tackled under Chehab, and then left to fester after 1964. Rural-urban migration increasingly made thousands of laborers, especially poor Shi'a from the South, available for new forms of political mobilization, which were not slow to emerge. Imam Musa Sadr's Movement of the Deprived, for example, rallied the Shi'a of the south and the Biqa' in the name of the grievances of the poor and oppressed against Israeli military strikes in the South and the "corrupt, monopolistic and socially insensitive establishment that ran the country." The Palestinians were happy to see Musa Sadr blame the plight of the South on the authorities and the Israelis rather than the commandos. And the conservative Sunni establishment were by no means unhappy at his "demanding full Muslim participation in the Lebanese State in equality with the Christians."[76] The other radical parties saw their best chances for mobilization among the Shi'a, and thus an increasingly broad opposition was formed.[77]

The Arab/Israeli conflict, fought on Lebanese soil, polarized the situation as much as any other single issue. On the one side, sectors of Christian Lebanese nationalist opinion feared the destruction of their country at the hands of Israeli reprisals if Palestinians continued to launch raids on Israel from Lebanon—a fear the Israelis did everything they could to confirm.[78] On the other side, pan-Arabists, leftists, the communists, pro-Palestinians, the Druze under Kamal Jumblatt, many Muslims, and the Palestinians themselves considered support for Palestinian nationalism in its attempt to regain a lost homeland a non-negotiable issue. Major armed clashes between Palestinian commandos and the Lebanese Army began in 1969, ending in the Cairo Agreement that autumn. The Lebanese Army itself was hobbled by political divisions, and by its relative weakness, stemming from Lebanon's role as a "nonconfrontation state" regarding Israel. In May 1973, when the second major armed clash with the Palestinians ended inconclusively, the Christians were now more than ever convinced that the Lebanon they knew could not be preserved without completely eliminating the commandos from Lebanon. With the arming by 1975 of tens of thousands of militiamen on all sides, and no political solution in sight, "Lebanon was . . . turned into a powder keg with a fuse attached, and there was no telling when it would be made to explode."[79] Once blood started to be shed afresh in April 1975, the slide toward civil war was relentless. In Jordan, the Palestinians were numerous but politically isolated, and they were successfully broken in Black September 1970 by the Jordanian army. In Lebanon, by contrast, the Palestinians had allies in a broad coalition of domestic opposition, and the attempt to break them split the country instead.

From the late 1960s, as the situation deteriorated, there was a political recasting of the meaning and role of Syrian workers, transforming them through the rearticulation of latent and newly forged symbols and meanings (in the eyes of Christian leaders, militias, and their propagandist allies) from "useful muscles" into "the enemy." In the 1960s, Maronite MPs and religious figures had occasionally articulated bourgeois, ethno-nationalist, and anticommunist fears about the poverty, unhealthiness, "noisiness," moral fiber, and foreignness of Syrians and others living in Beirut's slums, linking them to fears about outmigration and to foreign and predatory schemes as diverse as communism (coordinated through Syria), property acquisition (by Gulfis), and Palestinian "subversion."[80] Almost invariably, however, it was the Palestinians, not the Syrians, who were the chief target of these and related controversies.

With the changing political situation in the 1970s, Syrian workers started to be more clearly and prominently positioned within this pantheon of Maronite fears. Syria itself was not only firmly positioned in the pan-Arabist and "progressive" camp but, under President Hafez al-Asad, it was also becoming a regional power to be reckoned with for the first time. What implications did this have for Lebanon's regional position, particularly given the presence of so many Syrian workers in the country? Moreover, with dispossessed Shi'a and other groups starting to "raise their heads," domestic concerns over the sectarian balance were intensified and started to apply to Syrians for the first time. What if such groups—predominantly Muslims and Arabs—settled more permanently in Lebanon? Where would this leave the political representation of the Christians, where parliamentary seats were allocated according to the outdated census of 1932? What if such groups were politically mobilized and linked to the Shi'a, the Palestinians, the Druze, and the leftists? As Joseph reported of the early 1970s, "There was some tension building up about the presence of Syrian workers."[81] As a leading Maronite stated in 1971. "The demographic development of the alien population in the country is ominous. At least 300,000 Palestinians and 400,000 Syrians now live here" [in addition to Kurds, refugees, and other migrant workers]. All in all, there must be about one million aliens in the country. How shall we ever get these people out of the country?"[82] But these were still less polarized days, and the speaker did not have in view an all-Christian Lebanon, or armed confrontation, but pinned his hopes on "a just solution" to the Palestine question.

These fears were peculiarly associated with leading Maronites and their allies. When the French drew the borders of Grand Liban in 1920, adding to the Maronite *mutasarrifiyya* of Mt. Lebanon, the Sunni-dominated coastal cities, including Beirut, along with the predominantly Shi'a agricultural hinterland of the South and the Biqa', the Sunni notables were included against their will. At that time they preferred inclusion within a decentralized Syria.[83] While the National Pact of 1943 had put an end to Sunni recidivism in exchange for a measure of political power, pan-Arabism still found considerable support among Sunnis. As Muslims, Islam in general could hardly be seen as a threat to them, at least not in any straightforward and monolithic way. The Palestinian cause also had more appeal among Sunnis. Moreover, the issue of improving their political representation as against the Christians was increasingly on the table. For these reasons, they were more open to the "Arab-Islamic ocean" that surrounded them, and less likely to see Syrian workers as a threat. Speaking in the early 1970s, Rashid Karami, a veteran Sunni politician from a powerful Tripoli family and eight-times Prime Minister between 1955 and 1987, captured some of these sentiments well. He claimed that foreigners were no threat to the country. "Lebanon has always practiced an open-door policy. Arabs are part of the family here. Lebanon benefits from their presence: they provide labor we need but do not have. I do not believe that aliens in Lebanon present a danger. We are a sovereign state and in a position to do what is necessary."[84] These remarks—even with their potentially sinister *coda*—offer a glimpse of how the battle lines were being drawn, and how they owed as much to politics and various kinds of nationalism as they did to sect and economic interests. These lines were marked ever more heavily, with the Syrians in the opposition camp, as the situation deteriorated. The PLO was increasingly associated with Muslim parties and militias in opposition to predominantly Christian sectarian elites.[85]

Common Interests Frayed

Changing bilateral relations with Syria and political economy also played a role in undermining the dominant attitude in which Syrian workers were seen as trouble-free and useful muscles. In the early 1970s, the menial status of Syrian workers in Lebanon played an important role in a serious dispute between the two countries for the first time, and a blow was struck against the old deal in which Syrian workers were quietly conceived by Damascus and Beirut as an interest to be exploited.

Hafez al-Asad's Corrective Movement was a serious hegemonic project in that coercion was armored by the ways in which the corporate interests of the regime made concessions to wider constituencies, including peasants and workers, in order to win their consent.[86] Such policies combined ideology, strategy, and coercion. In 1971, for example, al-Asad told Hamud al-Shufi, one time Secretary General of the Ba'th Party and Syrian ambassador to the United Nations, that the people have "primarily economic demands"—a plot of land, a house, a car, and so on—and that he could satisfy these demands "in one way or another." Only "one or two hundred individuals at most," he added, seriously engage in or make politics their profession and will oppose him no matter what he does. "It is for them that the Mezzeh prison was originally intended."[87] In the context of this hegemonic project, the al-Asad government announced on March 9, 1971, that Lebanese working in Syria would benefit from social and health contributions. The corollary of this demand, more significantly, on the basis of the longstanding principle that workers in one country were to be treated in the same manner as workers in the other, was that Lebanon include Syrians in their own social security system.[88] The initiative was not welcomed by Lebanese elites, taxpayers, or employers who would have to bear its cost. The Lebanese Ministry of Work and Social Affairs responded that the measure would mean unfair competition with Lebanese workers for the Social Security Fund, and did not correspond to the principle of equal treatment, because there was no balance in the number of workers in the two countries. Indeed, the Ministry claimed that there were only 600 or so Lebanese working in waged labor in Syria.[89] On this basis, in spite of the repetition of the call in August,[90] the Syrian demand was rejected.

The demand reappeared in the summer of 1973, when Syria shut the borders for three months, protesting Lebanese suppression of the Palestinians, which was seen as a dereliction of pan-Arab responsibility.[91] By July, the Syrians were complaining about the "populist" route taken by the Lebanese, and at least one senior Syrian official maintained that Syria was still waiting for Lebanon's answers over its basic demands, "the first of these" being that the Lebanese treat Syrian workers in a suitable way and on the basis of Lebanese labor law.[92] "Informed" Lebanese sources saw the closure as being about the activities of Syrian political refugees in Lebanon, and the presence of Lebanese press criticism of Syria. At the same time, these sources maintained that the closure was also because Syrians were ignorant of Lebanese politics, were concerned about the Palestinians, and believed that Lebanese treatment of Syrian workers was unsuitable.[93] Maronite leaderships, reflecting the growing divisions within Lebanon itself, were most prominent in their protests. Pierre Gemayel (1905–1984), Christian powerbroker and founder of the Kataeb, expressed the hope in August 1973 that Damascus would shortly be opening the border, as the closure damaged the two economies. He made clear that no country treated the Syrian workers as well as Lebanon, and suggested that it was impossible to grant Syrian workers social security and health coverage in Lebanon while the system did not even cover all Lebanese.[94]

Nonetheless, the Syrian position held firm, bolstered by the fact that the Syrian government no longer viewed with equanimity what it was beginning to see as the loss of important manpower resources—particularly skilled manual labor—abroad.[95] As a result, as part of the bilateral negotiations regarding opening the border, it was agreed at Shtura on August 17, 1973, that "the Lebanese government will set in motion an urgent legal project to organize . . . Syrian workers in Lebanon," including work permits, minimum wages, weekly hours of work, weekly and sick holidays, and compensation for work accidents and for termination. The Lebanese government also agreed to explore the "possibility" of securing health coverage for Syrian workers.[96] The Asad government, both to maintain the pressure on those drafting and moving the legislation, as well as to organize, channel, and incorporate the activities, interests, and ideas of the great numbers of Syrians now working in Lebanon, moved in 1973–74 to sponsor the establishment of a League of Syrian Workers in Lebanon. The declared goal was to "remove injustice from the Syrian Arab workers in Lebanon and [achieve] their equality with the Lebanese in rights and duties in the field of work," as well as to "build the solidarity (*li-tawhid kalima*) of the Syrian Arab workers in Lebanon and tie them to the struggles of our Syrian Arab country . . . and its destiny."[97] An administrative body with a number of members was created in 1974, and some lawyers were appointed to move for the establishment of the League in Lebanon. The first meeting of this body came up with the future League's slogan: "Rights—education—health." As Jamil Muhanna recalled, "We chose these words from the dictionary of reality dominating the masses of workers, a reality of theft of rights and a reality of galloping illiteracy, and a reality of social misery causing disease to be rife [among workers]."[98] But before the League could be officially established, the civil war put a stop to all organization until 1977.

For the first time, the Syrian government had gone to bat for its workers in Lebanon. This dispute turned Syrian workers into a serious bone of contention for the first time, and undermined the older political economy in which Syrian cheap and disposable labor was a quietly held and achieved interest in common. The "problem of Syrian workers in Lebanon" was now on the diplomatic agenda as never before.[99] The dispute also further welded Syrian workers both practically and symbolically to leftism, pan-Arabism, the Palestinians, and Syrian policy, and opposed them more sharply to Maronite leaderships in Lebanon.

VIOLENCE AND KILLINGS

In the years and months before 1975, in terms of death tolls reported in the Lebanese press, Syrian workers had more to fear from accidents, negligent employers, criminals, and, to a lesser extent, Palestinian commandos than they did from Christian militias. In March 1973, for example, a building collapse because of the use of cheap and substandard metaling in Tripoli killed five Syrian tile workers. According to the police, the building owner fled and was nowhere to be found.[100] Lebanese construction sites where labor protection was minimal were clearly dangerous places to work. There were a number of other accidents, murders, and assaults in the early 1970s.[101]

Nonetheless, with the descent into the civil war, in 1975 and, above all, during the first six months of 1976 (especially January), massacres and identity card killings began. The Lebanese Forces, informally organized in 1976 as the military wing of the Kataeb under Bashir Gemayel, but becoming a coalition of Christian militias, killed and executed Syrian workers, among others, in numbers. Prior to April 1975, some Syrian interests had been attacked in Christian areas, an indicator of rising tension.[102] Armed clashes in April and May 1975 along the northern outskirts of Beirut pitted the Kataeb against Palestinian commandos, but also against the "slum dwellers (Sunnite or Shi'ite Lebanese, Syrian labourers, or Kurds) in the suburbs of al-Karantina and al-Maslakh, who enjoyed commando support, mainly from the Rejection Front."[103] It would seem, therefore, that certain links existed between Palestinian militias and Syrian workers in the slums. Armed incidents were accompanied with the expulsion of Syrian laborers among others.[104] Further, in May 1975, a wave of sectarian abductions and murders were carried out by militias.[105] In a new escalation, violence flared in late August 1975 in Zahleh between Shi'a and Christian groups and in Tripoli between Maronite and Muslim. Outside Tripoli, a busload of "Muslims" were executed in cold blood.[106] In October, the embryonic League of Syrian Workers in Lebanon protested the "silence of the Lebanese state regarding the oppression of isolationist elements against the Syrian workers," who, al-Buwari notes, were being physically attacked by the Kataeb and their supporters from the beginning of 1975.[107] When four members of the Kataeb were found murdered on the morning of Saturday, December 6, 1975, the Kataeb took the violence to a new level. As Robert Fisk reports, "Phalangist officers of the time insist that he [Bashir Gemayel, strongman, son of Pierre, and soon-to-be commander of the Lebanese Forces] told them to kill 40 Muslims in reprisal."[108] As a result, bands of Kataeb, members of the national Liberal Party (NLP), and other Maronite militiamen abducted hundreds of unarmed Muslims wherever they could be found "massacring over one hundred of them with the utmost brutality." Among the dead were workers in the Port area, presumably some Syrians among them. Muslim militias then "followed the Christian example."[109] "Black Saturday" led to a new eruption of fighting.[110]

Maronite leaderships had been hinting at a Christian Republic of Lebanon, including Mt. Lebanon and the eastern areas of Beirut, since at least 1975.[111] The slum area of Maslakh-Karantina, which until now had served as cheap accommodation for thousands of Syrian workers among others, including Palestinians, was now full square within the imaginative geography of the Maronite homeland. It was also in a strategic location on the main road-bridge between

Christian East Beirut and the Mountain, and close to both the Port of Beirut and the Kataeb headquarters. Just to make matters worse, parts of Karantina and Maslakh were on Maronite church land.[112] An attack on Karantina was only a matter of time, and the fact that it came just as the Maronite villages of Al-Damur and al-Saʿdiyyat south of Beirut were both under bloody siege by Palestinian commandos and their allies only intensified the violence. The Kataeb and NLP forces attacked on January 15, 1976. With the help of the Palestinian commandos, the slum held out, but only until January 18, when it was overrun and "razed from the map."[113] It is not clear how many were killed. Most historians speak of a massacre.[114] The League of Syrian Workers estimated in 1979 that more than 100 of its workers had been killed overall in Lebanon, and hundreds injured, between 1975 and 1979.[115] Thousands of survivors eventually made their way to the southern exit of Beirut, and took over the bourgeois beach cabins on the beaches of Saint-Simon and Saint-Michel.[116]

Over the next eight months, even after the Syrian intervention of June 1976, the Christian militias fought their way through the rest of East Beirut, killing, evicting, and destroying the homes and dwellings of Syrians, Kurds, and Palestinians. The Palestinian camp of Jisr al-Basha was destroyed in June 1976. Tal al-Zaʿatar finally fell after a long and bitter siege in August 1976. Other camps and slum districts such as Dubayya were attacked and destroyed.[117] Many Syrians fled or were expelled from these areas—according to one estimate 100,000 Syrians, their families, and Kurds were forced to flee. The less fortunate were tortured, killed, or dumped under bridges, in markets, and in Martyrs' Square.[118]

Hanna Awwad (1933–) from *wadi al-nasara*, who we encountered in the last chapter, was working as a master tiler in Lebanon by the time the war broke out. He was living, along with his wife and seven children, in Karm al-Zaytoun in Ashrafiyya (East Beirut), and was thus situated, as Hanna put it, "in the middle of the battlefield," primarily between the Kataeb and the Palestinians. The family endured heavy fighting from the start: "Missiles, artillery, people slaughtering each other. . . . My children used to go under the sofas to hide from the missiles. Apart from the snipers, all you saw were corpses! I picked out two bullets from my door." Christian brotherhood meant nothing: "The Kataeb and the [Lebanese] Forces were killing Syrians regardless of their religion." The paternal order was upturned: "You would see a little boy with a gun who would ask you to stop." The entire family, who aimed to settle in Lebanon, were reluctant to leave straightaway. They endured for a whole year, until late Spring 1976. Nonetheless, the intensity of the fighting, the notion that it was set to continue for a long time, and the fears for the fate of the children eventually made the situation intolerable. Hanna took some advice from a trusted acquaintance—a General in the Lebanese Air Force who was of Syrian origin and had been trained along with the generation of Hafez al-Asad. The General told him he should "seize the first opportunity and flee with my children whenever I hear that the road through Tripoli is open and safe. He told me that if I do not take my children away they will join their friends in street battles as soon as they are 13 years old. . . . The minute they join the militias and carry weapons they will start taking drugs and will forget about their families. They will believe that this gun is their father and mother. He advised me to flee away with my family."[119] Family values, in the end, provided the cultural code within which flight was conceived and made sense of, and the family managed to escape during the next lull in the fighting. Hanna Awwad started to take work in the Gulf on and off during the late 1970s. Ironically, just as "Syrian decision-makers . . . [were] institutionalized as the final arbiters of power"[120] in Lebanon, with the defeat of the leftist forces by September 1976, the overwhelming majority of Syrian workers, were forced out of increasingly homogeneous Lebanese Christian areas for the first time.

SYRIAN MILITARY INTERVENTION

The Syrian military intervention of June 1976 was by no means an attempt to save its workers, and no one has ever seriously suggested such, in spite of the ease with which many Lebanese (and others) have subsequently linked Syrian workers to the strategic objectives of Damascus. Above all, Syria was concerned with preventing either the division of Lebanon into separate states, or the total defeat of the Christians.[121] Syria did not want to see a raging conflict that could destabilize its own partly sectarian order.[122] More important was that Syria neither wanted a radical and uncontrollable Palestinian state fighting with Israel, nor a Maronite state possibly allied to Israel to come into being on the strategically, politically, and economically important adjacent territory of Lebanon.[123] On the basis of such a narrowly Syrian nationalist *raison d'etat*, Syria was ready to risk its pan-Arab and pro-Palestinian reputation.

Although the leftist and Palestinian forces were defeated by September, further Syrian "success" was elusive, and it was certainly beyond Syria's capacity to control Palestinian nationalism and unify Lebanon under Syrian hegemony in the 1970s and 1980s. A sea of blood came to separate the

Syrian army from various protagonists on the Lebanese stage. On the one side, the leftist and pan-Arab coalition was defeated by their erstwhile ally, and the Palestinians, their starving men, women and children, were slaughtered in Tal al-Za'atar in August 1976 after a grim siege. The Syrians, in what seemed a stupefying betrayal of the Arab cause, sat on their hands over long weeks, or were even said to have assisted. On the other side, Eastern Christian regions were quick to display open hostility to the Syrian armed presence, boycotts were organized, and the Kataeb and Chamoun's NLP, encouraged by Israel, which was backing Christian militias in the South, demanded by 1977 the "immediate withdrawal of the alien forces from the homeland."[124] In a reprisal for the assassination of the more pro-Syrian Christian, Tony Franjieh, the Syrians bombarded East Beirut from July 1978 until October. Amid the indiscriminate killing, and the flight of 250,000 Christians,[125] anti-Syrian sentiment greatly increased. The relatively conciliatory stance of the Christian clergy was finished.[126] During another round of clashes and Syrian shelling of the Christian sectors in East Beirut from January to April 1979, Chamoun declared, "For God's sake, let them leave the country, for this will be the only means of keeping some feeling of friendship between the Lebanese and Syrian peoples."[127]

Lebanese Forces propaganda posters from the late 1970s and early 1980s afford a glimpse of the attitudes of certain Christian militias toward the Syrian army. One such poster shows a map of Lebanon with a clearly Syrian Trojan horse entering the country. The caption reads, "Discover the traitor and right will be victorious." Another depicts a military boot topped with the emblem of the cedars kicking a Syrian tank out of Lebanon. In another, a scruffy Syrian soldier is being seen off to Damascus from a Lebanon colored as the national flag. The caption reads: "500 years of Ottoman rule could not dominate over the Lebanese." Another shows a stylized map of Lebanon. All over the map, in fine print, is the repeated injunction, "Know your enemy, your enemy is the Syrian." The same slogan is also the main caption for the print. The same print is reproduced in another form, this time emblazoned with the notorious comments of the Syrian Foreign Minister, Abd al-Halim Khaddam, on January 7, 1976: "Lebanon was part of Syria and we will return it to her if there is any serious attempt at division [of the country]. Best that I be clear: this does not refer to the four provinces or the coast alone, rather it also means Mt. Lebanon."[128] For many Christian Lebanese, and others besides, this statement crystallized the true, predatory, and annexationist intentions of the Syrians—what Amin

Gemayel (president from 1982 to 1988) called on French television in 1983 "the legendary scope of Syrian ambitions to put her hand in Lebanon."[129]

These images, understandings, judgments, and realities informed the attitudes of the Christian militias who barred, threatened, injured, or killed Syrian workers—regardless of their confession. Views of the army became views of Syria, and then of Syrian workers. There was no clear separation of the economic and the political, or the "base" and the "superstructure." Hanna Butros related, for example, that in 1982, the "[Lebanese] Forces and the Kataeb had forbidden Syrians from passing through. . . . Even though I was a Christian [the militias on the Tripoli road] "sent me back. They would not allow me to pass. They said go back to Hamra and die in Hamra, do not come here."[130] Just as before the war a bundle of interests, visions, and politics had ensured that Syrians were seen in a more expansive light, while exploited as "useful muscles," from 1975 onward, in the Christian areas, they were assaulted, excluded, and sometimes killed.

LABOR WITH THE ENEMY

At least until 1982, however, a limited number of Syrian workers still worked in the Christian areas. Among the Christian militias, the notion of Syrian workers representing "useful muscles" died hard. In one incident, elements from the Kataeb militia based in the Hilton Hotel captured a group of 15 Syrian workers for about six weeks during February–March 1977. The workers reported that they had been "maltreated and insulted" and forced to work in transporting the dead and carrying sandbags to all 20 floors of the hotel to build barricades. Syrians were still sought out as cheap and manipulatable labor power, but in the context of civil war and virulent ethno-nationalism, this implied a fleeting version of modern slavery. The workers were set free in an operation by the independent Nasserists (*al-Murabitun*) working with the Popular Front for the Liberation of Palestine-General Command. In the aftermath, the Nasserists held a press conference with all the liberated workers to publicize their feat.[131] Incidents such as these were not particularly widespread according to the evidence I have seen, but symbolized and confirmed the battle lines so recently drawn.[132]

In other cases, employers' economic interests in retaining their cheap and hard-working Syrian workers outweighed the threats, expectations, and sentiments generated by the division of the country and the descent into civil war. Hanna Butros and his wife told me a story about a Syrian Muslim worker who continued to work in East Beirut with a Lebanese Christian master plasterer from Ashrafiyya who was "with the Kataeb," no less, during the early years of the war. The Lebanese would take him in his car every day across the Green Line from West to East Beirut. Hanna Butros was clear that this employer was acting out of economic interest rather than any sense of tolerance. Butros reckoned that although this employer liked this particular worker, and paid him well because he was a good worker, he "did not like Syrians." Employing the Syrian was "about his business." Indeed, the Syrian was said to be a prodigiously hard worker: "He was mixing the cement for [as much as] three master plasterers!" Moreover, once the Syrian finally did leave (after 1982), because he wanted to go back to his family and "was getting stressed out because of the war," the employer was forced to employ Lebanese:

> He got three Lebanese instead of the one Syrian he lost. . . . At one o'clock his new workers put everything down. . . . They said work was over for the day. He then grabbed the shovel and hit it on the ground. He said, 'Curse on every Lebanese who wants to kick the Syrians out. The shoe of a Syrian works as much as all the Lebanese!'

This was understood by Aziz and Butros's wife, both present, as a story about how hard working the Syrians were and are, how this was the meaning of their migration (as opposed to their having a political agenda), and how the Lebanese were only cutting off their nose to spite their face when they clamored for Syria to leave Lebanon. However, the story also sheds some light on how certain workers continued to work behind enemy lines, at least before 1982, on the basis of the economic interests of employers, which could crosscut, rather than combine with, forms of communalism and ethno-nationalism. Even this unstable fix was broken up by the Israeli invasion of 1982.

FIGHTING, TENSION, AND CO-EXISTENCE

Outside the sectors controlled by Christian militias, Syrian workers were not targeted in the same way. They encountered the violence of a war zone, which became particularly dangerous at points, but not targeted for killing. During these periods, as Hanna Butros recalled, "you could not walk in the streets, everyone was armed and you could not tell who was what. I used to put on my working clothes before I left the house. When they saw that I was a worker, nobody bothered me." When things got really serious, Butros would escape back to Syria: "I would stay until it calmed down, then I would go back." Adib

Mahrus worked in the southern suburbs, which were particularly violent during the bitter struggles of the 1980s:

> There was fighting in the country. One couldn't live. You didn't know how to get through even the next day. There was fighting in the streets and mortar fire [during the] war. . . . At that time one couldn't stay in a secure place. It was a time of burning. . . . I worked in [construction] in Burj al-Barajneh and Haret Hreik.[133]

Abed, who survived periods of unemployment on money carefully saved during periods of work, was cool-headed about the conditions in al-Zarif:

> It was more or less a normal life. We used to work until there was fighting and shelling [at which] we stayed home. . . . In '77 and '78 work was not reliable, sometimes we used to work for a week and then stop for 10 or 15 days. Like we say in Arabic, "We barely made our living." After '78, things got better because the situation was a bit calmer. . . . During the Israeli invasion all work stopped completely for three months [June to September]. . . . After the Palestinians left Beirut there was a bit of stability and we were able to go out.

Relations with different communities and groups were highly uneven, but never descended, as far as my research has discovered, into political killing. Joseph—a Christian Syrian—recalled benign national and confessional relations in Caracas, West Beirut, during the war:

> The landlord was named Muhammad Shehab, a Muslim. I was living on the first floor, he was on the second, and above him was [another] Joseph, a Lebanese Christian. During the war when everybody was raging against Muslims or Christians, nobody bothered me. Nobody told me, your name is Joseph I want to kill you or shoot you. They were all Muslims over there and we were friends. They would say, "Good morning, Joseph, do you want gas, or do you want petrol for your car, we can bring you home some." And they were Muslims. . . . There was a lot of cooperation. They never harmed any [Syrian] Christians in [West] Beirut. They did not hurt Christians, unless they knew he belonged to the Lebanese Kataeb or something. I lived with them during the war.

With the war, however, sectarian thinking stole into the minds of even those who refused its values. Tony implicates himself rather than a demonized "other" to describe the new form of sectarian thinking:

If I went to … work in painting, if I found ten workers and we sat together to eat, I am an [orthodox] Christian and I myself would start thinking. … I would wonder whether the other worker was Muslim or Alawi and so on. We would watch what we say, not that we say anything bad.[134]

Nor was Joseph's account entirely rosy. He maintained that the atmosphere was poisoned, as discrimination increasingly appeared between Muslims and Christians. He said:

It is not that I lost them [Muslim friends], but their feelings towards us changed during the war. At one point, my neighbour, who had a cassette shop opposite American Dream—he used to love my company and ask for me constantly … however, after the division when the Christians left [West] Beirut and went to Ashrafiyya and Jounieh, he changed. … [In] his shop I would feel like an unwanted guest. Or if I wanted to borrow money from him or ask for a receipt, I could sense that he had changed his attitude to us.

These were stories not of systematic discrimination and assault, but of tension and co-existence.

A similar uneven picture of antagonism and broad co-existence was found in the political and communal landscape of the "Muslim" sectors. Vanishingly few held up Syria as an ideal model of national existence. In 1987, for example, a representative sample of Lebanese was asked to name their ideal country. Between one-third and one-half mentioned the peaceful countries of Switzerland, Austria, or Scandinavia. Arab countries were hardly mentioned and "Syria, the Arab brother country with the greatest influence on Lebanon's fate, was named by only 0.2 percent of the respondents."[135] The Amal movement and many Shi'a, however, remained tolerant or even friendly toward Syrians and Syrian workers,[136] particularly due to Syria-Amal alliances during the 1980s. The Sunni establishment evinced a mixed picture. Early in the war, for example, the Sunni politician Takieddine Solh included Syrian workers among the prewar foreign and impoverished elements taking advantage of Lebanon and undermining its unity: "Our qualities were exploited … our freedom, our prosperity and our progress. Anyone could enter Lebanon. Our economy attracted a lot of labour from neighboring countries."[137] Relations with Palestinians were not fatal, but they were tense, after both the Syrian betrayal of 1976 and the bloody, Syria-backed Amal sieges of Palestinian refugees in the "war of the camps" in the 1980s.

In this uneasy but liveable context, it was possible for Syrian workers to acquire some protection by asserting their identities as workers, or by ensuring that they did not publicly identify with the Syrian army. Hanna Butros described the latter tactic:

> Some friends of mine who were officers in the Syrian army had entered Lebanon, but I did not go to greet them. I did not go because I thought of the possibilities. I still wanted to work in Lebanon, and there were so many people against the Syrian army. I thought when the army leaves, I want to go to my work, I do not want anyone to have a grudge against me and kill me because of this. I would rather have peace of mind. And thank God, I spent three quarters of the war . . . without anybody ever asking me where I was going. Everyone I worked for were friends of mine and we maintained good relations throughout, whether he was a Christian or a Muslim. . . . The ones who created trouble got black points for themselves for being connected with the army.

In short, although Syrians working outside the Christian areas suffered from the violence of war, and assorted forms of tension and antagonism, they were not targeted. This was the decisive difference between the "Christian" and "Muslim" areas during the civil war and had a key impact on migrant trajectories and experiences.

SOCIAL PROTECTION SIDESTEPPED

Following the bilateral commitments made at Shtura, a law allowing foreigners to benefit from social security was passed in 1975.[138] All foreigners had to obtain from the Ministry of Labor and Social Affairs a work permit that gave the right of residence and the "right to bring family members under conditions to be later determined by decree." Permit holders would be covered by the Labor Code of May 1943, all laws and decrees relating to minimum wages, weekly holidays, sick leave, and the social security law of September 1963, along with related decrees on family allocations, indemnities for work accidents, and end-of-service compensation.

However, almost all Syrian workers were excluded from the social security law because they were defined as "seasonal or temporary" workers. This capacious category included all those engaged in "work not exceeding eight months, such as in summer tourism, winter tourism, skiing, gardening, and the fruit harvest . . . work which by its nature is temporary, such as on construction sites and public works." Moreover, "the seasonal or temporary worker will always be considered as such even in the case of re-employment." In this way, workers staying more or less permanently in Lebanon were defined as temporary and seasonal. Syrian seasonal workers in particular were not to receive work permits, but reduced-fee "work cards," which remained valid as long as workers returned to Lebanon within four months. Moreover, while seasonal Syrian workers were now to benefit from sick leave and accident indemnities, according to the 1943 Labor Code, as well as minimum wages and paid holidays, no fines or enforcement mechanisms are mentioned, making these provisions largely unenforceable.

Small wonder that neither social security nor the Labor Code and related legislation were a significant feature of workplace practice before or after 1975. Compensation was sometimes paid for death or injury, but usually through informal arrangements. Otherwise, social security was vanishingly rare, and paid holidays, legal minimum wages, maximum hours, and sick leave were unheard of. Joseph noted that after the law, "we started needing a residency and work permit. . . . I had to do it, it was the law, but nothing changed."[139] Even the new "work card" was not enforced in practice. Adib Mahrus, for example, reported that "in the 1970s and 1980s you came in without this [work] card. You just went in. Open borders. You didn't take a card or anything. . . . I didn't need anything. I came for 6 or 7 years and even the Syrian identity card wasn't necessary."[140]

In this way, Syrian demands regarding their workers' inclusion within Lebanese social security were thwarted, in line with the narrow interests of Lebanese elites, employers, and taxpayers. The *status quo ante* was largely preserved, while the open border without social protection was effectively regularized.

SYRIAN ORGANIZING

Civil war conditions, one might assume, would have induced Syrian workers to keep their heads down even more than before 1975. In fact, counterintuitively enough, the early years of the civil war were the setting for the only sustained period of labor organizing among Syrian workers in Lebanon. Few have touched on the topic, but it is insufficient to characterize this movement as simply the inevitable growth of discontent among an impoverished, noncitizen subproletariat.[141] Nor were these protests another inevitable manifestation of the predetermined and progressive struggle between capital and labor. Both views are too linear and mechanistic. The protests combined economic grievances with political and mobilizational opportunities and were informed by newly articulated languages of labor and social justice. And whereas the economic grievances were only ever partially addressed, the fact that the protests died away by the mid-1980s implies that they can be best explained by political and organizational conjuncture.

The organization established in 1974 to defend Syrian workers' rights was authorized to form a union during the first major ceasefire. The League of Syrian Workers in Lebanon (*Rabita al-'Ummal al-Suriyyin fi-l-Lubnan*), representing all Syrian workers in Lebanon, was established in October 1977 with the blessing of the "struggling comrade" (*al-rafiq al-munadil*) Hafez al-Asad and with Jamil Muhanna as president.[142] The League was linked to, and aimed to organize support for, the government whose troops were now in control of large sections of the country.[143] The League argued that Syrian workers complemented the labor-scarce Lebanese economy and made a significant contribution to the Lebanese economy and rebuilding. In this context, far from underestimating numbers, as the Syrians were later to do, the union was keen to point out that much of the Lebanese economy depended "completely or partly on Syrian labor."[144] An important early goal was to secure workers' social protection. This was a pan-Arabist and Ba'thist ideal because it enshrined the principle that Syrian Arab workers in Lebanon should be equal in rights and duties to their Lebanese Arab counterparts in Syria.[145] This thinking commemorated the 1930s and 1940s as a time when Arabs circulated without the discrimination that had arisen because of different national (*qutri*) legislation since the break-up of the customs union of 1950. The workers were said to feel unfairly treated and cheated (*ghabn*), oppressed by Lebanese workers and employers, unable to organize collectively, and lacking the most basic of their legitimate rights.[146]

The union's first major mobilization involved a protracted battle over end-of-service compensation for 3,000 workers who had been working as stevedores for the unloading companies in the Port of Beirut but were forced out by the security situation in 1975 and 1976. Negotiations with the firms of Makawi, Yafawi, al-Jamil, and Ghandour and Partners broke down by early 1979 and the League sent an open letter in March to the Lebanese government, the General Confederation of Labor in Lebanon, and the wider public, local and international. As an unusual glimpse of union, Syrian, and—to a degree—worker perspectives of the time, the rousing prose of this never-published letter is worth quoting in full:

In the name of three thousand workers, who expend in exemplary fashion their energies and lifeblood in the cause of selfless giving ('ata') and construction, [and who are] the axle driving the wheel of progress, the pillars of the system, and the bridge binding together two brotherly Arab peoples. In the name of blood and sweat, of tens of martyrs, and in the name of the orphans and the widows, in the name of human rights and international labour law, we call on your conscience to obtain justice and our rights from the bloodsuckers and abusers.

In the name of humanitarian values, [we declare that] those who rob our daily bread from the wide-open mouths of our children, those whose greedy ambition is carried on our shoulders, and [realized at the expense of] our hunger and our thirst, are the heads of the Lebanese unloading companies in the Port of Beirut.

[We declare] that the Syrian workers, who on their shoulders and in their hands have carried the burden of construction, and [suffered] from death . . . sorrow and misery . . . and [enjoyed] respect and honour among those who are hospitable, and preserved respect for the leadership in the days when transgressions were multiplied; who have kept [labour] competition to a minimum, preserved the solidarity of labour, and maintained a continuous flow [of manpower] in spite of the atrocities and destruction, [all] in order to keep the wheel of work turning.

They threw bombs at us and we replied with generosity and roses. . . . They discriminated but we did not discriminate, we all gave our own lifeblood and sweat. In the factories and in the streets they killed us, and in the open squares and for the sake of the peace of Lebanon we lost hundreds of our soldiers as brotherly martyrs doing their duty, and the blood of generosity was mixed with the blood of martyrdom.

They destroyed, but we built up. They called for help and we answered. They filled their stomachs and we went hungry. We said be just and they evicted us! . . .

The Syrian worker thus registered in the page of the Lebanese economy the most honourable and most sacred of sufferings in the feats of the labour movement. Hence it is his right, and legally necessary, that this generosity is properly recognized and this soldier is given a medal for work and honour. . . . [It is] as if the stories of the past and its pain for our workers has become the normal thing, regardless of workers' legislation for and [social security] payments to Lebanese workers, [and in spite of] legal codes . . . the social security

law, or the [1943] Labour Law, and in spite of Lebanese legal conditions granting such rights to the subjects of other states on the basis of reciprocity, [hence
we too should receive benefits] inasmuch as the law in our country, the Arab
Republic of Syria, does not distinguish between Lebanese and Syrian and all
Arab citizens in granting rights.

We have seen [little help] regarding this terrible situation, [even] after we
have lost everything, and [after] we have spent the flower of our youth [in Leb-
anon] and have worked in the fields and in sectors that no one but us will work
in, and we have put up with a great deal—a good deal of torture and hardship.
Many of us have been trampled underfoot, and even thrown into the sea. More
than a hundred martyrs have been killed from among us. Hundreds injured.
And amid this humanitarian crisis we are [still] waiting for assistance.

And when we came to demand our rights . . . we were refused by the owners in the unpacking companies . . . who continue to fail to learn from the
lessons of yesterday, afraid for their accumulated riches which they pile up at
the expense of our sweat and lifeblood, as if the images of widows and orphans
does not shame them and weigh on their consciences.

So we raise our voices to Lebanese, Arab and international public opinion
demanding justice . . . to pay [end-of-service] compensation and our [unpaid]
wages which exceed LL22 million, owed by [the unpacking companies of]
Makawi, Yafawi, Al-Jamil, and Ghandour in regard to a period exceeding 30
years, according to the spirit of the law and justice.

The letter aims to establish, with regard to end-of-service compensation, the
deserving, even heroic, status of workers who exert and sacrifice themselves in
the name of Arabism, the economy, labor solidarity, and manly honor in the
face of harsh conditions, legal discrimination, and the overweening ambition
and greed of the profiteering heads of the unloading companies. The letter opposed not the objective workings of capitalism, but war, discrimination, and
greed. Workers did not seek individuated material acquisition, but, as those
who gave selflessly in the cause of reconstruction, they laid claim to justice,
honor, and the wherewithal for proper familial provision. Workers were not
depicted as passive and fearful victims, marginals, an impersonal commodity, labor-power, or even rebels, but as heroic men, putting their very lives on
the line, loyal to properly constituted authority, heading families, showing no
weakness, and at the center of progress, wealth creation, and social order.[147]
In short, far from being an objective outgrowth of the means of production,

powerful themes in Ba'thism, pan-Arabism, and even anticolonial nationalism were present in defining the social subject the "Syrian Arab worker" and
his political and collective claims.

The letter was coolly received among employers and sectarian Christian
elites. *Al-Nahar* reported its existence in the tersest possible report.[148] Nonetheless, with the Syrian government backing the workers, and with the help of
various allies among Ba'thist politicians, leftist lawyers, and the Mufti of the
Republic, and with a relatively sympathetic Prime Minister, Salim al-Hoss, an
"amicable agreement" was secured in May 1979 with the firms agreeing to LL3
million/ $1 million in compensation.[149] By August, however, no compensation
had been paid. A sizeable group of workers, dissatisfied with the approach of
the League, and emboldened by links to Palestinian militias, decided to take
more direct action. One of the unloading companies was owned by a certain
al-Sayyid Abu Khalil al-Qayssi. On August 17, 1979, 400 workers, claiming to
represent all 3,200 workers, sat down on and around all 40 of al-Qayssi's grain
trucks in the latter's depot in Ra's al-Nab'a, West Beirut, effectively bringing
al-Qayssi's grain distribution business to a halt. The "amicable agreement"
of May had not been implemented, and the workers now lodged the original
compensation claim—LL20 million/ $6.67 million.

Al-Qayssi refused to concede, arguing that he dealt directly with the contractors and not the workers; that his company was fully legally compliant; and
that the forceful occupation of buildings as a means of exerting pressure was
dishonorable, illegal, and "a violence against the rights of citizens and their
freedoms." Al-Qayssi pointed out that wealth and honor were permitted by
law and he was forced to used legitimate self-defence when faced with attacks
on his home and family honor.[150] Al-Qayssi was supported by other employers, certain newspapers, and armed men from internal security, Brigade 16,
and the Kataeb. A handful of armed clashes ensued, injuring a Palestinian.[151]
Al-Qayssi was also reportedly trying to buy off individual workers, to "break
their solidarity" with "honeyed promises."[152]

The League initially opposed the use of violence by either side, and claimed
that the so-called nationalist militias were merely opportunists in bed with
capitalists and feudalists for a "handful of coins." Jamil Muhanna declared
that even murder would not intimidate the workers or the League, but warned
the workers in turn "against throwing his name around in connection with
any struggle or issue of protest or negative doings," and against using force
except in legitimate self-defense.[153] After meeting with politicians and the

Lebanese General Confederation, the League's position became more conservative. While exhorting solidarity among the workers, the League now sought a legal solution, and came out on August 23 for an end to the sit-in, while denying that the League had played any role in inciting the workers' action.[154] The solution, according to the League, was to be found in the good-faith efforts of officials. The workers were unimpressed. Their action stemmed precisely from the past failure of such efforts. They continued their sit-in at least until August 28, "leading to a serious situation regarding [grain] provisioning."[155]

Jamil Muhanna later stated that the workers "emerged with dignity" with "some of them getting some of their rights" because of the intervention of various political elements before the armed clashes got out of control. Muhanna maintained that of those involved in the sit-in at al-Qayssi, 300 workers obtained LL600,000/ $200,000.[156] He also stated that after a "tough and bitter" struggle, 1,200 workers previously employed by Makawi and Yafawi unloading companies also obtained LL2.8 million/ $930,000 in compensation.[157] Muhanna's League-friendly account is neither confirmed nor denied by other sources. It seems reasonable to suggest that through collective organization involving nonviolent institutional disruption—albeit with some links to militiamen in the civil war context—the workers achieved some results that, trusting to the legalism of the League and the good faith of "properly constituted authority," they would not have otherwise received, especially with the impending Israeli invasion and economic crisis.

But the activism of the workers was not able to change the basic stance of the union. Although the League expanded operations, established offices in Saida, 'Aley, Shtura, Tripoli, and Ba'albek, gained compensation for a number of individuals, and enforced contracts in certain cases, it was never again associated with direct collective action and popular confrontation. Instead, the League spoke increasingly of "social cooperation between the employer and the worker," and joint efforts to reconstruct Lebanon.[158] It established a newspaper in November 1979, Al-'Ata' (Giving), tackling issues related to the life of workers in Lebanon, aiming to raise their cultural level, encourage literacy, and represent pan-Arabist and progressive principles. The League was also involved in sport and theater, and opened a library. The League ran cultural and political seminars for workers and Syrian nationals to tackle public issues and explain the "struggle of our ruling party" and the nature of "our Syrian Arab country." It circulated Ba'thist viewpoints and recruited workers to the Ba'th party. Finally, the League set up an employment office, and started to act as a labor contractor, working with hundreds of workers.[159] In short, the League's activities diversified, and it became a labor contractor and social center with dirigiste political aims.

FOREIGN MANPOWER IN QUESTION

In the 1950s and 1960s, the Lebanon of the "miracle" economy had known few socioeconomic arguments against foreign migrant labor. In the 1970s, Syrians were designated as the "enemy" in isolationist-nationalist sectors for a host of political and ideological reasons: Economic arguments were not involved. However, the economic crisis of the mid-1980s, and the ideas that surrounded it, delivered a major blow against these inherited understandings. Migrant labor started to be seen for the first time as a cause of economic malaise.

Although numbers of migrants were diminishing and were at an historic low in the mid-1980s, their presence started to loom large in public debate as a pressing burden. "Lebanon faces an invasion—foreign workers" ran a headline in 1985. Amid a crippling economic and social crisis, 'Awwadi wrote, including hyper-inflation, the collapse of purchasing power, immiseration, and "armies of unemployed ... we see foreign labor attacking this country in a remarkable way," a "dreadful army" in numbers entirely abnormal for a country as small as Lebanon.[160] Two problems were especially emphasized. First, among a public not known for a prior history of solidarity with workers or concern with popular immiseration or unemployment, the unfair competition of cheap foreign labor received significant attention. 'Awwadi denounced the way businesses were firing Lebanese and replacing them with cheaper foreigners.[161] A more detailed study spoke of "serious competition" occasioned by the arrival of uncounted numbers of foreigners evading permits and working in ever more diverse sectors. Lebanese were left unemployed, a particular problem when work opportunities in the Gulf were heavily reduced.[162] Second, remittances— to the tune of $60 million a year—were said to contribute heavily to a drain on hard currency and the slide of the once proud Lebanese pound.[163]

While the power, range, and depth of the new thinking should not be exaggerated—older understandings were only slowly rearticulated, and certain sectors were willing to defend the standard views of conventional economics on open borders and labor mobility[164]—calls for state regulation and restriction on foreign labor became politically significant by 1985. In that year, the General Confederation of Workers mounted a campaign against an "invasion" of foreign workers onto the Lebanese labor market. Various constituencies supported the call for a more adequate employment strategy, labor market planning, and entry restrictions.[165] Prime Minister Rashid Karami, defender of the open door in the early 1970s, convened a committee to study the issue in February 1985.[166] In August, the Socialist Progressive Party announced the establishment of a National Organization for Migrant Affairs.[167] In the same month, the Lebanese Forces went further, issuing a ruling that foreigners were allowed only to undertake certain menial jobs—domestic service, construction, street cleaning, cooking, car-washing, and porterage—and only then if no Lebanese was willing.[168] This provoked some anxiety in the government, with Labor Minister Salim al-Hoss insisting in a letter to General Security that the Ministry of Labor is "the sole valid source for the validation of licences for foreign workers on Lebanese soil" and that other permits were illegal.[169] The Labor Ministry issued another warning, this time to employers, in November 1985, that nongovernmental permits were invalid and offenders would be fined.[170] In this context, the authority of the faltering Lebanese state was at stake, and following demonstrations, protests, and sit-ins by those maintaining that the state should ensure their subsistence, Salim al-Hoss, the Minister of Labor, issued law no. 261 in August 1986, preventing the employment of foreign labor in a variety of professions except those involving skills scarce in Lebanon. His adviser told a national daily that the measure was intended to protect Lebanese labor and to support the national economy at a time of political, economic, and social crisis and following popular protests.[171]

While these measures had little impact on the ground, the economic crisis and oppositional opinion it provoked created a new problem faced by Syrian (and other) foreign workers in Lebanon. And the discourse and interventionism of the mid-1980s was an important innovation on the Lebanese scene. From this point on, the economic benefit of migrant labor would have to be argued rather than assumed.

RETURNING TO SYRIA

High social costs, expulsion, violence, the Israeli invasion of 1982, and finally the economic crisis of the mid-1980s combined with family dynamics, gendered roles, and connections to Syria to drive increasing numbers of Syrian workers to return. Some Syrian families had left Lebanon, it is important to note, prior to the war, because of both high social costs in Lebanon, and family ties and resources in Syria. The family of Hanna Butros is a case in point. Butros first went to Lebanon in 1958. He married a woman from his village in

1964 and managed to bring her and their first child to Lebanon in 1965 once he was making LL11/ $3.50 a day as a painter. This wage, he said, "paid all our expenses. We were happy. We went out and everything." The family lived in Lebanon for six years, first in al-Dawra, north of Beirut, and then in Saqayet al-Janzir near Rouche in West Beirut. There, they rented a one-room flat with a Muslim landlord for LL70/ $30.57 a month. "Our eldest daughter was born there," reported the wife. In a nice detail, it was said that Butros was away attending a funeral at the time and so the wife was taken to hospital in the landlord's car by the landlord's son. He was "a married man," noted Butros.

Nonetheless, the wife and children returned to Syria in 1971. "We became a family [with two children] and we could not [afford to] get a big house . . . we could not get a bigger house than the one we had and we wanted to be stable [and settled]," said his wife. The high costs of housing in the merchant republic had meant that the family, even with Butros's wage, could not really plan on settling down on a permanent basis in Lebanon. On the other hand, things were different in Syria: "We had land here and an old house, so we came and started rebuilding, step by step." As Butros put it:

> When we came back here, when we moved the family, we decided on a specific goal, which was to build a house in our village. As long as we were in Lebanon we would not have thought about it. So she moved to live here and I would bring in money from work while that house was under re-construction. . . . I wanted to build a house because I saw that the family was getting bigger and would not be able to afford it [in Lebanon], so I started building it then.

Butros's wife assured me of her husband's proper behavior: "He visited regularly." Return was not just about the availability of adequate accommodation. The "weight of the ancestors" and attachments to home, village, and land also shaped and explained the move to return. Butros said:

> What tied us to this country is the land. We have a piece of land and olive trees that our father left us. How could we get rid of them? It is not right. This is it. I wish it wasn't so. . . . Believe me, no matter how long you stay away from your village, it [the land] stays in your chest.

Here, as elsewhere, culture is not merely resistant and creative, but weighed "like a nightmare on the brain of the living." Butros wished he did not have such ties, that he did not have to work in Lebanon and live in Syria, but such ties existed and shaped his activities and consciousness. As his wife added,

"We also worked the land" planting olives, grapes, and figs, "and we are living happily and are grateful to God." She continued, "You would find yourself a stranger away from it [the land], even if you were happy." Butros went on:

> If I go to live where you live, I might be living a beautiful life, but this remains to be my village. Childhood you cannot forget. Can you forget your friends, the good mates that you have lived with? You will always have a tender spot for them. Even though we were working over there, our minds were here. We would always ask what happened with this or that person.[172]

In this case, then, while Hanna Butros, with his mind in Syria, continued to work in Lebanon, his wife and children returned before the violence broke out, for socioeconomic and cultural reasons. High social costs in Lebanon, along with inheritance, goals, cultural pressures, and expectations worked to thin out a second generation in Lebanon even before the civil war.

Yet the civil war acted powerfully to reverse tentative settlement patterns, even in the mixed areas. Joseph, for example, was earning good money throughout the 1970s in the Hamra restaurant "American Dream," sufficient for his wife and family to stay in a respectable apartment in nearby Caracas. "We were living comfortably, we dressed elegantly and our home was nice. All my children were born in the American University Hospital [in West Beirut], all of them, Zizi, Micho, and Michelene, all of them at the American University. Three children at the American University Hospital [in 1975, 1979, 1982]. . . . All of them were born in Lebanon."[173] Joseph again repeated, as if in the early 2000s this was indeed something strange, a different world now lost: "All of them were born in Lebanon. Even here on their certificate it says they were born in Beirut." Joseph was even able to afford Lebanese private education: Zizi went to school in Beirut "all on my expense. Zizi went to a private school . . . I paid her tuition fees as well as the bus that transported her from home to school, and then from school back home." Nonetheless, with the Israeli invasion, siege, and bombardment of West Beirut, the family had to return.

> When Israel came in 1982 . . . there were bombs falling. My baby . . . would get afraid and cry . . . from the light and noise of the bombs. So I sent the family and the kids back to Syria. . . . My son, Michel, if he saw tanks on television, even if it [what he was seeing] were kids toys, he would scream and cry. . . . I did not have a house [in Syria], so she [my wife] came to live with my parents, she and the kids.[174]

Joseph's case is an important example of a worker with sufficient funds to settle his family respectably in Lebanon, paying costs of accommodation, health, education, and transport. Only with the Israeli invasion was the family driven home, while Joseph carried on working at "American Dream." He described how his domestic space was literally transported back piecemeal to Syria, while he remained, exhausted, in Lebanon:

> It was definitely tough sending my children away. I was mentally tired after that. I was not happy. I had a house and I left it. I brought my things and my furniture: the television, the refrigerator, the sofas. I brought everything. Even the washing machines and the refrigerator I brought to Syria. I would bring it to the borders. I am a resident of Lebanon so I had the freedom to move, and I had a paper from the mayor over there which allowed me to transport all my things without any trouble. I did not even have to pay. They let all my things pass. I had to certify that the television was mine, but that was it. I brought all my things to Syria.

In this way, while Joseph stayed in Lebanon for work for the time being, making quick return visits "every month or so," his family resettled in Syria, initially via their parents' house because, significantly enough, they had nowhere of their own. After some years, they built their own house in Syria with Joseph's remittances.

Few Syrian workers' families remained in Lebanon after 1982. Even many men who stayed in West Beirut without their families were driven back to Syria in that year. Tony Elias had returned from Libya in 1979 without even visiting his village. He was still single, and was embarrassed about a lack of earnings: "I had nothing to do in the village. I had not worked [only] to gain the price of the airplane ticket." So, "I thought going to work in Lebanon [even during the civil war] would be better." This was the familiar story of the migrant whose costs of transport eat up earnings, but it testifies to the power of social expectations, the importance of family ties, and economic compulsion in determining migrant trajectories, even in the face of grievous physical risk. Elias found an acquaintance in Hamra who connected him with a Muslim landlord in Hamra renting to workers: "I took a room, painted it and fixed it, and I brought a foldable bed, a little gas stove and a kettle. I lived there and went back to work in painting." He continued:

> When Israel entered Beirut, I was in Lebanon. [Israel] entered Hazmieh and surrounded the town, and entered Beirut Port with its tanks. I saw . . . Israeli

tanks in the Port. . . . I was afraid. I am Syrian and Israeli tanks were surrounding the city. They were even at the port and if I wanted to go back to
Syria I would have had to pass through them. . . . How could I pass? . . . I was
afraid because I was Syrian, and the Lebanese were angry with the Syrians
at this point. So I was afraid the Kataeb or the Israelis might catch me. . . .
I thought I should go to the village because there is no need to take a risk. I
thought it would only get bloodier and I'd have nowhere to go.

Elias paid LL100/ $27 to an acquaintance through work, a Lebanese Chris-
tian taxi driver, to take him out. "He came over to my place. I had my things
packed . . . and I locked my room. He drove me through different [side] streets
until we were past the Kataeb checkpoint in the Beirut Port, and took me to
Tripoli." From Tripoli, Elias made his own way home to Syria. During the rest
of the war Tony Elias worked as a painter in Lattakia, and did not return to
Lebanon until the early 1990s.

Some of the men who stayed on alone after 1982 were driven out by the
economic crisis after 1983. Joseph was eventually compelled to leave by hyper-
inflation, a falling salary, the lack of other economic opportunities, and the
need to support his family in Syria:

> After my salary [at American Dream] had reached $600, he decreased it to
> $400 then he made it $300, and then he said that I should take $200. I said,
> "From $600, you want to bring me down to $200." This would not even pay for
> my clothes, a pair of trousers, a shirt, and cigarettes! [Inflation now meant that
> three packs of cigarettes would have absorbed half his salary.] . . . There was
> no more work. All shops stopped working. Beirut became stagnant and busi-
> nesses went broke. People sold their shops and whoever had ten workers kept
> only two. . . . [By 1987] there were no tourists, no foreigners, and the Lebanese
> were not working, so there was no movement. So I decided to leave. . . . I also
> had to pay transport costs to come here [to Syria], and I also had to support my
> family's expenses here. Lebanon did not do it for me any more.

Joseph thus returned to Syria, defeated not by fear but by the dull forces of economic compulsion. He rejoined his family and took a job as a humble waiter
in a restaurant, earning far less than he had before.[175]

The only men who stayed on even beyond the economic crisis in my relatively small sample of interviews were those with no family to support. Adib
Mahrus, for example, stayed throughout the war, working mostly in construc-

tion, only marrying in 1992. Abed, who never married, remained in al-Zarif as a painter throughout the war: "Even after '75 . . . I stayed here. I worked in Hamra, Al-Zarif, Ra's Beirut, Mazra'a . . . . [I stayed] during the whole conflict. I was even hit by shrapnel in my shoulder. I had to stay for five days in the hospital after the surgery. . . . It came out and when the wound healed [after 12 days in hospital] I went back to work."

Abed's expenses were paid by the PLO. "Yasser Arafat's organization used to make rounds on the hospitals and check with everyone to see if they need help. . . . All I had to do is sign a paper on my way out and Yasser Arafat paid everything. . . . He would help anyone injured . . . an excellent deed."[176] Abed returned to Syria for the first time briefly in 1982 and a few times thereafter. He explained that family dynamics were crucial:

> People go [back to Syria] for family reasons, but both my parents are dead. I have my brothers there and [now] we stay in touch on the phone. . . . We live near Idlib, and I don't like the politics there. . . . [My family] live in a small village and . . . there was nothing there. Now it is different as there's a butcher and washing-machines. Before, you couldn't find bread. If you have a wife she will bake for you. Here [in Lebanon] I could [simply] go to the baker. Here there are public laundries, [whereas] there are none over there. It is shameful for a man to wash his own clothes. Days passed and I kept postponing going back and that is how I stayed here. [In spite of the] fighting, explosions, [and] bullets . . . going back to Syria, didn't cross my mind. . . . I was happy. I had friends. We used to play cards and dice [backgammon], and we used to go to work all day.

Abed was neither burdened with family responsibilities nor attracted to Syria by domestic comforts or filial obligations. More significantly still, Abed was positively repelled from returning by the fact that he had no home in Syria, no control over female labor, and so would have to wash his own clothes in shame, bake bread, prepare meat, and so on, exposing himself to ridicule (and domestic drudgery) in the process. Abed, therefore, had none of the reverse push-and-pull factors associated with family to drive him back to Syria, elements highly salient in his decision to stay throughout the war, in spite of the risks, and the injury he suffered.

High social costs, gendered roles, political violence, and economic crisis combined to leave the migrants' optimism of the 1950s and 1960s, and emerging forms of family settlement in Lebanon, in tatters. Men were left on their own in Lebanon—without family, sofas, and televisions. They worked in Lebanon but their minds were in Syria. Even many such men were ultimately forced to return to what was now, perforce, "home." Over 15 years of war, if the violence did not force them home, then, finally, the economic crisis did.

CONCLUSION

Against a common view, Syrians did not simply leave Lebanon at the first sign of violence in 1975, only to return with the reconstruction of the 1990s, nor was violence the only factor in the dynamics of migration and return. The picture was far more complex. Workers suffered a mass eviction from areas controlled by Christian militias during 1975–76. A significant proportion of the expellees returned to Syria, but many moved to areas of Lebanon outside of Christian control. The Israeli invasion of 1982 drove many back to Syria, at least temporarily. The economic crisis of the mid-1980s, finally, was highly significant in sending another wave of workers "home"—not because of tightened regulations or even due to the hostility that accompanied the crisis, but because employment and incomes were radically diminished. Patterns of family settlement were tentative even before the war, in spite of the open border, because of high social costs in Lebanon and existing family ties and resources in Syria. Nonetheless, the war blocked and set back even the existing, modest moves toward settlement and second-generation formation. Wives and children were the first to be sent home at the outbreak of violence, and, it has to assumed, even in default of any comprehensive statistical indicators, that few families remained after the economic collapse of the mid-1980s.

Although the borders of Lebanon remained to all intents and purposes remarkably open to Syrian workers, with only limited moves to regulate entry and work permits, the "borders" of the Christian-controlled areas became more or less impermeable to Syrians, who were seen as "the enemy" after 1975–76 and especially after 1982. Syrians in various sectors were replaced by Asians. Christian areas of Lebanon thus preserved the formal structure of economic migration but transformed its content. Syrians were excluded as Syrians, because of what they came to represent in political and cultural terms, in the face of particular economic interests, which were overwhelmed by the political and sectarian division of Lebanon. The strategic interests, political economy, and national vision that had worked to produce Syrian workers as manpower were upturned by political change. So-called useful muscles became the enemy. It was not that the free market vision itself was transformed through ethno-nationalism. This vision had always been segmented—but Syrians, in all their particularity, had been acceptable whereas Palestinians had not. What changed was that Syrians now became designated as to be excluded, and certain other groups—predominantly Asians—were now seen as desirable for menial labor. Outside such areas, the picture was a mixed one of coexistence, tension, and cooperation, but not targeted, fatal violence. During the economic crisis of the 1980s, economic arguments against the presence of migrant workers were widely mobilized for the first time.

Direct collective action by workers had emerged where specific grievances combined with a particular political and ideological context, but dissipated as political opportunities closed down. Efforts by the Syrian government, and then by the League, to gain state-backed social provision and protection for Syrian workers failed, although mobilization had achieved compensation in some cases. The League slowly lost its focus on collective social rights, and morphed into a labor contractor. After 1982, the political and ideological terrain for those fighting for social rights became increasingly inhospitable, with economic crisis and antimigrant campaigns in the press, and the diminishing will of the Syrian government on the matter.

This history suggests that antimigrant campaigns, an old theme in the history of the United States and elsewhere, do not necessarily depend on the formation of an assertive second generation in the receiving country. In fact, largely ungrounded fears about Syrian settlement, which in reality was particularly tentative, combined with politically and ideologically constructed fears about all the other things that they came to represent, were responsible for antimigrant agitation and for the mass expulsion from the Christian areas. These events show the extent to which economic interests could be overwhelmed by political and cultural articulation. On the other hand, sectors controlled by Christian militias still found *someone* to do the menial labor. Although particular economic interests were overwhelmed by politics, the economic structure of appropriation and accumulation remained in spite of the ways the labor market came to be segmented.

The fact that Syrian workers continued to go to Lebanon, especially in the 1976 to 1982 period, even sometimes at quite significant risk to life and limb, powerfully underlines the power of the dull forces of economic compulsion combined with social aspirations and expectations in driving migration. Tony Elias, for instance, on returning to Damascus from Libya relatively penniless in 1979, did not even dare to show his face at home, but went directly to war-torn Lebanon. This point draws attention to the forms of structural coercion that underpin so-called voluntary and economic labor migration. The poor of the Syrian countryside had no choice about the range of options with which they were presented. At one end of that range lay social stigma and poverty; at the other end was migration, with all the possibilities and miseries that that involved. The terms of this battle—the circumstances transmitted from the past, and transformed by state policy, world economy, and so on— were not chosen by economic migrants. To speak as if such migration was therefore "voluntary" or "spontaneous" is profoundly misleading. It belies and ignores the whole structure of economic power, and assumes that culture is simply creative, resistant, and manipulated by individual agents, rather than constitutive and sometimes repressive. Hanna Awwad, we recall, lamented his ties to the land, and the "weight of the ancestors"—while his wife insisted that such ties were the keys to the good life.

Finally, the interpretation advanced in this chapter underlines the ways in which the labor market is constructed not just out of economic forces, but is laden with power and freighted with meaning. Migrants are not simply faceless units of labor power, or purely commodified inputs to production. Outside of conventional economics, economist Marxism, and various other particular visions, they are not viewed as, and do not act as "muscles," hands, arms, stocks, reservoirs, or surpluses. Their movements are not best understood by a theory based on individuals as maximizers working among the simple operations of exchange and supply and demand. History, politics, culture, and particular economic and social purposes intrude at every turn. Before the civil war, Syrians' status as muscles was given by a complex orchestration of forces. Likewise, the ways in which these practices and ways of seeing were broken up also stemmed from historical conjuncture, civil war, political economy, interpellation, and the particular projects and ties of migrants themselves.

4 PAX SYRIANA

INTRODUCTION

When I mentioned my research, in 2004, to Raghid el-Solh, political advisor to the United Nations in Beirut (ESCWA), his response was terse: "controversial." Indeed, from public commentary on the question of Syrian migrant workers in Lebanon in the 1990s and 2000s, one might assume that the most important issue was the controversy surrounding their "invasion." "The subject of Syrian workers is the most thorny question occupying the minds of the Lebanese in general," wrote Jani Nasrallah in December 2000.[1] Certainly this controversy must be given its due. But it must also be put in context and set alongside other important questions. The more surprising point, perhaps, is that during the 1990s, Syrian workers returned to Lebanon in large numbers, perhaps in larger numbers than ever before, to work all over the country, even in Christian areas where only a few years previously they had been subjected to killings and eviction. By the end of the civil war, Lebanon was in economic crisis, politically unstable, and Syrian activities and policies could hardly be said to be suddenly popular in many sectors of Lebanese society. Meanwhile, Syrian migrants felt anything but relish at the prospect of returning to the lands of the Christian militias. Nonetheless, by the mid-1990s, hundreds of thousands of Syrian workers were working all over Lebanon: "The Lebanese have the impression of seeing them everywhere," reported *L'Orient-Le Jour*, "at crossroads, under bridges, at the exits of factories, in the fields, in the destroyed buildings of downtown [Beirut] and even in the smallest alleyways of the capital."[2] In spite of the reappearance of those harshly stigmatized during the war, moreover, hardly a word of opposition to their presence was uttered by officials or appeared in the press before 1994, and the controversy emerged only slowly and haltingly after that time, and was not inevitable, but depended on changing circumstances. Indeed, the Francophone daily, *L'Orient-Le Jour*, in the article just cited, was the first newspaper to mention the presence of Syrian workers in a critical fashion. As I will argue, it is too simple to view the reappearance of Syrian workers in the 1990s as only imposed on Lebanon by Syria, or the silence over Syrians in the early 1990s as stemming from a simple fear of Syrian reprisals, although these factors were certainly part of the story. The reappearance of Syrians in their hundreds of thousands in Lebanon in the 1990s, in demand among many employers, Christian and Muslim, and the telling silence that greeted them, has something more fundamental to tell us about how migratory systems are constructed.

PAX SYRIANA

The return of Syrian workers to Lebanon in the 1990s did not come without important (geo)political, economic, social, and cultural changes. But the Pax Syriana was not made by Damascus, and certainly not by God, as Hafez al-Asad famously claimed. Its construction reached from the White House to Syrian households, and from pan-Arabism to the entrepreneurs of the "new" Lebanon. The civil war finally came to an end, with Syria holding overall strategic and military power in Lebanon, apart from the territory in the South occupied by Israel. The blueprint for a postwar settlement, to which most of the major parties to the conflict acquiesced, had been signed in the Saudi Arabian town of Ta'if in 1989. The Maronite General Michel Aoun led the last major opposition to the Ta'if Accords in the name of a "free" Lebanon. In October 1990, however, the Syrians were given the green light by the United States to use air-power against Aoun, based in Baʿabda Palace—dubbed the "people's palace" by supporters. The United States was willing to allow Syria some increased measure of control in Lebanon in return for Syrian support in the Arab coalition against Iraq in the 1990–91 Gulf War. With U.S.-backing, Syrian geopolitical power was in the ascendant, in spite of the loss of its Soviet patron. Maronite-led Lebanese nationalism was defeated. Saudi and the Gulf states had been moving to secure Syrian support against the expansionism of Saddam Hussein's Iraq. Israel had been pegged back: The use of the Syrian air force was a clear breach of the Red Lines agreement between Syria and Israel that regulated the parameters within which each country had been operating, but Israel could not respond. Israeli political clout in Lebanon had been all but broken, along with its ties to Maronite leadership. The Israeli occupation of the South, and the struggle against it, only strengthened the Syrian interpretation of Ta'if.[3] Long-standing Syrian hostility to Ba'thist Iraq was vindicated, and Hafez al-Asad even found a way to portray his support for the United States against a fellow Arab country in pan-Arab and anti-imperialist terms: As he put it, "If we want the foreigners [the Americans] to leave quickly, then let us quickly resolve the problem [Saddam Hussein's invasion of Kuwait], so as to remove any pretext for their stay."[4]

In Lebanon, then, the Syrian Arab Republic became the undisputed guardian of the Ta'if Accords, with American and Saudi blessings.[5] The Ta'if Accords allowed for Syrian troop deployment in Lebanon for a limited but unspecified period, and mandated the disarming of the militias except for Hizbullah, charged with the liberation of the South from the enemy. The Accords retained Lebanon's fundamentally sectarian political structure, but handed more power to the Sunni and Shi'a Muslim political leadership, historically more sympathetic in general to the Arab and Islamic world, by diminishing the presidential writ and boosting the powers of the Sunni Prime Minister and the Shi'a Speaker of the parliament. In 1943, Prime Minister Riad al-Solh had declared that Lebanon was a country that drew "great good" from the "civilized West," while having an Arab "face," and refusing to be "a passageway or base for any [colonial] power or state or organization aiming at disrupting its security or the security of Syria."[6] The Ta'if Accords situated Lebanon more firmly in the Arab world and emphatically underlined its links to Syria. There was no mention of any good, let alone any "great good," that Lebanon derived from the West. And Lebanon was said not just to have an Arab face, but to be "Arab in identity and belonging."[7] Moreover, it was declared that "between [Lebanon] and Syria are special relations (*mumayyaza*), their power extending from roots of kinship and history, and from joint brotherly interests." It was understood that the two countries would engage in "coordination and cooperation" in subsequent agreements, albeit in the context of the "sovereignty and independence" of both countries.[8] Close relations between the two countries were accordingly signed into being with the Treaty of Brotherhood, Cooperation, and Coordination of May 1991.

The basis of Syrian power in Lebanon was not only geopolitical. Apart from the political arrangements that favored the advance of Shi'a and Sunni Muslims, and thus had an obvious appeal to those constituencies, the Lebanese in general craved security after more than a decade of war, which appeared increasingly senseless to so many. Popular mobilization against the fighting and war-time conditions dated back, in fact, to the mid-1980s.[9] Many said that war was *kidhb*, a lie, whereby people's passions were manipulated by wealthy faction leaders lining their own pockets, or by foreigners with their own agenda. As a Lebanese upholsterer, Ibrahim stated, "In Lebanon it is the government and rich individuals who instigate blind hatred and sectarianism in the country."[10] Syria appeared to be the only credible guarantor of security, and the delivery of such security during the 1990s, after 15 years of civil war, was widely cited as one of the most important achievements of the Syrian role in Lebanon.

Such security was linked to the hoped-for revival of the economy. Lebanese workers looking for jobs, (ex)middle classes who had lost their savings and property, and businessmen searching for profit hoped for the economic reconstruction of what had once been the "Switzerland of the East." Here, their interests and hopes meshed with the policies and interests of Damascus, which was fully aware that it stood to gain much from the economic development of Lebanon. Far from seeking to impose a Ba'thist solution for the destruction of war and economic crisis in Lebanon,[11] Syria sought, in the context of cautious "market reform" at home, a regional free-trade bloc that would in theory benefit and develop the two economies in the name of Arabism in the face of both globalization and Israeli, Turkish, and Western machinations.[12] As a Lebanese economist, central banker, and government minister put it in the mid-1990s: "I believe the future is in our hands to create an appropriate environment for Lebanon and Syria to become a 'regional hub' for the Middle East and the countries of Central Asia."[13] This was a strategic, and not simply an economic, plan. A Syrian-led Arabism was battened onto Washington consensus-style economics, an elective affinity few predicted, with the approval of many in both countries: businessmen; the new, war-rich economists in Lebanon; and regime figures in Syria looking for lucrative contracts and commissions.[14] Nasser Saidi argued in the late 1980s and early 1990s that reconstruction required foreign investment, low taxes and social charges, banking secrecy, currency convertibility, unhindered capital movements, and "freedom to repatriate capital dividends and profits."[15] Not for the first time, an economic principle of order stitched together diverse subjectivities and projects. Christians were no longer dominant among Lebanon's wealthy elite in any case.[16] Coming from outside the well-established families and confessional strongmen (*zu'ama*) of Lebanon's political class, of humble origins, a Sunni Muslim and self-made billionaire, and with good connections in Saudi Arabia, Rafiq al-Hariri was a near-perfect candidate for leadership and reconstruction in the Lebanon of Syrian "guardianship." As al-Hariri reported in 1993, "There are no parties with any reservations about the full and complete coordination between Lebanon and Syria."[17] In line with the economic thinking of the pax Syriana, indeed, al-Hariri soon cut corporate taxes to 10 percent.[18]

The pax Syriana drew strength from association with pan-Arabism, a powerful theme among officials and popular intellectuals in Syria and Lebanon, and reiterated and appropriated by Syrian workers in widespread fashion, as we shall see. In pan-Arab thinking, those interested in Arab unity (al-wahdu-yiyyin), long opposed to colonial designs of divide and rule, were pitted against isolationists (al-infisaliyyin), who stood for a sectarian Lebanese nationalism with a long association with colonialism. Without Arabism—based on the historic ties, brotherhood, and common destiny of one people separated into two states—Lebanese citizenship would remain incomplete, and the "Lebanese would continue to be a stranger in his own surroundings, if not a belligerent."[19] The hegemonic reach of pan-Arabism meant that even those attacking Syria opposed not Arabism but its betrayal. It was argued that Syria stood only for narrow regime or Syrian nationalist interests, or even more tellingly, the interests of outsiders, including the United States and Israel. As one Christian "isolationist" put it: "Syria is Israel's best friend. They allowed them [the Israelis] in in 1982, they didn't raise a finger. The deal [now] is that Israel can keep the Golan as long as Syria has a free hand in Lebanon."[20]

The Islamic accommodation—perhaps with a Sunni face—of the new Lebanon, along with its discontents, was symbolized by the large size, grandeur, and location of the Ottoman-style mosque that al-Hariri's companies started to plan and build in the middle of downtown Beirut (although construction was only completed in the mid-2000s). Maronite-led, isolationist nationalism had been defeated, and for some of its former partisans, if an accommodation with the Arab and Islamic world was the price for peace and reconstruction, then so be it. Indeed, a distinctly pragmatic strain developed among some of the erstwhile "defenders of the cedars." Joseph Abu Khalil, long-time editor of the Kataeb newspaper, Al-'Amal, argued that Lebanon had no choice but to "breathe" through Syria, as routes south (meaning ties to Israel) were largely closed, and routes to the sea (meaning ties to the West) were weaker than before, particularly as European borders were increasingly restricted. The prosperity and independence of Lebanon was now said to depend on ties to

Syria and hence the rest of the Arab world.[21] Other Christians looked askance
at such reasoning, where a relative loss of power, status, wealth, and position
meant a sense of alienation—feelings that bolstered support for the Christian
boycott of the first nation-wide elections, held in 1992, following the exile to
France of General Michel Aoun. Many felt they could not ratify a system that
made them feel no longer at home in their own land and made emigration,
now reinterpreted as a "national hemorrhage," the only viable option. Lebanon had been a beacon of freedom and a refuge in a hostile and despotic Arab
and Islamic world. Now, some said, it was under occupation by a totalitarian
regime.

Migrant Labor

The changing geopolitical, economic, and cultural landscape was crucial in
defining patterns of labor migration, and attitudes toward it, in the 1990s.
The notion of an Arab free-trade bloc, and the conventional economic thinking and business interests that underpinned it, supposed that Syria, rich in
labor-power but capital-poor, would supply Lebanon, rich in capital but lacking an abundant labor supply, with cheap abundant labor.[22] Both countries
would benefit: Lebanon from labor-power, and Syria from remittances (not
to mention a political safety-valve regarding a young population demanding
jobs and new consumption patterns). Defenders of the pax Syriana saw the
movement of labor-power in the region as part of a positive process of globalization. "While it is said," wrote Mikhail Awwad, "that there are tens of thousands of Syrians in Lebanon . . . there are more than 600 thousand Egyptian
workers in Syria . . . and 1.5 million Sudanese in Egypt." These movements
had deep roots. Lebanon, too, from ancient times, had benefited from significant emigration and immigration. In the 1950s, the Lebanese economy was
built on the shoulders of the Arabs: Syrian capitalists fleeing nationalisation,
oil money searching for financial services, and summer tourists. Further, as
many as 400,000 Syrians worked in Lebanon under proper regulations until
1975.[23] In this view, Syrian labor came to Lebanon not for political reasons,
but because of market forces, to which the Lebanese political establishment
had always been committed. "The Lebanese economy is based on the free-
market," argued Awwad, "and labour power is a commodity which submits
entirely to the laws of the market, just as any other commodity."[24] Lebanese
war-time emigration left a gap in the labor force, which Syrians filled; the war
and militia culture had caused Lebanese workers to lose their work ethic and

become lazy, expensive, and ineffective. The war had exacerbated individualism, "boss mentality," intolerance, and neglectfulness, and diminished workforce skills and training, while the Lebanese refused to take exhausting or shameful work, preferring consumption over production. The major growth sectors after the war, contracting and construction, had always been done with foreign labor in Lebanon. In fact, Syrian labor was said to be a golden opportunity for employers and reconstruction. Legal and other costs were minimal, and workers had both high productivity and professional skills.[25] Nor was Syrian labor a drain on hard currency or economic activity: Unlike Egyptian or Asian labor, Syrian labor was not costly in terms of insurance, communications, and transport. Moreover, unlike other foreign labor, Syrians are not contracted immediately, and so do not start sending hard currency home straightaway, but spend what they have or acquire debt that is later paid off. Also, many Syrians use earnings to buy consumer goods (to send home) in Lebanon, while spending at least half their earnings in Lebanon on subsistence, thus stimulating the economy. By transferring Lebanese consumption habits to Syria, return migrants stimulate Lebanese (re)exports and Syrian shopping trips to Lebanon. Migrants were said to open Lebanese bank accounts and reinvest their remittances, unlike Asians.[26] According to some, only Lebanese chauvinism could oppose these positions, which were tied to pan-Arab aspirations,[27] not to mention to the interests of the foreign and Lebanese business community.[28]

The open door was rationalized by the 1994 Bilateral Labor Agreement, which established joint border offices granting entry and temporary work permits for seasonal workers, who were supposed to obtain a written work contract detailing duration, wages, hours, and holidays, among other things.[29] The work contract was not a condition of the border work permit, and hence the contract provision was a dead letter, a point that must have been clear to the drafters. In practice, at the border, workers merely had to assert (where it was not automatically assumed) that they were temporary seasonal laborers. They would then be issued a card and stamped in. Technically, Syrian workers without contracts contravened the Agreement, and were hence in some sense illegal, but in practice this illegality was rarely invoked, except in the writings of those agitating against the workers' presence.

Lebanese employers, foreign investors, and economists were already decidedly hostile to hardly generous existing social provisions—denounced as backward—for Lebanese workers (involving sickness and maternity, family allowances, and end of service indemnity).[30] These sectors were thus chiefly concerned to ensure that Syrian workers were not enrolled in the social insurance system, a point ensured by the Bilateral Labor Agreement.[31] As the Finance Minister Fu'ad Siniora put it in 2000, the imposition of regular Ministry of Labor work permits on Syrian workers would add to the burdens of employers and create an "outcry" among them.[32] The Agreement also in practice freed employers of the potential bureaucratic and labor hassles of the employment contract. Workers were wanted who would work cheaply, be easily hired and fired, and work long hours at different times and intensities in greatly variable numbers. The regulation in effect regularized this situation.

This free-market logic, the theme of Arab unity, the interests of Western, regional, and local business, the Syrian government, and the open border all implied that the labor unions in Lebanon be firmly controlled. Organization by Lebanese labor in general, but particularly against Syrian workers, was not to be tolerated, while Damascus, in a reversal of its position in the 1970s, effectively undertook not to raise demands on behalf of Syrian workers upsetting to Lebanese employers and foreign investors. Al-Hariri, indeed, attempted (with only partial success) to prevent unions from striking or demonstrating by making such activities illegal.[33] The Lebanese Ministry of Labor was headed by a number of pro-Syrian officials. Abdullah Amin had been head of the Lebanese branch of Syria's Ba'th Party. Asad Hardan was an important official in the Syrian Social Nationalist Party (SSNP). Michel Moussa, another former Labor Minister, was a close ally of Nabih Berri, known for his pro-Syrian positions. Ali Qanso was a one-time head of the SSNP. Even outside the union movement, neither official agencies such as the United Nations, nor nongovernmental organizations felt that the political climate could allow them to research the question of Syrian workers: not just the issue of numbers, residence patterns, and so on, but also and especially that of workers' labor rights. The Syrian workers were sensitive—a taboo topic.[34] Syrian control and Lebanese "collusion," as Samir Kassir called it, in other words, implied that the workers should neither be opposed nor supported; rather, as the "muscles" of reconstruction, they should simply be left alone by opinion at large. Certainly the press observed this taboo until 1994 at least, and the subject only slowly came to be a matter of contention in the public sphere thereafter.

The Role of the Military

An unusual feature of the pax Syriana was that a poorer, labor-sending country had a powerful military presence—the term *occupation* was increasingly

used among the opposition by the early 2000s—in the richer, receiving country. The view among pro-Lebanese came to be that Syrian workers were practically untouchable because of military protection and were in league with Syrian intelligence to boot. Vivid stories regarding the power and effectiveness
of these links circulated, especially among Christians opposed to the postwar
settlement. For example, a retired lawyer for the Iraq Petroleum Company of
prenationalization days, told me that in the early 1990s, the wife of the Lebanese Commander of the Preventive Forces had a dispute (the details were not
specified) with her Syrian maid. The following day the house was surrounded
by Syrian tanks. Even powerful Lebanese, it seemed, were vulnerable to the
ways the Syrian army rallied round their own and engaged in an unreasonable defence of their workers.[35] Many took the position that many if not most
of the workers would have to flee if the army withdrew.

These positions are highly misleading. It is true that there is some evidence
to suggest that the Syrian military did, in particular cases, defend their compatriots, most likely in an unofficial and *ad hoc* manner. It was reported, for
example, in March 1992, that "when Lebanese police tried to evict scores of
Syrian vegetable vendors from sidewalks along the airport highway . . . [there
followed] a gun battle with Syrian soldiers that left six dead and many more
wounded."[36] Moreover, the provision of jobs was also not beyond the workings of patron-client linkages between officers and workers, particularly where
officers secured positions for work gangs in road building, hotel renovation,
agriculture, or elsewhere. Military service in Lebanon was also a common
route to finding employment. In Khoury's sample, for instance, 23 percent of
Syrians had been on military service in Lebanon.[37] Finally, it was the case that
some workers, from a vulnerable position, would assert or show off real or
imagined links to particular officers or the army in general.

None of this vitiates that fact that, contrary to the pro-Lebanese position,
the Syrian army in Lebanon was one among many forces underpinning the
overall system of labor control envisaged and established by the pax Syriana.
The military was an important pillar of the regional free-trade bloc, union
control, and the open labor market, and did not protect workers in any general
sense against the conditions of menial labor, or support their collective organization, or any progressive change in their pay, conditions, or status. In the
early 1970s, the Asad government did lobby for extended social security and
other protections for Syrian migrant workers—a policy the Lebanese always
managed to reject. But after the Syrians were in overall control during the
1990s, Damascus made no mention of such demands: Lebanese business would

be tapped through deals and levies, official and unofficial, but it would not be antagonized by Syrian support for workers' rights. Indeed, the forms of labor contracting in which the Syrian army was engaged, or the way it operated as a vehicle for the acquisition of jobs, linked workers to employers on terms no less exploitative than the norm. An agricultural engineer with good contacts in the Syrian army, for example, told me the following story. Tenders went out for a road-surfacing contract in Lebanon. A Syrian company got the contract from the government because of the influence of an army officer, who in this case had a controlling stake in the company itself. In this instance, when the Syrian company arrived at the work site, a Lebanese company, also employing Syrian workers, was already there doing the work. The police and the military resolved the situation such that both companies ended up with the work. But when the work was found to be substandard, bribes had to be paid to keep this quiet. The supposedly "protected" Syrian worker was exploited by all parties. In fact, the workers supplied by the military—those on military service—were in fact *far worse* off than Syrian workers not on military service, as the former were paid $150 per month, whereas those not on military service and paid directly received $250 to $300 per month.[38]

Syrian workers were often anxious about the arbitrary and sometimes abusive role of Syrian officers in contracting and employment in Syria, and these sentiments did not suddenly change in Lebanon, where the activities of the feared Syrian intelligence services were more significantly a source of anxiety than of comfort. There were many powerful distinctions of class, religion/sect, region, and education between officers and workers. Some Syrian workers did have connections, but so did wealthy Lebanese businessmen. For every second- or third-hand anecdote about the ways in which Syrians in Lebanon somehow had the protection of the army and the Lebanese authorities, my own interviews threw up plenty of first-hand anecdotes pointing in the opposite direction. Jo Farah, for example, reckoned that one could not go to the police in Lebanon if one were Syrian, as "even if it was not your fault they do not believe you just because you are Syrian." He related the following incident: "My car was severely damaged by a Lebanese guy while it was in a parking place. He refused to pay me any money. I complained to the police and told them that he had damaged my car. But they did not do anything just because I am Syrian and he is Lebanese. They did not want a Lebanese to pay some money to a Syrian."[39]

Moreover, the army enforced eviction orders on workers. For example, in the wake of fatal attacks on Syrian workers in South Lebanon by an obscure armed group called "Citizens for a Free and Independent Lebanon" in spring 2000, it was reported that "Damascus has ordered Syrian workers to leave a number of villages in South Lebanon."[40] In other words, rather than defend the livelihoods of workers against this kind of violence, strategic considerations induced Damascus to order the workers to leave. There was nothing unofficial about this policy. Moreover, Syrians did *not* flee when the army withdrew in April 2005, as some Lebanese predicted. On the contrary, they fled during February, March, and April, *before* the withdrawal, owing to the hostility that the military presence stirred up in Lebanon. After the withdrawal, it became increasingly safe for Syrians to *return* to Lebanon. In other words, the stigma and hostility that the military presence exacerbated, a stigma of which many workers were acutely aware, was a very serious problem for Syrian workers: It could and did lead to violence and even fatality. The Syrian military presence, then, played an important role, not in protecting workers but in the reproduction of the menial and increasingly insecure labor regime.

RETURNING TO LEBANON

With the Syrians in overall control, the Christian militias disarmed and their isolationist nationalism either abandoned or disempowered, and with the beginnings of economic reconstruction, Syrian migrant workers began to return to Lebanon. Accurate statistics on Syrians in Lebanon are elusive and were a matter of intense controversy in Lebanon from the late 1990s until the Syrian military withdrawal in April 2005. Whereas the Lebanese Minister of Finance, Fu'ad Siniora, estimated in November 2000 that there were 150,000 Syrian workers in Lebanon, the university professor, Bassam al-Hashim, estimated in the same month, in an academic paper delivered to a conference on the issue of Syrian-Lebanese relations, that there were 1.5 million such workers.[41] Respected centers of opinion thus disagreed on the matter by a factor of ten, a powerful measure of how acute the dispute had become.[42]

Numbers

The fact is that neither side had a powerful method for determining how many Syrians there actually were in Lebanon. The statistics on Ministry of Labor work permits were more or less irrelevant because, in practice, Syrian workers rarely obtained them. Comprehensive sampling was difficult, not only because of the sensitivity of the question to the Syrians but also because of the interests of Lebanese employers. For example, when the National Employment Agency undertook a "labor market" study in 1996, fully 97 percent of the enterprises in the sample refused to furnish the exact total of foreign workers they employed.[43] Such were employers' interests—in line with those of the pax Syriana—in keeping such workers out of sight of potential regulators and/or "agitators." Most estimates, therefore, were based on the only set of figures available: the highly problematic General Security statistics on entries into and exits out of Lebanon, totaled by nationality. The basic idea was that the sum of entries minus exits on the land borders would equal the net number of Syrians staying behind in Lebanon.

The most important problem, though, is that these numbers are unreliable. Some Syrians were at times waved in and out of the country by the busload, whether or not they showed their "red cards." Some showed their cards but were not counted. Others gained entry or exit without a red card and were therefore uncounted. Still others came in via military routes used by the army—whether as full-time workers or as soldiers to begin with who then worked during off hours, or as full-time soldiers who worked as part of their military service. And others avoided both border posts and military routes altogether, instead using small routes on the long and winding border, or by special arrangements. In order to avoid paying the Syrian exit tax, many avoided registering exits and reentries, thereby making their stay in Lebanon look continuous. These problems seriously undermine attempts to use the statistics in anything more than an impressionistic way.

But there are further problems. The statistics do not register whether the Syrian is a worker, a student, a tourist, a visitor, a child or nonworking dependent, a businessman, a Syrian resident of Lebanon, or an official, so it is inaccurate by some significant proportion to assume that all entries and exits were accounted for by workers. Moreover, the numbers do not count individual persons, but entries and exits. In other words, if the same person entered and exited the country 12 times in a year, the statistics would show 12 entries and 12 xits, making the global statistics far larger than they would have looked had they counted individuals, and making for some curious statistical results, depending on the methods adopted. Finally, the internal workings of how counting procedures at the border are translated into the numbers published by General Security itself may be subject to a variety of logistical, practical, and political exigencies, about which little is known.

The kinds of inaccuracies and ambiguities inherent in the figures only stoked the controversy. The highest estimates were obtained by simply totaling the number of Syrian entries, subtracting the number of Syrian exits, and positing that the sum remaining equaled the number of Syrian workers in Lebanon. The problem for the opposition was that this exercise produced figures that were improbably high, even by their standards. For example, General Security recorded 9.9 million Syrian entries and only 7.3 million exits from 1991 to 1997, implying that 2.6 million Syrians were left in Lebanon.[44] This number was not plausible to most, in a country where the total population was considered to be about 4 million, and the Lebanese resident workforce about 1.25 million. Thus, the opposition had to find some credible way of reducing the numbers, but not by too much. The main idea was that the entry figures were more reliable than the exit figures, inasmuch as Syrians avoided registering their exit so as to make their stay in Lebanon seem continuous. Economist Michel Murqus, for example, the leading public protagonist of these methods, reckoned on a 40 percent error on exits, so he reduced his mid-1990s estimate from 2.3 million Syrians to 1.4 million Syrians.[45] No real justification was ever produced, however, for this 40 percent margin of error, or in other studies that assumed a 10 percent margin of error on entries and a 30 percent margin of error on exits.[46]

The far lower estimates produced by the defenders of the status quo in Lebanon were dogged by similar problems stemming from the basic unreliability of the statistics, and the problematic nature of the assumptions made to bring down the numbers. A study undertaken in 1998 for the Syrian-Lebanese Supreme Council by demographer Roger Sawaya argued that there were between 110,000 and 253,000 Syrian workers in Lebanon. The study basically involved stronger assumptions about how many times individual workers entered and left the country each year (in this case, 12), how many of the entries and exits were accounted for by tourists, students, shoppers, and Syrian residents (often professionals) in Lebanon, and how inaccurate the exit statistics were.[47] On this basis, the Council study suggested that only 110,085 workers entered Lebanon in 1995, and 99,868 workers entered Lebanon in 1996. Given that most workers were temporary and seasonal, and returned to Syria fairly regularly, these figures were said to give a more accurate picture of how many Syrians were actually working in Lebanon. Even if Roger Sawaya's governing assumptions were less arbitrary, less heroic, and usually justified in more detail than those of Murqus, al-Hashim, and especially Khoury, the idea that workers entered and exited Lebanon 12 times a year on average is generous,[48] while the basic unreliability of the initial data-set could not be transcended.

A more satisfactory attempt to estimate numbers works through drawing together diverse indications from surveys, samples, and educated guesses as to the sectoral distribution of Syrian workers. These judgments seem to have implicitly informed a number of knowledgeable economists, academics, and journalists. Taken together, they estimate totals of workers at 200,000 in 1992, 450,000 to 700,000 in 1995–96, falling to 225,000 to 450,000 by the year 2000.[49] These imperfect estimates, which are only educated guesses, are likely the most convincing figures available. They are broadly consistent, for example, with the results of a sample of 243 enterprises undertaken in 1995 by the Centre de Recherche pour le Développement et la Paix (CRDP), which concluded that 34 percent (or about 700,000) of the total working population of Lebanon in 1995 was foreign.[50] These kinds of figures also pass the test of educated common sense: If it is true, for example, that there were 194,000 businesses of all kinds employing 720,000 workers in Lebanon in 1997, as one credible survey suggested,[51] then it is simply not difficult to imagine—on the basis of many small samples, general observations, and numerous partial indications—that Lebanon employed almost as many Syrian workers at the peak of reconstruction. Likewise, if 724,707 Lebanese workers were employed in sales and services, artisanal and related trades, machine operation and driving, and unskilled labor taken together in 1997, then it is not difficult to imagine similar numbers of Syrians working in Lebanon in these categories overall.[52] Although these estimates are insufficient, they do provide an approximate quantitative guide to Syrian migration to Lebanon. If, by the mid-1990s, Syrians came to comprise roughly one-third of the total workforce (Lebanese and nonLebanese, resident and nonresident) in Lebanon, then these were significant proportions by global standards, although in relative terms broadly comparable to patterns already seen in Lebanon in the boom years of the early 1970s, and rather small proportions compared to some of the Gulf economies.[53]

Unfixing

In spite of toil spanning at least three working lives of Syrians abroad—two before independence and at least one since the 1950s, and in spite of remittances in vast sums so diligently sent home, pressures on livelihoods, land hunger, cash pressures, social expectations, and so on bore down just as heavily on the generation coming to working age in Syria in the late 1980s and early 1990s as it did on their fathers and grandfathers. In fact, these pressures were only becoming more widespread, as, by the 1980s, the needs and wants of the cash economy had incorporated almost every corner of the country, and in larger numbers than ever before, men and increasingly, women felt obliged to leave their home communities for cash. Social networks—brothers, fathers, uncles, friends, and so on—connecting migrants or would-be migrants to jobs, housing, contacts, and so on in Lebanon existed in almost every village and hamlet, from al-Hasaka in the North to Darʻa in the South. Transport to Lebanon remained cheap and convenient, and the border remained open, whereas European, North American, and other borders were increasingly closed. In some senses, pressures were intensified as new needs became more expensive. Whereas tea, coffee, tobacco, sugar, and clothes had been the new consumer goods of the 1950s and 1960s, and white goods, furnishings, and televisions those of the 1970s and 1980s, the 1990s and 2000s saw the advent of computers, satellite dishes, and mobile phones. A period of high economic growth (7 percent a year) in Syria from 1990 to 1995, accompanied by U.S. geopolitical support, Gulf monies, and foreign funds and investments (including French investment by Elf-Aquitaine), amounting to an estimated $8 billion between 1990 and 1995, served to deepen Syria's linkages to the transnational economic system. Yet, the low and even negative growth of the later 1990s exacerbated the forms of dependency so produced. Moreover, the teaching and civil service salaries marking respectable status and assuring a middle-class lifestyle in the 1960s and 1970s were diminishing in relative terms over time, and good quality public health and education was slowly eroded and started to involve certain costs.

A measure of the acute systemic pressure on those seeking livelihoods is an estimate that every year there were 200,000 to 300,000 new entrants to the Syrian labor market, but only around 80,000 new jobs within the Syrian economy.[54] These pressures were primarily economic and political rather than demographic. As I have argued, for demographic growth to translate into outmigratory pressure, a series of political, institutional, and economic conditions must be present. It should be noted, in addition, that contrary to the sometimes loose talk of overpopulation in Syria, the crude birthrate in Syria actually started to fall after 1985 due not only to the higher age of marriage, perhaps in turn a result of growing expenses, but also due to the expansion of family planning programs, as natalist thinking started to be moderated by the 1970s.[55] Economic pressures were compounded not just by the civil war and recession in Lebanon, which forced many Syrian migrants to return, and the fall in the oil price in the early 1980s, but also by the Gulf crisis of 1990–91. It has been estimated that 4 to 5 million Arabs, Kurds, and Asians were displaced and expelled from Iraq and the Gulf between 1989 and 1992,[56] but the number of Syrians in the Gulf may have fallen by just under a half to 110,000 by mid-1992.[57] The acute vulnerability to expulsion of those migrating "against community" was again underlined.

As the migrant generation of the 1960s started to retire and return, their sons and increasingly, daughters, had to begin again the process of finding a livelihood, establishing an independent household, getting married, perhaps buying land, or investing in a taxi or a shop, and then acquiring the forms of housing, health, education, and durable and disposable consumer goods that were rapidly becoming needs and not wants.[58] Some of the older generation continued to work in Lebanon until the 2000s. The same forces driving workers into the labor market in their early teens lengthened working lives. Hanna Butros (1945–), encountered earlier, was a painter from *wadi al-nasara* who started working in Lebanon in 1958. His wife and children returned to Syria in 1971 to cultivate and build on their grandfather's land, while he worked during much of the civil war in Lebanon. The pressures on Butros to continue to provide for his wife and children, and his own desire to work for good money, kept him in Lebanon for much of the 1990s and early 2000s, although he was also taking lower-paid work in Syria by then. He said that he wanted to work in Lebanon "because it is comfortable. I work less . . . and make more money. . . . Moreover, you would find that an architect is responsible for a construction site, you could speak to him. Here, you do not know who is in charge."[59] He recounted a long story about a struggle he had had with a Syrian client who had contracted him to paint his house in Damascus. The client knew the head of the Syrian prisons, and used this connection, in Butros's story, to delay and cut payment and make unreasonable demands. Butros intended the story as an illustration of the difficulties of working in Syria as compared to Lebanon. He maintained that "if I got the chance now I would return. I would not stay here, because [over there] I was feeling comfort and happiness." At this point, his wife, who did not want to be identified by name, interjected: "Over here he is comfortable as well." But her husband went on: "It is not the same over here. I will speak the truth. When I was in Lebanon I did not envy the highest salary in this country. I did not care. People from here shopped in Homs; I dressed my children from Lebanon in the best clothing. That is because I was comfortable. If I did not have the money, where would I get that from? Over here only the thief lives. If one is a thief he will manage, this is it."

Others from the prewar generation were approaching retirement by the time I interviewed them in 2004, while their progeny were looking for ways to earn a livelihood. We encountered Hanna Awwad (1933–) from *wadi al-nasara* fleeing with his family from Karm al-Zeitoun (East Beirut) during the heavy fighting during spring 1976. He worked on and off in the Gulf before returning to Lebanon for work in 1992, traveling back and forth regularly for much of the 1990s, before entering semiretirement in Syria in 2002. By the late 1980s, his son Roger, born in 1968, one of the new postwar generation of Syrian workers in Lebanon, was thinking about how to establish himself independently. We last heard of Roger, who was born in Beirut, cowering under the sofa as a small boy amid mortars and bullets.[60] He had memories of armed Palestinians from Tal al-Zaatar in the area, the snipers, and the escape from the war. He went to school in Syria, completing his studies in 1989, but failed to get the necessary marks for university.[61] There was no opportunity in the second half of the 1980s to go to Lebanon because of the war, and so Roger worked with his father, Hanna Awwad, in the summers in Syria, helping the family as a good son, and learning the tiling trade and earning some pocket money in the process. He did his military service, working in radars in Syria, from 1989 to 1992. But tiling work was no more available in Syria than it had been in the 1960s, and so Roger, now a skilled tiler, went to Lebanon with his father to find work in 1992.

They returned to Karm al-Zeitoun, the scene of the fighting. Awwad had contacts and friends who remembered him there. The atmosphere was tense: "The Syrian was hated in the Christian areas, in Achrafieh [including Karm al-Zeitoun]. . . . The Syrian generally [was hated], they do not discriminate [between Muslim and Christian Syrians]." Roger managed to avoid trouble, however, mostly because "from my accent people would think that I am Lebanese, because I was born there and speak Lebanese, they would not know that I am Syrian." Father and son lived together in a single-room apartment rented for $200 per month from a Christian landlord, a confessional affiliation that mattered amid the "fear and religious discrimination" then and since. Through his father's connections, and by passing as a Lebanese, even for employers who refused to employ Syrians, Roger went to work all over Mt. Lebanon. He mentioned Broummana, Mansourieh, Farayya, 'Ayoun el-Siman, and Souk el-Gharb. He said that working as a skilled tiler—and being in charge of 3 to 5 workers (Syrians who were usually Sunni Muslim who he would pick up for particular jobs from under the bridge at Dawra or the Fu'ad Chehab bridge)— he could earn the significant sum of $800 to $900 in a month. These times of prosperity lasted until the depression of the late 1990s.

A new generation of migrants from poorer backgrounds in other parts of Syria was also appearing. Brief mention was made in Chapter 2 of al-Hajj Ali (1946/7–), from a landless, Syrian Kurdish family of agricultural laborers in the Aleppo region, who went to work in construction for a short period in Lebanon during the construction boom in 1970.[62] His various migrations, and a lifetime of hard work, did not result in enough money by the early 1990s for him to realize his ambition of buying a small plot of land. His nine sons, born from the 1960s to the 1990s, were therefore expected to help, while thinking of how they could themselves become independent (through land acquisition or small business), marry, and raise a family. Ibrahim, born in 1969, was the pioneer. He said his father wanted him to continue with schooling, but his own desire to earn money—forged from the circumstances in which he lived—meant that he preferred to leave school and find work. He wanted, like everyone, he said, to obtain "a home, a car, a family. This is something that you have in Europe when you are young." Ibrahim continued:

> [I would like] a house in the country, which always [in my imagination] has three or four rooms, with a garden, for example. I saw it myself . . . in my imagination. . . . I would put it together in my own way, without an engineer. . . . I would see, for example, a carpenter, and tell him [how to do the work]. . . . I would want to be in charge without an engineer. . . . I would bring people, meaning workers, they would work for me, and I would pay them money.

Ibrahim went first to Jordan in 1987 to work in construction before returning to Syria for military service. He then left for Libya in 1990, staying for a year and a half. He returned to Syria in 1992 "with nothing," having lost all his money thanks to not being paid by unscrupulous Libyan employers who paid out wages in small installments that never amounted to the total agreed. He went home, but needed money, so stayed for only "a week, with no money, no work." "I wanted to travel for a very long time since my childhood. I hear that in Lebanon there's work, [so] I packed my bag and came, I didn't know anyone here at all. I stayed [the first night] with someone I met on the road. . . . I came without knowing anyone. By my own effort."[63]

Ibrahim introduced his younger brother Radwan, born in 1972, who became a friend of mine, to work in the vegetable market in 1994. Radwan came to Lebanon "in order to improve my condition, my life." He was single, had finished his military service (1990 to 1992), and had already worked for two summers during the last years of secondary school in Jordan in 1989 and

1990. After military service, he said, "I started another stage. In order to build a house, in order to marry, I was looking for something better." He was not seeking to come to Lebanon in particular, he assured me, Jordan would have been just as good, but the opportunity to go to Lebanon came up through his brother. His real ambition, never given up, and held from the age of 10, was to become a sports journalist. As a small boy he had supplied his own commentary to football matches, and from the age of 12 was contributing small pieces to readers' letters pages in sports magazines.

Radwan's migration to Lebanon in search of money was neither a mechanical response to abstract pressures, nor a simple product of individualistic ambition. Instead, a complex warp and weft of necessity, social obligation, family values, and an individual work ethic were involved. "When I . . . go back to Syria, they don't say to me, what did you eat, what did you drink? [Instead they ask] how much money did you bring? Yes. The society there [has high expectations]." These pressures, however, were part of a wider set of kinship norms described as "sympathetic" and "caring." "I benefited," said Radwan. "The family, my family, the family of the father [benefited]. We are Easterners. We love the family. We love our fathers and mothers—the opposite of you in Europe. I'm not telling you that everyone [in Europe does this], but . . . when you get to about 18, 19, or 20 years of age, [many Europeans] leave their father and mother, and go. [As for us] we stay [figuratively speaking], we spend on the house and the father and mother, until the end of our lives."[64] Finally, Radwan pointed out that if one gets a chance to work, even if temporarily, one "must seize these opportunities. And we Arabs say to people, God gave us one chance in life. If you benefit from it, you benefit, if you don't benefit, well, peace be on you."

From a similarly poor background and region, and a friend of the family of al-Hajj Ali, Abd al-Qadir, a Sunni Kurd from Tal 'Aran on the plain east of Aleppo, came to Lebanon for the first time in 1989 aged 13.[65] His father had been a construction worker in Aleppo in the 1950s, and then worked in Lebanon for 2 to 4 years pouring cement in the 1960s. The father then had at least one spell working in Saudi Arabia, where he did the Hajj pilgrimage to Mecca, but nonetheless, by the late 1980s, the family was in a "very harsh" financial situation. The pressure on Abd al-Qadir, as with Ibrahim and Radwan, was not simply that he was looking to establish himself independently, or to provide for his brother's education, for example, as we saw with Abu Yussuf who went to Lebanon as a young teenager in the early 1970s. Abd al-Qadir, as he made clear, also felt the need to provide for his mother and father, even at the age of 13. Abd al-Qadir's work was not merely during school holidays—he had to leave school completely. Abd al-Qadir told me in 2004 that his father had for some time been basically inactive, increasing the need for the son to provide. The fact was, Abd al-Qadir explained, "Syrians are unable to make a living [in Syria]," and hence "we want, by necessity, to go, for example, to Cyprus, Libya, Jordan . . . so where ever there is work one has to go and work. We don't necessarily want to come to Lebanon [in particular] . . . [instead] we want to work; wherever there's an opportunity for work, we work, we do it, we work, we do it."

Abd al-Qadir was physically too young to work in cement pouring, or in the Port in loading and unloading, where his father had also worked. But the family had contacts in the wholesale vegetable market next to the Kuwaiti embassy near Sabra, in southern Beirut. Without an identity card of any kind, Abd al-Qadir crossed the border with his father who took him to find work as a porter there. From then on, Abd al-Qadir returned to Lebanon only for short breaks. His father would come every month or two to collect his son's earnings and then return with them to Syria, often leaving Abd al-Qadir behind. "Once," said Abd al-Qadir, in the manner of a convict or conscript, "I spent 11 months and 20 days in a row [in Lebanon]." After starting his own family, he continued to work primarily for his children:

> I hope to give them a good education because education is everything. The most important thing for a child is to be educated. And not to suffer the way I have suffered. I suffered a lot when I was a child. Like I told you I came here when I was 13 or 14 years old. In 1989, I had to work night and day and suffered a lot. I want my children to work in their own business or at a company. I will support them in achieving this.

Omar, a Sunni Arab from near Aleppo, first came to Lebanon to work with the help of his uncle during the summer as a 14-year-old in 1995, while remaining at school. He was earning money to pay for family expenses. His main goal was education.

> This was my aim from the beginning. I always wanted to study, but our condition at home was bad. We are 9 boys and 5 girls, and so had lots of expenses. We needed 5 kilos of rice, a box of potatoes, and a gallon of oil every day. . . . I was the third oldest. There are 2 older than me. We did elementary school

because it was free. But later studies were not. We had to buy our own books and stationery.[66]

The pressure was hardest during 1998 and 1999 when Omar was paying for two brothers' education while working in Lebanon. He completed his Baccalaureate in 1999 and had to choose between university and full-time work. Being too poor for the former, he started working full time in Lebanon for $10 per day at the Coop, continuing to defray family expenses until late 2003. Finally, in 2004 he was able to start saving for himself. He chose to save with a bank account in order to keep the money safe from untrustworthy relatives:

> I am waiting for the amount to be complete, and then I'll open a supermarket in Syria and . . . import the [Lebanese] way of work. Work there is different. . . . People here help the customers in a different way, [in Syria] . . . we don't have the system of credit cards. . . . I need 5 more years. I have already done 2 and in total I need 7 or 7½. God willing I will get the supermarket ready and send my applications to the different businessmen for them to give me quotas. And most importantly I will have exemplary workers who know how to treat customers properly. I learned in Beirut that when a woman is having problems getting her stuff, workers would come to her and help her out. In Syria this would not happen. In Beirut you could easily talk to strangers.[67]

RECONSTRUCTION

The neoliberal economic thinking behind the reconstruction of Lebanon in the context of the pax Syriana and the wider post-Soviet, U.S.-based global economy demanded that Lebanon, in order to attract investment, needed a "state-of-the-art physical infrastructure," and at least an "acceptable social infrastructure." The physical infrastructure not only took priority in quality but also in timing, and in fact, by the mid-1990s, when the government turned its attention to the social infrastructure—housing, education, and the like—a yawning budget deficit prevented the execution of even the merely adequate projects that had been planned. After the infrastructure was completed, it was hoped, investment and economic growth would create budget surpluses to pay for almost half the cost of reconstruction. The government paid hundreds of millions of dollars to European multinationals such as Siemens, Ansaldo, and Bouygues for electricity and telephone networks, marine defenses, the airport, and so on.[68] The government raised soft loans from the international community, funds from Arab investment and development banks, and costly loans from Lebanese banks, in the form of T-bills to be paid back at a yearly interest rate of 20 to 40 percent. In practice, foreign multinationals often contracted work back to local companies at cheaper rates.[69]

Political security and reconstruction underpinned a return to macroeconomic stability and economic growth in Lebanon. The Lebanese pound was tied to the dollar. Inflation came under control. Important sections of the local and international business community declared that policies on interest rates and taxation were responsible. Some Gulf money flowed toward Lebanon, especially in association with tourism, hotels, entertainment, and real estate. Some Lebanese capital and entrepreneurs abroad returned to the country. Local bankers made money from T-bills and high-end real estate boomed. Reconstruction projects directly created tens of thousands of jobs. Syrians made up much of the basic labor of Lebanese reconstruction, and their numbers rose through the mid-1990s, before falling again in line with economic growth and the intensity of reconstruction.[70] The rebuilding of the Beirut Sports City alone by Kvaerner for $60 million employed at its peak a small army of 1,600 Syrians as "basic labor."[71] Thousands of other Syrians were employed in other projects: building roads between Sidon and Tripoli, and in Beirut (around downtown, the airport road, the southern suburbs, and the Beirut circular); constructing four major electricity plants, the electricity network, pylons and substations; rebuilding most of the piped drinking-water network in Beirut; constructing a water sanitation plant in Dubayya; rebuilding and expanding the Beirut international airport; (re)constructing a series of major hotels in Beirut; and extensive rebuilding of housing destroyed during the war.[72]

Many jobs offering earnings sufficient to attract Syrians were newly available in Lebanon. In Khoury's sample, 96.5 percent of Syrians said that salaries were better in Lebanon than in Syria, and for 94 percent of respondents this was the main reason for coming to Lebanon.[73] Khoury estimated that incomes in Lebanon were three to four times what Syrians could expect to earn in Syria.[74] Wages and incomes varied greatly, but the majority of Khoury's workers were paid $7 to $13 a day.[75] The poorest—those earning $4 to $6 a day—were female agricultural workers in the Biqa', working in teams brought over by contractors, and living in huts in the fields during the harvest season. Newly arrived, young male building workers also earned as little as $6 a day. Rubbish collectors, street sweepers, more established construction and male agricultural workers often earned daily amounts from $7 to $10. Ambulant sellers often did better, according to Khoury's research, making $10 to $13 a day. Taxi-drivers could make up to $20 a day.[76]

Occupations

In large-scale reconstruction projects and beyond, Syrian migrants mostly worked in four kinds of jobs in Lebanon.[77] First, they worked primarily in unskilled labor. Syrians were and remain day laborers, pickers and harvesters, both male and female, in agriculture. They are employed extensively as basic labor in construction (cement pouring, heavy carrying, excavating), road building,[78] and in quarries.[79] One 1990s estimate claims that 75 percent of building workers were Syrian.[80] They also provide the majority of Lebanon's unskilled services, outside of domestic labor, where south and east Asian labor predominates. Syrians work as ambulant fruit, vegetable, food, water, lottery-ticket, and other sellers; as porters (in warehouses, wholesale markets, docks, and elsewhere), as packers and baggers in supermarkets and groceries; as delivery boys and errand runners; as street sweepers and rubbish collectors; as dish-washers in hotels; and as doormen and guards in apartment buildings, offices, and elsewhere.[81] Syrian workers were widely employed by al-Hariri's companies, including the major waste-collecting company, Sukleen.

Second, Syrians labored as plant and machine operators, assemblers, and drivers in the direction and control of machinery and vehicles. They worked as digger operators in road building; as mechanics; in car-servicing and repair; as truck, bus, and taxi-drivers; as private drivers; as certain kinds of machine operators on construction sites; and so on.[82] A Lebanese union source estimated in 1996 that there were as many as 12,000 Syrian taxi-drivers in Lebanon.[83]

Third, Syrians worked in numbers as service workers and shop and market sales workers. They were waiters, shawarma makers, all kinds of sandwich and kebab makers, coffee makers, chefs, assistant chefs, juice makers, arguileh workers, and small shopkeepers (clothes, cheap electrics, and so on), or those with more responsible positions in shops or restaurants. Syrian secondhand clothing sellers, for example, appeared in the slum area of Hayy al-Sillum in the mid-1990s when Syrian import restrictions on clothes from the United States and Germany were increased.[84]

Finally, Syrians worked, although in lesser numbers, in crafts and related trades in more skilled positions in the direct production and transformation of durable and consumer goods. Here, they were mostly skilled workers in

(1) construction and related trades (stone-cutters, carpenters, roofers, tilers, glaziers, electricians, plumbers, plasterers, painters, furniture makers, upholsterers); (2) metalwork and mechanics (metalworkers, lathers, key-makers, mechanics of various kinds); (3) food (butchers, bakers, and patisserie-makers); and (4) garment-making (tailors, dressmakers, shoemakers, and so on). One source from the mid-1990s estimated that 90 percent of bakers were Syrian.[85] Syrian butchers and meat sellers were certainly noted in Sabra.[86] There is much anecdotal evidence to suggest that the Syrian presence in these trades was diversifying.[87] Stone masons, for example, were increasingly in demand among the war-rich, building large villas with pools, balconies, and so on.[88]

The Division of Labor

Syrians sold services and wares or found employment in Lebanon not because they were a perfect structural complement to the Lebanese economy that simply lacked unskilled labor, or because the Lebanese refused low-status jobs. This view eviscerates the operations of power, forms of state regulation, social interests, and economic disciplines at work in the migratory regime. Syrians found work because they were cheaper and more manipulable than their Lebanese counterparts. The big employers surveyed by Oweijane Khoury in her doctoral research were practically unanimous in their assertions that they employed Syrians because they were cheaper and caused fewer problems than their higher-waged, less hard-working, more regulated, and more assertive and collectively organized Lebanese counterparts.[89]

Among medium-sized and small employers, the picture was no different. Sami Harb, a Beiruti architect and engineer who has built seven or eight apartment buildings and similar construction projects since the 1970s, has always employed Syrians as unskilled labor on site because they were easily available in quantity, could be taken on and dropped at will, and "they accept conditions that the Lebanese do not accept. In Lebanon there is a minimum salary, it is well known . . . [and] the Lebanese do not want to work below this figure, so one takes Syrians, who . . . are known for their hard work and motivation." Moreover, regulations were minimal: Project managers did not have to list or record any details about such workers, or provide them with social security. Site insurance insured workers for injuries and death, but it was in fact optional whether this coverage extended to Syrian workers.[90] As Abu Subhi, a Lebanese Sunni shopkeeper and employer of five or six Syrians in Beirut (including Abd al-Qadir) put it, "We work Sunday—seven days a week—without stopping—therefore I want a worker who is willing to sacrifice himself."[91] Employers large and small overwhelmingly preferred Syrians and foreigners because they could be paid lower wages, worked harder, were more obedient for longer hours, and could be fired at any moment.[92]

In this political economy, recession and low profitability did not always throw Syrians out of work. On the contrary, such conditions put employers under stronger pressure to find the cheapest labor possible. This could mean Syrian workers were hired and Lebanese workers were fired. It was said that this trend was particularly marked in manufacturing in the late 1990s and early 2000s, where clothes, tiles, metalwork, and furnishings businesses, for example, were suffering higher utility costs (especially electricity), lower domestic demand, and some lower customs duties as Lebanon's market was opened somewhat to foreign competition.[93] Certainly this substitution was observed in the garment-making industry by a case study conducted by Fadi Bardawil at American University in Beirut (AUB).[94] Similarly, where monopolies, middlemen, high input costs, and lack of state protection for growers drove up costs and hit profits for often indebted small growers, heavy pressures continued to be exerted in agriculture to employ Syrian workers, especially women, who were the cheapest available labor.[95] Women came seasonally in labor gangs under a contractor from the age of 15 to farms in the Biqa' to do the tedious, repetitive work of weeding, and of harvesting fruits and potatoes for $4 to $5 a day. They lived in shacks on the farm or built tents themselves out of canvas bags.[96]

Because the indirect control of combined and uneven capitalism is an unfinished business, and it combines with direct forms of control, employers were interested not only in low wage rates but also the qualities Syrians reputedly had. Syrians are "known" to be docile, hard-working, and ready to follow orders. Such characterizations are overwhelmingly given as reasons for hiring them. Syrians are also said to be uneducated and "backward" or "rural," qualities that further denote—in employers' eyes—their resilience, naïveté, and exploitability. Syrian workers hold regional, sectarian, or ethnic identities that supposedly render them ready for hard work and exploitation. Syrian Kurds, in particular, were reputed by some to be tough and indefatigable workers, their racial stock and minority status in Syria purportedly endowing them with strong constitutions and formidable stamina. Or, one middle-class professional told me that her sister still hired Syrian Druze for domestic work, known "to be honest and sincere" being from "how can I say it? A primitive kind of area."[97] As young males, moreover, workers are commonly seen as capable of looking after themselves, and suited to hard and strenuous labor.

Others are thought to be suited to monotonous or menial tasks because of their provincial provenance. Omar shed light on these Lebanese attitudes:

> If a Lebanese asks me [who I am], I tell him I am a Syrian from the city of Aleppo and not from the outskirts. . . . [This is] because the Lebanese have a weird way of looking at people coming from the rural areas of Syria. It's as if they see people from the Hawran. When a worker does something wrong they say, "You Hawrani!" Its always a Hawrani when thing go wrong.[98]

The attribution Hawrani thus stood in for a range of "rural" and "backward" characteristics that served to designate persons as fit for certain kinds of labor.

The Lebanese, in contrast, are said to be different. They are known to refuse hard work, to sit behind computers, to work in offices, and to be unused to hard, manual labor. They would not accept, it is said, the kinds of wages paid to Syrians.[99] As Abu Subhi declared roundly:

> All of the Lebanese they want to work as Prime Minister, or President of the Republic! . . . The Lebanese are liars. . . . They say there is no work, but there is plenty of work. There's plenty of work. But you've got to want to work, you've got to want to work. You want to play games! . . . This one [here he points at one of his Syrian employees] works here for ten or eleven hours [a day]. The labor law requires, for example, that he [a Lebanese worker] works for eight hours. The Lebanese will say, 'Oh! Eight hours. I'm done!'

Palestinians are regarded as something else again: One commonly hears that they are proud and refuse dirty or degrading work. In these ways, then, Syrian nationals are culturally constituted as those who may be commodified. The indirect controls of exploitation work through these qualitative particularisms.

These ascriptions can change, of course, and they cut both ways. Prior to the 1970s, female Syrian Alawis were widely employed as domestic servants in Lebanese households. They were seen as poor, rural, hard-working, "primitive," and undemanding. But with the sect's ascendancy in Syria, accompanying the rise to the presidency of the Alawi Hafez al-Asad, their status was raised, and such employment almost completely disappeared. Domestic maids now come predominantly from Sri Lanka and the Far East.[100] Finally, certain

Syrians, such as the Dom—gypsy-like groups who often work as unofficial dentists in the Biqa' valley—are stereotyped as being unreliable, lazy, and unfit for hard, manual labor, and therefore are not sought out as menial labor by employers.[101]

Employers' attitudes and practices are informed by other cultural materials. Indeed, beyond the seemingly endless focus of cultural studies on identity, the "savage god" of free-market "theology" also plays an important role.[102] The notion that the free operation of market forces was an unalloyed good with regard to the labor market was strikingly dominant in public discourse at large in Lebanon. This orthodoxy had a formidable genealogy. Ottoman reformers and French colonial discourse had long before written the peoples of the historic *bilad ash-sham* into a language of the *mise en valeur* of territory, population, and human and natural resources. Lebanese laissez-faire and Syrian statist developmentalism alike adopted this colonial legacy. From the 1970s, the language of market economy, and the identification of migrants as "manpower," "resources," and "labor supply" was heavily reinforced by the oil boom and the ways the World Bank and other institutions tended to monopolize the representation of migration to and within the Middle East in academic and policy-making circles.[103] Those with the authority to speak on the economy in Lebanon, who headed powerful institutions and whose policy prescriptions were adopted by a state that consulted them not solely on a whim but as a matter of institutionalized practice and law, were economists trained in the neoclassical and monetarist tradition in the United States and Europe.[104] The reduction of social subjects to menial "manpower" worked not just by chauvinistic stereotypes diminishing complex persons to essentialist caricatures of the "backward" or the "rural" but also through imagining such persons as the commodity labor-power sold supposedly as a matter of choice and contract. Whether or not these different kinds of reductionism produced each other in general terms, they certainly work together to produce and specify those who were to be subject to the disciplines of commodification. Such disciplines, in this case, were therefore a double effect of the particularism of identity and quality on the one hand, and the supposed universalism of free-market principles on the other.

MENIAL LABOR

Syrians in Lebanon both suffered and flung themselves into a menial labor regime involving low pay, long hours, hard labor, insecurity, and poor conditions.

The 84-hour weeks worked in double shifts by Ibrahim as a street sweeper for a large company (Ogero) when he first arrived in Lebanon in 1992 were nothing unusual. He worked two shifts a day, 5 a.m. to 11 a.m. and 5 p.m. to 11 p.m., seven days a week.[105] Abd al-Qadir eventually obtained a responsible job at the till in Abu Subhi's grocery in Ra's al-Nab'a, Beirut. Between 1999 and the present, he has worked 14- or 15-hour shifts. He typically arrives at 7 a.m. and works until 9.30 p.m., Monday through Friday. Saturday is a half-day, and the Sunday shift lasts from 9 a.m. until 9.30 p.m. He usually gets a two-hour break at some point in the afternoon, although not when the shop is busy.[106] At festivals and at certain other times, however, Abd al-Qadir is allowed to take a few days off to see his family. In other words, Abd al-Qadir, whose hours are not unusual, is at work 90 hours a week 6½ days a week, while breaks and holidays are insecure. His wages are less than $1 per hour, in a country where utility bills and other costs often rival those of OECD countries.[107] As he tells me, "I don't want to return to Syria to do what I do here. I would like to rest a bit. Have you noticed that it's been two years and I'm still thin? I can't even eat during meal times because I have so much work. . . . I keep saying to myself I will finish with this customer and then eat."[108]

Others worked longer hours, or in dirtier, less responsible, and less secure jobs. I interviewed a Syrian from the Aleppo region who rented a small shop in Saida selling cheap electrical goods, and who worked over 100 hours a week as a norm. He stated that he worked from around 7 a.m. to 10 p.m. "Every day?" I asked. "Yes," he responded. "Seven days?" "Yes. Eight days. I don't take holidays. No Saturday, no Sunday, no Friday. I don't close at all." "Is that difficult?" I asked. "[It's] normal," came the response.[109] Even Muhammad's 105 hours a week looked relatively straightforward compared to Radwan's sleep-destroying double shifts. From 1994 to 2000, Radwan worked in bagging and packing in supermarkets for 17 hours a day, seven days a week (119 hours a week), with only a few holidays. He chose to work double shifts at the supermarket, 1 a.m. to 7 a.m., then 11 a.m. until 10 p.m. "In 24 hours I sleep 6 hours," he told me. He eventually switched to a shorter 7 a.m. to 3 p.m. shift: "Why? Because I was tired. Had I carried on doing evening hours, you wouldn't have found me. I'd have gone back to Syria long ago."[110]

Work hours in construction and agriculture were shorter. Here, 10 hours a day was common—but the work is generally more intensive, dirtier, and more exhausting than in retail and services. Workers also had to work harder as deadlines loomed. Such working conditions, which included sleeping on the construction site, had exhausted and almost broken Adib Mahrus. As he explained phlegmatically: "I worked a lot, and tired myself out. Because of that I stopped. For two years I did nothing, and lived off my savings." In the end, Adib Mahrus managed to start earning again by obtaining lighter work as a concierge. Such "light" work involved being on call 24 hours a day, seven days a week.

Furthermore, Syrian laborers have few social protections. In Khoury's sample of Syrian workers, 84.5 percent were not protected by contract. More than 90 percent had no social security and no end-of-service compensation. Around 50 percent reported no work insurance at all, and 25 percent felt that their employers could fire them arbitrarily.[111] Indeed, in 20 years working in semi-skilled construction work in Beirut, Adib Mahrus never saw a written contract.[112] Terms of employment, if they are discussed at all, are set verbally at the outset. Social insurance is out of the question. And, if the contractor or employer tells you that "whatever happens you are responsible for yourself," then you know there is to be no accident compensation.[113] Those working by the day are usually entirely unprotected as casual labor, and Lebanese labor law is not seen to be applicable.[114] Workers have to be willing to forgo basic safety standards, such as hard hats on construction sites.[115] Adib Mahrus gave me an example in which two construction workers died after a fall resulting from a defective lift. The employer paid death compensation of $5,000, whereas Adib Mahrus thought the minimum should have been $25,000. Moreover, when working on illegal construction, common in slum areas, such as Hayy al-Sillum, workers have no legal recourse.[116] I asked Armange, who worked in both radiography and decorating, if employers offered him accident insurance. He replied, "No. And we don't even ask. We don't know [whether we're insured]. You know, when we look for a job, we don't care about insurance. All we care about is [getting] the work. . . . Because of necessity. If we asked . . . [about insurance], the employer would say, are you here to work or to flirt? So we don't ask."[117] Norms of manliness, in other words, are here part of the substance of labor discipline. Armange related an accident, while decorating, in which he and his co-worker fell six feet because of a broken ladder. His colleague broke his leg. The employer paid no insurance and no indemnity, and the co-worker had to return to Syria for treatment. "Where was the employer?" I asked. Radwan quipped, "He was with his wife!"[118]

Syrian laborers are hired and fired at will. Abu Subhi explained, for example, the secret honesty tests he gave employees. He would leave small sums of money on the floor, or arrange to have a customer give a certain tip to the worker. If the worker did not return the money found on the floor, or declare the tip, Abu Subhi would fire him on the spot. "Allah Ma'ak!" ["Goodbye!"] he declared. I asked him how many times he had done this from his mini-market employing five or six workers: "Five times or ten times, more than. Yesterday I sent away . . . one." Further, "everyone who doesn't behave properly with customers: bye bye!"[119] Armange had been fired from his work in a clinic after threatening to quit in search of a pay rise. Nazir, a brother of Radwan, had been fired, "just like that," from Abu Subhi's shop.

Menial workers are expected to perform a striking variety of tasks. As a concierge for an apartment building in Hamra, Abed, in his twenties, and who came to Lebanon for the first time in the 1990s and had also worked in construction, had to be on hand for virtually whatever the Asif family—who owned the building—wanted him for.[120] This meant not only numerous dirty and manual tasks around the building, unblocking sinks and toilets, carrying bags and gas cannisters, parking cars, removing rubbish, shining shoes, and so on, even in the middle of the night, but also delivery for the sandwich shop that was on the ground floor of the building.

This labor regime stretches working lives, shortens childhood, retirement, periods of downtime, sickness, holiday, and unemployment, and thus diminishes maintenance time (in the language of social costs theory). Combinations of cost, motivation, and employer control also reduce the quantity and quality of "renewal time," periods of rest during the day, in the evening, and on weekends. Abed, for example, pointed out that after a 10- or 12-hour shift on the construction site:

we cook here at home and go to bed. We have no spare time so we don't go out to coffeehouses or elsewhere. We cook at home. This is much, much cheaper. Sandwiches would be much more expensive—especially because being so hungry I would eat about four. We can buy chickens for good prices and cook them ourselves.

This is perfectly natural, Abed explained, given that "we don't have our mothers or sisters around." He added, "When I am working as a concierge I also cannot go to coffeehouses and the like, because Asif or the Hajj might want me for something." Moreover, when I arrived, Abed was cutting the hair of a co-worker, and simultaneously, "renewal" costs. Adib Mahrus did not "go out" in Lebanon either. "I cook in the house. There's no possibility of going out to coffeehouses or restaurants or the like. Definitely [I cook] in the house. . . . I don't go out. I'm committed to this work."[121] One Lebanese academic told me about her grandmother's 20-year-old Syrian maid, employed because the grandmother preferred a Muslim to a Sri Lankan. The maid was said not to be "treated like a human being. . . . She is not allowed to be tired, and not allowed to have a date."[122]

The quality of renewal time is reduced further because in order to cut housing costs, Syrians live in huts and shacks in the fields where they work, on construction sites, at the backs of shops, in the basements or outhouses of apartment blocks, in exceedingly cheap hotels, or in dilapidated rooms in urban slums. Rents are cut by having 6 or 10 workers share a room. Heating and cooling costs are cut by not having heaters or air-conditioners. Health costs are cut by not going to the doctor, or by returning to Syria, where treatment is largely free. "We can't go to the hospital and pay $2,000 or $3,000 for a cure. So, many of our friends who get ill—if an accident happened or something like that—we put them in a service taxi and [go] to Syria."[123] Renewal time was especially vulnerable to depredation as employers felt that they owned not just the labor power of the employee, but their person too, regardless of the niceties of law. The French sociologist, Franck Mermier, for example, reported that a wealthy Lebanese housewife said, without embarrassment, of a Syrian Alawi maid she had hired: "We bought her."[124] Domestic workers and concierges were particularly vulnerable to being on call around the clock.

Labor Discipline

Crucial to this menial labor regime is the self-activation of workers in seeking out employment, expending energy on the job, obeying commands, delivering goods and services, cultivating good relations with employers in the face of direct controls, seeking to develop their skills in the face of indirect controls, and disciplining their manners, speech, bodily movements, costs, and time, while avoiding the temptations of alcohol, women, and gambling, and keeping their heads down in terms of residence, social space, and wider political and cultural issues. These apparently self-imposed disciplines certainly by no means all depend narrowly on fear and coercion, or the "whip of hunger." Nonetheless, they are necessary techniques and tactics for securing hopes and goals and negotiating the exigencies of a hierarchical system riddled with direct and indirect forms of control, and they are activated by the ways in which exertions can result in local gains.

Abd al-Qadir exemplifies some of the survival strategies associated with worker self-discipline. He cultivates good relations with his employer. He is his right-hand man. As one patron mentioned, "You might mistake him for the owner's son," as Abu Subhi allows him to man the till and leaves him in charge of the shop for hours on end.[125] Through the self-discipline necessary to obtain trust, Abd al-Qadir was therefore able to make gains which, while small to those looking in from outside, were substantial in terms of the many fine gradations within which Syrians perforce worked. "Perhaps you've noticed," Abd al-Qadir told me, "that here's a Syrian working in a [responsible position] in a Lebanese shop. My position is very good compared to the other Syrians here. Why? Because Abu Subhi is a man who spends much on me and he likes me, and I do the same in return. . . . Other friends of mine who are Syrian, they don't get treated like I get treated. . . . [Other employers] treat them worse and tire them out more." "This man [Abu Subhi] has a good heart. . . . He can get angry sometimes, but he soon calms down."[126] Abd al-Qadir refused to accept tea or soda from Abu Subhi (something I witnessed on several occasions), and always paid for whatever he consumed from the shop. With Abu Subhi within earshot, I ask Abd al-Qadir, "Do you take holidays?" He replies, "No, no. I don't want holidays. Here is my work." He repeats that he gets Saturday afternoons off.[127] The model employee, it seems, it supposed to say that he does not want holidays, even in the context of 90-hour work weeks. This model, Abd al-Qadir faithfully fulfils. Forms of self-discipline were written into Abd al-Qadir's body language: While in the shop he was a model of the quiet, industrious worker, he spoke quietly, his eyes returned to the floor, and his shoulders were slightly forward. At home, however, or with friends, the difference was striking: His voice rose, his chin came up, his shoulders went back, and his physical presence appeared more commanding.

Abd al-Qadir had adopted, consciously or not, similar ways of being with a previous, Christian employer in the hostile environment of Bikfaya in Mt. Lebanon, in the early 1990s shortly after the cessation of armed hostilities. He established excellent, filial relations with his employer, who was said to be "very, very good and he loved me, and trusted me like his son."[128] As for the wider environment:

There were [problems], a little. . . . They say, for example, be afraid, be afraid, but we were not scared. We say that when a person's time has come, he will die wherever he is. Death can come at any time. So I worked without fear—that was normal. But . . . my family said to me, "My son, don't go there, don't work in that place." perhaps there are [militant] Christians or [militant] Islam. I said to them, "I don't have a problem myself. I work."[129]

Abd al-Qadir kept his head down, established a quasi-filial form of trust with his employer, and did little else but work, and in this way managed to secure his main objective: cash.

In other instances, Syrian workers were actually working for their fathers, such as Ayman, who worked in a small shop in Saida with his father, Muhammad (who we encountered earlier working "eight days"). Such relations undoubtedly acted as a formidable disciplinary mechanism. I asked Ayman how he found his work, within earshot of his father: "Me? What can I think about it when I work with my father. How does someone work with their father? Of course, truthfully, faithfully, trustworthily, right? A son wants his father's work to improve."[130] Here, actual kinship relations were the nexus through which the controls of menial labor were secured. Ayman also underscored the importance of personal effort, initiative, and responsibility: "If I had the opportunity to work on a farm I would. If I had the opportunity to work in transport—taxi [driving]—I would too. . . . A person must try hard to insure his future."[131]

Since workers could be fired at any time, one tactic was to develop the disciplines of honesty and rectitude. Workers refrained from talking back, kept their heads down, tried to be scrupulously honest, and followed orders. Ibrahim explained how he attracted, through his honesty, the attention of a shopkeeper who used to visit the wholesale market, which then landed him a job. "He [the shopkeeper] came to the market to buy. I carried his things. . . . He saw me . . . [working] well. . . . There were boxes with cherries, apples, and such. There are some who carry and eat. I didn't eat. For example, if I want a cherry, I pay for it." On the strength of this, it was said, the shopkeeper offered Ibrahim a more established job in a shop.[132] Such practices were not only pragmatic, but sanctioned by religion and honor. As Radwan said, "We love life and living with honor. . . . If my brother had wanted to obtain money illegally, then today he could be at a very high level, but he knows God well and he is trustworthy in his work."[133]

Keeping one's head down in the face of direct forms of control could also mean evincing "no opinion" on wider political and cultural questions. Khoury's doctoral research involved a questionnaire asking Syrian workers about their experience in Lebanon. Many workers reported no problems whatsoever.[134] As Muhammad told me a little hastily, "Everything is good, everything is good. Nothing is bad. . . . Everything I have [experienced]: the people, the way they treat you. Everything. Everything is good here."[135] In this way my informant attempted to shut down further discussion of this sensitive topic. Certainly a plethora of tactics aims at social invisibility and acceptance. Ambulant sellers often display the Lebanese flag as a kind of protection against Lebanese hostility. On the corniche such flags could be dated from serious incidents. Above all, fresh flags appeared in great quantities after the assassination of al-Hariri, widely blamed on Syria. Other vendors insist that their products are not from Syria but made in Lebanon.[136] Others change their accents, clothes, and manners in order to appear Lebanese. "How are your relations with the Lebanese?" I asked Armange. "Lots of Lebanese don't know that I'm Syrian . . . from my looks."[137] In a service-taxi with Radwan, he nudged me to prevent my telling the Lebanese service-driver that he was Syrian. He did not want to generate any problems. Syrians pick up local fashions in clothes and their accents are unobtrusive or accepted.[138] Radwan insists that he tries not to cause trouble: "I have been here since '94. Until today I have not gone to the police, I have not done anything wrong. [I go] from work to home and from work to home."[139] According to Armange, "We're here for subsistence, not for politics."[140] "What can I do?" asked Jo Farah, in the face of discrimination. "I cannot change the Lebanese. What I care about is to work and earn money. I do not care about the way they think of us. If they talk about us in that negative way, it does not mean that I am inferior to them. . . . Even a 5-year-old boy will tell you that we do not want the Syrians in Lebanon. Of course he is repeating what he hears from his parents."[141]

Others found ways to make gains with the finely differentiated system. Salim al-Dahash, a concierge who started out in the 1970s as a construction worker, said, "You must come and learn a skill, whether in painting, paving, carpentry, or in plastering." These skills could enable those operating amid forms of indirect control to improve their position. Nonetheless, such learning occurred in the context of direct control also: "Even if there are personal problems between you and the employer," al-Dahash continued, "you have to keep quiet and learn a skill." He had learned to excavate foundations using compressor machines and small explosives, thus increasing his earnings.[142] Small gains provided reasons for self-discipline. Jo Farah, a Maronite from Tartus, told me that he worked so hard—14 hours a day—as a worker in gypsum and decoration on $10 a day to gain skills and thereby raise his earnings closer to $20 per day.[143] Others reckoned that workers could and should learn ways to hold on to their dignity and thus improve their positions in the face of overbearing employers. Omar, who worked in cigarette selling all over the wholesale market as a teenager, observed this "ugly image" and learned from what he saw:

> Some [workers] were well treated and some were humiliated. Some of them had nothing to do and others were carrying out very tough jobs. . . . You have to learn the viewpoint of your employer. You have to know how to keep your dignity. Some people from Hawran [for example], come to the employer and tell him we will do anything for you. But this is wrong. The employer will then pressure them and insult them. I say, "I will work for you but I have conditions. . . ." I didn't understand why they accepted being treated this way. They even worked in gambling, and they even worked for people who drink [on the job]. That is not good. Once I saw an employer hitting his Syrian worker while he [the employer] was drunk. He was kicking him. It is also the worker's fault [for telling] him "I will do anything for you." This is wrong. Workers should know how to ask, and know their rights.[144]

According to Omar, such tactics could mean important gains. "In my first summer," he said, "I saw the difference between those who did ask for their rights and those who did not. Some people ask for $400 [per month], for a 5 p.m. finish, and for breakfasts!"

Michael Burawoy's study of the labor process argued for the importance of the "manufacture of consent" at the point of production. Such consent, in Burawoy's account, operates through the sorts of games set by employers under monopoly capitalism in which through piece work and competition, individual workers became intensely interested in expending energy in increasing their individual earnings and outdoing their co-workers.[145] Consent sprang from the larger structure of the factory, established by employers according to a deliberate plan. The labor disciplines evident among Syrian workers, by contrast, only a minority of whom were factory workers, sprang not from a factory structure designed by employers, but from larger sets of differences in which they were enmeshed. Processes of capital accumulation and the extension of market relations did not divide the workforce into a clearly defined wage-labor proletariat on the one side, and a homogeneous bourgeoisie on the other, or into fundamental classes (bourgeoisie and proletariat) on the one side, and subaltern social groups (peasantry, lumpen proletariat, petty bourgeoisie, and floating population) on the other. Instead, the structure of accumulation involved a differentiating field of small gains, and was riddled with many fine gradations of status. Energies were activated in attempts to make small gains, and to cross and overcome the finally graded and layered status differences produced within the system.

Justification

Workers were highly capable of justifying their positions and roles. Certainly Syrians did not in any simple sense internalize negative stereotypes about them. They knew about, and were able to articulate, many a narrative of self-worth, and they were able to draw on discursive resources—from Arabism, to free-market economics and beyond—depicting their labor in a positive light and defending their positions in Lebanon.

Just as the free-market for labor had been conceived in terms of Arabism, Syrian workers in turn grew great strength from Arabism in justifying their movement from Syria to Lebanon. Arabs are one people, it was said, with a common history, and borders between states were artificial, colonial creations. Radwan puts it eloquently: "Before the [colonial] division, Syria and Lebanon were the *bilad as-sham*. . . . Our ancestors came to Lebanon, for example, during a particular season, and then in another season went to Syria, or Iraq, or Palestine. They were going for trade to Palestine, to Lebanon, or Syria, and there were no problems and no borders." Nowadays, there has to be a "special law allowing the movement of Syrians to Lebanon. I am against the [need] for this to exist."[146] Look, a Syrian taxi-driver, told me, "All the Arabs are one. It's been that way for ages. The borders that have been created between the Arab states and between Syria and Lebanon are artificial."[147] Said another, more bluntly, "Syrians have the right to be here! Work or no work. They have a right to be here. This is one country!"[148] Such Arabism claims deep historical roots. Radwan said, "If you go back to history, you find that Syrian work has been present in Lebanon since the distant past. . . . President Hariri says, 'When I was a student I went to the Arab University, and there were Syrians working in construction.'"[149] Radwan goes on: "We and the Lebanese are a complete circle whether we like it or not."[150] Workers also assert that their presence is legal. "We enter [the country] according to regulations . . . and no one can tell us that [we] are [illegal]; no one can question us about our presence. We have the 'card' and we have official entry [permits]."[151]

Syrian workers also articulated the liberal economics so important in the design of the free labor market of the pax Syriana, and familiar in the stories of Lebanese employers. Syrian workers hence claim that their work does not so much compete with that of the Lebanese, but efficiently fills an economic gap. Salim al-Dahash told me that "Syrians are distinctive for their labor, particularly in construction. The Lebanese are simply not accustomed to this kind of heavy labor, they don't want to do it. They want to sit in offices, in banks, to work with computers. They can't carry heavy things on their shoulders, or work with their hands."[152] Radwan makes the same point: "There are many kinds of jobs that the Lebanese do not undertake—they are not able to undertake them. The Lebanese don't work in cleaning, in Sukleen, in the vegetable market."[153] He also tells me, appropriating the language of mutuality and exchange, that "even now, there are Lebanese who go from here to work over there. Now in 2004, when we're living, there are Lebanese who work in Syria in the communications sector and in the dam building sector, on roads. This means that there are processes of exchange [between Syria and Lebanon]."[154] The mutuality works out well, it is said, because "Syrian people are well-known for their skills. They are very talented in the work that they do, meaning that when they build, they build in a good way; when they work, they work in a good way."[155]

Syrian workers have an armory of further notions responding to wider opprobrium in Lebanon. Radwan told me that Syrian's work was not shameful, as even the Lebanese do exactly the same when they go abroad, something which made their superior attitude incomprehensible.[156] Others depicted the role of the Syrian military in Lebanon as positive and well intentioned. One Alawi small-holder from Homs, who was deployed as a soldier in Lebanon as well as working there in construction and tourism from the 1970s until the present, told me that Syria's role in Lebanon during the civil war was to "keep Muslims and Christians from killing each other." He argued that "we did the impossible and unified the country—with 15,000 martyrs and 40,000 soldiers," something for which the Lebanese were grateful.[157] In a less strident vein, Radwan related, "I know many Syrian soldiers and relatives who died and sacrificed themselves for the sake of Lebanon. They died for the sake of the Lebanese when Israel invaded." It was true that the Syrians had been sympathetic to the Lebanese, Radwan argued, for "there was a song by Julia Butros, a Lebanese singer: [starts to sing] 'The sun of justice has gone, The dawn of deception has come. . . .' This song broke records. It was a great success in

Syria, and was very popular. Why? Because we were sympathetic to the Lebanese!" Moreover, the Syrians made other sacrifices for the Lebanese during the civil war: "While we [in Syria] were waiting in long queues [to buy cement]," he goes on, lorries went from Syria to Lebanon "loaded with cement and came to be distributed for free [in Lebanon]. On whose account?"[158]

Others justified Syrian intervention in a narrower language, referring to the "harsh realities" of Syrian national security, paying less attention to either Arabism or to the wishes and interests of the Lebanese. An older and relatively wealthy male member of the Awwad household, who had worked in Abu Dhabi for many years, waved away my suggestion that Syria's position in Lebanon benefited the Syrian economy. Syria's position in Lebanon was about nothing other than the protection of Syria from an outbreak of chaos in Lebanon that would spread the war to Syria, he asserted. It was a matter of security, which he said was the most important thing in the turbulent Middle East divided by sect into Kurds, Sunnis, and so on, all of whom could make problems at any time. This was why Saddam Hussein's rule in Iraq had been necessary, he averred. He went on: "Syria has a very long border with Lebanon. It's very difficult to defend. Only this year there was the discovery of a substantial arms cache under a mosque near Homs. And where did those arms come from? Lebanon of course!" Syria must now be in Lebanon, he concluded, to prevent the place from dissolving into chaos and exporting such chaos to Syria.[159]

Yet not all workers combat opprobrium by defending the Syrian position *in toto*. Others make distinctions between the people and the government. How can humble workers, especially in a dictatorship, be held responsible for the actions of the regime? Indeed, workers are ready to criticize the role of the military in Lebanon, and of the powerful and the corrupt in Syria. Radwan told me that like any army, the Syrians in Lebanon did "really bad things" such as "rape, plunder, and pillage." This is the reason, said Radwan, why the Lebanese look on all Syrians as members of the Syrian army.[160] There are criticisms of the ruling Alawis. It is said that they do not work. Instead they just sit in Ladhiqiyya. They can do what they like. Their "backs are covered." They're involved in all the illegal trades, such as drugs, and arms. One night, I took Nazir and Radwan to a relatively expensive restaurant near Hammam al-Askeri in Beirut. Seeing a passing group of young men, Nazir muttered to Radwan, "The biggest proof!" Nazir explained that they were Alawi, he could tell by their accents, and that their coming to an expensive restaurant proved their corrupt and wealthy lifestyle.[161] Nazir went on, "We are supposed to be a

Republic! But the Arab regimes, including those round here, are keeping it in the family—something unfortunate, indeed!"[162] Abd al-Qadir told me that the problems between the Lebanese and the Syrians were

> not the people's fault. There are lots of Lebanese people working in Syria, and Syrian people should not mistreat them. We [Syrians] are people just like them [the Lebanese]. Ministers and governments and those big shots out there should deal with their own issues by themselves because they are the ones that are ruining everything for everyone else. . . . There are a lot of poor Lebanese as well, may God help them. The big leaders are the ones ruining everything, stealing, [mismanaging] the economy, [and engaged in] bribery.[163]

Others criticize the lack of social freedom in Syria. As Armange tells me:

> We are simple people, you see. We are very, very, very simple. All we seek is our means of living. . . . But if there was a few freedoms, which we are deprived of [in Syria], we find them here [in Lebanon]. We can speak. We can hear opinions. We can see nice scenes. We can see girls. We're not that free in Syria. There is no such freedom. It's much simpler there. But first we try to assure our means of living.[164]

More broadly, Radwan says, "We are not able to say that all Syrians are good. . . . There are good and not good, and this goes back to upbringing."[165] Finally, not all aver that the Syrian homeland is the dearest treasure, and that their one ambition is to return there. Armange says, on the contrary, "We wish to live . . . wherever the person has some value."[166]

CONCLUSION

This chapter has explored how Syrian migrant workers were once again drawn on a mass basis into the menial labor regime in Lebanon during the pax Syriana of the 1990s and early 2000s. Workers migrated neither because of coercion or hunger on the one side, or because they chose among equally viable options to maximize returns and develop entrepreneurial skills in Lebanon. The free market and the open border through which they moved was an effect of a complex orchestration of social power—a pax Syriana with diverse origins—including geopolitics, politics, economics, and culture. In a mere handful of years, Syrians returned without direct coercion to a country that had only recently been the scene of eviction and recession. The stabilization and reconstruction of Lebanon, both growth and recession in Syria, along with rising expectations and pressure on livelihoods there combined to underpin the flow of migrant labor. Within this structure, workers strove to establish themselves and their families on an independent footing, to access independent means of subsistence, and to raise their wealth and status. In the process they once again became vulnerable to the violence of the system in which they were now enmeshed—a vulnerability that became acutely evident during the break-up of the pax Syriana.

Omar in his shared room in Sabra, Beirut, August 2005.

Radwan (*left*) and Abd al-Qadir celebrating Radwan's final departure from Lebanon, August 2005.

Radwan outside his falafel shop in Syria, August 2006.

Al-Hajj Ali's family, at home in the Aleppo region following the Israeli attacks, August 2006. (*From left to right*): Imad, Nussein, Nazir, two unidentified friends of the family, Khayriyya (Al-Hajj Ali's wife), Ibrahim's son, and Ibrahim

5 INSTABILITY AND EXILE

INTRODUCTION

A new generation of Syrians set out to Lebanon in the 1990s and 2000s to improve their lives, as we have seen. Hoping to escape privation and lack of status, and aiming to raise families and renovate homes and communities of production, it seemed instead that material goods "gained an increasing and finally inexorable power" over their lives,[1] and their toil contributed in unintended ways to a polarizing system of accumulation, labor exploitation, and competition, while the making and breaking of the pax Syriana meant hostility, violence, expulsion, unsettlement, and ultimately a particular form of exile. Both the construction and the unraveling of the pax Syriana forced migrants to return, and the break-up of the pax Syriana unleashed hostilities against them, which although at their most intensive during spring of 2005, and at particular moments since, remain an unsettled question at the time of writing.

ACCUMULATION

Workers' energies were activated, as I have argued, beyond the dull force of sheer necessity, by the possibility of making small gains in wealth and status. But wealth accumulated in a polarizing fashion, and goalposts defining social status constantly shifted. What was regarded as modern one year came to be seen as backward the next. The small gains for which migrants worked so hard played their own role in driving forward the very systemic features of accumulation and status differentiation that impoverished them in relative terms, and worked to define them—in ever-changing ways—as backward and "other," multiplying forms of indirect and direct control in the process.

Unwittingly reinforced by diverse migrant projects were a series of institutional features crucial to accumulation and market relations. Rival and exclusive property rights, title to land usually being held by the father or head of the family who was understood in the law as an individual, were the basis of the functioning of this system of remittances and saving. The key to independence and status was the acquisition of property. The economic importance of domestic communities of production diminished, and the reliance on the market system became more acute. The control and ownership of property armored itself with forms of direct control (patriarchy, hierarchy, and so on) while stripping away the forms of reciprocity previously associated with such direct control: social obligation, patriarchal care, "feudal" protection, and guarantees of existence. Direct control emerged as domination when reciprocity and guarantees were stripped away by the market system. Migration thus played its part in sedimenting the institutions of a world of rival and exclusive rights. Here, one man would eat his neighbor and the old spirit of cooperation and solidarity, it was repeatedly lamented, had been lost. Small wonder at the resentments and tensions that outmigration stirred among those who stayed behind.

The system was polarizing because the bulk of workers' earnings were required to pay for reproduction, maintenance, and renewal, and relatively little found its way into capital investment and factor accumulation. As for the costs of daily renewal, accurate figures are unavailable, but it is plausible to estimate that between 25 and 50 percent of workers' earnings were spent in Lebanon on food, rent, and other daily costs.[2] Much of the unspent earnings (usually remittances) went on maintenance during periods of sickness, unemployment or retirement, reproduction, housing, food, clothing, and other costs associated with families who were often back in Syria. The sums involved in a migration flow involving perhaps a tenth of Syria's workforce amounted to hundreds of millions of dollars a year, comprising perhaps 8 percent of Syrian GDP in the 1990s.[3] Certainly some remittances became capital in Syria. They were invested in a small shop, a taxi, or some means of production in land or petty commodity production. But these businesses, operating in crowded and competitive sectors where demand was weak and fluctuating, supplied little profit above subsistence. Further, heroic thrift on the one hand, or profligacy on the other could make positive or negative differences to individuals at the margins. Nonetheless, the great majority of earnings and remittances overall were spent on renewal, maintenance, and reproduction. Profits turned by all of those who controlled and employed Syrian labor were often used in factor accumulation and capital deepening. In short, the structure of accumulation was a polarizing one in which workers became relatively poorer than accumulators over time, and inequality deepened.

We have already seen the relatively large sums that Syrians operating as small contractors or as skilled masters made once they exploited and controlled the labor of, say, two or three fellow Syrians. Many small Lebanese employers tended to accumulate at similar or higher levels. Abu Subhi's grocery in Ra's al-Nab'a, for example, employed four to six Syrian workers. Their labor supplied him with the working capital necessary to rent a shop and establish himself in grocery. Abu Subhi took sufficient profits in 2004, on an annual labor bill totaling $18,000, to pay $20,000 a year in total for his son's private education at a local engineering college and his two daughters' schooling. In 2005, the son went to Concordia University in Quebec. His training and skills were largely paid for by the disciplined labor of Syrian workers. Recall, by contrast, the case of the worker Omar, who, in spite of his own careful planning, self-discipline, and hard work, was unable to go to university because he had to pay for his own and his family's subsistence. In this case, the exploitation of labor was decisive. Levels of accumulation are obviously higher among those employing scores of Syrians, such as at the national and regional levels, local construction companies and supermarkets (for example, Monoprix, BHV, Spinneys, or the co-ops owned by Lebanese or Gulf capital), and at the international level, the multinational firms contracted to rebuild Lebanon's physical infrastructure,[4] both in the 1990s and since the devastating Israeli attacks in summer 2006. Kamal Dib estimated that the employment of Syrians, who were cheaper than other available workers, represented a saving to employers in Lebanon in wages and in social, legal, and bureaucratic costs of $1.22 billion a year.[5] These sums effectively found their way into the pockets of employers of all kinds in Lebanon, including local and international banks and the multinational companies contracted for reconstruction. No wonder Abed averred that "the poor don't own anything. It is the rich who own."

While small, individual material gains turned out to be impoverishing in relative terms, small apparent gains in status were similarly wiped out by the continual production of new differences, in reference especially to the social meaning of region, religion, sect, accent, livelihood, gender, culture, and so on. Hawranis, for example, may have been working in Lebanon to raise their status since the 1940s, but status criteria changed, and Hawranis were continually redefined as falling on the wrong side of status gradations heavily colored by bourgeois-colonial modernity. Omar reckoned that villages from the Hawran were not necessarily poor, but they "never liked education. They don't know how to read or write. . . . The area they come from looks like nothing. They sleep next to their cows, and eat with cats all around. Little children grow up on the streets and don't go to school."[6] In similar fashion, it was clear that in the eyes of Jo Farah, more than a generation of hard labor by workers from the grain-producing plains had not improved their status in relative terms at all. He stated,

> I am a Syrian from Tartous. People [mostly Christian and Alawi] from Tartous and Lattakia, I mean the Syrian coast, are very good workers. I mean they work in gypsum, restaurants, clothes shops, or in hotels. While people [mostly Sunni] from the inner part of Syria, like Hama or Idlib, they do jobs like digging, carriers and porters in Lebanon. While other people from Aleppo, the city, work in trading. People from the countryside around Aleppo work in cultivation. People from Masyaf work in planting vegetables and fruits. So Syrians from special parts in Syria have their special style of work down in Lebanon. People from the coast dress all the time very well and they do just specific type of work which is clean and elegant. While people from the inner part of Syria . . . there will be fifteen persons living together in one room![7]

One might say that Jo Farah's multiple social differentiations were based on the way old bottles (categories of status, honor, and modernity) were continually filled with new wine (status criteria as well as different groups, such as the Alawis, whose status had been dramatically raised by political change). It was the very fact that Syrians from the grain-producing plains crowded into one room—a practice intimately related to their efforts to earn money, send back remittances, and raise their status—that marked them off as "backward" and of low social status. The consumption of mass-produced, processed sugar, for example, was regarded as a marker of modernity in the grain-producing plains of Syria in the 1950s, whereas by the 2000s, it was increasingly made to look backward by new notions of health and diet, and the search for more "authentic" or sugar-free sweeteners. Many other aspects of everyday life—manners, comportment, leisure, and so on—were implicated in this mobile border. The youth culture surrounding dating and nightclubbing, for example, was a relatively new addition to the Lebanese scene after independence, but the fact that

Syrian migrants did not generally and were not expected to attend quickly became a new border dividing "their" backwardness from "our" modernity. This point was illustrated by Jo Farah, who told a story of being mistaken for a Lebanese because he went to a nightclub with his girlfriend—something that was assumed Syrians simply did not do.

OUR RIGHTS ARE DESTROYED!

It's no wonder that Radwan told me that the rights of Syrians in Lebanon were destroyed. As Chapter 4 argues, workers were (self-)disciplined, could justify their position, and often asserted in public that there were no problems in Lebanon. Moreover, there was little labor organizing, and few formal complaints from workers about their treatment.[8] None of this means, however, that workers believed that the conditions under which they worked were just or legitimate, or that they felt well remunerated, valued, and content. We have already seen some of the ways in which the menial regime of migrant labor exhausted workers' physical capacities, in which the work of reproduction had been invested, diminished maintenance periods by lengthening working lives, and restricted and squeezed renewal times. Workers were also aware of, and antagonistic toward, the humiliation, indignity, poverty, violence, and the exhaustion and physical pain associated with hard work and poor conditions, which violated many a principle of moral economy. Syrian workers were not desensitized, backward folk, insensible to, or inarticulate in the face of, their own sufferings or exploitation. Nor did they miraculously shed status consciousness and become amoral, individuated, maximizing units because of their geographic distance from home and community. Indeed, the narratives by which Syrians justified their position in Lebanon and asserted their self-worth, far from being an element of consent or an indicator of well-being, reinforced their sense of indignation and grievance.

Radwan, for example, had a strong sense of the exhaustion, exploitation, and injustice of the menial labor regime. "I'll tell you about the conditions [here]," he said. "If the Lebanese did not benefit 100 percent from us, they would not pay us this income that we take from them. They can fire us easily. We don't have yearly holidays . . . a worker works all week. And every fifteen days he takes a one-day break." Radwan quips, "Beyond that, there is no thirteenth or fourteenth month in the year" in which to take a holiday. "Where I work . . . there are many holidays taken by the Lebanese [none of] which I take."

[In Lebanon] the first time I worked in this work [was very difficult]. In Syria, [among] my family, [things are] . . . easy and comfortable. We have a house, we have things. I was in school you know. It was true that I was tired at work in Syria, but nothing like this exhaustion which I found here. Why? Because in my life I had not worked at night. I worked at night. Worked.

Radwan condemned night work in religious terms: "God made the day for things, for income, for going about [one's affairs] and for work. We inverted the [Qur'anic] verse. We inverted the system . . . and made it the opposite. The night was made day and the day night." He asserted that compared to other migrants who have work contracts, health coverage, and travel arrangements on the employers' account, "we, the Syrians who work here—our rights are destroyed!" Compared to working in Europe, things were even worse: "I tell you if I was working in Europe . . . I would have become like Bill Gates. . . . We don't force them [the Lebanese] to pay us for nothing. We work."[9]

The idea that workers from poor and rural backgrounds are used to tough conditions and grateful for the excitements and comforts of the big city looks problematic in this context. First, Radwan was not at all used to tough conditions, which were a product of the menial labor regime in Lebanon, and did not inhere in the conditions he was brought up with. Second, the supposed comforts and excitements of the big city were remarkably elusive in the context of the menial labor regime. They existed, in some cases, as we shall see, but often at the expense of other values that workers held dear. In other cases, they were barely present. Third, it was not as if Radwan's background had provided him with a moral economy incapable of designating menial labor unjust. In contrast to the assimilationist literature on migration, Radwan did not need to learn the dominant values of the host society in order to hold a sense of grievance, as Radwan's reference to the Qur'an shows.

Radwan spoke more openly with me a year later:

Syrian laborers always sacrifice. They sacrifice at their own personal cost, whether bodily or personally, their own rights. They sacrifice for the sake of earning a living. . . . Because they are in need. When I go from one country to another and not just Lebanon, I sacrifice because I want to work for my children and for my family, even if it comes at my own personal cost. I will take a lot, emotionally. I might hear a lot of insults or racist talk [and do nothing]. Or I might work a lot more than other people. Sometimes around 13 to 14 hours for only 7 dollars. It's difficult for a donkey to work like this, let alone a human being.

Radwan continued:

> Today a type of incident occurred which makes . . . you go crazy. There are two Syrian laborers that work for us at the co-op. They work for 13 to 14 hours for only $7 per day . . . and the bosses keep the salaries in the bank for a longer time to get interest. . . . [So] sometimes they don't have enough to eat. . . . The other day . . . [they] were really hungry, so I gave them two tomatoes. . . . Imagine! Isn't it the right of a laborer who works for 14 hours to eat when he is hungry so that he can function? At least at work? . . . There is no mercy. . . . A huge hall 100 meters by 100 meters with only two people keeping it clean. Imagine! . . . Then someone comes to ask why the hall is dirty, why the bathrooms aren't clean, then [they say] "Go downstairs and get me things from the storage room" [or fix the air-conditioning] and so on and so forth.

Omar, from near Aleppo, first arrived in Lebanon in 1995 as a 14-year-old schoolboy to work summers in ambulant cigarette-selling in the wholesale market near the Kuwaiti embassy. He was shocked to see the undignified conditions under which his uncles and relatives worked in Lebanon, and the humiliation they suffered. As he told me:

> The idea of going to Lebanon came after my uncles and relatives all went there. . . . I kept hearing Lebanon, Lebanon, Lebanon. [But] I never thought I would see them in such a [bad] condition. When they were in Syria, they were more straightforward [and] had more dignity. But after I came here I heard so many Lebanese swearing at us as if it was the normal thing to do. . . . "You donkey!" [they would shout]. . . . When someone is carrying a light load, they say, "You donkey carry more."[10]

Expectations, notions of justice, and moral economies journeyed from Syria to Lebanon—they were not simply formed by assimilation to host-country values. Omar had also encountered a good employer, measured at least in part by his hospitality in insisting on getting his wife to provide Omar with breakfast every morning as they parked their pick-up and sold vegetables outside the employer's house. This moral economy—with all its forms of obligation, sociability, and generosity—was in part brought from Syria and formed a basis for judging conditions and persons in Lebanon.

Armange told me that he simply was not capable of doing the hard labor in construction that someone like Ibrahim, Radwan's older brother, could do. He was a trained radiographer, but his qualifications were mostly not recognized in Lebanon, and so he had to work in décor. He lived in a single breeze-block room with five or more male compatriots and few amenities in a slum area of Sabra. If he did get work in radiography, it was unofficial, which meant that in spite of his toil and long hours, his pay was significantly reduced (to $400 per month). Worse, his Lebanese boss was solely interested in making money off him, ignoring his needs and treating him like an object rather than a faithful younger brother or loyal son:

> [My boss] said "I consider you to be my little brother" [and] I said "[And I con-sider myself] to be your son" and so I was working in the clinic [for more than 19 months] as if the clinic belonged to my father, taking care of the patients, dealing with them in a very polite way.... My salary was little.... I said, "Doctor, we are friends and you [said] you considered me a brother to you.... [The clinic was doing good business] so I asked for a raise. He said that busi-ness wasn't very good.... But I wanted him to understand that I was in exile, away from my family, that I needed to start my own family. That's what I told him. But he wasn't sympathetic, and the salary didn't change. He kept saying "God willing, God willing...." But the salary didn't change, so I said "If you don't improve my salary, I'm going to quit." He said "Go then," just like that! ... His words [about friendship and brotherhood]—it was just talk![11]

Here, economic injustice was measured against the codes of fictive kin, codes rooted in the local histories of Syrians themselves. As Armange mentioned in a different context, "I don't care about what people say, but I like to prove I'm a man [by earning good money] to my parents and get their respect."[12] Part of being a successful migrant was gaining the respect of parents; part of proving that success was through material gain. But the "respectful son" model, in a pattern of elective affinities, bound Armange to menial labor while being de-stroyed by that same regime, producing betrayal and grievance in the process. Syrians felt acutely the burden of their lowly status in Lebanon as "muscles," hands-for-sale, not persons.

Abed, in his mid-twenties, and asserting his physical strength in masculin-ist mode, reckoned that one good aspect of hard labor in construction was that it kept him fit.[13] Adib Mahrus, on the other hand, after the tough experience of intensive work in construction for almost 20 years, was less sanguine than the younger man. On the one side, he asserted that one got used to such work, which was normal and a necessity among the poor: "Definitely this is hard work! You know the Lebanese people they don't do this kind of work—each to his own. But this [hard work] is something normal among the poor . . . that you work in concrete. You work at it and you get used to it." One might "get used" to such toil, but it was hardly a condition that defined the limits of one's horizons, or one that Adib Mahrus embraced. "By God!" he told me, during a discussion of contracting, "If I was a contractor, I wouldn't work, you know what I mean?"[14]

The way Syrians could be fired "just like that" and without compensation came up repeatedly as a grievance. Nazir, for example, told me with a passion that when he and Ibrahim started working with Abu Subhi's shop, "It was nothing . . . just vegetables." The very idea to start a shop came from Ibrahim, not Abu Subhi.[15] Now the shop is successful, it is a well-supplied and diverse mini-market. "All of this was on our shoulders!" declares Nazir, bowing his head and touching his shoulders. "And in the end, what? Nothing! I was fired. . . . In Britain, don't you have compensation after four years' work?"[16] Here, the notion of just rewards for labor, that Abu Subhi had gained disproportionately from Syrian toil, was linked to notions of social rights regarding compensation. The history of labor activism in both countries, and in particular the strikes of the 1970s over end-of-service compensation, were part of the background to this way of thinking. Joseph, one of the older generation who had worked in "American Dream," also dwelt on the fact that after "serving for 27 years" he lost his job without compensation. His employer "ate it all." For Joseph this was a key grievance in Syrian-Lebanese relations in general.[17]

Workers were not congenitally thick-skinned. They felt the opprobrium directed at them, especially as the pax Syriana started to unravel in the later 1990s and early 2000s. As Armange told me, "When they find out I'm Syrian they don't take me on for no reason."[18] Radwan told me that he heard a Lebanese mother scare her child by invoking a Syrian bogeyman right in front of him in the supermarket.[19] Jo Farah, who had to work with employers who thought he was Lebanese and insisted on hiring only Lebanese, stressed the "arrogance" of the Lebanese.[20] Nazir was more direct. "The Lebanese hate us and that's it. That will never change. And we get angry about this, we get angry, really we do." Nazir continued, "Especially because we care about our reputation outside our country, and it hurts to have to walk around perhaps not in the best clothes, not having just had a bath, maybe not smelling good. It hurts not to be respectable. We really care about this. And they judge us badly for our appearance."[21] Contrary to stereotypes, migrants new and old felt acutely the stigma of dirty clothes and low-quality habitation.

Migrants were perfectly ready to blame not themselves, but the bourgeoisie itself, for the backwardness of the poor and rural areas. As Abed told me, "From 1943 till 1975 the governing political elite [in Lebanon] are the people responsible for backwardness [in the countryside, through lack of social investment]. It's the same elite that you call 'bourgeois.' I call them the rotten bourgeois."[22] Bourgeois morality and honor was impugned in other ways. Nazir expressed his anger, perhaps, by seeking to prove false the norms of bourgeois respectability and honor that the Lebanese claimed to hold so dear. He told me that all Lebanese women were prostitutes and that he had slept with many Lebanese women, and boasted of his own conquest of a married Lebanese woman, only days after her wedding. His was a fantasized reconquest of Lebanon, perhaps, through the corruption of its women and the dishonor of its men.

COMPETITION

Syrian workers did not intend to put Lebanese workers' wages and conditions under pressure: They were searching for cash, independence, status, and so on. But the way Syrian, other foreign, and Lebanese workers combined with the larger political economy did exactly that. Contrary to the free-market position, which, wedded to the pax Syriana, argued that Syrian workers were simply a structural complement to a Lebanese economy that lacked unskilled labor, Syrian workers were in fact thrown by the pax Syriana into severe competition with sections of the Lebanese (and non-Lebanese) labor force—a point frequently made, if often instrumentally and vaguely, by those opposing the Syrian presence.[23]

The civil war, the recession of the 1980s, and the process of reconstruction enriched a few, significantly truncated Lebanon's middle classes, and greatly increased numbers in lower-income groups.[24] Average real wages may well have declined by 30 percent during the 1990s; average spending on food in family budgets climbed between 1966 and 1997, and, in the 1990s, 35 percent of Lebanese households were defined as subsisting below the poverty line.[25] A large number of Lebanese (797,763 persons) were wage-earners (neither employers nor self-employed) in industry, agriculture, construction, commerce, hotels and restaurants, and transport and communications.[26] The average income for wage-workers in Lebanon was a hardly wealthy $387 per month.[27] A surprising 18.2 percent of total Lebanese workforce was in seasonal or temporary work—mostly in agriculture, construction, and transport.[28] Moreover, almost half the entire Lebanese workforce (45.2 percent) had only a primary education or less.[29] Just as before the war, there were far more unskilled, low-income, and partially educated workers in Lebanon than common perceptions admit. A Lebanese friend of Abu Subhi's, for example, declared that the Lebanese did not accept menial labor, yet it turned out that his son was washing dishes in a hotel. Realities did not accord here with perceptions. Lebanon's small, globalized elite existed alongside "a pauperized, expanding minority, stuck with a receding economy, limited horizons and declining opportunities."[30]

Competition took place in specific sectors, and the middle and upper classes were mostly insulated from such "market" forces. Roughly half a million Lebanese worked as (1) legislators, senior officials, and managers; (2) professionals; (3) technicians; and (4) clerical workers. Syrians rarely worked in these occupations. It is likely, moreover, that Syrians were only slightly in competition with the further 68,111 Lebanese working as skilled agricultural and fishery workers in Lebanon.[31]

Nonetheless, as many as 724,707 Lebanese workers, or over half the resident labor force, were in occupational categories where jobs, pay, and conditions were at least potentially vulnerable to the competition of Syrians.[32] This total included, first, 137,585 service workers and shop and market sales workers, working as waiters, shawarma makers, all kinds of sandwich and kebab makers, coffee makers, established retailers, and so on.[33] The average income among this group of occupations was $449 per month, and wage-workers in this sector worked for $369 per month.[34] Syrians were extensively at work as wage-earners and self-employed across this sector, although numbers are lacking. One anecdote can give a glimpse of the pressures involved. Roy was a Lebanese in his late twenties working as a kebab maker at Berber, a well-known kebab shop in Hamra, Beirut. He explained to me that he needed $500 a month "just to get by," whereas any Syrian worker could do his job for $250. His co-worker, Mahmud, was one such Syrian, working in exactly the same profession, for a much reduced wage. For this reason, Roy was profoundly resentful of the Syrian presence, and wanted "all of them to leave." The explosiveness of the issue was quickly revealed because Mahmud overheard what Roy was saying, was highly offended, and a standoff resulted. The atmosphere was tense, with Roy visibly shaken. The till operator physically interposed himself, declaring, "Let's have no politics in here!"[35] Such scenes may not have been unusual, and did not depend on a wider political opposition to the pax Syriana.[36]

Second, there were 305,140 Lebanese workers in crafts and related trades, mostly working in industry, construction, and commerce, earning on average

$443 a month.[37] Wage-workers in this category were making only $306 per month.[38] Syrians were extensively at work in these occupations. Conflicts between Syrian butchers and Lebanese Shi'a butchers were reported in Sabra.[39] Syrians were said to undercut Lebanese, Palestinians, and others in the skilled building trades. In decoration and painting, for example, I was told that Lebanese and Palestinians offered $1.30 to $2.50 per square meter, whereas Syrians offered $0.75. In plastering, Lebanese and Palestinians offered $6 to $14 per square meter (especially skilled Palestinians), whereas a Syrian plasterer would offer a maximum of $5 per square meter. Competition was muted where the labor market was segmented by local networks, such as where the Palestinians maintained a monopoly as carpenters of furniture and windows in Tripoli.[40] On the other hand, Lebanese stone masons were relatively few, and charged around $25 per meter to cut stone. Syrians, on the other hand, charging $6.5 per meter, had become much in demand among the war-rich, profiteers, and so on, who now had a taste for large villas with pools and balconies.[41] Contractors using electrical fitters in construction work also hire Syrians at much cheaper prices than those offered by Lebanese electricians.[42]

Third, there were 119,876 Lebanese machine operators and drivers, mostly working in industry and transport, earning on average $432 per month. Wage-workers in this category were paid on average $335 per month.[43] Syrians were to be found in many occupations in this sector, in direct competition with their Lebanese counterparts. Syrian mini-buses, for example, from Msharifiyya and the Hadi Nasrallah road in the southern suburbs, undercut the existing Lebanese intercity mini-bus service from Cola.[44] I interviewed a Lebanese Shi'a taxi-driver from the South who was married with children. He spoke passionately of tough competition. He said he could not compete because his expenses were higher. He had to pay for his whole family at Lebanese prices, whereas the Syrians did not have to because they often left their families at home. His expenses were therefore very high in comparison. He said his subsistence expenses came to about $21 per day, $630 per month, "just for the very basics, . . . before anything." He paid $7 a day rent for a flat, much more than the Syrians pay because they sleep 10 to a room. He paid $5 a day for a respectable school, which is more than the Syrian pays because schooling is free in Syria. The remainder went to the rent for the taxi and food for himself and his family—the latter costing far more than the $1 per day for food paid by the Syrians, who without family, paid "just for themselves." In short, he told me, it was a "very serious situation" involving "many problems."[45] Where more

Syrian taxi-drivers were on the road, it is easy to see how Lebanese drivers lost out, especially if lower-end fares were determined more by social costs in Syria than in Lebanon. This situation put a powerful squeeze on the ability of Lebanese to defray the social costs of reproduction.

Finally, there were 162,106 Lebanese unskilled workers at work in agriculture and fishery services, commerce, and construction, earning an average of $291 per month. Wage-earners in this category earned only $236 per month.[46] In these occupations, where Syrians were probably working in higher numbers than anywhere else, the pressure of the open labor market was particularly acute. Agricultural laborers were pressured by Syrian migrant labor,[47] as were porters and related trades. In Barbir, for example, it was reported that Lebanese removal men complained about their Syrian competitors who charged half the fee for the same work. "The Syrians themselves don't have rent to pay, nor family to maintain. They can therefore lower their prices."[48] Ambulant sellers were another group in which Lebanese livelihoods were pressured or displaced.[49] An illustration is furnished by a story related by a Palestinian, Maher al-Yamani.[50] In the early 1990s, he told me, there were two Lebanese men selling lotto tickets in the vicinity of Café Rawdat al-Bahr in Ra's Beirut, who he knew personally. Ten years later there in which about 20 sellers of these tickets, and about 15 of them were from Syria. Al-Yamani explained that it was particularly difficult for the Lebanese to compete. They earned 7.5 to 10 percent of what they sold, and so only made about $67 to $100 per month—at a time when $266 a month was a minimum, survivalist wage in Lebanon. The lottery administration, of course, does not care who sells their tickets. Hence, wages for Lebanese were squeezed, whereas Syrians could afford to work in Lebanon because their costs were lower. Al-Yamani also told me that Syrian concierges had replaced Palestinians during the civil war, partly for political reasons—where Palestinians were fighting the Kataeb in Christian areas, and where Lebanese building owners, in Muslim areas, were making connections to the Syrian army.

Lebanese workers were therefore directly in competition with Syrian workers in numerous specific occupations. Far from the Lebanese being too proud, wealthy, or educated to take on such jobs, they were already working in great numbers in occupations similar to those in which Syrians worked, at low rates of pay, and often with little education. Historically and socially determined expectations and costs of reproduction, rather than pride, meant that Lebanese could not effectively compete with Syrians in many of these sectors. As a result, the way Syrian workers combined with the Lebanese political economy undermined the jobs, pay, and conditions of Lebanese workers.

WAR OF WORDS

Lebanon inherited from the economic crises of the 1980s a set of economic arguments against foreign migrant labor in general. With economic and currency crises recurring, such opinions appeared in the press in the early 1990s. For a certain Ali Safa, foreign labor was a "frightening spectre, quietly on the march in the darkness."[51] Carol Samaha reported that over 15,000 foreign workers arrived in 1991. The government, she argued, was failing to protect Lebanese, while handing out work permits all-too-easily to queues of foreigners, their "white, black and yellow faces looking at you, each talking some language and all asking for directions." The result was unemployment and a subsistence crisis among the Lebanese.[52] Immigrants, it was said, pressured the pound, which meant a drain of $1.2 billion a year in hard currency.[53] And emigration, which before the war had often been seen positively as part of the Lebanese destiny and "ambition to realize their humanity,"[54] was increasingly worrisome, seen as a "vast emigration of the national potential"[55] and more and more viewed as a *result* of immigration (rather than as a cause).[56]

A new assault on the role of specifically Syrian workers, led by *Al-Nahar* and encouraged by those who rejected the pax Syriana, drew on this current of opposition to foreign labor, and developed it extensively throughout the 1990s. The taboo on explicit mention in the press of Syrian workers in Lebanon was broken by the Francophone *L'Orient-Le Jour* in 1994. Appearing shortly thereafter, a brief article, tucked away in the center pages, under a small headline in *Al-Nahar*, was the first implicitly critical mention of Syrian workers in the Arabic press. Critical pieces trickled out through the mid-1990s, developing the demographic and economic aspects of the issue, while broadening the debate to include regulatory, fiscal, and legal problems associated with Syrian workers. The pace of criticism increased as the 1990s wore on, explicit debate became routine, and the growing movement started to attract prominent supporters. The authority and recognition of the oppositional discourse was given a boost, for example, in August 1997 when the Maronite Patriarch Cardinal Mar Nasrallah Butros Sfeir stepped into the fray, speaking of the abnormal situation in Lebanon, and endorsing the figure of 1.2 million Syrian workers, citing their competition with Lebanese workers as one of the "basic problems" facing the country.[57] By the later 1990s, the controversy expanded beyond articles in the press to official and academic studies and reports, meetings, talks, and panels.

The Economy

The growing debate focused extensively on the economy, above all on remittances, consumption, taxation, and labor competition. First, Lebanon's regional role had relied on a strong currency and macroeconomic position, it was argued, but billions of dollars in Syrian remittances put immense pressure on Lebanon's currency, liquidity, and balance of payments. A weak currency diminished Lebanon's spending power internationally, increased the price of much-needed intermediary goods, and caused inflation (by making foreign goods more expensive).[58] One of the chief protagonists in the debate, the economist Michel Murqus, argued that Syrian remittances amounted to $4.2 billion yearly, a vast sum only paid for by a growing and unsustainable national debt.[59]

Second, it was repeatedly argued that Syrian workers spent practically nothing in Lebanon and thus did little to stimulate the local market. As it was popularly remarked, "They even bring their bread." Khoury reckoned that Syrians spent only half their earnings in Lebanon, and even used Syrian transport where possible.[60] Muhammad Zabib made similar points, adding that workers sleeping under bridges, on building sites, or in overcrowded rooms did nothing to benefit the all-important real estate market.[61]

Third, opponents of the pax Syriana—not noted for any prior history of solidarity with Lebanese labor—emphasized unfair labor competition. Murqus emphasized the entry of Syrians into new sectors, such as industry, transport, ambulant selling, hotels, restaurants, hospitals, fuel distribution, retail, the public sector, and bus stations, as Lebanese employers sought to increase profits and as the market suffered from inadequate regulation. Zabib argued that the competition of around 700,000 Syrian incomers on the Lebanese workforce of 1.2 million put significant downward pressure on wages and increased unemployment and emigration. Workers came from countries with relatively low living costs, and hence could afford to take work with no benefits and wages 35 percent lower than the absolute poverty line, said to be over $600 per month for a family of five in Lebanon. Contrary to the common idea, not all Lebanese job-seekers are skilled: There were Lebanese cleaners in municipalities forbidding foreign labor, such as in Saida, Sur, Nabatieh, Junieh, Tarablus, and Ba'albek. Foreign competition, moreover, reduced Lebanese wages, which in turn accounted for a large proportion of the weakening of consumer demand.[62]

Finally, it was argued that unregulated and hence untaxed Syrians were a fiscal burden: The Treasury still subsidized services like electricity, which foreign labor consumed but did not pay for, and the Social Fund lost out because foreigners were not registered in it. Moreover, revenue loss led to capital flight and meant a growth in debt.[63] Zabib estimated that the Treasury lost roughly $180 million a year because of untaxed foreign labor—a sum that if raised would cover 14 percent of the Lebanese external debt, estimated at that time to be about $1.3 billion.[64]

Overall, far from being a sign of prosperity as some officials claimed, the presence of foreign labor was said to seriously hamper Lebanon's economic development. The emergence of an economy strong in finance but with no industrial base and a heavy reliance on foreign labor meant a regression "toward the level of backward countries."[65] Hidden in these arguments was the point that intensive coordination with Syria and the Arab and Islamic world that Syria represented for many, far from allowing Lebanon to play its long-standing intermediary role in the region, was hampering Lebanon's efforts to rebuild its position.[66]

Economics became a relatively protected battleground for political debate. Arguments by acknowledged experts donned the protective garb of technocracy and objectivity regarding central issues of economic development, while implicitly addressing sensitive political issues. A defense of the Lebanese nation against invasive and heavy-handed Syrian direct control—in security, the constitution, politics, the law, commerce, and beyond—could take the form of analysis of modes of indirect control, on which Syrian control in turn relied.[67] The Syrian "occupation" was engaged through a debate over the management of things. Significantly enough, the economic focus played into the hands of the pro-Lebanese as the economy started to fail during the second half of the 1990s. The sale of contracts to build Lebanon's physical infrastructure mortgaged the country's finances and saddled it with increasingly unmanageable debt. The government had optimistically expected about half (47 percent) the financing for the $11.7 billion projected public investment goals in all sectors at constant 1992 dollars to come from budget surpluses after 1996.[68] These surpluses never appeared, and by 1997, the remainder of the Horizon 2000 program—that is, the social infrastructure including housing, public health, social services, education, culture, and sport—was suspended.[69] Reconstruction contracts were only temporary and should not be confused with foreign direct investment, which was limited in scale and value, and deterred by the limited size of the market, the high cost of factors of production, the lack of skilled labor and technicians, the lack of a suitable legal framework, the prevalence of red-tape and bureaucracy and corruption, and economic and political instability.[70] Many in the business community saw Dubai, afloat on petrodollars, zero-tax zones, and an even more numerous, menial, rotating labor force than Lebanon, as the real financial hub in the Middle East of the 1990s and the early 2000s.[71] Lebanon's once starring regional role had been eclipsed, and the hard realities of the new regional environment were grist to the economic arguments of the opposition, who found a convenient scapegoat in the Syrian workers and by extension Syrian control in general. The controversy expanded and deepened with the recession, which affected all Lebanese. The appeal of the provocative articles of al-Nahar was expanded. Whereas economic order could stitch together diverse subjectivities, debates about that order had the power to put them asunder.

Numbers

Competing with the economic debate in importance was the question of numbers. Murqus's opening salvo in 1994 claimed that there were as many as 1.4 million Syrians in Lebanon. If the Lebanese population was about 3 million, wrote Murqus, then "one Syrian lives in Lebanon for every two Lebanese." Meanwhile, Murqus warned, Lebanese emigration was increasing. There was a veritable substitution of "Lebanese labour power for foreign labour power."[72] Others warned luridly that Lebanon was "drowning" with an "invasion of foreign labour," representing a "dark danger" threatening "political and social explosion." Foreign workers were said to number "half the Lebanese population."[73] Bassam al-Hashim, a professor at the Lebanese University, and his doctoral student, Nada Oweijane Khoury, supported similar or higher figures in 2000 and later.[74]

In a country where the political power of the different sects is supposed to correlate to their relative demographic weight—a factor that has long made demography a sensitive subject in Lebanon—the possibility that Lebanon's highly sensitive "sectarian balance" was to be upset by the arrival of large numbers of mainly Muslim Syrians was particularly upsetting. Certain Christian constituencies already felt alienated by both the long-term changes displacing Maronite sectors from the core leadership of Lebanese nationalism as well as by the more specific loss of political power and status under the pax Syriana. Decree no. 5247, of June 20, 1994, through which some tens of thousands of Syrians obtained Lebanese citizenship, quickened such fears significantly.[75] Such sensitivities are clearly elaborated in Khoury's Ph.D. thesis, written in French, supervised by a prominent opponent of the pax Syriana, and hidden away in three volumes in the Rabieh section of the Lebanese University, linked to the Université Réné Descartes in Paris. She writes of a "foreign invasion" of mostly Muslim migrants, whose "massive presence" affects "acculturation, influences styles of life, traditions, national comportment, and increases the number of crimes and of all sorts of transgressions." Syrian immigration meant "sectarian disequilibrium" and emigration amounting to a "veritable national hemorrhage," and hence an impending "revolutionary transfiguration" of Lebanese society. "Galloping Syrianization," driven by the desire of Syrian migrants to become citizens in a Lebanon that was for them "the paradise of the Middle East," put in question the "identity of the country itself," threatening its very existence. Syrian migrants were involved in nothing less than "colonization" and displayed a "colonizing attitude," comporting themselves as if they were "at home or in a conquered country."[76] Meanwhile, Lebanon's image was disfigured by tents, the presence of workers under bridges, on pavements, and in public places.[77] Khoury suggested that the migration might even be about "the annexation of Lebanon to Syria."[78] Khoury predicted (erroneously) that by 2007 there would be a Syrian majority in Lebanon.[79] And while Lebanese employers hire Syrians and fire Lebanese, the government under Syrian tutelage does nothing, merely multiplying accords and protocols rationalizing the situation.[80]

Syrian workers were certainly in some measure a "sacrificial lamb,"[81] a foil for concerns about Syrian control, economics, and the sectarian balance. As Picard puts it, "These slaves submitted to the projects and ambitions of Lebanese entrepreneurs, have become the metaphor for the military and political domination that Syria exercises on Lebanon.[82] Yet, opposition to Syrian workers was also animated by a "structure of feeling" that was more than a simple cipher for the changing distribution of power. Larger assumptions about the poor, peasants, illiterates, Syria, the Arab world, Islam, civilization, backwardness, and modernity in general were in play. How can they live like this? wondered literate opinion. Have they no shame? Where are their homes? Do they live like this at home? These are the sons of "modern Syria!"[83] A Muslim Lebanese professional, for example, urged me to consider the distasteful situation (indicated more with facial expression and gestures than with words) in Tripoli. There, the Syrians lived in a shanty town, she told me, next to the coast in poor shacks. They even keep women and children there in such conditions. The children beg; the men do menial day labor. These conditions, she indicated, are connected to social problems and to crime.[84] Lebanese migrants, it was asserted, were different. Whereas Syrian workers come to Lebanon without education, without degrees, and without skills, the Lebanese, in contrast, take their degrees and set off abroad, providing skills to the outside world.[85]

Miscellaneous news carried reports of misdemeanors, suspects, and arrests in which Syrians play a starring role.[86] According to Picard, many "easily confuse the illegal market in work with the workers themselves."[87] The United Nations claimed that "for some time now observers have noted, even in the absence of accurate data, a relation between the presence of poor foreign workers and certain disorderly behavior patterns."[88] Joseph, a Christian motorbike mechanic in his thirties from East Beirut, reckoned that "Syrians come and commit many crimes as a result of their mentality, which is shaped by their dictatorial regime, which is like the Soviet Union. . . . 99 percent of them [are like this]. They don't have any concept of freedom." For this reason, when they come to a free country like Lebanon, their rigid mentalities are confused and overexcited in ways that lead them to commit crime. Joseph's preferred solution? "America should come and free Syria like Iraq."[89]

A raft of jokes armored and expressed this structure of feeling, identifying Syrians and Syrian workers as incompetent, irrational, country-bumpkins, naïve in the face of sexual relations, technologically backward, self-regarding, illiterate, innumerate, devious, and uneducated. To give an example: "A Syrian is buying a color TV for the first time," ran one joke. "He asks, 'Do you have a color TV?' The salesman says, 'Sure.' Replies the Syrian, 'Give me a green one.'"[90]

FROM WORDS TO ACTIONS

Geopolitical tectonics were shifting at the turn of the millennium as the political dispensations of the 1991 Gulf War receded. With the break-down of the Oslo process and the failure of related peace negotiations between Syria and Israel, Syria's relationship with the United States cooled, and the country became increasingly isolated internationally. The Israeli withdrawal from the occupied South in May 2000 may have been a success for Hizbullah, and by extension its ally Syria, but its very success reduced the security rationale for

the Syrian presence in Lebanon, hastened demands for the redeployment en-
visioned in the Ta'if Accords, and diminished the appeal in Lebanon—no longer suffering a major occupation—of the more confrontational, anti-Zionist
Arabism of Syria.[91] Moreover, in June 2000, the death of the Syrian president,
Hafez al-Asad, eliminated from the scene a powerful leader in Damascus, in-
spiring confidence among the pro-Lebanese in Lebanon. Thousands of Syrian
workers returned to Syria temporarily as a result: Some were seeking to do the
right thing, sincerely and for the sake of propriety, during the period of official
mourning; others wanted to be with their families during a time of uncertainty in Syria; and still others may well have been unsure about what this
development meant for their status in Lebanon and hence thought it best to
return. But the spectacle of busloads of returning Syrians was interpreted by
many Lebanese as a sign of the Syrians' fragile position in Lebanon and a har-
binger of hoped-for things to come.[92] Moreover, Syrian troop redeployments
under international pressure—some checkpoints were removed from Beirut
in June 2001, for example—made the military presence less visible, embolden-
ing the opposition.[93] With Syria's growing weakness and isolation, and the
recession deepening, the movement opposing the now fraying pax Syriana
gathered strength, and opponents of what was now widely seen as the "invasion" of Syrian workers, moved from talk to action, from articles and lectures
to demonstrations, protests, and sporadic violence.

Anti-Syrian street protests and demonstrations appeared for the first time
in the spring of 2000. In particular, students linked to Aoun's Free Patriotic Movement, beginning in the second week of May, engaged in various
high-profile campaigns, such as selling "Lebanese" produce on the streets
(in place of Syrian vendors). The banners they carried read "Lebanese produce, Lebanese worker, Lebanon money." They urged Lebanese workers to
join the "insurgency" against the Syrian occupation. The students declared
that at a time when Lebanese workers faced a social and economic crisis, and
lacked a voice to defend them, the students undertook their initiative, not to
substitute for the unions but to pose questions of the labor movement and
of the government with regard to the regulation of the labor market and the
unfair and illegal competition represented by Syrian workers and vendors.[94]
The movement received wide coverage. It was a powerful issue around which
to mobilize because of its appeal well beyond the "Christian right." Leftists
and intellectuals, for example, could hardly remain aloof from the question of
labor competition—and while eschewing racism, demanded proper regulation
of the labor market.[95] Free-marketeers could readily agree to the importance

of sound regulation of the labor market. For the mass of the population, the issue resonated with everyday economic frustrations in general and the competition of Syrian workers in particular. The student protests also highlighted Syrian control, because they underlined the complicity of the unions and the Lebanese government with Syrian designs.

The authorities played into the hands of the opposition when they arrested 5 to 10 university students for selling bread without permits on Ain al-Mreisseh Corniche in July. This action drew an outraged reaction because it revealed that the authorities would regulate *Lebanese* would-be workers, and prevent them from working, while turning a blind eye to the ways in which *Syrian* workers violated the regulations. Moreover, the government, by arresting the students, was scorning their "magnificent initiative" and doing everything it could to protect the Syrian workers themselves over the Lebanese.[96] Certainly the General Labor Confederation, which had been making occasional critical noises since 1997, was moved to speak out against the government for allowing foreign laborers to live and work freely in the country, where there were so many unemployed, contributing to Lebanon's economic crisis.[97]

Demonstrations and protests continued to be met with force. Photographs were circulated of plain-clothes intelligence officials beating student protestors in August. Information about Lebanese taken to Syrian jails circulated. Students protested against the Syrian occupation on November 21, 2000, on the campus of Saint Joseph University in Beirut. They carried Lebanese flags draped with black sashes symbolizing Lebanon's loss of sovereignty, and included members of the Free Patriotic Movement, and other Christian opposition groups, of Walid Jumblatt's Progressive Socialist Party and some Communists. Their protest was put down by Lebanese security forces, who tore down posters and flags but made no arrests. The Beirut Bar Association and several MPs condemned the raid. Gibran Tueni wrote that the state was behaving as if "it is the enemy of its own people." On November 26, Saint Joseph University and Notre Dame University canceled classes to allow students to demonstrate against the raid, while thousands of students at Balamand University, the Lebanese American University, and the American University of Beirut boycotted classes in protest. In general terms, discussions of Syrian withdrawal became far more frequent and public, and even the use of the word occupation became increasingly routine.[98]

In November, a widely publicized academic conference in Antiliyas, convened by the Cultural Movement, repeated high-end estimates for the number of Syrian workers in Lebanon and concluded that "Lebanon was drowning in inadequate agreements and her sovereignty, independence, and *wifaq* were just words on paper."[99] Prime Minister Rafiq Al-Hariri was moved to respond. He ridiculed the high estimates of the number and remittances of Syrians, suggesting that there were fewer than 300,000 Syrian workers in Lebanon, and 95 percent of them worked seasonally in construction and agriculture and this was "nothing new." He dismissed the conclusions of the conference as "political talk," stating that "Beirut is committed to strengthening economic, political and security ties with Damascus," He continued, "Some want Lebanon to be an island, but if we wanted to slip away from Syria, where would we go—into the sea or towards Israel?"[100] The Finance Minister, Fu'ad Siniora, reckoned there were only 150,000 Syrian workers in Lebanon. Officials, for all their apparent equanimity, were now drawn into the fray as never before, and those who felt obliged to defend their own records now started to blame employers more frequently for taking on Syrian workers, undermining their own free-market stance, and antagonizing powerful interests in the process.[101]

In Sunni, Shi'a and Christian areas, and in town and country, attacks on Syrian workers reappeared for the first time since the civil war. On April 4, an organization apparently called Citizens for a Free and Independent Lebanon carried out two dynamite attacks on Akaidia, a shantytown housing 1,500 Syrian workers in the southern outskirts of Sidon. This obscure group issued a statement: "We are against the presence of all the foreign troops in our country and we demand them to withdraw and get their citizens out of Lebanon." Two further attacks against Syrian workers took place in Sidon and Zahrany on April 19 and 20.[102] The group carried out another attack on workers in Nabatiyyeh on September 23.[103] The perpetrators may have been linked to those arrested by Lebanese security forces in May 1999, who were plotting to carry out operations against Syrian targets, including workers, and said by the Lebanese authorities to have links to Israeli intelligence.[104]

Other violence was more spontaneous. On October 23, 2000, residents of al-Khiyam, for example, in the South started a fight with Syrian workers employed by the Swedish telephone company, Ericsson, which was upgrading phone line networks in the region. The Syrians were employed to cut off illegal lines used by residents of the village. About 40 persons were involved in the scuffles and a few suffered light injuries before police intervened and arrested a handful of individuals. Local residents said they were angered by the fact that since the Israeli withdrawal of May 2000, numerous unskilled, low-wage Syrian workers had arrived in the area, taking away their jobs in the process.[105]

Other similar incidents were reported in the South. Residents in Sunni Muslim Shebaa, for example, beat up seven Syrian workers and threatened to shoot them if they did not leave within 48 hours.[106] There were further incidents in the southern suburbs, in Sidon, in Zahleh, and in North Metn.[107] One source estimated that six Syrian workers were killed in 2000, but the exact details of these killings are not clear.

Such attacks did nothing to stir the sympathies of the public. On the contrary. When an American University at Beirut politics professor, Omar Nashabe, published an article raising the question of the human rights of Syrian workers, he received a sizeable postbag of protest. "How can you talk about Syrian rights!?" his antagonists expostulated. "What about the rights of the Lebanese?"[108] Indeed, the workers had come to be seen as a problem in their own right. They were no longer simply a cipher for other concerns. They were held in such low regard that they had "become a problem in themselves."[109] Regardless of who was attacking whom, it was the workers who were said to be guilty of inciting the Lebanese. The workers were not just in Lebanon for subsistence, it was now claimed, but were imposing their opinions and position "by force" on people, and showing disdain for the "feelings of decent Lebanese."[110] Only in the late 1990s and early 2000s did commentators skeptical of the pro-Lebanese position start to use the word racism with increasing frequency in regard to Lebanese attitudes toward Syrians.[111] Moreover, by the 2000s, the issue was no longer a narrow sectarian concern. The pattern of attacks shows that the issue crossed confessional boundaries. Shi'a, Sunni, Maronite, Greek Orthodox, Armenian—all such groups used a variety of registers to express antagonism or concerns about Syrian workers: "One of the disasters that has befallen this country," said one Sunni Muslim Lebanese taxi-driver to me, pointing to a Syrian dressed in poor clothes pushing a barrow holding cardboard at the roadside. Said another: "Fuck them. Send them back. They come here, they steal our money. They take it all back with them."[112]

VIOLENCE

After September 11, 2001, Syria was increasingly isolated internationally, being added by the United States to its "axis of evil" in May 2002. Moreover, some read in the rapid collapse of Saddam Hussein's strongman-led, Ba'thist government following the U.S. invasion in March 2003 an indicator of the fragility of Ba'thist Syria, led similarly by a "strongman" (and his son) since 1970. The geopolitical move that set in motion the decisive break-up of the pax

Syriana, however, did not come from the usual suspects (Lebanon, Syria, other Arab states, Israel, or the United States). Instead, in 2004, France, seeking to mend fences with the United States after French opposition to the attack on Iraq, and snubbed by Syria on various diplomatic and economic initiatives, emerged as a crucial force. French President Jacques Chirac decided to support the U.S.-led, U.N. Security Council Resolution 1559 of September 2004, passed on the narrowest of margins, and calling for "all remaining foreign forces" (that is, Syria) to withdraw from Lebanon and the "disbanding and disarmament" of all Lebanese and non-Lebanese militias there (that is, Hizbullah). Rafiq al-Hariri, a personal friend of Chirac, and whose government had been bailed out by Chirac's sponsorship of Paris II, which provided upward of $10 billion in grants and loans to ailing Lebanon in late 2002, was now said to have moved into—or at least toward—the French camp, putting himself on a collision course with Damascus. From a position of considerable weakness, Syria could either withdraw quietly or reassert its writ in Lebanon. The decision taken by the Lebanese parliament, the day after the U.N. Security Council Resolution passed, to amend the constitution to grant pro-Syrian President Emile Lahoud a three-year extension of office showed that Syria had no intention of going quietly. In October, Bashar al-Asad declared that "Syria will not allow those who have never fired a bullet against Israel to give it lessons." On February 14, 2005, Rafiq al-Hariri, erstwhile pillar of the pax Syriana, was killed in a massive car bomb. Syria was widely blamed. Half of Lebanon took to the streets—on the one side demanding Syrian withdrawal, and on the other thanking Syria for its role in Lebanon. Washington claimed the "Cedar Revolution" as its own, and the Western media feted the "westernized"-looking demonstrators on the pro-Lebanese side.

Assumed Syrian culpability in the assassination of a man who quickly came to be hailed as "Mr. Lebanon"—symbol of national unity and embodiment of the aspirations of an embattled nation—made long-reviled Syrian workers an immediate target for the wrath of the Lebanese male youth. Syrian workers suffered numerous violent attacks across the country, and a number of workers, perhaps no more than 10, were murdered.[113] The great majority of workers were forced to flee the country for fear of physical security. Omar experienced the assassination as a decisive turning point:

> I lived the shock of my life . . . after the explosion happened. We went down [to the site] after three hours and we saw people walking on the streets and calling for Syria to get out. . . .

I have had two experiences, one before [the assassination] and one after. Before the fourteenth, I was living by myself, I was working and going home after work, and I used to go [to Syria] every two months and put my money in the bank. After the fourteenth, I couldn't go to Syria every two months, [as] I might have been killed on the way. Lebanese people could stop you outside your work and take the money from you. I noticed that a lot especially in Sabra. My older brother was stopped and they stole his money and ID card. It happened at the end of Sabra Street. They are hooligans. . . . Before the 14th, Syrians felt stronger. If I had a fight with a Lebanese I could hit back, and then take him to prison. Syrians felt they had the power. . . . I felt safe before the 14th, we used to go anywhere and felt safe. [But now] every day a Lebanese official states that the Syrians have stolen the country. And the next day on the streets the Lebanese start repeating whatever is said.[114]

Omar's brothers, uncles, and most of his friends left. He stayed, but was "afraid to walk the street." "Some Lebanese," said Omar, "are racists. Some of them come to you and they have an angry look. Then I don't tell them I'm Syrian because you could start a fight or a problem."[115]

Abd al-Qadir's parents expected him to return, but he felt relatively safe in Ra's al-Naba', given his friends and contacts there and that he was in a trusted position in Abu Subhi's shop. He said:

After the assassination everything became negative. But I'm one of the least people that got affected. But some people had it worse than others. Many left their jobs and returned to Syria. Many of them had vegetable places that got burned and attacked. And if they didn't get attacked, there were threats of attacks. . . .

[My wife] would worry [more than me]. She would watch more TV and see all the demonstrations, the flag burning, and the slogans, such as "Syria out!" But we both know that our fate is in God's hands. Even our children started singing the slogan, "Hey, hey, Syria out!"

Interestingly enough, Abd al-Qadir regarded money rather than ideology or politics to be the source of the problem:

Some things bother me, like when they blame the Syrians for anything and everything. But I just get upset and stay quiet about it because I can't really defend Syria openly. Everything is possible, any side could be to blame. At this time, money is making people blind. People will kill their own mother or father for money. I don't think this should affect us. We are two brotherly nations. But actually there have been problems; wherever you go there are problems.

Not for the first time, then, Syrians were forced to flee Lebanon in fear for their physical security, property, and lives.

BETWEEN ISRAEL, THE ARABS, AND THE SEA

Under considerable international pressure, and after massive demonstrations in Lebanon, Syrian troops packed up and withdrew in April 2005. A coalition, which came to be known as "March 14," which included many of the old pro-Syrian leaderships, and now rebranded as pro-Western and hailed as one of George W. Bush's few foreign policy successes, took up the reins of power in Lebanon following Spring elections. Against those who always asserted that the army was the great protector of the Syrian workers, the withdrawal in fact was crucial in defusing hostility toward Syrian workers, who could not now be seen as proxies for an occupation. As Omar put it a few months subsequent to the withdrawal: "After the Syrian army left, things calmed down. It felt like all the trouble was caused by the Syrian army. As soon as they crossed the borders in . . . April, people went out on the streets and rejoiced as if nothing is wrong anymore."[116] Abd al-Qadir was more cautious but conveyed the same idea:

> I have been hoping that things will calm down. After all . . . the two popula-
> tions are like brothers, there should not be any problems between them. The
> crisis has now eased a bit, thank goodness. There are no problems now.[117]

For the first time in decades, articles appeared in *Al-Nahar* suggesting that perhaps Lebanon needed those Syrian workers after all. It was expensive and inconvenient, employers discovered, to grapple with the bureaucracy surrounding the hiring of South Asian workers. Syrians were indispensable, it became quickly clear, for heavy lifting and hard graft in the Lebanese economy, whether in town or country.[118] By the autumn of 2005, probably the great majority of those who had fled Lebanon trickled back into the country, which in spite of a trickle of explosions and outbreaks of sporadic violence was relatively stable for the time being.

Syrians were to flee again in large numbers, however, in July and August 2006. The Syrian withdrawal was not enough for Washington. Lebanon's stability was to be held hostage to a larger geopolitics. U.S. attention was drawn to Hizbullah, which Washington viewed as a proxy for Iran, against which regional power the drums of war were beating. Israel had been looking for a way to strike back at Hizbullah since the withdrawal of 2000 and to extend in Lebanon its writ, which had been shrinking since the disastrous invasion of 1982. Those who had warned that a Syrian withdrawal would expose Lebanon to "Israeli designs," a prediction that seemed pessimistic to the forgetful or the naïve at the time, were proven correct.[119] Possibly both Washington and Tel Aviv thought they would be cementing the power of the new government in Lebanon if they "took out" Hizbullah. Certainly U.S. and Israeli *political* calculations about the Arab world have often been in error. Whatever the case, the pretext for the Israeli attack was a border skirmish in which Hizbullah captured some Israeli soldiers. Israel immediately launched a bombardment and then a ground invasion. The Israeli Defense Force, used to fighting against relatively defenseless Palestinians in the Occupied Territories, became quickly bogged down in the valleys of South Lebanon against the well-organized, well-equipped and determined resistance of Hizbullah. Once the spectacular failure to destroy or even degrade Hizbullah became clear, a U.N. resolution was pushed through and Israel withdrew, dropping millions of cluster bombs in civilian areas south of the Litani River as it went. The bombardment and invasion drove around a million people from their homes, and was sufficiently threatening to send many Syrians home to their families.

Once the ceasefire was called, Syrians trickled back into Lebanon once more. Pressures in Syria itself were growing again with an influx of Iraqi refugees from a country, invaded and occupied by the United States, that had now collapsed into anarchy and civil war with the comprehensive political failure of the occupiers. On the other hand, following the destruction wrought by Israel in Lebanon, it was U.S. loans, soft-money, and grants that now backed the March 14 government of Fuad Siniora and guaranteed the start of another round of reconstruction, in which Syrians once again took their place as menial laborers in hostile and precarious circumstances. The fault lines dividing a resurgent opposition and the U.S.-backed government meant instability and polarization for the time being.

EXILIC ROTATION

While settlement processes remained heavily truncated in Lebanon, Syrian migrants increasingly became strangers to their home communities in Syria. Indeed, whether they liked it or not, most Syrians have had to live with a footprint in both countries, a pattern which has now become intergenerational.

And while ongoing rotation implied a certain mobility, male privilege, and personal freedom, it also ensured that migrants remained poor, fragmented, vulnerable, and subject to a many-headed hydra of direct and indirect control. A migratory movement that started as a temporary expedient, and a means to an end, became an increasingly permanent condition of exilic rotation.

Unsettlement in Lebanon

Patterns of community formation and family settlement in Lebanon have remained limited and patchy to the present. There is no sizeable second generation of Syrian workers' children in Lebanon today. This does not mean that Syrians were simply the "muscles" of reconstruction, labor-power abstracted from persons, for all the heavy limits placed on the quantity and quality of maintenance and renewal time in Lebanon. Employers and the state may have sought out Syrians as commodities, but labor-power inevitably came attached to persons. Syrians may have initially aimed simply to make money and return as soon as possible, but social needs in Lebanon took them in unintended directions. Syrian workers developed social networks in Lebanon and found ways to fulfil social needs and to create familiarity out of strangeness. Some walked the Corniche in Beirut with acquaintances at night, and paid visits to friends or other workers or extended family during days or afternoons off. Some went to cafés or stepped out to look for bargains in cheap neighborhoods. Others frequented the super-nightclubs in Hamra, Beirut, where sexual services could be purchased at low prices. Ibrahim told me that as long as he was not too tired after a day of work, he would head to a super-nightclub in Hamra and spend up to $100 per month there. Others visited Sri Lankan prostitutes.[120] And still others made Lebanese friends and picked up Lebanese accents and styles of dress. Wealthier migrants could afford to go out on dates. Jo Farah, for example, went out to clubs with girlfriends in Junieh. Some did manage to bring their wives and children to Lebanon. Marriage to Lebanese women was by no means unheard of. Salim al-Dahash lived with his Lebanese wife (the daughter of a local chauffeur) and their children in his concierge's room underneath his apartment building in Verdun. Salim had many Lebanese friends. Some Syrians passed themselves off as Lebanese, or came to appear so over time. Syrians were constantly in the process of reconstructing community and social relations. Cooperation in finding jobs, accommodation, and so on, kinship ties in Lebanon itself through relatives, and relationships forged at work were the nuclei out of which more extensive social relations were forged.

But this drive toward community formation, underpinned by communal needs more than by any particular love for Lebanon or in accordance with any long-term plan, was heavily constrained, not so much by the sheer proximity of Syria, although this played a role, but more by a combination of high social costs, hostility, and violence. In Khoury's sample of 150 Syrian workers, only a handful were married to Lebanese (2.6 percent), about a quarter had their families with them, but the families of the great majority stayed in Syria.[121] Most importantly, reconstruction in the 1990s, and the new round of reconstruction after the summer of 2006, did nothing to reduce high social costs in Lebanon. Health and education remained in private hands.[122] Lebanon purchased a "state of the art" physical infrastructure, but electricity, telephone, and other bills associated with that infrastructure became extremely high. Rents remained high and subsidies for basic commodities nonexistent. There were no significant social funds or charities, governmental or nongovernmental, that Syrians could draw on. On the Syrian side, "market reform" was not pushed very far, and the Syrian government maintained its tradition of supporting agriculture.[123] Health care is mostly state-provided and schooling remains free and provided by the state.[124] Utilities such as irrigation and electricity remain relatively cheap. A variety of basic commodities continue to be protected against international price fluctuations. Indeed, the "slum planet" has yet to appear in Syria, which has kept its distance from debt and structural adjustment programs.[125] Such differential social costs mean that Syrians have reasons to return from Lebanon for maintenance and reproduction—that is, to return to Syria during unemployment, sickness, and retirement, and to defray the costs of raising and maintaining a family there, rather than in Lebanon, where expenses are so much higher. In this way, Syrian government policy and the domestic labor of women under patriarchal and indirect controls operate to produce a cheap labor "reserve." As Khayriyya, the wife of Al-Hajj Ali, told me, "We [women] do everything around here [the farm and household]. If we didn't, nothing would work."[126]

Adib Mahrus, born in 1959, had come to Lebanon as a teenager in the 1970s, and worked in construction before taking a job as a concierge in the early 1990s. He used all his savings to get married and brought his wife to Lebanon in 1992. While the children were still of preschool age, his wife's labor bore the costs and labor of reproduction. When the first child became of school age, Adib Mahrus was lucky in that the large construction company he was working for paid for the schooling initially. The job was only temporary, however, and once it was finished, after about a year, there was no way Adib Mahrus, on

$200 per month, could afford to keep his child in school in Lebanon. Reluc-
tantly, his wife and children had to return to Syria. In the early 2000s, even
with the family in Syria, all his salary went on daily expenses. Indeed, liberalization in Syria had started to mean expenses even there that he said had not
previously existed. As he put it:

> 100 percent is spent. . . . Before the marriage, of course, there are savings. After
> the marriage you have a family and a house. Impossible! Impossible that you
> could save [just] LL10. . . . It's impossible to save . . . if you get $200 per month.
> . . . The one goal of work is to make a house and build a family and bring
> children, and [pay for] education, but the circumstances are very difficult and
> earning [money] is difficult. For example, regarding schools, back in the days
> of the deceased Hafez al-Asad, the schools didn't demand anything or any
> money from you. Except nowadays they demand books from you. It's very,
> very difficult. There's lack [of funding] now. The state doesn't help out.

In a similar pattern, Radwan brought his wife and children to Beirut in the
mid-1990s, but he had to send them back mostly because of the cost of a flat in
a more respectable area (Khaldé) was more than his salary could bear.[127] Likewise, Abd al-Qadir's wife and children came in the early 2000s to Lebanon but
they had to leave because of education and health costs.

On the other hand, Abd al-Qadir was able to bring his family—his wife,
four boys, and one girl all born between 1997 and 2005—back once again in
2004, where they have stayed until the time of this writing.[128] The family is able
to stay because Abd al-Qadir's employer is ready to pay the rent, as it means
that Abd al-Qadir is closer to the shop, would not keep returning home, and
is indirectly controlled in powerful ways. As Abd al-Qadir said, "He pays. He
pays the $200. To tell you the truth I work very hard for him. I talked to him
about this idea and it works better for him. If I get my family here I won't have
to go every time to Syria and stop working."[129] Staying in Lebanon did mean
some savings. Abd al-Qadir told me that it was expensive and inconvenient to
continue to return constantly to visit his family near Aleppo, particularly as
presents had to be given on return to immediate family, including his parents,
presents that would cost a minimum of $100.[130] Nonetheless, the burden of
expenses in Lebanon was acute. Abd al-Qadir spoke of his "suffering" in keeping his family clothed, fed, and schooled. Schooling for two of the boys—8
and 6 years old—in a nearby school called al-Rawda al-Haditha was currently
costing $1,000 a year, something he could only manage with the help of dona-

tions from Lebanese friends in the neighborhood, for whom he also did favors in return. He was thinking of finding something cheaper. School in Syria was cheaper, of course, but not as good, he thought, in terms of education. As for health,

> Here it's very expensive. But my wife after having five children knows a lot about that. Every time she goes to Syria she gets a collection of medicines worth SL2,000 Syrian Pounds [$40] and as soon as the child coughs she gives him what is needed directly. . . . Only when she is unable to treat him we go to the doctor. And a lot of them are our customers at the shop so they help me out with the cost.[131]

Without dependents, it was far more possible to settle in Lebanon. Abed, a painter who we encountered in Chapters 2 and 3, has spent almost his entire working life in Lebanon (since 1963) and was used to hostility and violence and hence unruffled by the events of early 2005. In the early 2000s, he lived in a small room in a condemned building in Zarif, Beirut. He was among those who obtained citizenship in 1994:

> I was living here, had my working permit, bills, and rent. And I could prove that since '63 I was living here. . . . I handed in a whole file to the authorities. . . . There is an acquaintance of mine who is a lawyer in the government since the French mandate. He advised me to keep every paper that has to do with the government because at some point I could get the nationality. . . . I kept every paper ever since.[132]

Abed was sure he would never return to Syria because of the absence of family ties there. He had prepared for sickness and retirement by saving, but although in his seventies, was still having to take plenty of work when I interviewed him in 2005.

The best paid of the Syrian workers could more or less afford the costs of family settlement in Lebanon, as long as they hunted out bargains in cheap areas and at least while business was good. Roger Awwad married in 2001 and took his family to Lebanon, which had become his main "place of residence." He wanted his wife to come because

> my wife would be at my side. After work I would return home to her and rest. I would feel comfort at home and she would help me out with things. It is better than returning from work and having to think about what to eat and things like that. She would help me and serve me.

Once in Lebanon, they lived in a flat for $250 per month in the lower-middle class Armenian area of Jeytawi. The wife did her best to hunt out cheap clothes and goods for the household. As she told me, "When we are looking to buy something cheap they would tell us to go to Chiah or Sabra or Na'ma. We would find the same thing but for a cheaper price." On the other hand, after a few months the family had to return because there simply was not enough work in Lebanon to keep Roger employed during the recession. Roger left Lebanon shortly thereafter also and found work in Abu Dhabi.[133]

The hostile and sometimes violent context of the drawn-out instability that has accompanied the break-up of the pax Syriana since the late 1990s also has had an important impact on the plans and hopes of migrants vis-à-vis settlement. I asked Omar if he thought of settling in Lebanon. "God forbid!" he replied quickly. "No. It is out of the question. Beirut is no good. Every month or so, you have explosions going off somewhere." Even before al-Hariri's assassination in February, Omar had thought Lebanon too hostile for settlement:

> Under the Syrian guardianship . . . the majority [of Lebanese] were afraid of Syrians. If you were spotted alone somebody could kill you or stab you . . . just because you are Syrian. . . . You always had to avoid groups of people. I used to see them with knives and guns. And then, whenever they saw a group of Syrian solders they would run away. Hooligans would run away because the Syrian army used to catch them.[134]

Radwan decided to leave Lebanon for good in the summer of 2005. Accumulated exhaustion, poor living conditions, humiliation, stifled ambition, dead-end jobs, and separation from family had all taken their toll. Although he had stayed, while most ran, throughout the peak of the violence during February and March 2005, the hostility, stigma, and insecurity were wearing on him. He now had saved enough to open a small falafel shop in Tal 'Aran (near Aleppo) on premises owned by family friends not far from his home village. It was time, finally, for him to leave.

The oft-repeated notion that Lebanon and Syria have deep historical links, customs, and language in common, and enjoy ties of Arab destiny and brotherhood implies that Lebanon is in some sense a home away from home for Arab Syrian migrants. But this is far from being the case. The language of Arabism is deployed by workers as a response to antagonism directed at them by Lebanese isolationism and chauvinism. Its level of assertiveness is a barometer not of the homeliness of Lebanon, but of the hostility faced by workers there. Moreover, the language of Arabism, inasmuch as it is genuinely felt and internalized, works in important ways to accentuate feelings of exile among migrants. This is because the Arabist story creates an "ought"—that of brotherhood and commonality—that is constantly shattered by experiences in Lebanon. Arabism *ought* to generate cooperation, brotherhood, and solidarity. The Lebanese *ought* to respect and honor their fellow Arabs. But instead, their rights are destroyed, their work undervalued, their dignity impugned, and their persons physically assaulted. The idea that the Arabs should be unified by the crossing of borders between the "regions" of the Arab nation works to create antagonism and exile where lived experience, defined as it is by a shifting moral economy, shows Arab brotherhood to be sham, and reveals what comes into view as distinctively Lebanese discrimination, sectarianism, and division in its place.

Joseph was emphatic that Lebanon had given him nothing:

> I have [Lebanese] citizenship but I hate Lebanon. . . . I was given the citizenship in the last decision they made. I had proof for having a house and paying my rent, a work and residency permit, my children were born at the American University, I had paid all my taxes to the government and the city council, all was right. Therefore when they made the decision for citizenship, I was the first one to get it. I now hold a Lebanese citizenship, as well as the Syrian. I have got two nationalities. The law in Syria allows the Syrian to hold two citizenships. My children, my wife and I are all Lebanese.

Such citizenship was meaningless, however. Joseph told me that he "regretted" the whole experience of working in Lebanon. "I am the only man in Syria," he said, "who would say that staying in Syria is better." He continued:

> [In Syria] I would have achieved something; over there I did not achieve anything. . . . I mean with money and a decent future, I did not reap anything from over there. I worked but I had an income to spend on my children, their school and transportation, and the food. Everything you work you spend. . . . I could not save any money in Lebanon.

Joseph seemed to be saying that his long years in Lebanon added up to very little because they had been lived purely hand to mouth, a temporary condition that had become semi-permanent, but one that absorbed all his earnings, meaning that he could not neither build up any enduring resources nor social status. Whatever he had was lost on his return, and even his acquisition of

Lebanese citizenship was of no value. Even after 27 years in the country, his repudiation of Lebanon seemed to be complete.

Even for those with the money to stay in Lebanon, and to go out on dates and to nightclubs, such as Jo Farah, the process of settling and feeling at home was never comfortable. It was assumed by many that he was not Syrian, and at many points he simply had to pass as a Lebanese in order to avoid unwanted hassle. He had no illusions about Lebanese attitudes:

> The Lebanese generally do not like the Syrians and especially Christians who are very arrogant down there. . . . The Christian Lebanese, specifically, does not like the Syrians from all religions and sects . . . even the Christian Syrians. They look at the Syrians as inferior to them. This is a general attitude toward the Syrians from the Lebanese. If a Lebanese wants to have jobs done, like digging the earth or lifting some slabs up to the roof of the building, he will say: Go and bring a Syrian to do the job for you. He will not say: Go and bring a worker. He will specify: Go and bring "a Syrian." . . . I do not care if he says: "Go and bring a Syrian," though it is a bit humiliating. I might be sitting there [among them, the other Lebanese] when they say such things. They do not care about me sitting there!

Strangers to Home

Unsettlement and exile may have been powerful themes of Syrian migratory existence in Lebanon, but this did not imply that Syria continued to be a familiar and unproblematic home for migrants who spent much of their working lives in Lebanon, even if Syria was spoken of as such in many registers. In fact, from the moment of departure from Syria, forms of distance, difference, and alienation seemed inexorably to multiply, deepening the space between migrants and their domestic communities.

Migrants often assert that Syria is very close, that one can be back there in just a few hours, that one can always pick up the phone any time to talk to relatives, that working in Lebanon does not really imply separation from home, family, and nation. Adib Mahrus, for example, claimed with some sharpness that working in Lebanon involved no real separation from his family. I asked him how he viewed his travel to Lebanon:

> What do you want me to tell you? For us, with regard to this separation, there is no separation. For example, what do you think if I say that in one hour and twenty minutes I can be in my house. There is the telephone, for example. You

don't feel like you have emigrated [literally, "become a stranger"] from your home. Every day you speak to your home. If I want to go, I can get there in an hour, an hour and 20 minutes, an hour and a half is the maximum to get home. We are only 35 km from Tripoli. From the capital, Tripoli, of the province, we are only 35 km.[135]

In this way, migrants assert that their "temporary" work in Lebanon and their easy proximity to Syria means that by working in Lebanon they have not really left home. Powerful interests collaborate in this discourse, which "defends" the workers against the charge that they are coming to settle in Lebanon, while absolving the state of any responsibility to provide for their costs of maintenance or reproduction.

Over time, I came to see this idea regarding the proximity of Syria, in spite of the obviously veridical elements it contained, as relating not so much to some objective truth about strong ties to Syria and to home. Instead, it was arguably part and parcel of the way migrants negotiated and negated the multiple antagonisms that the dislocation of prolonged rotation involved. The notion of being in Lebanon only temporarily, and being close to home just across the border, was in part a response to Lebanese hostility, and, in the case of my informants, to the assumed or potential hostility of a Western, white, bourgeois, Christian, British academic. As long as Syrians insisted that they were only in Lebanon to work—in other words, that they were there temporarily, with no political intentions, cultural footprint, or social demands, and that they could return home at will—they deflected and defused Lebanese hostility, which turned heavily, as we have seen, on fears of settlement.

Just as important, however, migrants were tackling forms of antagonism present in relations to wives, children, relatives, and the community at large back in Syria. Migrants were often so insistent that Syria was so close, and one could return at any time, precisely to try to avoid the unacceptability of actual separation from domestic communities. Wives expected spouses to be in touch regularly, to send back remittances for themselves and the children, to return for festivals, and to allow them to purchase goods that would raise their status in the village, goods that would make up, in a sense, for the practical and affective problems associated with separation. Migrants felt acutely the burden of these responsibilities, which were in some senses the *raison d'etre* of their migration in the first place. It was said among the family of Hanna Awwad that he had spent far too much money gambling on the horses, especially in the 1990s, and hence remittances were not nearly as lavish as they should have been. His son Roger was also indirectly reprimanded in my presence for not paying sufficiently frequent visits home. When Roger told me that he returned regularly to see his family when in Lebanon, one of the women present interjected in an admonishing tone: "He would spend months there before he visited." It was not impossible to detect a note of resentment in the statement.[136] As Abd al-Qadir told me, before his wife came to Lebanon, "she hated the word Lebanon because I was coming here so much."[137] Here was a glimpse of the strain under which kin were placed by outmigration and the domestic tensions involved. Indeed, some of the very activities that made life bearable or sociable in Lebanon—sex, alcohol, and gambling—squandered much-needed cash through a host of transgressions in Lebanon, and became a source of tension, suspicion, and distance between migrants and their families. The good migrant, then, was one who maintained his ties to home, and Syrian workers were thus understandably ready to protest in the face of those who enquired as to issues of separation.[138] In so doing they revealed the intensity of the tensions that dislocation and separation provoked.

Some of these tensions revolved around the ways in which migrants were perceived to take on airs and graces, to spend their remittances unwisely or unfairly, or the ways that migrants did in their own minds start to put a distance between them and their "backward" country cousins. Salim al-Dahash admitted to me that with the comforts he enjoyed, the fine and "civilized" surroundings in which he worked, and because of the wealthy and educated people he mixed with, he did not feel that he could possibly go back to live in his village, to which he had grown unaccustomed. Nonetheless, in the face of political upheaval, his position in Lebanon was by no means guaranteed. Migrants' ways of doing things and attitudes were often subtly changed by their experiences in Lebanon. Abed admitted that "sometimes when I go back to my village in Syria I don't relate to the way things are done over there. Some people are still living 'ala al hilli.' They have a backward way of thinking. The villagers still cling to their traditions." Abed added that he was not judging the villagers: "I am not saying that this is a wrong way of life."[139] But his remarks clearly indicated certain new patterns of thinking after many years in the Lebanese city. Abd al-Qadir had acquired status through his work in Lebanon, which had helped him to "marry well" to a woman from the village. In the process, his own attitudes had changed, and his distance in this regard was noted—and perhaps emphasized—by those who stayed behind: "Abd al-Qadir has become Lebanese," it was said.

The tensions between those who stayed and those who left were amply revealed in the relations between Aziz, a semi-retired schoolteacher and Ba'thist of the 1960s who worked all his life in Syria, and the migrants who I interviewed in his presence. Aziz, as the father of the woman who had introduced me to the village in the first place, was present in a series of interviews I conducted in *wadi al-nasara*. Aziz acknowledged the wealth that outmigration could bring. He showed me the houses in the village. The largest and most ostentatious were those of the former "feudalists" (*iqta'iyyin*) who had left in the 1950s and 1960s but still maintained houses locally. Aziz pointed at houses that were still fairly ornate: "America," he said, "Canada," or, pointing at another, "Australia." The more modest but still roomy houses with some wrought iron and stone-work on gates and balconies were designated as "Saudi Arabia," "the Emirates," and even "Lebanon." His own house and small-holding was more modest (although he also owned an apartment in Homs). As for the rest, Aziz pointed toward the stables and outhouses of the agricultural laborers. Disparities of wealth were stamped in the layout and architecture of the village, and Aziz's tour of the village vividly underlined not the simple resentment of the less well-off but how wealth acquired abroad went into private hands, was used for private consumption, and had nothing to offer to the public in the village as a whole. And Aziz was clearly uncomfortable with coded or openly disparaging remarks that migrants might make about the village, the region, and Syria itself. To give one example here: Hanna Butros, author of the remark, possibly within earshot of Aziz, that only the "zeroes" stayed behind, told a long story about working in Syria, the point of which was to explain how impossible it was to work in a country where one was intimidated by people with connections to security and the regime, and how good it was to work in Lebanon as a result. Aziz's interpretation, however, was that the story showed that if you struggled for your rights in Syria, you would be able to obtain them, and to do so with the support of the union. On the other hand, such forms of protection simply did not exist in Lebanon.

Migrants who had spent some time in both countries, themselves under the inexorable pressures of providing for kith and kin, unsurprisingly felt caught between two countries and between different ways of life. Abd al-Qadir, with his family in Lebanon, but knowing that this arrangement might not last forever, clearly felt precarious in Lebanon and uncertain about whether a return to Syria was possible or desirable.

> In the end of it all, I will return to my country, I don't know when exactly but I will . . . . [I have to stay at the moment] because at this time in Syria there is no way I will find work like I have here. My work here earns money, good money. . . . And I have five children. I can't just sit there and ask for money. From where? Unless of course I get a good opportunity there. Of course if I could guarantee a good job there, along with the ability to save there like I do here, or even a bit less than here, then I will leave. As long as I don't have work there, then I will stay here. Even when I go to my village for a visit, I don't know anyone anymore. I have been living here for so long. These things push me to stay here. But again if I get a good opportunity there, I will go back.[140]

Caught between Syria and Lebanon, hesitating between different economic possibilities, wanting to return to his country, yet hardly knowing anyone in the village anymore, Abd al-Qadir was betwixt and between, a stranger, in different ways, to both worlds. Hanna Butros was clearly torn between two kinds of life. He maintained, "If I got the chance now I would return. I would not stay here, because [over there] I was feeling comfort and happiness." Nonetheless, Butros was in fact living in Syria, in semi-retirement, and, as his wife insisted, "Over here he is comfortable as well." Omar, although still in his early twenties, was already torn in some respects by his life in two countries:

> [Lebanon currently] is my home. . . . First, I see all my friends here, and second, I am working under very good conditions . . . and I am very happy. But sometimes I am not happy and especially when I am going to sleep. That is when I think about home and wonder why I am here. [I wonder] why I'm not doing the same work while at home. [I wonder] why I don't go home after work and eat with my mother. It feels very far from home. . . . Every person likes to be close to his family.[141]

Indeed, Syrian homes and villages were also spoken of in rosy terms by migrants when in Lebanon. These depictions are constructions of circumstances in Lebanon, not a faithful indication of how life in Syria is experienced by returnees. These rosy images stem above all from the need to negotiate antagonism in Lebanon. Some of these depictions, especially when they relate directly to the government, stem from the need to say the right thing and to avoid trouble with the regime and the security services. They are also an assertion of Syrian patriotism in the face of real and perceived enemies, and they act as a riposte to bourgeois-colonial stereotypes. Muhammad, from the Aleppo region, and working as a shopkeeper in Saida, told me when I clumsily broached the question of how expensive it must be to bring up 10 children: "Ten children is not too much. . . . Back in Syria life is very good, it's very cheap: food, clothing, housing, it's heaven. . . . I own a house, I own a car, I own the farm and everything. It's great in Syria, wonderful."[142] Muhammad was responding to an apparent (although unintended) attack launched by his interviewer on the size of his family, a sensitive question even absent paranoia over sectarian balance or bourgeois-colonial notions of overpopulation. His defense included veridical elements relating to relatively inexpensive social costs in Syria, but it was also part of an image of Syria as a haven, built up in different modes by Syrians facing antagonism in Lebanon, and constituting a tissue of representations imagining a homeland where antagonisms would be extirpated and identity and social being allowed to flourish.[143]

Inasmuch as this tissue of representations took on a life of its own in the minds of migrants, through familiar psychologies of nostalgia and absence, rosy views of Syria were dashed on return. The sense of restlessness, boredom, and tension was palpable in the household of al-Hajj Ali when I stayed with them in August 2006, where some of his sons had been forced to return from Lebanon because of the devastating Israeli bombardment of July and August. In particular, my own working notion that Nazir had been a particular antagonist of Lebanon was shattered, when, seeing him in his natal household for the first time, I realized that he suffered from a series of different, but equally pressing, frustrations in Syria. Instead of hard labor, boredom; in place of earning, poverty; in place of personal freedom, family responsibilities and paternal authority; and in place of employment, unemployment and restlessness. If Syrians abroad had started to imagine a homeland where antagonisms would melt away, these dreams were quickly crushed by the very reality of repeated returns, partly in the context of violence in Lebanon. Workers caught in a cycle of migration and return, in short, had not even the luxury of nostalgic delusion. And sitting at home on the plain outside Aleppo, Lebanon, for all its exploitation and violence, could also be imagined as a place of particular friends and occasional pleasures, and Beirut conceived as a place of glamour through which the world passed, especially when those who stayed behind made remarks that revealed they did not understand Lebanon or were antagonistic to it.

Some of Hajj Ali's sons had been driven home by the violence of 2006, but even those returning amid economic pressures and projects had to cope with a loss of earnings and of status (in the eyes of their families and communities), and dead-end and thankless work. Radwan returned in 2005 to set up a falafel shop in Tal Aran. He had already built a house on his father's land. He renovated a shop premises owned by family friends on a side street, and set to work from dawn to dusk selling sandwiches. He had to start early to catch agricultural laborers heading out to the fields, and finish late for those coming back. Although he was working for himself, his earnings were far less than in Lebanon, and his hours were just as long, and the work was boring, dirty, and tiring. In the summer of 2006, Radwan closed the shop and, determined to remain close to family in Syria, obtained thankless and physically tough work in Aleppo working six or seven days a week for about $200 a month as a machinist in a factory spinning and weaving plastic sacking. Radwan explained to me when I visited in the spring of 2008 that his costs had doubled over the last two years, primarily because of the rising price of wheat and rice. Working flat out, he had had virtually no time to pursue his lifetime ambition of journalism. Radwan's brother, Ibrahim, had returned to Syria in 2004 to work, no less thankless. His expectations had been raised by a brief period earning higher wages in Cyprus, but he was deported in an immigration crackdown, and work in Lebanon looked even less appealing than before. He had sufficient savings to build a small house on Hajj Ali's small plot of land and set to work driving a taxi in nearby Aleppo. Work was slow, earnings slight, family responsibilities heavy, and hours long.

Returnees no longer enjoyed the status conferred by working abroad, where local perceptions of living conditions in "civilized" and "westernized" Lebanon were often rosier than the hard realities of slum living. Many took jobs of lower or similar status to those they had had in Lebanon. Roger Awwad, forced out of Lebanon by recession, reckoned there was nothing for him in Syria, and in 2004 was back in Syria but thinking of Australia or America.[144] Joseph had earned good money in Lebanon, in a responsible position in charge of the finances of an up-market restaurant, including paying the employees' salaries and supervising the staff (and kitchen). He returned to Syria in the late 1980s during the war-time recession. He did not have sufficient savings after family expenses to start his own business or open a restaurant of his own. He therefore took a job as a humble waiter in a restaurant called Al-Douwar. Certainly he managed to become head waiter after six months, but his status and earnings had taken a major cut. Nonetheless, he was quite sure that even though he had spent most of his working life in Lebanon, Syria was now his home:

> When I decided to return to Syria I decided that I want to live here and I am happy here. . . . My final home and my refuge is Syria. If I was now offered 1,000 dollars to work in Lebanon compared to 300 dollars for working here, I work for the 300 here and would not go there for 1,000 dollars. . . . It is my country, it suits my feelings and I know the people here. Moreover, there is no discrimination over here. Syria is a country that does not discriminate. . . . There is no discrimination between a George or a Mohammad and Hasan, we are all friends. We are all brothers, we eat together and drink together, and there are no such problems. . . . [Syria] is better than Lebanon concerning this particular issue. There is no discrimination like over there.

Syria is also home, maintained Joseph, because "my children are here. My son could go do his military service in Lebanon, it is just one year over there but it is two years and a half here, but he decided to serve here, not in Lebanon." Joseph, who saw most of his life in Lebanon as simply a waste, was now determined to make a proper home in Syria. Gnawing away at this vision of home, hearth, and kin, apart from Joseph's own quarter-century abroad, was the fact that his own sons were now migrants. Michel, his younger son, for example, had gone to America and been there now for two years.

It is striking that the main grievances cited by workers in Khoury's sample were related very closely to some of the key features of exilic rotation discussed here. Workers said they were mainly unhappy with distance from friends, family, and country; the cost of living in Lebanon; and the Lebanese attitude of superiority toward them.[145] The first point—distance from friends and family—was squarely about the dislocation and fragmentation of home involved in migration. And the second two points—the cost of living and the hostility in Lebanon—may not simply have been about the admitted importance of material security and personal dignity, but the fact that it was the cost of living and Lebanese hostility that were the two key obstacles to community formation, settlement, and constructing a home in Lebanon.

The foregoing suggests that Syrians were neither settled in Lebanon, with the luxury of making occasional visits home to explore their roots (as in some versions of transmigration), but nor were they entirely at home in Syria, while making occasional and temporary forays across the border to sell their labor or services before returning post haste, as in conventional models of temporary and rotational labor migration. Instead, migrants circulated in a world in which sought-after and socially desirable models of community and home were constantly broken down and made unrealizable. This was a process of considerable symbolic violence and constituted what is meant here by exilic rotation. Syrians were not simply privileged males who made instrumental or liberatory use of multiple identities (Arab, Syrian, male, and so on) to enjoy personal and sexual freedom in Lebanon, while returning to Syria for home comforts whenever nostalgia struck. Certainly men exercised direct and indirect control over women's labor, which included all the menial tasks of child rearing and household management, but also farm work and off-farm wage-labor, including increasingly migration itself. Subordinated women's labor was integral to the production and circulation of male labor. But Syrian men asserted their Arab identity in neither liberatory nor instrumental mode, but in the context of antagonism, as we have seen. Moreover, personal freedoms in Lebanon can hardly be exaggerated in a menial labor regime that reduced renewal time to a minimum and left migrants with very low spending capacity. More significantly, Syrians were not possessed of an essential *homo economicus* "set free" by spending money. They felt acutely the burdens and inspiration of the moral economy within which they worked, and satisfactions and strains were lived out through cultural and social codes. Nor did Syrians merely express a shapeless multiplicity, which, unrepressed by definition could not be set free. Their aims and goals were definite, and their pleasures and woes were substantive and determined through the dense fabric of practices, hopes, and historical materials. Syrians did not return to Syria for the sake of nostalgia or simple choice, but in pressured, economic, social, political, and geopolitical contexts, wherein they were exposed to exploitation, hostility, and violence. If some did experience Lebanon as personal freedom, and Syria as home, then this psychology worked to bind migrants ever more tightly to the unstable system in which they were enmeshed. Once in Syria, moreover, "home comforts" had become problematic. In short, circular migration, even between the two brotherly countries of the historic *bilad ash-sham*, built of economic control armored by direct forms of violence and hierarchy, was strongly associated with dislocation, dismemberment, and exile.

CONCLUSION

In Baxter's view the care for external goods should only lie on the shoulders of the "saint like a light cloak, which can be thrown aside at any moment." But fate decreed that the cloak should become an iron cage.[1]

This book has recovered for the first time a history of a little-known but important cycle of migration and return between Syria and Lebanon from independence to the present. I have sought to understand how Syrian migrant subjects were bound to a prolonged pattern of migration, hard labor, and return. The question is posed in this way because existing histories and theories of migration have arguably had far too little to say, not just about the Arab world and the global South in general, but about how migrant subjects are bound to structures and vice versa. The recovery of popular agency and explorations of hybridity and multiple identities, prominent in subaltern studies and cultural history, risk confusing active with empowered subjects, and in their more idealist variants, overemphasize agency and potency by dissolving structures of inequality, violence, and coercion into hermeneutics. Whereas migration conceived in terms of individual material maximization is no closer to taking structure seriously, economic sociology only introduces social context shorn of power and politics. Conventional economic assumptions about how individual self-interest leads to structures of equilibrium, rising prosperity for all, and even civilization are no more plausible where asymmetry and inequality reign and civilization remains an artifact of colonial discourse. On the other hand, the laws of accumulation, and the hydraulics of class power and mystification so prominent in Marxist writings are flawed by their automatism, and are difficult to connect to flesh and blood individual subjects, their existential demands, and political and cultural projects, especially if those individual subjects do not match the model of proletarian agency that Marxism recognizes.

The exploration of this question guides the history recounted in this book, the main chapters of which, along with being broadly chronological, have alternated between examining how subjects are combined with structures (Chapters 2 and 4), and the ways in which subjects are then alienated within these changing structures (Chapters 3 and 5). The trajectories of migrants through time and space have been understood in terms of election, affinity, and alienation. My argument throughout has been to understand migrant circulation and menial labor in terms of hegemonic economic control. "Economic" because migrants, who were neither slaves nor colonizers, were unfixed and subordinated above all by the indirect controls associated with the ownership of things, an idea derived from Marxism. "Control" because at every point these indirect controls were stitched together by forms of direct control, an idea consistently downplayed in the Marxist tradition. "Hegemonic" because this structure of power depended on its ability to aggregate, channel, and transform energies deriving from diverse individual and localized projects and aspirations.

Migrant circulation and hard labor were not above all a product of direct control. Labor migration did not entail the direct coercion supplied by the institutions of slavery—forceful seizure, labor bondage, and property in the person of the direct producer. Through the course of the book there have been glimpses of the *language* of slavery with regard to female Alawi Syrian domestics, commonly employed in Lebanon in the 1950s and 1960s: Recall the Lebanese bourgeois madame who spoke of buying her servant. Outside the ranks of the Syrian migrants, the ways in which female, mostly Sri Lankan and Filipina domestic workers are bound to particular employers in Lebanon since the 1970s through passport-withholding, the absence of rights, *de facto* treatment as if their whole persons were employers' personal property, and high levels of physical repression are justifiably referred to as contract slavery, as long as it is made clear that Sri Lankans and Filipinos were neither forcibly seized from sending-countries by direct coercion, nor did they become *de jure* private property in law. In the wider world, of course, forms of debt slavery are by no means uncommon among migrants.[2] The apparently "voluntary" migration studied here, however, is fruitfully distinguished from slavery of the direct and "unveiled" kind, which, in its capitalistic form was little known in the Ottoman Empire historically, and in many ways decisively dissolved on a world scale during the nineteenth century, when labor relocation and control became more subtle. The occasional use in Lebanon of the language of ownership redolent of slavery was part and parcel of a superior attitude—familiar in many countries and not an essential property of the Lebanese—rather than of a legal institution. Predominantly male Syrian workers may have lacked social and political rights, and they certainly encountered derogatory and abusive language associated with categories of civilization, race, and so on. But they were neither obtained by forcible seizure, nor were they property in law, they were legally free to change employers, they were not bound to employers by debt or contract slavery, and they were not physically beaten (by employers) or sexually abused at work on any significant scale.

On the other hand, Syrian migration was not above all a result of migrants' own access to forms of direct control. Contrary to some of the more unlikely assertions of Lebanese nationalism, Syrian workers were not colonizers, moving within a structured community violently to seize control of land, means of production, and resources, and exterminating, expelling, or subordinating existing native populations after the manner of different forms of settler colonialism. In the early to mid-1990s, the sizeable presence of Syrian workers in Lebanon certainly played a role in strengthening the pax Syriana, inasmuch as it tied the two economies together in a way that made an isolationist Lebanese nationalism unviable. In this context, it was hard to envisage an alternative for Lebanon but to live and breathe through coordination and cooperation with the Syrian "big brother." Further, Syrian workers did compete on a broad scale with Lebanese workers, putting heavy pressure on their jobs, wages, and conditions, while Syrian powers in Lebanon assuredly worked to guarantee the open border against pressure for restriction. Moreover, Syrians were in Lebanon, unusually enough, alongside the Syrian army (between 1976 and 2005), and there were certain senses in which the lives, properties, and persons of Syrians were protected by this military presence.

However, as I have argued in detail, the workers became increasingly controversial in Lebanon, and eventually became a stick that the campaign to get Syria out of Lebanon used, to tremendous effect. It became one of the key issues on which diverse sectors of opinion, including popular opinion, were able to agree, and at best a major problem for those arguing for the continued necessity of "special relations." In this way, the Syrian workers did not serve the purposes of Syrian control, but were an important feature of its attrition. Furthermore, heavy pressure on Lebanese workers—not to mention the intense competition among Syrian workers themselves—was part of an expanded, menial labor regime not only acceptable to, but actively sought by key interests in both countries and internationally, a regime servicing unequal processes of capital accumulation.

The open border, it is important to emphasize, both pre- and postdated the Syrian military "occupation" of Lebanon, owed much to the interests of employers and accumulation, and was part and parcel in any case of an exilic and prolonged rotation, as I have argued, rather than any pattern of settlement and colonization. The very openness of the border meant that workers did not have to make a final choice about where to settle. Indeed, the "Galloping Syrianization," before which certain sectors of Lebanese opinion trembled, never materialized. Moreover, as I have also argued, the role of the Syrian military in Lebanon was to defend not the workers, as such, but the stability of the pax Syriana itself, which was based on a menial labor regime. Here, the army played an important role in the reproduction of this exploitative system. When opposition to the army started to rub off on the workers themselves, exposing them to hostility, violence, and even fatality, the military presence exacerbated the physical insecurity of Syrian workers in Lebanon. This was demonstrated by the way the hostility to workers peaked in February–March 2005, and died down during and after the Syrian withdrawal. At the time of this writing, with the Syrian army three-years gone, the workers have lost their prominence as a central national issue in the Lebanese media, in spite of their continued physical presence, and ongoing attacks against them. Finally, as we have seen, it was the Syrians, not the Lebanese, who were stigmatized in bourgeois-colonial discourses as backward, dirty, brown, uneducated, uncouth, rural, and the like.

Only with considerable simplifying violence can the migrant labor regime be understood to work through the "invisible" hand of benign market forces and processes of equal, complementary, and autonomous exchange in a free labor market whose unfettered operations—based on either maximizing individuals or the growing awareness on the part of the ambitious or the talented—tend toward prosperity, equilibrium, and a higher level of liberty and civilization. This view mistakes what I have called "election" under conditions of structural pressure, for choice and empowerment, and renders invisible the forces of structural affinity, direct control, and alienation that have been consistently present throughout the history recounted here. There is no transcendent warrant for supposing that the migrant subject who seeks to leave home in order to earn cash is somehow a liberated subject, throwing off the shackles of tradition and superstition, and embracing the world of reason and modernity. This is a conceit of modernism. It can be sustained only by a leap of faith, a simple inability to subject normative assumptions to critical analysis, or an avowed language of civilizational, racial, national, or communal superiority. The history recounted here underlines Claus Offe's point that in an apparently "free" labor market, workers are at a structural disadvantage vis-à-vis capital. Unlike capitalists, workers cannot afford to withdraw their labor in order to take advantage of market shifts, but are constantly forced to "sell up," even in a buyers' market, in order to acquire the resources to eat, drink, and survive.[3]

Further, even though for much of the period in question, conditions approximating a free, unrestricted, "flexible," and unregulated labor market pertained, there is no justification for assuming that this was either the most efficient and productive arrangement, or that it involved rising prosperity for all through comparative advantage, complementarity, efficient market signaling, and the like. Where labor was cheap and manipulatable, incentives for productivity and efficiency gains were limited. The Lebanese economy has long been in a parlous state. And where social costs of reproduction, maintenance, and renewal were born by Syrian workers, their families, and the Syrian state, and surplus appropriation went ahead in Lebanon and internationally, factor accumulation in Syria was limited, and material inequality rose. Syrians were not driven from the countryside by the failures of state capitalism and Ba'thism. On the contrary, Ba'thist protection gave Syrians a reason to return, while the domain of economic liberalism *par excellence*, Lebanon, had long suffered from what it increasingly considered a national hemorrhage in the form of emigration rates as high or higher than almost any other country on the globe.

Above all, and contrary to the self-understandings of various policy-makers and attendant technicians and experts, the "free" migrant labor market was not a natural state of affairs, the effective functioning of which political powers simply strove to ensure. The open border, the lack of work permits and contracts, the distance from Lebanese social funds, and the other regulatory instruments underpinning the open door to labor, stemmed from two distinct political settlements. The first was led by the mercantile and financial mostly Maronite elite of the merchant republic in the 1950s and 1960s, a leadership underpinned by larger geopolitical conjunctures. The migratory system broke down during the civil war in the very sectors controlled by isolationist Christian militias, where there was a mass expulsion of Syrian workers. The second settlement was led by the Syrian government and the diverse coalition of forces it assembled and the geopolitical conjuncture that supported it in the 1990s. The pax Syriana then broke down with the shifting geopolitics and mobilization of the 2000s, causing the mass flight of Syrian workers, who then trickled back as circumstances permitted. Ultimately, these forms of political order, the interests and identities they represented, and the geopolitical conjunctures within which they operated, dominated the policies relating to the migratory labor regime. To read this as a system driven by market signals, the abstract forces of supply and demand, and state attempts to ensure their functioning on principle, is to eviscerate understanding of the forms of structural power and political order at work in the construction of an economy in general, and the transnational labor market in particular.[4] The putatively universal project of the "free market," and its attendant hubris of liberty and civilization, could only ever be a tool in the hands of those fighting for one order over another. As a model it is less an explanatory tool in the hands of the historian, and more a weapon in the hands of specific projects of leadership.

The forms of election, decision making, and subject formation at work in the lives of labor migrants were not an expression of their own empowered and hybridizing agency. Cultural studies is right to criticize the essentialism of approaches that insist that migrants must dwell in particular kinds of heteronormative families, patriarchal clans, neighborhoods, authentic homelands, and particular civilizational and racial categories. It was not that there was once a pastoral idyll in the Syrian countryside based on human nature and organic community, a pre-lapsarian Eden shattered by the advent of the labor market. As we have seen, communal land tenure in the Syrian plains was relatively easily dominated by predatory tax-farmers and landlords, and new forms of "second serfdom" associated with the world market, whereas forms of property ownership on Mt. Lebanon and on the coastal plains were sometimes able to guarantee some security against such exactions and new combinations. Older forms of exploitative direct control were overturned by the actions of the state (in land reform, for example) as much as by the market, which in parts of Syria as well as north Lebanon had often meant debt peonage. The notion of an authentic and unsullied past is simply not necessary for an appreciation of how multiple statuses, identities, "faces," and modes of belonging were actually the *modus operandi* of the circular migratory regime. This multiplicity worked to activate subjects and stitch together migrants and markets. The trajectories of Syrian migrants, just as those of the Lebanese migrants during the period from 1870 to 1920 studied by Khater, did little to unpick civilizational and status hierarchies. In many ways, just as Khater documented with regard to Lebanese returnees without emphasizing the point, Syrian returnees actively brought such hierarchies back with them. The content of these hierarchies changed, while the form persisted and was reconstructed. Sites of what Mignolo called "colonial difference" were mobile.[5] The boundary between the civilized and the primitive, the modern and the traditional, the white and the colored, kept shifting and their content was continually redefined. "Mixing and matching" meant a change only of content, not of form. The production of difference persisted and ramified. As one bridge was crossed, another gulf was constructed, what was à la mode quickly became quaint and old-fashioned—in consumption patterns, dress codes, accents, personal hygiene, gender codes, and so on. Migrants were not upwardly mobile except in the most individual and local of settings, which in turn worked to conceal the ways that their disciplined labor was operative in the construction of unequal, surplus-generating processes on a regional and global scale and in new social hierarchies. As Hanna Butros cuttingly remarked of his compatriots in Syria, "Only the zeroes stay behind." As Talal Asad pointed out with regard to migration, the "dominant power realizes itself through the very discourse of mobility."[6]

The celebration of hybridization, moreover, downplays the social suffering involved in constant attempts to rework and reestablish forms of belonging, recognition, identity, and community. It is not that male migrants, for example, belong at home with the wife and children, and any deviation from this model is a form of alienation. The perspective here is not that of those, for example, who moralized about the "perversion" of black African migrant homosociability in the shantytowns of the Witwatersrand. It is that the cycle of migration and return involves the constant re-creation of new forms of belonging and recognition under conditions of poverty, menial labor, stigma, humiliation, and sometimes violent hostility. Many of the more subtle changes in migrants' lives are hardly chosen, the different indicators of status are highly fraught and contested, and many of the faces tried on by migrants were attempts to stave off hostility. There is no reason to view these difficult changes and struggles as necessarily liberatory. Far from tackling colonial discourse, such a view is complicit with the type of bourgeois-modernism criticized by Gyan Prakash, a discourse placing the whole burden of coercion and power on the past, and mistaking change for progress. The "discovery" of pluralized subaltern experience does not imply the disappearance of coercion and exploitation. Indeed, coercion and exploitation often work through such forms of pluralization.

Migrants' choices were sharply limited and pressured by existing structures of power, as the need to obtain cash was not something about which workers had a significant choice. However, they were not driven *en masse* from the countryside through violent dispossession and starvation to become "doubly free" waged-labor, speedily stripped of all access to means of production and atomized as equivalent individual subjects related through the cash nexus outside the motley ties of direct domination and subordination. Nor was it simply automatic reification, the hydraulics of class power, or false consciousness and the slough of traditional culture (backwardness, rural stupidity, or nostalgia) that worked to subordinate them within the circulatory migrant regime. Still less did migrants leave because foreign capital penetrated Syria, disrupted the "traditional" economy, schooled workers in new consumptions patterns, and established linkages to the receiving country. Nor, finally, was the circulation of menial labor from sending-areas where reproduction costs were low to receiving-areas where costs were high the automatic outgrowth of the objective interests of capitalists and imperialists. These understandings, so common in the Marxian tradition, rely on rigid and monolithic notions of precapitalism and advanced capitalism, and underplay, in automatist mode, the role of politics in general, and, in particular, the fact that Syrian workers' own decisions, as well as many direct forms of control, were stitched into the system at every turn.

Migration stemmed from an assault on, and the break up of, the independence of existing livelihoods and domestic communities of production. But it also represented an attempt to renovate and restore access to viable means of production and domestic community, an attempt that usually began well before existing forms of economic independence had been completely destroyed. The slide toward proletarian status, not that status itself, was crucial in activating migration, partly because those who were not reduced to penury had some of the resources necessary with which to undertake migration. It was the attempt to escape a potential future as "doubly-free" waged-labor that drove many workers to leave for Lebanon, a project activated but by a ramifying field of small gains and differentiations in wealth and status. The partial success of migrants on an individual basis in their attempts at such forms of renovation was partly responsible, in turn, for the fact that primitive accumulation was generally incomplete. Male migrants, unpaid female domestic, farm, and sometimes off-farm, and migrant labor, as well as forms of state subsidy and protection, ensured that migrants returned over decades to viable forms of production and reproduction in Syria, involving some, albeit highly differentiated, access to means of production and subsistence. This pattern also worked to maintain forms of patriarchal control in particular forms.

In pursuing projects of renovation, Syrian workers were not dupes, doltish and simple, who, unable to face up to the reality and dignity of the proletarian struggle, were chasing a nostalgic pipe dream for a vanished village community. They had specific goals derived from their local histories and the heavy social and economic pressures under which they labored. They did not constitute a class in themselves or for themselves and cannot be seen as constantly failing to live up to this supposed reality. Their status and access to wealth was relentlessly differentiated. Syrians worked within a system of fine gradations and mobile sites of difference, not a situation of objective class equivalence, and they labored under a many-headed hydra of direct control. As we have seen, migrants began mostly as men whose remittances worked to shore up a renovated form of patriarchal control over women. They were also sons or fathers aiming to provide for, and linked to relations of power in, families. They were marked by nationality, gender, region, sect, age, accent, comportment, and so on. These elements, mediated through changing hierarchies of civilization, nation, and race, fed into direct forms of control, including hostility and violence, in Lebanon—in the workplace and beyond. Accumulation and market relations in Lebanon did not inevitably break down or necessarily cut against these kinds of relations, but worked through forms of direct control at many levels. New kinds of essentialism, and the collectivization of personal status and honor/dishonor, made these forms of direct control more potent and generalizable. In addition to goods and services, command over persons was also sold for cash, a form of command greatly cheapened by forms of hierarchical ascription and direct control. Workers were not in any simple sense deluded because they *did* earn more in Lebanon than they could by staying at home, and their migration meant, at least in the first instance, that through hard labor in Lebanon they could acquire forms of status and wealth in Syria, where the social costs of reproduction were lower. Migrant agency was incorporated not through any simple mechanism of mystification, but through the fact that in localized contexts and contests, workers could make particular gains. This structure was hegemonic, but *not* because migrants themselves consented to dominant arrangements in any simple sense, or because migrant subjectivities were dominated from the start in their substance by preestablished forms of cultural power. It was hegemonic because in eliciting self-activation, it offered to individual subjects the possibility of conceiving of themselves as subjects in their own right, pursuing goals and taking decisions in local contests that were in some part their own.

But the migratory regime was hegemonic also because it aggregated, channeled, and transformed migrant choices in the forging of a larger structure. Forms of election resulted in new combinations and affinities, sedimented powerful structures, and involved unintended consequences and the displacement of consent. The menial labor regime reduced the quantity and quality of renewal time, exhausting workers. Hours and conditions provoked significant antagonism among workers in a variety of registers. Contrary to the claims of some economic sociologists, migrants did not shed status consciousness the moment they crossed the international border; rather, they felt acutely forms of stigma and humiliation. It was nobody's dream to work in menial labor. Ambitions in regard to economic activity often centered around some form of self-employment, small business, or farming. Menial labor was regularly rationalized as a temporary condition, soon to be overcome. The economic system was polarizing and increasingly unequal, as wages, earned in competitive, fragmented, and unprotected environment, were spent primarily on reproduction and maintenance, while profits on a billion-dollar scale were available for accumulation in Lebanon and beyond. As "muscles," and as "commodities" stripped of cultural and sociopolitical claims and rights, especially in the absence of significant community-formation and settlement, workers were exposed to generalized stigma and high levels of hostility and violence at particular moments, both during the civil war and the break-up of the pax Syriana and the instability that followed. While doubtless at some points the desire for the city and the longing for home comforts activated circulation, this circulation involved the rude shattering of dreams about city freedoms or country comforts, neither of which were experienced as freedom or comfort for very long. Patterns of unsettled rotation also involved the constant work of cobbling together forms of identification, recognition, and belonging under hostile and impoverished conditions, where existing schemas were continuously broken up as Lebanon remained hostile and Syria and "home" became strange. Contrary to the hopes of pan-Arabism, the unsettled circulation of migrant workers did little to forge a sense of pan-Arab identity. If persistent claims to belonging and recognition involve attempts to euphemize, deny, domesticate, control, or render invisible the antagonism of instrumental social relationships, then migrant circulation constantly denied migrants the chance to euphemize instrumental relationships. Employers may have spoken the language of kin, but in reality, it was said, they cared only about their pockets. Perhaps this was why the lack of end-of-service compensation was so acutely felt: It was final confirmation of the purely hour-by-hour, wage-based instrumentality of relations to employers. Moreover, actual kin may have spoken the language of love and affection, but migrants knew that they were in Lebanon to earn money and send it back. There were some distinctive ways, therefore, that constant circulation exposed instrumentalism in forms that could not be stably euphemized. Perhaps this constant exposure of instrumentality was what prevented the development of extended hegemony as such, wherein migrants would start to conceive of themselves as subjects in the context of dominant arrangements, rather than just within the narrower frame of family and village.[7]

The pessimism of the history told here is that workers clearly acquired stakes in their subordination, and their hard labor worked to ensure the reproduction of the vertiginous hierarchy, and collective, empowering, and cumulative transformation remained a distant prospect. Forms of subordination and accumulation were all the more unpleasant because this was clearly not just a victim's tale, but one of dignified subjects wrestling with circumstances. But for all their efforts and hopes, the hard labor, debt, poverty, hostility, and exilic rotation remained. Attempts to hold together personal dignity in the face of stigma concealed the rank humiliations involved.

The optimism of the story, on the other hand, is that powerful structures needed to elicit consent in order to function, and that migrant workers were neither easily duped nor congenitally backward, nor did they suffer from false consciousness. Indeed, where the possibility of collective action arose in the late 1970s, workers were quick to join strikes and protests. The system did not function through wooden behavioral conformity, or nostalgia, but through concrete, particular possibilities pursued by workers. Precisely because decision-making agency was required by the system, there was always a possibility—especially in the context of ceaseless structural and social change, fracture, and contradiction—that such agency was put to purposes other than those that worked to reproduce the dominant form of power. Partly as a result of this structural instability, this potential contradiction, it may be true that what

Zygmunt Bauman calls "order-building" works all the more ferociously to categorize, to exclude, to essentialize, and to distinguish Self from Other, citizen from alien, sane from insane, normal from transgressive, modern from traditional, and civilized from barbarian.[8] But there is no reason to presuppose in advance that such order-building can contain all possibilities of instability and insurrection, and all forms of counterhegemonic rearticulation, particularly as order-building, can introduce fractures and contradictions of its own.[9] Whereas the different elements in the changing combinations of elective affinity in Goethe's novel "attract, seize, destroy, devour [and] consume one another," they may also "emerge again from this most intimate union in renewed, novel and unexpected shape."[10] The search for the renovation of independent access to the means of existence could be seen as a reappropriation of the means of production by other means, and if articulated as a collective rather than an individual project, could yet hold out possibilities for empowerment.

ENDNOTES

Introduction

1. Cited in Francis Wilson, *Labour in the South African Gold Mines (1911–1969)* (Cambridge: Cambridge University Press, 1972), p. 14.

2. Lydia Potts, *The World Labour Market: A History of Migration*, published in German 1988, trans. by Terry Bond (London: Zed Books, 1990), pp. 218–289. Wilson, *Labour in the Gold Mines*, p. 1. Labor surpluses were not uniform, of course. Only in the 1960s, for example, did the South African gold mines have a surplus, p. 87.

3. Rosa Luxemburg, in spite of her groundbreaking concentration on the colonial world, does not seem to have considered this possibility in her monumental *Accumulation of Capital*, published in German 1913, trans. by Agnes Schwarzschild (London: Routledge, 2003).

4. Potts, *World Labour Market*, p. 199, pp. 205–206.

5. Saskia Sassen, *The Mobility of Labor and Capital: A Study in International Investment and Labor Flow* (Cambridge: Cambridge University Press, 1988), p. 31; Michael J. Piore, *Birds of Passage: Migrant Labor and Industrial Societies* (Cambridge: Cambridge University Press, 1979), pp. 25, 98.

6. Bauman identifies 1870 as the moment that the notion of "overpopulation" started to be significant in the Anglophone world. Zygmunt Bauman, *Wasted Lives: Modernity and Its Outcasts* (Cambridge: Polity Press, 2004), p. 34.

7. As Portes puts it, "Spontaneous migration, when people move without any coercion or without inducement by their future employers, is mostly a twentieth century phenomenon." Alejandro Portes, "Economic Sociology and the Sociology of Immigration: A Conceptual Overview," in *The Economic Sociology of Immigration: Essays on Networks, Ethnicity, and Entrepreneurship*, edited by Alejandro Portes (New York: Russell Sage Foundation, 1995), p. 21.

8. The rules for indentured workers covered, for example, industry, docility, and obedience on the job; cleanliness and regularity in personal habits; bedtimes; and personal and barrack hygiene. Such rules passed into disuse by 1900. Clarence E. Glick, *Sojourners and Settlers: Chinese Migrants in Hawaii* (Honolulu: University Press of Hawaii, 1980), pp. 34–35.

9. Richard Williams wrote that whereas slaves were extracted from Africa in the eighteenth century by military force, the Irish were driven from Ireland in the nineteenth century by economic force. Richard Williams, *Hierarchical Structures and Social Value: The Creation of Black and Irish Identities in the United States* (Cambridge: Cambridge University Press, 1990), pp. 133–134.

10. Adam Smith, *The Wealth of Nations*, edited by Edwin Cannan (Chicago: University of Chicago Press, 1976), Vol. 1, Book II, p. 291 and Vol. 2, Book V, pp. 302–303; Gary Becker, *The Economics of Discrimination* (Chicago: University of Chicago Press, 1957); Barry R. Chiswick, "The Effect of Americanization on the Earnings of Foreign-Born Men," *Journal of Political Economy* 86, 5 (Oct. 1978), pp. 897–921; George J. Borjas, *Friends or Strangers: The Impact of Immigrants on the US Economy* (New York: Basic Books, 1990). Free marketeers in this tradition occasionally advance the 'almost unthinkable' panacea of open borders for labor. See Nigel Harris, *Thinking the Unthinkable: The Immigration Myth Exposed* (London: I. B. Tauris, 2001).

11. Wilson, *Labour in the Gold Mines*, pp. 140, 141–144, 154.

12. Emphasis in original. Frederick Engels, *Anti-Dühring: Herr Eugen Dührings's Revolution in Science* (New York: International Publishers, 1939), p. 205. In medieval society, wrote Marx, personal relations of dependence between "serfs and lords, vassals and suzerains, laymen and clerics" characterized "the social relations of material production." Here, personal relations of dependency are "not disguised as social relations between things." Karl Marx, *Capital*, Vol. 1, published 1976 by Pelican Books, intro. by Ernest Mandel, trans. by Ben Fowkes (London: Penguin, 1990), p. 170. See also Marshall Sahlins, *Stone Age Economics*, published 1972 (London: Routledge, 2004), p. 92.

13. Stephen Castles and Godula Kosack, *Immigrant Workers and Class Structure in Western Europe* (2nd ed.), published 1973 (Oxford: Oxford University Press, 1985); History Task Force, *Labor Migration under Capitalism: The Puerto Rican Experience* (New York: Monthly Review Press, 1979); Saskia Sassen-Koob, "The New Labor Demand in Global Cities" in *Cities in Transformation: Class, Capital, and the State*, edited by Michael Peter Smith (Beverly Hills: Sage Publications, 1984); Robin Cohen, *The New Helots: Migrants in the International Division of Labour* (Aldershot: Avebury, 1987); Sassen, *Mobility of Labor*; Williams, *Hierarchical Structures*; Paul Ong, Edna Bonacich, and Lucie Cheng, eds., *The New Asian Immigration in Los Angeles and Global Restructuring* (Philadelphia: Temple University Press, 1994); Bridget Anderson, *Doing the Dirty Work? The Global Politics of Domestic Labour* (London: Zed Books, 2000); Grace Chang, *Disposable Domestics: Immigrant Women Workers in the Global*

Economy (Cambridge, MA: South End Press, 2000); Gilbert G. Gonzalez and Raul A. Fernandez, *A Century of Chicano History: Empire, Nations and Migration* (New York: Routledge, 2003); Catherine Ceniza Choy, *Empire of Care: Nursing and Migration in Filipino American History* (Durham: Duke University Press, 2005).

14. Marx, *Capital*, Vol. 1, pp. 873ff.

15. An excellent summary of Marx's ideas as set out in *Ireland and the Irish Question*, *Grundisse*, and *Capital* is in History Task Force, *Migration under Capitalism*, pp. 36–57. Marxian readings are not entirely absent from the history of migration in the Arab world. Ignacio Klich, "*Criollos* and Arabic Speakers in Argentina: An Uneasy *Pas de Deux*, 1888–1914," in *The Lebanese in the World: A Century of Emigration*, edited by Albert Hourani and Nadim Shehadi (London: I. B. Tauris, 1992), pp. 243–284, p. 246ff.

16. Elizabeth McLean Petras, *Jamaican Labor Migration: White Capital and Black Labor, 1850–1930* (Boulder: Westview Press, 1988).

17. See especially Edna Bonacich and Lucie Cheng, "Introduction: A Theoretical Orientation to International Labor Migration," in *Labor Immigration under Capitalism: Asian Workers in the United States Before World War II*, edited by Lucie Cheng and Edna Bonacich (Berkeley: University of California Press, 1984), pp. 1–56, pp. 3, 27, 46; Chang, *Disposable Domestics*, p. 4.

18. Claude Meillassoux, *Maidens, Meal and Money: Capitalism and the Domestic Community*, published in French 1975 (Cambridge: Cambridge University Press, 1981); Michael Burawoy, "The Functions and Reproduction of Migrant Labor: Comparative Material from Southern Africa and the United States," *The American Journal of Sociology 81*, 5 (March 1976), pp. 1050–1087. See also Gary P. Freeman, *Immigrant Labor and Racial Conflict in Industrial Societies: The French and British Experience, 1945–1975* (Princeton: Princeton University Press, 1979), pp. 216–258.

19. Hourani and Shehadi's account bears some of these characteristics. Hourani and Shehadi, "Introduction," *The Lebanese in the World*, p. 4; Glick, *Sojourners and Settlers*, p. ix; Samir Khalaf, for example, goes as far as to argue that "more than poverty and oppression" it was the "image of a promised land" that drove emigration from Lebanon before 1914. Samir Khalaf, "The Background and Causes of Lebanese/Syrian Immigration to the United States Before World War I," in *Crossing the Waters: Arabic-Speaking Immigrants to the United States Before 1940*, Eric J. Hooglund ed. (Washington DC.: Smithsonian Institution Press, 1987), pp. 17–35, p. 33; Alan Dowty, *Closed Borders: The Contemporary Assault on Freedom of Movement* (New Haven: Yale University Press, 1987), p. 18. In a victory for Cold War fantasy, Dowty saw Syria, a country with a long-tradition of outmigration, as one of the great culprits in restricting the exit of citizens.

20. Milton M. Gordon, *Assimilation in American Life: The Role of Race, Religion and National Origin* (New York: Oxford University Press, 1964). For a particularly

negative view of "traditional culture" and how it supposedly operates in these contexts, see Dino Cinel, *The National Integration of Italian Return Migration, 1870–
1929* (Cambridge: Cambridge University Press, 1991), pp. 67, 121, 163, 217. The conventional non-Soviet historiography on Eastern European migrants made much of
how "peasants in the factory" brought backward ways with them and were prone
to traditional violence. Inge Blank, "A Vast Migratory Experience: Eastern Europe
in the Pre- and Post-Emancipation Era (1780–1914)," in *Roots of the Transplanted:
Volume One, Late 19th Century East Central and Southeastern Europe*, edited by
Dirk Hoerder and Inge Blank (New York: Columbia University Press, 1994), p. 216;
Miller's account is premised on a negative view of traditional, Irish Catholic cul-
ture, deemed incapable of understanding the true basis of Irish migration: Kerby A.
Miller, *Emigrants and Exiles: Ireland and the Irish Exodus to North America* (New
York: Oxford University Press, 1985); Robert T. Averitt, *The Dual Economy* (New
York: Norton, 1968).

21. Portes, "Economic Sociology and Immigration," pp. 1–41; Aristide R. Zolberg,
"Response: Working-Class Dissolution," *International Journal of Labor and Working-
Class History* 47 (Spring 1995), pp. 28–38.

22. Piore, *Birds of Passage*, pp. 54, 64–65.

23. Ibid., p. 82.

24. Ibid., pp. 25, 98.

25. Homi K. Bhabha, *Nation and Narration* (London: Routledge, 1990); James
Clifford, "Traveling Cultures," in *Cultural Studies*, edited and with an introduction by
Lawrence Grossberg, Cary Nelson, and Paula A. Treichler (New York: Routledge, 1992),
pp. 96–116; Arjan de Haan, *Unsettled Settlers: Migrant Workers and Industrial Capital-
ism in Calcutta* (Calcutta: K. P. Bagchi & Co., 1994), pp. 15, 24, 26–28, 237–238; Katy
Gardner, *Global Migrants, Local Lives: Travel and Transformation in Rural Bangladesh*
(Oxford: Clarendon Press, 1995), pp. 12–16; Rob Wilson and Wimal Dissanayake, eds.,
Global Local: Cultural Production and the Transnational Imaginary (Durham: Duke
University Press, 1996); Ahn Nga Longva, *Walls Built on Sand: Migration, Exclusion
and Society in Kuwait* (Boulder: Westview Press, 1997), pp. 1–2; Hondagneu-Sotelo,
Gendered Transitions; Akram Fouad Khater, *Inventing Home: Emigration, Gender,
and the Middle Class in Lebanon, 1870–1920* (Berkeley: University of California Press,
2001); Lara Putnam, *The Company They Kept: Migrants and the Politics of Gender in
Caribbean Costa Rica, 1870–1960* (Chapel Hill: University of North Carolina, 2002).

26. Khater, *Inventing Home*, pp. 16, 180–181.

27. Cf. Carine M. Mardorossian, *Reclaiming Difference: Caribbean Women Rewrite Postcolonialism* (Charlottesville: University of Virginia Press, 2005), p. 19.

28. Basch, Nina Glick Schiller, and Cristina Szanton Blanc, *Nations Unbound:
Transnational Projects, Postcolonial Predicaments, and Deterritorialized Nation-States*
(Amsterdam: Overseas Publishers Association, 1994).

29. Compare similar arguments in Mardorossian, *Reclaiming Difference*, pp. 19–21; Aihwa Ong, *Flexible Citizenship: The Cultural Logics of Transnationality* (Durham: Duke University Press, 1999), pp. 11, 12–13; Gonzalez and Fernandez, *Chicano History and Migration*, p. 46

30. Subaltern studies, seeking to escape Marxian materialism at pace from the late 1980s and early 1990s, left the category of the economy oddly unscathed. Revised subaltern studies, it was said, now encompassed elite texts and practices, went beyond the discipline of history, tackled issues of "contemporary politics and politics of knowledge" and "dominant formations and representations," and went beyond the narrow study of subaltern groups such that "nothing—not élite practices, state policies, academic disciplines, literary texts, archival sources, language—was exempt from effects of subalternity." Nothing, that is, except the economy. Gautam Bhadra, Gyan Prakash, and Susie Tham, eds., *Subaltern Studies X: Writings on South Asian History and Society* (Oxford: Oxford University Press, 1999), pp. v–vi.

31. Gonzalez and Fernandez, *Chicano History and Migration*, pp. 97–98, 101–102. In Gonzalez and Fernandez's work, moreover, cultural and economic imperialism work hand in hand (pp. 73–74). Similarly, in Anderson's book, domestic paid labor was taken on in Europe in the 1990s so that middle-class couples could avoid the difficult work of renegotiating gender norms regarding the division of domestic labor. Anderson, *Doing the Dirty Work?*

32. Choy, *Empire of Care*, pp. 4–5. The distinction between a work such as this and the standard works of economic sociology is its critical attention to issues of imperialism, gender, race, and class.

33. Eley, *Crooked Line*, pp. 181, 201. For similar points, see Ong, *Flexible Citizenship*, p. 15, and Nugent, *Rural Revolt in Mexico*, p. 21.

34. Hegemony is considerably more sophisticated than the notion of legitimacy, which assumes far too much about the autonomy and rationality of the subject who confers legitimacy. It is also richer than the concept of authority, which tends to ratify power by ignoring the ways that its authoritative exercise is linked to violence, oppression, and social interests.

35. Such leadership involved certain compromises in regard to the narrow corporate interests of the fundamental class in order to win the consent of the subaltern groups to the domination of that class over the general direction of social life.

36. The point here is to distinguish the critique of a certain form of structural determinism and teleology from an idealist rejection of objective social structure *in toto*. Resnick and Wolff call surplus generation "class processes." Stephen A. Resnick and Richard D. Wolff, *New Departures in Marxian Theory* (London and New York: Routledge, 2006).

37. Wolfgang von Goethe, *Elective Affinities*, published 1809, trans. by R. J. Hollingdale (London: Penguin, 1971), p. 35. See especially pp. 50–56.

38. Ibid., pp. 53–54.

39. Max Weber, *The Protestant Ethic and the Spirit of Capitalism*, published 1930, trans. by Talcott Parsons (London: Routledge, 1992), pp. 180–183.

40. Ong urges that "the *regulatory effects* of particular cultural institutions, projects, regimes, and markets that shape people's motivations, desires, and struggles and make them particular kinds of subjects in the world should be identified." Ong, *Flexible Citizenship*, pp. 5–6. My position reverses this logic. Instead of searching for the ways systems constitute subjects, I am interested in the ways subjects are alienated within systems.

41. As Claude Meillassoux stated, "Marx showed that what appeared to the liberal economists to be purely economic and material, for example, commodities or capital, was, in fact, the *crystallization of social relations*, in particular those which dominate the wage earning process." My emphasis. Meillassoux, *Maidens, Meal and Money*, p. 6.

42. For this argument in regard to contractarian theory, see Carole Pateman, *The Sexual Contract* (Cambridge: Cambridge University Press, 1988).

43. Anderson, *Doing the Dirty Work?*, p. 6.

44. The reference here is to the remarks of Senator Borah of the U.S. Senate in 1937: "No business has a right to coin the very lifeblood of workmen into dollars and cents." Cited in Marc Linder, *Migrant Workers and Minimum Wages: Regulating the Exploitation of Agricultural Labor in the United States* (Boulder: Westview Press, 1992), p. 95.

45. Emphasis in original. Claus Offe, *Disorganized Capitalism: Contemporary Transformations of Work and Politics* (Oxford: Polity Press, 1985), pp. 16–18, 23–28, 55–57.

46. Picard, *Lebanon: A Shattered Country* (rev. ed.), trans. by Franklin Philip (New York: Holmes and Meier, 2002), p. 193.

47. "It is sometimes difficult to make a clear distinction between . . . voluntary and involuntary flows, [but] the distinction is an important one, and, when separated conceptually, the two phenomena raise very different questions." Sarah Collinson, *Europe and International Migration* (London: Pinter Publishers, 1993), p. xiii.

48. Parnwell's working distinctions between (1) forced migration involving displacement, evacuees, and slave trade; (2) impelled migration, involving refugees and indentured labor or the coolie trade; and (3) free migration, involving push and pull factors, are broadly serviceable here. Mike Parnwell, *Population Movements and the Third World* (London: Routledge, 1993), p. 25. See also Sassen, *Mobility of Labor*, p. 53.

49. Women were more commonly present among migrant workers, even in the late nineteenth and early twentieth centuries, than is commonly recognized. S. M. Gualtieri, "Gendering the Chain Migration Thesis: Women and Syrian Transatlantic Migration," in *Comparative Studies of South Asia, Africa and the Middle East,* pp. 69–80.

50. Regarding, for example, eastern Europe, see Blank, "A Vast Migratory Experience," p. 244. For a summary of these points regarding pre-1945 migrants from Asia, see Ong et al., *Asian Immigration*, p. 3.

51. In West Africa, for example, precolonial migration involved movements as a community or with community, whereby whole tribes moved long distances to escape hostilities or find fertile land or greener pastures. These kinds of movements were broken up with colonial labor policy, the development of market relations, and associated forms of labor migration. Paulina Makinwa-Adebusoye, "The West African Migration System," in *International Migration Systems: A Global Approach*, edited by Mary M. Kritz, Lin Lean Lim, and Hania Zlotnik (Oxford: Clarendon Press, 1992), pp. 63–79, p. 63.

52. June Mei, "Socioeconomic Origins of Emigration: Guangdong to California, 1850–1882," in *Labor Immigration under Capitalism*, pp. 219–247, 220.

53. Nakano Glenn, *Issei, Nisei, Warbride: Three Generations of Japanese American Women in Domestic Service* (Philadelphia: Temple University Press, 1986), p. 9. The vast late nineteenth-century migrations from eastern Europe were seen by Inge Blank as different from previous migrations because they stemmed not from escape from the plague or from a particularly harsh landowner, but were linked more structurally to the "internationalization of the labour market." Blank, "A Vast Migratory Experience," p. 201.

54. Bauman, *Wasted Lives*, p. 73.

55. Saskia Sassen, *Guests and Aliens* (New York: The New Press, 1999). As Mei stated, "The Chinese were wanted overseas only for their labor power and not for their persons." Mei, "Guangdong to California, 1850–1882," pp. 220–222. See also Samir Amin, "Modern Migrations in Western Africa," in *Modern Migrations in Western Africa*, edited by Samir Amin (Oxford: Oxford University Press, 1974), pp. 65–126, p. 66; Piore, *Birds of Passage*, pp. 52–55; Glenn, *Issei, Nisei, Warbride*, p. 9; Hondagneu-Sotelo, *Gendered Transitions*, p. xv. Regarding Syria and Lebanon, see Robert Widmer, "Population," in *Economic Organization of Syria*, edited by Sa'id B. Himadeh (Beirut: American University of Beirut Press, 1936), pp. 3–26, pp. 13, 17; Albert Hourani, "Introduction," in *The Lebanese in the World*, pp. 3–13, pp. 5–6. According to Sassen, "colonizing migrations" belong to an earlier phase and were about the "process of capitalist penetration into previously unincorporated, autonomous regions of the world." Sassen, *Mobility of Labor*, p. 32.

56. Janet Abu-Lughod, "Recent Migrations in the Arab World," in *Arab Society: Social Science Perspectives*, edited by Saad Eddin Ibrahim and Nicholas S. Hopkins (Cairo: American University in Cairo Press, 1985), pp. 177–188, p. 177. Many a scholar agrees that "colonialism integrated the peasantry into the international capitalist market and traditional social and subsistence patterns were disrupted." Richard Lawless,

ed., *The Middle Eastern Village: Changing Economic and Social Relations* (London: Croom Helm, 1987), p. 1.

57. Hondagneu-Sotelo, *Gendered Transitions*, p. 29.

58. Aristide R. Zolberg, "Labour Migration and International Economic Regimes: Bretton Woods and After," in *International Migration Systems*, pp. 315–334, p. 321. Note the euphemistic use of the term *relocation*.

59. Sassen, *Mobility of Labor*, p. 34.

60. Similar patterns have been noted in West Africa, China, Yemen, South Africa, and elsewhere. See, for example, Amin, *Migrations in Western Africa*, pp. 69–71, 94–97; Mei, "Guangdong to California," p. 227; Jon C. Swanson, *Emigration and Economic Development: The Case of the Yemen Arab Republic* (Boulder: Westview Press, 1979), p. 2; Colin Bundy, "The Transkei Peasantry, c.1890–1914: 'Passing through a Period of Stress,'" in *The Roots of Rural Poverty in Central and Southern Africa*, edited by Robin Palmer and Neil Parsons (London: Heinemann, 1977), pp. 201–220, pp. 201–202.

61. Burawoy, "The Functions and Reproduction of Migrant Labor"; Hondagneu-Sotelo, *Gendered Transitions*, p. 17.

62. This is Piore's useful definition of jobs commonly filled by migrants in Europe and the United States. Piore, *Birds of Passage*, p. 17.

63. Basch et al., *Nations Unbound*, p. 4.

64. Castles and Kosack, *Immigrants in Europe*, pp. 492–494, 500; Chang, *Disposable Domestics*, pp. 4–5.

65. See Daniel Kubat, ed., *The Politics of Return: International Return Migration in Europe* (Roma: Centro Studi Emigrazione, 1983), p. 2.

66. Basch et al., *Nations Unbound*, pp. 5–7.

67. Sassen, *Mobility of Labor*, pp. 40–41; Sassen-Koob, "Global Cities," p. 165.

68. Bonacich and Cheng, "Theoretical Orientation," pp. 27–28.

69. Collinson has argued that to ensure the temporary labor recruitment of foreigners, policy attempted to induce a "state of dependence and insecurity" among migrants. Hence, the Aliens Act of 1965 noted that "foreigners enjoy all basic rights except the basic rights of freedom of assembly, freedom of association, freedom of movement, and free choice of occupation, place of work and place of education." Collinson, *Europe and Migration*, p. 95. The act intended to create a rotation of workers, to ensure a "match in supply and demand in the labour market"—underlain by a consensus that all would gain economically. Collinson, *Europe and Migration*, p. 51.

70. Chang, *Disposable Domestics*, pp. 7–9, 14.

71. "Border enforcement is a mechanism facilitating the extraction of cheap labor by assigning criminal status to a segment of the working class—illegal immigrants." The strengthening of the nation-state hence creates the conditions for immigrant labor as a distinct category in the labor supply. Sassen, *Mobility of Labor*, pp. 36–37.

72. Migrant jobs in Buenos Aires, for example, a regional hub with some similarities to Beirut, are characterized by "low-wages, instability, limited benefits, and hazardous working conditions." Alicia Maguid, "Immigration and the Labor Market in Metropolitan Buenos Aires," in *International Migration*, pp. 104–119, pp. 104–107. Massey and Taylor argue uncontroversially that "the concentration of immigrants is highest in those sectors which have always been more flexible and unfavorable in terms of salary levels and working conditions" in *International Migration*, p. 6; Sassen speaks of an "underclass." Sassen-Koob, "Global Cities," p. 153. Piore speaks of low-paid, insecure, low-status jobs. Piore, *Birds of Passage*, p. 17. Portes notes the overrepresentation of migrants in "informal, menial and badly-paid activities." Portes, "Economic Sociology and Immigration," p. 30. See also Collinson, *Europe and Migration*, p. 36; Blank, "A Vast Migratory Experience," p. 222; Castles and Kosack, *Immigrants in Europe*, pp. 6–7; Gonzalez and Fernandez, *Chicano History and Migration*, pp. 123–124.

73. See Kitty Calavita, *Inside the State: The Bracero Program, Immigration, and the INS* (New York: Routledge, 1992). Also see Piore, *Birds of Passage*, p. 166.

74. Hondagneu-Sotelo, *Gendered Transitions*, p. xxiii.

75. Cited in Wilson, *Labour in the Gold Mines*, p. 3. See also R. Mansell Prothero, "Foreign Migrant Labour for South Africa," in *International Migration Review, VIII* No. 3 (Fall 1974), pp. 383–394, pp. 383–384.

76. Sassen, *Guests and Aliens*, p. 143. See, for example, Blank, "A Vast Migratory Experience."

77. See, for example, Cinel, *Italian Return Migration*, p. 1.

78. "Circulation is often the most prevalent type of movement in Third World countries." Parnwell, *Population Movements*, p. 28.

79. Andrzej Kapiszewski, *Native Arab Population and Foreign Workers in the Gulf States* (Kraków: TAiWPN Universitas, 1999), pp. 17–18.

80. Bridget Anderson, *Labour Exchange: Patterns of Migration in Asia* (London: Catholic Institute for International Relations, 1997), p. 7.

81. Swanson, *Emigration and Economic Development*; Fred Arnold and Nasra M. Shah, "Asian Labor Migration to the Middle East," *International Migration Review, 18* 2 (Summer 1984), pp. 294–318; Kritz and Zlotnik, eds., *International Migration*; Parnwell, *Population Movements*; Amin, *Migrations in Western Africa*; Scott Whiteford and Richard N. Adams, "Migration, Ethnicity, and Adaptation: Bolivian Migrant Workers in Northwest Argentina," in *Migration and Urbanization: Models and Adaptive Strategies*, edited by Brian M. du Toit and Helen I. Safa (The Hague: Mouton Publishers, 1975), pp. 179–199; Dawn I. Marshall, "International Migration as Circulation: Haitian Movement to the Bahamas," in *Circulation in Third World Countries*, edited by R. Mansell Prothero and Murray Chapman (London: Routledge & Kegan Paul, 1985), pp. 226–240; Seteney Shami, ed., *Population Displacement and Resettlement:*

Development and Conflict in the Middle East (New York: Center for Migration Studies, 1994); Putnam, *The Company They Kept.*

82. Sassen, *Guests and Aliens*, p. 142.
83. Castles and Kosack, *Immigrants in Europe*, p. 12.
84. Piore, *Birds of Passage*, p. 81.
85. Ibid., pp. 84–85.
86. Longva, *Walls Built on Sand*, p. 44.
87. Wilson, *Labour in the Gold Mines*, p. 5.
88. Anderson, *Labour Exchange*, p. 5.
89. Kubat, *The Politics of Return*, p. 2.
90. Hondagneu-Sotelo, *Gendered Transitions*, p. 12.
91. Ibid., p. 11.
92. See also (on Mexico) Chang, *Disposable Domestics*, p. 5.

Chapter 1

1. Cited in Moh Bourhan Chreitah, *L'Economie Syrienne et les Relations Economiques et Douanières de la Syrie Avec les Voisons Arabes*, Doctoral thesis, University of Fribourg, Switzerland (Geneva: Imprimerie Fornara, 1958), p. 21.

2. Khater, *Inventing Home*, p. 187. Migration peaked from 1900 to 1914 at 15,000 persons a year.

3. Cited in Charles Issawi, "The Historical Background of Lebanese Emigration, 1800–1914" in *Lebanese in the World*, pp. 13–31, p. 31.

4. Robert Widmer, "Population," in *Economic Organization of Syria*, edited by Sa'id B. Himadeh (Beirut: American University of Beirut Press, 1936), pp. 3–26, p. 15.

5. Richard Thoumin, *Géographie Humaine de la Syrie Centrale* (Paris: Libraire Ernest Leroux, 1936), p. 334.

6. Ibid., pp. 334–337.

7. Widmer, "Population," p. 18. The population of two French Mandates was estimated at three million in the 1930s (p. 4).

8. Hourani, *The Lebanese in the World*, pp. 5–6.

9. Widmer, "Population," pp. 23–24; Abdul-Rahman Hamidé, *La Région d'Alep: Etude de Géographie Rurale* (Paris: Université de Paris, 1959), p. 557.

10. Widmer, "Population," pp. 13, 17; Hourani, *Lebanese in the World*, pp. 5–6.

11. Roger Owen, "Lebanese Migration in the Context of World Population Movements," in *The Lebanese in the World*, pp. 33–39, p. 33.

12. Thoumin, *Syrie Centrale*, p. 142.

13. André Latron, *La Vie Rurale en Syrie et au Liban* (Beirut: Institut Français de Damas, 1936), p. 84.

14. Widmer, "Population," p. 23; Latron, *La Vie Rurale*, p. 112.

15. Thoumin, *Syrie Centrale*, pp. 159–160. Wealthy families started to spend their winters on the coast during the same period.

16. Jacques Weulersse, *Paysans de Syrie et du Proche-Orient* (n.p.: Gallimard, 1946), p. 170.

17. Ibid., p. 172.

18. Latron, *La Vie Rurale*, p. 86.

19. Weulersse, *Paysans*, p. 172.

20. Martha Mundy and Richard Saumarez Smith, *Governing Property, Making the Modern State: Law, Administration and Production in Ottoman Syria* (London: I. B. Tauris, 2007), p. 188.

21. Thoumin, *Syrie Centrale*, p. 146.

22. Ibid., pp. 150–154.

23. Thoumin, *Syrie Centrale*, pp. 154–156.

24. Latron, *La Vie Rurale*, p. 112.

25. Ibid., p. 87.

26. Weulersse, *Paysans*, p. 172.

27. Latron, *La Vie Rurale*, p. 86.

28. Widmer, "Population," p. 16; Khater, *Inventing Home*, p. 70; Thoumin estimated the ratio of Christian to Druze migrants on Mt. Lebanon at 5:1 in the 1930s. Thoumin, *Syrie Centrale*, p. 334.

29. Khater, *Inventing Home*, p. 23; Thoumin, *Syrie Centrale*, p. 334.

30. Basim Faris, "Internal Trade," in *Economic Organization*, pp. 199–226, p. 201.

31. Weulersse, *Paysans*, pp. 100–101. For *musha'* arrangements in the 'Ajlun district, see Mundy, *Governing Property*, pp. 156–163, 179–180.

32. Latron, *La Vie Rurale*, p. 112.

33. For a groundbreaking study of the ways in which these codes were shaped by Ottoman legal reinterpretation, as well as by implementation, regional elites, and local production arrangements, see Mundy, *Governing Property*, passim.

34. Weulersse, *Paysans*, pp. 100–102, 116.

35. Ibid., pp. 102–103.

36. Weulersse, *Paysans*, p. 105. Hawwara in 'Ajlun seems to have presented a similar structure. Mundy, *Governing Property*, pp. 186–207.

37. Abdullah Hanna, *Al-Fallahun wa Mallak al-Ard fi Suriyya al-Qarn al-'Ashrin [Peasants and Landowners in Twentieth Century Syria]* (Beirut: Dar al-Tali'a, 2003), p. 50ff.

38. Weulersse, *Paysans*, p. 105.

39. For the importance of access to grazing land, see Mundy, *Governing Property*, p. 187.

40. Husni Sawwaf, "Natural Resources," in *Economic Organization*, p. 42.

41. Daher, *Ta'rikh Lubnan*, p. 199ff.

42. Mundy, *Governing Property*, p. 201.

43. For a good exposition, see Iliya F. Harik, "The Impact of the Domestic Market on Rural-Urban Relations in the Middle East," in *Rural Politics and Social Change in the Middle East*, edited by Richard Antoun and Iliya Harik (Bloomington, Indiana: Indiana University Press, 1972), pp. 337–363; Weulersse, *Paysans*, pp. 124–125.

44. Weulersse, *Paysans*, pp. 231–244.

45. Jean Hannoyer, "Le Monde Rural Avant les Réformes," in *La Syrie D'Aujourd'hui*, edited by André Raymond (Paris: Centre National de la Recherche Scientifique, 1980), pp. 273–295, pp. 286–287; Albert Huri, "Agriculture," in *Economic Organization*, p. 98; Weulersse, *Paysans*, pp. 114–115.

46. Weulersse, *Paysans*, p. 125.

47. For the consolidation of landowner power in the nineteenth century, see also Philip S. Khoury, *Urban Notables and Arab Nationalism: The Politics of Damascus 1860–1920* (Cambridge: Cambridge University Press, 1983); Michael Gilsenan, *Lords of the Lebanese Marches: Violence and Narrative in an Arab Society* (Berkeley: University of California Press, 1996), p. 79ff ; James A. Reilly, *A Small Town in Syria: Ottoman Hama in the Eighteenth and Nineteenth Centuries* (Oxford: Peter Lang, 2002), p. 117ff.

48. Weulersse, *Paysans*, p. 129.

49. Khater, *Inventing Home*, p. 26.

50. Weulersse, *Paysans*, p. 131.

51. Khater, *Inventing Home*, p. 22.

52. Ibid., pp. 20–21.

53. Ibid., p. 43.

54. Ibid., pp. 43–44.

55. Sidney W. Mintz, *Sweetness and Power: The Place of Sugar in Modern History*, first published in 1985 (New York: Penguin, 1986), p. 183.

56. For the case of sugar, see ibid., p. 169.

57. Weulersse, *Paysans*, pp. 114–115.

58. Khater, *Inventing Home*, pp. 31, 202, fn 53.

59. Ibid., p. 31.

60. This process vividly recalls Marx's descriptions of the "herod-like slaughter of the innocents" that accompanied the birth of the factory, staffed by orphans and occupants of poor-houses, in Lancashire. Marx, *Capital*, Vol. 1, p. 923.

61. Khater, *Inventing Home*, pp. 13–14.

62. Ibid., p. 37.

63. Ibid., pp. 36–37.

64. Ibid., p. 32.

65. Ibid., p. 13.

66. Ibid., pp. 20–21.

67. Hourani, *The Lebanese in the World*, pp. 5–6.

68. Widmer, "Population," p. 17. See also Dominique Chevallier, *La Société du Mont Liban à L'époque de la Révolution Industrielle en Europe* (Paris: Librairie orientaliste Paul Geuthner, 1971).

69. Engin Akarlı, "Ottoman Attitudes Towards Lebanese Emigration, 1885–1910," in *The Lebanese and the World*, pp. 109–138, pp. 134–135.

70. Widmer, "Population," p. 14.

71. Ibid., pp. 13–14.

72. Khater, *Inventing Home*, pp. 59–60.

73. As Mike Davis puts it, demography was no "self-acting archimedean lever" but certainly mattered at the level of "*local* population-resource relationships" [emphasis in original]. Mike Davis, *Late Victorian Holocausts: El Niño Famines and the Making of the Third World* (London: Verso, 2002), p. 309.

74. Ussama Makdisi, *The Culture of Sectarianism: Community, History, and Violence in Nineteenth-Century Ottoman Lebanon* (Berkeley: University of California Press, 2000), especially Chapter Two.

75. "The economic development and prosperity of Syria, therefore, must be sought through a more complete and intensive utilization of the available resources through more efficient and up-to-date methods." Husni Sawwaf, "Natural Resources," p. 47.

76. Albert Huri, "Agriculture," p. 98.

77. Widmer, "Population," p. 17.

78. George Hakim, "Industry," in *Economic Organization*, pp. 119–173, p. 171; Dominique Chevallier, *Villes et Travail en Syrie: Du XIXe au XXe Siècle* (Paris: G.-P. Maisonneuve & Larose, 1982).

79. For a detailed examination of these processes with regard to Egypt, see John Chalcraft, *The Striking Cabbies of Cairo and Other Stories: Crafts and Guilds in Egypt, 1863–1914* (Albany: State University of New York Press, 2004).

80. Abdullah Hanna, *Dayr Attiya: al-Ta'rikh wa-l-'Umran [Dayr Attiya: History and Civilization]* (Damascus: Institut Français d'études Arabes à Damas [IFEAD], 2002), pp. 255–283. Abdullah Hanna, interview, 15 August 2006. See also Philip S. Khoury, *Syria and the French Mandate: The Politics of Arab Nationalism, 1920–45* (London: I. B.Tauris, 1987), pp. 10–12, 286–293.

81. Abdullah Hanna, interview, 15 August 2006. May Seikaly, *Haifa: Transformation of an Arab Society, 1918–1939* (London: I. B. Tauris, 2002), pp. 20, 24, 144.

82. Elias, interview, 10 August 2004.

83. Jubran Hilal, *Dhikriyyat al-Niqabi [Memoirs of a Trade Unionist]*, foreword by Abdullah Hanna (Stockholm: Al-Yanabia, 2005), p. 71.

84. Piore, *Birds of Passage*, p. 141ff; David M. Gordon, Richard Edwards, and Michael Reich write of the "continuous erosion of independent farmers' and artisans'

economic bases" in *Segmented Work, Divided Workers: The Historical Transformation of Labour in the United States* (Cambridge: Cambridge University Press, 1982), p. 11.

85. The quotation is from Noel Ignatiev, *How the Irish Became White* (New York: Routledge, 1995), pp. 180–185. See also Williams, *Hierarchical Structures*, p. 7. The language of co-production is used by Kaushik Sunder Rajan, *Biocapital: The Constitution of Postgenomic Life* (Durham and London: Duke University Press, 2006), p. 4.

86. Luiz Maria Martinez Montiel, "The Lebanese Community in Mexico: Its Meaning, Importance and History of Its Communities," in *The Lebanese in the World*, pp. 379–392, p. 380.

87. Alixa Naff, *Becoming American: The Early Arab Immigrant Experience* (Carbondale: Southern Illinois University Press, 1985).

88. History Task Force, *Labor Migration under Capitalism*, pp. 8, 15.

89. Karl Polanyi, *The Great Transformation: The Political and Economic Origins of Our Time*, first published in 1944 (Boston: Beacon Press, 2001), p. 73.

90. Hanna, *Dayr 'Attiyya*, p. 267.

91. The evidence in regard to the social suffering of families left behind to cope is remarkably persistent in other locations during these years and later. See, for example, Mary Eleanor Cygan, "Polish Women and Emigrant Husbands," *Roots of the Transplanted*, pp. 359–374, p. 360.

92. Khater, *Inventing Home*, p. 77.

93. Ibid., p. 181.

94. Bauman, *Wasted Lives*, p. 73.

95. Khater, *Inventing Home*, pp. 14, 85–88.

96. Ibid., p. 14.

97. Ibid., pp. 14, 89.

98. Ibid., pp. 104–106, p. 113. Irish Americans—absent the constructs "East" and "West"—expressed similar themes. Miller, *Emigrants and Exiles*, pp. 4–5.

99. History Task Force, *Labor Migration*, p. 8.

100. The reluctance on the part of those operating their own means of production to work for wages for someone else, and the temporary nature of such work, has been discussed in many times and places. Edna Bonacich, "United States Capitalist Development: A Background to Asian Immigration," in *Labor Immigration*, pp. 79–129, p. 80; Piore, *Birds of Passage*, p. 95; Gardner, *Global Migrants, Local Lives*, p. 39.

101. A common finding. See Portes, "Sociology of Immigration," p. 20.

102. Weulersse, *Paysans*, pp. 131–132.

103. Albert Huri, "Agriculture," pp. 98–99.

104. Cf. Meillassoux, *Maidens, Meal and Money*, p. 87.

105. Hourani, *The Lebanese in the World*, p. 7; Jeff H. Lesser, "From Peddlers to Proprietors: Lebanese, Syrian and Jewish Immigrants in Brazil," in *The Lebanese in the World*, pp. 393–410.

106. Hourani, *The Lebanese in the World*, p. 8; Naff, *Becoming American*. Cf. Glenn, *Issei, Nisei, Warbride*, p. 10.

107. Qasim al-Haymani al-Biqa'i, *Dalil al-Muhajirin* (Havana, Cuba: Monte St., 1931).

108. Khater, *Inventing Home*, pp. 1–2, 9–10. Cf. Widmer's emphasis on migrants' determination to return, "Population," p. 15.

109. Khater, *Inventing Home*, p. 15. These are common patterns among migrants who often return to some form of self-employment. Kubat, *Politics of Return*, p. 5.

110. Thoumin, *Syrie Centrale*, pp. 183–184.

111. Owen, "Lebanese Migration," p. 36.

112. Klich, "*Criollos* and Arabic Speakers," pp. 278–279.

113. In Britain the key legislation was the Aliens Act of 1905 and the Aliens Restriction Act of 1914. Castles and Kosack, *Immigrants in Europe*, p. 18.

114. Widmer, "Population," pp. 19–20.

115. Weulersse, *Paysans*, pp. 311–312.

116. Widmer, "Population," pp. 19–20.

117. Idem. The same idea was repeated by other "foreign experts" in the 1940s. See analysis of Abdulhadi Yamut, *Al-Iqtisad al-Lubnani wa Afaq al-Sharq Awsatiyya wa-l-'Awlima [The Lebanese Economy, the Middle East and Globalization]* (Lebanon: Al-Shirka al-'Ilmiyya li-l-Kitab. 2005), p. 21.

118. Eric Wolf aimed to write history not as a developmental scheme involving the unfolding of timeless essence but as "a complex orchestration of antagonistic forces." Eric R. Wolf, *Europe and the People Without History*, illustrations by Noel L. Diaz, first published in 1982 (Berkeley: University of California Press, 1997), p. 5.

Chapter 2

1. See Stephen Castles and Mark J. Miller, *The Age of Migration: International Population Movements in the Modern World* (3rd ed.) (Houndmills: Palgrave Macmillan, 2003), pp. 122–177.

2. Chreitah, *L'Economie Syrienne*, p. 21; Mouna Liliane Samman, "Aperçu sur les Mouvements Migratoires Recents de la Population en Syrie," in *Revue de Géographie de Lyon*, 53, 3 (1978), pp. 211–228, p. 212.

3. Samman, "Les Mouvements Migratoires," p. 212.

4. Ibid., pp. 213–214.

5. Huda Hawwa, "Linkages and Constraints of the Syrian Economy," in *State and Society in Syria and Lebanon*, edited by Yussuf M. Choueiri (Exeter: University of Exeter Press, 1993), pp. 84–102, p. 86.

6. In 1970, Syria's GDP was estimated at $2.1 billion ($342 per capita). Nasser H. Saidi, *Growth, Destruction and the Challenges of Reconstruction: Macroeconomic essays on Lebanon* (Beirut: The Lebanese Center for Policy Studies, 1999), p. 352.

7. Unskilled Syrians also went in small numbers to other neighboring countries, such as Turkey. Hamidé, *La Région d'Alep*, p. 563.

8. Samman, "Les Mouvements Migratoires," p. 213.

9. Günter Meyer, *Ländliche lebens- und wirtschaftsformen Syriens im Wandel [Changing Forms of Social and Economic Life in Rural Syria]* (Erlangen: Selbstverlag de Fränkischen Geographischen Gesellschaft in Kommission bei Palm und Enke, 1984), p. 303.

10. Joseph Chami, *Le Mémorial du Liban, Tome II: le Mandat Béchara el Khoury 1943–1952* (Beirut: Chemaly & Chemaly, 2002), p. 363.

11. Ibid., p. 407.

12. Ibid., p. 433.

13. Reported in *Makhbar Sahaf*, March 6, 1958, cited in *Al-ʿAlaqat al-Lubnaniyya al-Suriyya 1943–1985: Waqaʾiʿ, Bibliyughrafiyya wa Wathaʾiq [Lebanese-Syrian Relations: Events, Bibliography and Documents]*, 2 Vols (Antiliyas: Markaz al-Tawthiq wa-l-Buhuth al-Lubnani, 1986), p. 168.

14. Ibid., p. 17.

15. The key turning point was 1958 for André Bourgey, "La Guerre et ses conséquences géographiques au Liban," *Annales de Géographies*, No. 521, 94th year (1985), pp. 1–37, p. 3.

16. Al-Jumhuriyya al-Lubnaniyya, *Al-Majmuʿa al-Ihsaʾiyya al-Lubnaniyya li-ʿam 1963 [Lebanese Statistical Totals for 1963]* (Beirut: Wizarat al-Tasmim al-ʿAm [Ministry of Planning], n.d.), pp. 46–48; Al-Jumhuriyya al-Lubnaniyya, *Al-Majmuʿa al-Ihsaʾiyya al-Lubnaniyya li-ʿam 1973 [Lebanese Statistical Totals for 1973]* (Beirut: Wizarat al-Tasmim al-ʿAm [Ministry of Planning], n.d.), pp. 68–71.

17. Joseph Chami, *Le Mémorial du Liban, Tome IV: le Mandat Fouad Chéhab 1958–1964* (Beirut: Chemaly & Chemaly, 2002), p. 307.

18. *Al-ʿAlaqat al-Lubnaniyya al-Suriyya*, vol. 1, p. 18.

19. This estimate was given by Lebanese General Security, responsible for regulating entries and exits at the border. André Bourgey and J. Pharès, "Les bidonvilles de l'agglomeration de Beyrouth," *Revue de géographie de Lyon*, 48, 2 (1973), pp. 107–139, p. 121. The Lebanese report of a net migration of 101,000 Syrians between 1959 and 1970 noted by Samman seems to refer to an attempt by the Lebanese to estimate how many Syrians had moved permanently to Lebanon. As such, it does not contradict these other figures, which refer to seasonal as well as permanent work. Samman, "Les Mouvements Migratoires," p. 212.

20. The number of resident Lebanese in work or looking for work in 1970 was 572,000 according to an "exhaustive enquiry" published in November 1970 by the *Direction Centrale de la Statistique*. See *Etude Annuelle sur L'Economie Libanaise de L'Année 1972* (Beirut: Bureau des Documentations Libanaises et Arabe, 1973), p. 98.

21. Syria's workforce numbered approximately 1.89 million out of a populace of 6.3 million in 1970. Onn Winckler, *Demographic Developments and Population Policies in Ba'thist Syria* (Brighton: Sussex Academic Press, 1999), p. 6.

22. Bourgey and Pharès, "Les bidonvilles," p. 120.

23. Marwan Maouia, "Lebanese Emigration to the Gulf and Saudi Arabia," in *The Lebanese in the World*, pp. 651–659, p. 652.

24. Abdullah Hanna, interview, August 15, 2006.

25. The Palestinian exodus and dispossession of 1948–49 can be described as "mass explusion" in the sense defined by the International Law Association in 1986: "Mass expulsion results from the use of coercion, including a variety of political, economic and social measures which directly, or even more so indirectly, force people to leave or flee their homelands for fear of life, liberty and security." See Nicholas Van Hear, *New Diasporas: The Mass Exodus, Dispersal and Regrouping of Migrant Communities* (London: UCL Press, 1998), p. 10.

26. *Al-'Alaqat al-Lubnaniyya al-Suriyya*, vol. 1, p. 79.

27. Bourgey and Pharès, "Les Bidonvilles," pp. 116–119; Interview, Abdullah Hanna, August 15, 2006.

28. Jean Hannoyer, "Le Monde Rural Avant les Réformes," in *La Syrie D'Aujourd'hui*, edited by André Raymond (Paris: CNRS, 1980), pp. 273–295, pp. 286, 289.

29. Cf. Meyer, *Syriens im Wandel*, p. 303. Eviction by capitalistic landowners, especially in the face of peasant resistance, was also a factor. Hanna, *Al-Fallahun wa Mallak al-Ard*, p. 61.

30. Meyer, *Syriens im Wandel*, p. 303.

31. Hanna Batatu, *Syria's Peasantry, the Descendants of Its Lesser Rural Notables, and Their Politics* (Princeton NJ: Princeton University Press, 1999), p. 32.

32. Ibid, p. 32.

33. Ibid., p. 35; Meyer, *Syriens im Wandel*, p. 302.

34. Batatu, *Syria's Peasantry*, p. 42.

35. Fathi Muhammad Abu-Aianah, *Al-Sukkan fi-l-Watan al-'Arabi: Dirasat Giyudimughrafiyya [Population in the Arab World: Geodemographic Studies]* (Alexandria: Dar al-Ma'rifa al-Jama'iyya, 1994), p. 245.

36. Tabitha Petran, *Syria: A Modern History* (London: Ernest Benn Ltd., 1972), p. 136.

37. Batatu speaks of "glaring inequalities," *Syria's Peasantry*, p. 35.

38. For similar processes in Eastern Europe, see Blank, "A Vast Migratory Experience," pp. 214–215, 235–236, 243.

39. Cited in Batatu, *Syria's Peasantry*, p. 59.

40. Ibid., pp. 59–63. Cf. Lawless, *Middle Eastern Village*, p. 1.

41. This latter position is surveyed in Ilan Pappé, *The Modern Middle East* (London: Routledge, 2005).

42. Meyer, *Syriens im Wandel*, p. 303. Meyer argues, however, that "relatively few former sharecroppers decided to work abroad." Everything depends here on the definition of *former sharecropper*, a category encompassing a very wide variety of land tenure arrangements, including beneficiaries of the land reform, who were now small landowners, but included former sharecroppers in their ranks. Certainly, sharecroppers rarely migrated, but my research suggests that *former* sharecroppers certainly did, especially to Lebanon, where resource constraints were less of an issue because it was so cheap to migrate there.

43. Batatu, *Syria's Peasantry*, p. 25. Usurers were dealt a decisive blow in 1963 when Ba'thists expanded the Agricultural Cooperatives bank (p. 55).

44. Louise E. Sweet, *Tell Toqaan: A Syrian Village*, Anthropological Papers No. 14 (Ann Arbor: University of Michigan, 1960), pp. 1–3.

45. Ibid., pp. 5–8.

46. Ibid., p. 72.

47. Ibid., p. 34.

48. Ibid., pp. 117–118.

49. Ibid., p. 130.

50. Ibid., p. 205.

51. Ibid., pp. 235–236.

52. 1 dunum = 900m² hence 10 dunums is just under 1 hectare.

53. Interview, Abu Yusuf, August 10, 2004.

54. Noted briefly in the Hawran, for example, by Hannoyer, "Le Monde Rural," p. 292.

55. Meyer, *Syriens im Wandel*, p. 304. He adds that 18 percent of returnees to the Euphrates Valley spent their money on building houses "while 11% needed their savings to raise the bride-money for their *marriage. Productive investments* to help improve the earning opportunities of the migrants in their native village *are very rare.* Less than 4% of the migrants had used their remittances for such purposes—i.e.. buying agricultural machinery, livestock, or a car which could be used as a taxi, or opening a retail-shop." Italics in original.

56. Tony Elias, interview, August 12, 2004.

57. Hanna Awwad, interview, August 11, 2004.

58. Ibid.

59. Hanna Butros, interview, August 11, 2004.

60. Ibid.

61. Ibid.

62. Meyer, *Syriens im Wandel*, p. 302.

63. To give the US$ figure, I have used a 1959 exchange rate.

64. Chami, *Béchara el Khoury*, p. 433.

65. Joseph, interview, August 10, 2004.

66. Hanna Butros, interview, August 11, 2004.

67. *Al-'Alaqat al-Lubnaniyya al-Suriyya*, vol. 1, p. 168.

68. Hanna Awwad, interview, August 11, 2004.

69. The US$ rate is calculated using the 1974 exchange rate.

70. Tony Elias, interview, August 12, 2004

71. Abed, interview, August 9, 2005.

72. *Al-'Alaqat al-Lubnaniyya al-Suriyya*, vol. 1, p. 298.

73. Joseph, interview, August 10, 2004.

74. Timothy Mitchell, *Rule of Experts: Egypt, Techno-Politics, Modernity* (Berkeley: University of California Press, 2002), pp. 209–244.

75. Winckler, *Demographic Developments*, p. 8.

76. The Syrian population increased by 50 percent again from 1947 to 1960, to number 4.5 million. But Syrian outmigration during the 1950s remained on a limited scale compared with what was to come in the 1960s. The great increases in outmigration to Lebanon and hence overall came in the 1960s, but the rate of population growth does not seem to have increased, moving from 4.5 million in 1960 to 6.3 million in 1970, or an increase of 40 percent on the decade. Figures cited in Winckler, *Demographic Developments*, p. 6.

77. Abu-Aianah, *Al-Sukkan fi-l-Watan al-'Arabi*, p. 240. Damascus housed 220,968 migrants in 1970, hence total internal migration in Syria during these years was estimated to be a little short of 1 million persons, although it is not clear how this figure is derived.

78. Abu-Aianah, *Al-Sukkan fi-l-Watan al-'Arabi*, pp. 244–245.

79. Hamidé, *La Région d'Alep*, pp. 558–559.

80. Ibid., pp. 561–562.

81. Idem.

82. Abu-Aianah, *Al-Sukkan fi-l-Watan al-'Arabi*, pp. 244–245.

83. Ibid., p. 245.

84. Hamidé, *La Région d'Alep*, p. 562.

85. Ibid., p. 562.

86. Ibid., p. 558.

87. Hannoyer, "Le Monde Rural," p. 290.

88. André Gibert and Maurice Fevret, "La Djezireh Syrienne et son Réveil Economique," in *Revue de Géographie de Lyon, 28* (1953), pp. 1–15.

89. The actual figure in 1970 was +3,994. Abu-Aianah, *Al-Sukkan fi-l-Watan al-'Arabi*, pp. 244–245.

90. Hannoyer, "Le Monde Rural," pp. 291–292. See also Jean Hannoyer, "Industrie et changement social en Syrie: Deir-ez-Zor et sa région," in *Industrialisation et*

changements sociaux dans l'orient arabe, edited by André Bourgey (Lyon: Lyon University Press, 1982), pp. 401–428.

91. Hamidé, *La Région d'Alep*, pp. 558–560.

92. Gilsenan, *Lords of the Lebanese Marches*.

93. ʿAbed, interview, August 30, 2005.

94. Ibid.

95. François Metral, "State and Peasants in Syria: A Local View of a Government Irrigation Project," in *Arab Society: Social Science Perspectives*, edited by Saad Eddin Ibrahim and Nicholas S. Hopkins (Cairo: American University Press, 1985), pp. 336–354.

96. Meyer, *Syriens im Wandel*, p. 302.

97. Abu-Aianah, *Al-Sukkan fi-l-Watan al-ʿArabi*, pp. 244–245.

98. Janet Abu-Lughod, "Recent Migrations in the Arab World," in *Arab Society*, pp. 177–188, p. 181.

99. Joseph kept out of Syria for 10 years (1956–66) to avoid conscription. Joseph, interview, August 10, 2004.

100. Samman, "Les Mouvements Migratoires," p. 212.

101. Meyer, *Syriens im Wandel*, p. 303.

102. Samman, "Les Mouvements Migratoires," p. 213.

103. Hanna Awwad, interview, August 11, 2004.

104. Fahed Agha al-Barazi, interview, February 27, 2004.

105. Elizabeth Picard, "Managing Identities Among Expatriate Businessmen Across the Syrian Lebanese Boundary," Unpublished paper, MESA 2004, p. 16.

106. Rania W. Ghosn, "Syrian Elites' Practices and Representations of Beirut: The Intimate Nearness of Difference," Unpublished MSc Dissertation (London: University College London, 2003).

107. Hanna Awwad, interview, August 11, 2004.

108. E. Kanovsky, "The Economic Aftermath of the Six Day War: UAR, Jordan and Syria," in *The Middle East Journal*, 22, 3 (Summer 1968), pp. 278–296, p. 279.

109. Hamidé, *La Région d'Alep*, pp. 557–563.

110. Al-Hajj Ali, interview, August 10, 2006.

111. Bourgey and Pharès, "Les Bidonvilles," p. 132. Abdallah Hanna, with a substantial track record of research and publication in Syrian social history, dated migration flows from northern Syria to Lebanon from around the mid-1960s also. Abdallah Hanna, interview, August 15, 2006.

112. Kamal Matar, "Rubʿa miliyun ʿamil Suriy yadhubun kulla masa' ka-al-sukkar fi-l-shay [Quarter of a Million Syrian Workers Melt Away Every Evening Like Sugar in Tea]" in *Al-Sayyad*, April 27, 1972.

113. Cited in Chami, *Béchara el Khoury*, p. 207. The pipeline was to terminate between Sur and Saida in Lebanon. Syria's agreement was announced by Prime Minister Riad al-Solh (the Tapline Agreement) on September 1, 1947 (p. 213).

114. "'Amal al-Bahhara [Shipping]", *Al-Aswaq al-Tijariyya*, October 21, 1951, p. 6.

115. Carolyn L. Gates, "Laissez-Faire, Outward-Orientation, and Regional Economic Disintegration: A Case Study of the Dissolution of the Syro-Lebanese Customs Union," in *State and Society in Syria and Lebanon*, pp. 74–83, pp. 77–79.

116. Gates, *The Merchant Republic*, pp. 85–86.

117. *Al-'Alaqat al-Lubnaniyya al-Suriyya*, vol. 1, p. 14.

118. Chreitah, *L'Economie Syrienne*, p. 53.

119. Ibid., pp. 129–130.

120. Gates, "Laissez-Faire, Outward-Orientation," p. 81.

121. Idem. It should be noted that persons (*ashkhas*) did not mean workers who were few in number but businessmen, tourists, students, shoppers, officials, and so on.

122. *Al-'Alaqat al-Lubnaniyya al-Suriyya*, vol. 1, p. 15.

123. Ibid., p. 64. The Agency (*Maslahat al-Shu'un al-Ijtima'iyya al-Lubnaniyya*) was to become the Ministry of Social Affairs.

124. *Al-'Alaqat al-Lubnaniyya al-Suriyya*, vol. 2, p. 168.

125. Samman, "Les Mouvements Migratoires," p. 213; *Al-'Alaqat al-Lubnaniyya al-Suriyya*, vol. 1, p. 18.

126. Joseph, interview, August 10, 2004.

127. Adib Mahrus, interview, March 9, 2004. As we shall see, this card was an innovation of the 1975 regulation.

128. "This rapid adaptive potential permits him to easily familiarize himself with modern installations." Chreitah, *L'Economie Syrienne*, pp. 36–37.

129. *Al-'Alaqat al-Lubnaniyya al-Suriyya*, vol. 1, p. 321.

130. Ibid., p. 229.

131. Ibid., pp. 243, 245.

132. Opposition to Syrian workers played a limited role in union organization, strikes, and the labor movement more generally. See Traboulsi, *History of Modern Lebanon*, pp. 145ff, 166–169, 174; Ali Shami, *Tatawwur al-Tabqa al-'Amila al-Lubnaniyya fi Ra'smaliyya al-Lubnaniyya al-Mu'asira [The Development of the Lebanese Working Class in Contemporary Lebanese Capitalism]* (Beirut: Dar al-Farabi, 1981), esp. 373ff; Waddah Sharara, *Al-Salm al-Ahali al-Barid: Lubnan al-Mujtami' wa-l-Dawla, 1964–1967 [The Cold Peace: Lebanon, state and society, 1964–1967]* 2 Vols. (Tripoli, Libya: Ma'had Al-Anma' Al-'Arabi, 1980); Elias al-Buwari, *Ta'rikh al-Haraka al-'Ummaliyya wa-l-Niqabiyya fi Lubnan [History of the Labour and Union Movement in Lebanon]* 3 Vols. (Beirut: Dar al-Farabi, 1986–87), Vols. 2 and 3.

133. Bassem Sirhan, "Palestinian Refugee Camp Life in Lebanon," in *Journal of Palestine Studies*, 4, 2 (Winter 1975), pp. 91–107, p. 99.

134. See, for example, the parliamentary debate of December 27, 1951. Chami, *Béchara el Khoury*, p. 415.

135. Ibid., p. 433.

136. Joseph Chami, *Le Mémorial du Liban, Tome III: Le Mandat Camille Chamoun 1952–1958* (Beirut: Chemaly & Chemaly, 2002), p. 33.

137. "Tatarrud li-l-Lubnaniyyin [Sacking Lebanese]", *Al-Aswaq al-Tijariyya*, June 15, 1951, pp. 1, 4.

138. Batatu, *Syria's Peasantry*, p. 6.

139. *Al-'Alaqat al-Lubnaniyya al-Suriyya*, vol. 1, p. 16.

140. Broadcast from the *Rabitat al-'Amal al-Lubnani*, February 5, 1958, reported in *Al-'Alaqat al-Lubnaniyya al-Suriyya*, vol. 2, p. 200.

141. *Al-'Alaqat al-Lubnaniyya al-Suriyya*, vol. 1, p. 279.

142. See, for example, the language surrounding the proposals on economic unity in 1955. *Al-'Alaqat al-Lubnaniyya al-Suriyya*, vol. 2, p. 173.

143. For example, in Autumn 1968, economic delegations from both countries met and discussed a wide range of commercial issues: legal fees, the division of revenues from the Tapline Agreement, the 1953 economic agreement, the 1965 agreement on transport, the Arab transit agreement regarding trucks and commodities, the question of goods to Iraq, Syrian cars, passenger vehicles, finance, the 1951 legal agreement, the railway line, and Lebanese property in Syria. Workers were not even on the agenda. *Al-'Alaqat al-Lubnaniyya al-Suriyya*, vol. 2, pp. 232–244.

144. Cited in Joseph Chami, *Le Mémorial du Liban, Tome IV: Le Mandat Fouad Chéhab 1958–1964* (Beirut: Chemaly & Chemaly, 2002), p. 61.

145. *Etude Annuelle sur L'Economie Libanaise de L'Année 1970* (Beirut: Bureau des documentations Libanaises et Arabe, 1971), pp. 61–62.

146. From this dynamic stemmed the long tradition of Syrian-backed assassination of journalists and dissidents in Lebanon.

147. *Al-'Alaqat al-Lubnaniyya al-Suriyya*, pp. 12–13.

148. Gates, "Laissez-Faire, Outward-Orientation," p. 80.

149. This does not mean that "Finance and Business Services" as an economic sector employed many manual or day-workers itself—only 360 in 1973 according to *Al-Ihsa'iyya al-Lubnaniyya 1973*, p. 94.

150. Bourgey, "La Guerre," p. 32. The Syrian Pound was pegged during Mandate to the French Franc at 1SP = 20 Francs. It was no longer officially accepted in Lebanon as of 1948.

151. Fahed Agha Al-Barazi, interview, February 27, 2004.

152. Bourgey and Pharès, "Les Bidonvilles," p. 132.

153. Matar, "Like Sugar in Tea."

154. Hanna Awwad, interview, August 11, 2004.

155. Mouvement Social, *Recensement des Habitations et des Résidents dans les Bidonvilles de Beyrouth et de sa banlieue* (Beirut: Ministry of Public Works, General Directorate of Urbanism, 1971), p. 22 ; Bourgey and Pharès, "Les Bidonvilles," p. 120.

156. Bourgey and Pharès, "Les Bidonvilles," pp. 134–136.

157. Gates, "Laissez-Faire, Outward-Orientation," pp. 79–80 ; Yamut, *Al-Iqtisad al-Lubnani*, p. 21.

158. Siksek et al, *Manpower Resources*, p. 22.

159. Mission-IRFED-Liban, *Besoins et possibilités de développement du Liban* (Beirut: Ministère du Plan, 1960–61), vol. 1, pp. 147–148.

160. Ibid., p. 161.

161. Yamut, *Al-Iqtisad al-Lubnani*, pp. 68–69. The proportion of the labor force taken up by agricultural workers had fallen from 48 percent in 1948 to 38 percent in 1970 (p. 80).

162. The study was conducted by Doxiadis and Associates, and put the total Lebanese labor force at 434,000. Siksek et al, *Manpower Resources*, p. 34.

163. Abu-Aianah, *Al-Sukkan al-'Arabi*, p. 240; See also IRFED, *Besoins et possibilités*, Vol. 1, pp. 49, 53.

164. IRFED, *Besoins et possibilités*, Vol. 1, pp. 95, 148–149; Gilbert Beaugé and Alain Roussillon, *Le Migrant et son double: Migrations et Unité Arabe*, Preface by Bruno Etienne (Paris: Publisud, 1988), p. 143; Bourgey and Pharès, "Les Bidonvilles," p. 120.

165. Bourgey and Pharès, "Les Bidonvilles," p. 109.

166. Mouvement Social, *Recensement des Habitations*, p. 8.

167. Bourgey and Pharès, "Les Bidonvilles," pp. 121, 127.

168. Meyer, *Syriens im Wandel*, p. 304.

169. Meyer makes this last point, *Syriens im Wandel*, p. 304.

170. IRFED, *Besoins et possibilités*, Vol. 1, p. 93.

171. See *Etude Annuelle 1972*, p. 162. Of 571,755 resident Lebanese in work or looking for work, 90,420 persons had a primary education, 200,340 less than primary, and 164,280 no formal education at all.

172. There were a further 20,893 self-employed (excluding farmers) and 24,566 employees. Siksek et al., *Manpower Resources*, p. 33.

173. Siksek et al., *Manpower Resources*, pp. 35–36. A further 8,476 were recorded as skilled workers, mechanics, carpenters, electricians, blacksmiths, machine operators, and plumbers.

174. *Al-Ihsa'iyya al-Lubnaniyya 1973*, pp. 92–93.

175. Ibid., pp. 92–94.

176. Ibid., p. 94. The census itself gives a total of 118,680 day workers or laborers among resident Lebanese.

177. As Gaspard has shown, the Lebanese economic growth was only average among developing countries, and "even less than what was achieved by the neighboring non-oil countries." Toufic K. Gaspard, *A Political Economy of Lebanon, 1948–2000: The Limits of Laissez-Faire* (Leiden: Brill, 2004), pp. 72–73, 222ff.

178. Cited in Bourgey and Pharès, "Les Bidonvilles," p. 127.

179. *Etude Annuelle 1972*, p. 100.

180. Abed, interview, August 9, 2005.

181. Cf. Annika Rabo, *Change on the Euphrates: Villagers, Townsmen and Employees in North East Syria* (Stockholm: Studies in Social Anthropology, 1986), pp. 52, 56–57.

182. Bourgey and Pharès, "Les Bidonvilles," p. 132; Mouvement Social, *Recensement des Habitations*, p. 22. This was not always true. In Wata Mussaitbé near the Cola roundabout in Beirut, Syrian Druze families lived together, reproducing "the atmosphere of a Druze village in Syria" (p. 29).

183. Bourgey and Pharès. "Les Bidonvilles," p. 109.

184. Ibid., p. 122.

185. A certain Jamila Hasan Iskandar, described as "15 years old, Syrian, brown coloured, stout," was advertised as missing from a household in Ashrafiyya, Beirut in October 1977. *Al-Nahar*, October 30, 1977, p. 12.

186. This helps explain why even forms of labor antagonism between Lebanese and Syrians on the eve of the civil war were not taken up by Maronite leaderships as major issues. See, for example, the dispute in the Port of Beirut referred to below, reported in *Al-Nahar*, June 1, 1974, p. 4.

187. See, for example, al-Buwari, *Al-Haraka al-'Ummaliyya*, Vol. 3, p. 317.

188. Elias, interview, August 10, 2004.

189. Cited in Chami, *Béchara el Khoury*, p. 345.

190. Ibid., p. 349.

191. The announcement came on June 29, 1950. Cited in Chami, *Béchara el Khoury*, p. 350.

192. Ibid., p. 407.

193. Ibid., p. 413.

194. *Al-'Alaqat al-Lubnaniyya al-Suriyya*, vol. 1, p. 78.

195. Idem.

196. Idem.

197. *Al-'Alaqat al-Lubnaniyya al-Suriyya*, vol. 1, p. 78.

198. Idem. Lebanese government press release, June 12, 1951.

199. Antagonism in the Port of Beirut continued to flare up occasionally in the years before the civil war. In June 1974, for example, a fight broke out involving Lebanese seamen from the ship Faris, the head of their union, Syrian and Egyptian seamen, and General Security. The Lebanese seamen were demonstrating in front of General Security in the Port of Beirut. The Lebanese were at odds with the "strangers" over taking their jobs, and were requesting that the ship captains hire them instead. The head of the union was at odds with some of the Lebanese aggrieved that their work permits had been withdrawn by him without justification. After a fight broke out among these three parties, General Security weighed in to impose order. *Al-Nahar*, June 1, 1974, p. 4.

200. Restrictions were discussed by officials in 1958 (*Al-ʿAlaqat al-Lubnaniyya al-Suriyya*, vol. 1, p. 168) and a highly restrictive list of professions from which Syrians were supposedly excluded appeared in 1968. *Etude Annuelle sur L'Economie Libanaise de L'Année 1968* (Beirut: Bureau des Documentations Libanaises et Arabe, 1969), p. 99.

201. Joseph, interview, August 10, 2004.

202. Abed, interview, August 9, 2005.

203. Hanna Butros, interview, August 11, 2004.

204. Hanna Awwad, interview, August 11, 2004.

205. *Al-ʿAlaqat al-Lubnaniyya al-Suriyya*, passim. Compare Breman's account of migrants "who remain invisible, as it were, in the South Gujarat plain." Jan Breman, *Of Peasants, Migrants and Paupers: Rural Labour Circulation and Capitalist Production in West India* (Delhi: Oxford University Press, 1985), p. 442.

206. Matar, "Like Sugar in Tea."

207. Ibid. This incident may have been one of the security searches that followed the "series of mysterious explosions which rocked Beirut" in January 1972. Kamal S. Salibi, *Cross Roads to Civil War: Lebanon, 1958–1976* (London: Ithaca Press, 1976), p. 60.

Chapter 3

1. Bourgey, "La Guerre," p. 4.

2. Winckler, *Demographic Developments*, p. 95.

3. Estimate given in January 1985 in a report issued by the Beirut Chamber of Commerce and Industry. Yussuf Dib, ed., *Al-Yawmiyyat al-Lubnaniyya 1985 [Lebanese Daily Events 1985]* (Beirut: Shirkat al-Fahrasat li-l-Intaj al-Thaqafi, 1986), p. 10.

4. "Hawl Awdaʿ al-ʿUmmal al-Suriyyin fi Lubnan [The Condition of Syrian Workers in Lebanon]", *Al-Baʿth*, December 31, 1981.

5. Salim al-Dahash, interview, March 11, 2004.

6. *Al-Nahar*, September 9, 1975; *Al-Nahar*, October 20, 1975, p. 5.

7. *Al-Nahar*, August 18, 1979.

8. Adeed I. Dawisha, *Syria and the Lebanese Crisis* (London: The Macmillan Press, 1980), p. 187; Salim Nasr, "The New Social Map," in *Lebanon in Limbo: Postwar Society and State in an Uncertain Regional Environment*, edited by Theodor Hanf and Nawaf Salam (Baden-Baden: Nomos Verlagsgesellschaft, 2003), pp. 143–158, p. 148ff.

9. Winckler, *Demographic Developments*, p. 95.

10. Adib Mahrus, interview, March 9, 2004.

11. Maher al-Yamani, interview, February 14, 2004.

12. Winckler, *Demographic Developments*, p. 9.

13. Ibid., p. 91.

14. Meyer, *Syriens im Wandel*, p. 305.

15. Hani el-Zein, "Foreigners Provide Basis of Labor Force," *The Daily Star*, April 4, 1984.

16. Bourgey, "La Guerre," p. 4.

17. Amal Isma'il, *Al-'Ummala al-Ajnabiyya fi Lubnan (Halat al-'Ummal al-Srilankiyya) khilal al-Fitra 1982–1986 [Foreign Labor in Lebanon and the Condition of Sri Lankan Workers, 1982–1986].* Unpublished MA thesis, Lebanese University, Institute of Social Sciences, Branch 1, 1987, pp. 1, 10–11.

18. Isma'il, *Al-'Ummala al-Ajnabiyya*, pp. 22–23.

19. Alawis were no longer employed as maids in Syria, too, where Kurds and especially Filipinos and Indonesians were employed. Conversation, Khaled Malas, August 12, 2006.

20. Winckler, *Demographic Developments*, p. 3. Syria's population was 3 million in 1970, 9 million in 1981, and 13.8 million in 1994.

21. Batatu, *Syria's Peasantry*, p. 36.

22. Ibid., p. 37.

23. Ibid., p. 53.

24. Ibid., p. 6.

25. Ibid., p. 47.

26. Emphasis in original. Meyer, *Syriens im Wandel*, p. 302.

27. Syria had previously been a net exporter of food. Batatu, *Syria's Peasantry*, p. 6.

28. Idem.

29. Rabo, *Change on the Euphrates*, p. 35.

30. Ibid., p. 49.

31. For a consummate discussion of this regarding Akkar in north Lebanon during the 1970s, see Gilsenan, *Lords of the Lebanese Marches*, pp. 263–298; see also Johnson, *All Honourable Men*, especially pp. 17–21.

32. Norman N. Lewis, *Nomads and Settlers in Syria and Jordan, 1800–1980* (Cambridge: Cambridge University Press, 1987), pp. 195–197; cf. the fact that according to Lawless, in Oman, numerous Pakistanis are employed as Omanis become unwilling to "work as labourers on other people's land." Lawless, *The Middle Eastern Village*, p. 8.

33. Marina Leybourne, Ronald Jaubert, and Richard N. Tutwiler, *Changes in Migration and Feeding Patterns among Semi-Nomadic Pastoralists in Northern Syria.* Network Paper, Pastoral Development Network (n.p.: Overseas Development Institute, 1993), p. 18.

34. Batatu, *Syria's Peasantry*, pp. 63–66.

35. Al-Hajj Ali, interview, August 10, 2006.

36. Rabo, *Change on the Euphrates*, pp. 52, 56–57.

37. Idem.

38. Malika Abdelali-Martini, Patricia Goldey, Gwyn E. Jones, and Elizabeth Bailey, "Towards a Feminization of Agricultural Labour in Northwest Syria," *Journal of Peasant Studies* 30, 2 (Jan. 2003), pp. 71–94.

39. Batatu, *Syria's Peasantry*, p. 47.

40. Rabo, *Change on the Euphrates*, p. 48.

41. Winckler, *Demographic Developments*, p. 94.

42. Rabo, *Change on the Euphrates*, pp. 101–103.

43. Ibid., pp. 101–103.

44. Ibid., p. 51. Rabo makes no mention of Lebanon here.

45. Winckler, *Demographic Developments*, p. 105.

46. Batatu, *Syria's Peasantry*, p. 44.

47. The estimate here for the monthy wage in Damascus is SL250 per month, or $68. Winckler, *Demographic Developments*, p. 91.

48. In 1974, $1,415 per head, whereas in 1982, $2,011 per head. Cited in Najem, *Lebanon's Renaissance*, p. 16.

49. Isma'il, *Al-'Ummala al-Ajnabiyya*, p. 9.

50. One estimate puts this at 14 percent. Najem, *Lebanon's Renaissance*, p. 16.

51. Bourgey, "La Guerre," pp. 5–7.

52. Adib Mahrus, interview, March 9, 2004.

53. Isma'il, *Al-'Ummala al-Ajnabiyya*, p. 8.

54. Idem. See also *In'akasat al-Ahdath 'ala al-Yad al-'Amila fi Beirut [Effects of the Civil War on Labour Power in Beirut]* (Beirut: Beirut Chamber of Commerce and Industry, n.d.), pp. 5–25.

55. Bourgey, "La Guerre," pp. 5–7.

56. Patricia Nabti, "Emigration from a Lebanese Village: A Case Study of Bishmizzine," in Hourani, *The Lebanese in the World*, pp. 41–63, p. 60.

57. Hani el-Zein, "Foreigners Provide Basis of Labor Force," *The Daily Star*, April 4, 1984.

58. Bourgey, "La Guerre," pp. 5–7.

59. Isma'il, *Al-'Ummala al-Ajnabiyya*, p. 8.

60. Yamut, *Al-Iqtisad al-Lubnani,* pp. 68–70. The source for this is a UN Report. The figures seem only to count males.

61. In 1982, $1 still equaled only 3.7 Lebanese lira. Bourgey, "La Guerre," p. 33.

62. Saidi, *Challenges of Reconstruction*, p. 100. For rising unemployment estimates, see Dib, Al-Yawmiyyat, p. 10. Reported in *'Al-Masar al-Iqtisad fi 'Ashar Sanawat 1974–1984 [The Course of the Economy Over Ten Years, 1974–1984] Al-Safir*, January 1, 1985; Dib, *Al-Yawmiyyat*, p. 393.

63. Saidi, *Challenges of Reconstruction*, p. 214. The purchasing power of the minimum wage fell drastically between 1984 and 1987. Kamal Hamdan, "Les Libanais

face à la crise économique et sociale: étendue et limites des processus d'adaptation,"
Maghreb-Machrek 125 (JulySeptember 1989), pp. 19–39, p. 27.

64. Remittances fell from $2.2 billion in 1980 to only $300 million in 1987 according to Najem, *Lebanon's Renaissance*, p. 17. For employment, see Bourgey, "La Guerre,"
p. 8.

65. Reported in *Al-Safir*. Dib, *Al-Yawmiyyat*, p. 33.

66. Theodor Hanf, *Coexistence in Wartime Lebanon: Decline of a State and Rise of a Nation*, trans. by John Richardson (London: I. B.Tauris, 1993), p. 477.

67. Bourgey, "La Guerre," pp. 5–7.

68. Saidi, *Challenges of Reconstruction*, p. 233.

69. For this understanding of "mass expulsion," which stresses that expulsion does not simply involve loading people onto trucks and removing them, but also involves indirect measures, see Van Hear, *New Diasporas*, p. 10.

70. Hanna Butros, interview, August 11, 2004.

71. See, for example, Piore, *Birds of Passage*, pp. 1–2, 65–66; Glenn, *Issei, Nisei, Warbride*, pp. 10–11; Hondagneu-Sotelo, *Gendered Transitions*, p. xv.

72. Abed, interview, August 8, 30, 31, 2005.

73. See, for example, Robert Fisk, *Pity the Nation: Lebanon at War* (Oxford: Oxford University Press, 1990), p. 82.

74. Johnson, *All Honourable Men*, p. 7.

75. Sharara, *Al-Salm al-Ahali al-Barid*.

76. Salibi, *Civil War*, p. 78–79. As Imam Musa Sadr stated in 1971, "We want a share in the economy, the culture and the political power of this country in accordance with our strength," cited in Hanf, *Coexistence in Lebanon*, p. 367.

77. Salibi, *Civil War*, pp. 62–63.

78. Hanf, *Coexistence in Lebanon*, pp. 3–4.

79. Salibi, *Civil War*, pp. 69–70. The main Christian militias were the Kataeb Party (Phalange) of Pierre Gemayel, the Marada Brigade of Suleiman Franjieh, the National Liberal Party (NLP) of Camille Chamoun, and the Guardians of the Cedars of Etienne Saqr.

80. Traboulsi, *History of Modern Lebanon*, pp. 147–149.

81. Interview, Joseph, August 10, 2004.

82. Cited in Hanf, *Coexistence in Lebanon*, p. 371.

83. Copies of the Sunni petitions are reproduced in Yasin Sawayd, *Al-Masa'la al-Lubnaniyya: Naqd wa Tahlil [The Lebanese Question: Critique and Analysis]* (Beirut: al-Shirka al-'Alimiyya li-l-Kitab, 1998), pp. 285–290.

84. Hanf, *Coexistence in Lebanon*, p. 372.

85. Cf. Salibi, *Crossroads to Civil War*, p. 82.

86. Dawisha, *Lebanese Crisis*, pp. 45–46.

87. Cited in Batatu, *Syria's Peasantry*, pp. 205–206.

88. For this principle, see Chapter 2. Also see "Copy of the Proposed Lebanese-Syrian Economic Unity Agreement," offered by the Lebanese delegation to the Syrian delegation, Beirut, March 24, 1955, *Al-'Alaqat al-Lubnaniyya al-Suriyya,* Vol. 2, p. 174.

89. *Al-'Alaqat al-Lubnaniyya al-Suriyya,* Vol. 1, p. 273.

90. Announced on August 18, 1971. Ibid., p. 278.

91. The closure had very little to do with the fringe benefit of diverting Iraqi and Gulf tourists to Syria instead of Lebanon, as some Lebanese averred. Ibid., p. 18.

92. See, for example, a statement by Suhail Sukriyya, member of the national leadership of the Syrian Ba'th Party, July 20, 1973. Ibid., p. 303.

93. Ibid., p. 305.

94. Ibid., p. 204.

95. M. E. Sales, *International Migration Project Country Case Study: Syrian Arab Republic* (Durham: Durham University, 1978), p. 63.

96. *Al-'Alaqat al-Lubnaniyya al-Suriyya,* Vol. 2, pp. 248–249.

97. So said the leader of the League, Jamil Muhanna, in an interview in 1981: "Hawl Awda' al-'Ummal al-Suriyyin fi Lubnan [The Condition of Syrian Workers in Lebanon]", *Al-Ba'th,* December 31, 1981.

98. Ibid.

99. Literally so, for example, at the Franjiyeh-Al-Asad summit of January 7, 1974. Traboulsi, *History of Modern Lebanon,* p. 182.

100. *Al-Nahar,* March 9, 1973, p. 12.

101. A report of two Syrian workers who died in a building accident appeared in *Al-Nahar,* December 7, 1972, p. 5. Two more deaths were reported in *Al-Nahar,* April 4, 1973, p. 3. A Syrian female worker was murdered for money south of Tripoli. *Al-Nahar,* June 21, 1973, p. 5. A Syrian worker was fatally shot in a robbery near Saida. *Al-Nahar,* November 20, 1974, p. 5. A Syrian shopkeeper was injured by a Palestinian commando in a debt dispute. *Al-Nahar,* August 14, 1973, p. 4. A Syrian was fatally shot in murky circumstances in Beirut, *Al-Nahar,* November 22, 1973, p. 5. A Syrian student was fatally shot in his car in unclear circumstances in Ain al-Rumana, *Al-Nahar,* May 3, 1975, p. 3.

102. For example, the Syrian and Lebanese bank in Furn al-Shubak was attacked in December 1974, *Al-Nahar,* December 29, 1974, p. 5.

103. Salibi, *Civil War,* p. 103.

104. Ahzab al-Haraka al-Wataniyya al-Lubnaniyya, *Al-Muhajjarun: Dahaya al-Mukhatat al-In'azali [Forced Migrants: Victims of Isolationist Plans]* (Beirut: Lajnat al-Wataniyya li-l-Muhajjarin, n.d, [c.1980]), p. 73.

105. Ibid., p. 109.

106. Ibid., p. 123.

107. Al-Buwari, *Al-Haraka al-'Ummaliyya,* Vol. 3, p. 316.

108. Fisk, *Pity the Nation,* p. 79.

109. Idem.

110. Salibi, *Civil War,* pp. 146–147.

111. Ibid., p. 117.

112. Johnson, *All Honourable Men,* p. 63.

113. Bourgey, "La Guerre," pp. 24–25. Fisk maintains that this finally brought the PLO officially into the conflict. Fisk, *Pity the Nation,* p. 79.

114. For example, Johnson, *All Honourable Men,* p. 62.

115. League of Syrian Workers in Lebanon, "Kitab Maftuh [Open Letter]", March 26, 1979, in *Al-Nahar* Press Cuttings Archive.

116. Bourgey, "La Guerre," pp. 24–25.

117. Johnson, *All Honourable Men,* p. 63.

118. Al-Haraka al-Wataniyya, *Al-Muhajjarun,* pp. 75–76, 78.

119. Hanna Awwad, interview, August 11, 2004.

120. Dawisha, *Lebanese Crisis,* p. 186.

121. This line of argument is fairly well established in Fisk, *Pity the Nation,* pp. 81, 83; Salibi, *Civil War,* pp. 129, 159. Further, Syrian Foreign Minister Abd al-Halim Khaddam insisted to the Kuwaiti newspaper, *al-Ra'i al-'Am,* in January 1976, that Syria's primary interest was to avoid the division of Lebanon. Interview reproduced in *Al-'Alaqat al-Lubnaniyya al-Suriyya,* Vol. 2, p. 254. Asad himself stated in a speech in April 1976 that Lebanon should remain united in the face of sectarianism. *Al-'Alaqat al-Lubnaniyya al-Suriyya,* vol. 2, pp. 266–268. See also Patrick Seale, *Asad of Syria: The Struggle for the Middle East* (London: I. B. Tauris, 1988), pp. 276–277, 280ff.

122. Fisk, *Pity the Nation,* p. 83.

123. Asad maintained that the Palestinians were part of the pan-Arab cause, and hence there should be no independent Palestinian national decision. Batatu, *Syria's Peasantry,* p. 313.

124. Dawisha, *Lebanese Crisis,* p. 186.

125. Bourgey, "La Guerre," p. 9.

126. Dawisha, *Lebanese Crisis,* pp. 187–188.

127. Ibid., p. 189.

128. I obtained these images courtesy of Zena Maasri to whom thanks are due.

129. *Al-'Alaqat al-Lubnaniyya al-Suriyya,* vol. 2, p. 325.

130. Hanna Butros, interview, August 11, 2004.

131. *Al-Nahar,* March 31, 1977, p. 3.

132. Asian workers suffered in similar fashion. "When any militiaman sees Asian people cross at a checkpoint he orders them to fill sandbags or move arms and munitions closer to the front line," said one Bangladeshi bakery worker. Hani el-Zein, "Foreigners Provide Basis of Labor Force," *The Daily Star,* April 4, 1984.

133. Adib Mahrus, interview, March 9, 2004.

134. Tony Elias, interview, August 12, 2004.

135. Hanf, *Coexistence in Lebanon*, pp. 509–510.

136. In 1977, for example, Imam Musa al-Sadr spoke of "close brotherhood and integration" between the two countries. Al-Imam al-Sayyid Musa al-Sadr, *Hawarat Sahifa (2) al-Wahda wa-l-Tahrir [Dialogues with the Press (2) Unity and Liberation]* (Bir Hassan, Beirut: Imam al-Sadr Centre for Study and Research, 2000), pp. 334–338.

137. Hanf, *Coexistence in Lebanon*, p. 373. Solh was primarily thinking of the Palestinians.

138. "Projet de loi réglementant le travail des étrangers au Liban." *L'Économie des pays arabes*, [monthly, Beirut] 18, 211 (August 1975), pp. 51–54. See also *Al-Muharrar*, January 7, 1975.

139. Joseph, interview, August 10, 2004.

140. Adib Mahrus, interview, March 9, 2004.

141. Hanf, *Coexistence in Lebanon*, p. 199.

142. *Al-Nahar*, October 30, 1977, p. 5; see also 'Abd al-Rahman al-Hamadi, "Arba' Sanawat min al-Nidal al-Niqabi [Four Years of Union Struggle]", *Al-Sharq*, October 30, 1981. The League was founded on October 16, 1977, via regulation 545.

143. "Rabitat al-'Ummal [Workers' Union]", *Al-Nahar*, January 30, 1978.

144. Al-Hamadi, "Arba' Sanawat"; "Hawl Awda' al-'Ummal al-Suriyyin fi Lubnan [The Condition of Syrian Workers in Lebanon]" *Al-Ba'th,* December 31, 1981.

145. "Rabitat al-'Ummal" *Al-Nahar*, January 30, 1978.

146. Al-Hamadi, "Arba' Sanawat."

147. League of Syrian Workers in Lebanon, "Kitab Maftuh" March 26, 1979, in Al-Nahar Press Cuttings Archive. Another similar letter of the same date added that the employers were not just bloodsuckers but "eaters of human flesh," whose "hands and feet are still soaked in the blood of innocents from among us." It emphasized that "we have justice on our side and no weakness enters our hearts." "What are these castles," the letter went on, "except that which our hands made, built on the skulls of our martyrs and mixed with the sweat of our workers?"

148. *Al-Nahar*, March 27, 1979.

149. The union thanked the Prime Minister, the Mufti of the Republic, Hasan Khaled, and the lawyers Suhail Sukriyya, member of the national leadership of the Ba'th Party, 'Asim Qansu, Regional Secretary of the Ba'th Party, Najjah Wakim, Nazim al-Qadiri, and three others. *Al-Nahar*, May 20, 1979.

150. *Al-Nahar*, August 19, 1979.

151. Ibid, p. 4; *L'Orient-Le-Jour*, August 19, 1979, p. 10.

152. "Jamil Muhanna: Ba'd mada'i al-wataniyya nasabu anfusahum hama li-l-iddtihad [Jamil Muhanna: Some of the So-Called Nationalists Are Making Every Effort to Protect Oppression]", *Al-Rayya*, August 25, 1979.

153. *Al-Nahar*, August 18, 1979.

154. *Al-Anwar*, August 22, 1979, p. 4; *Al-Nahar*, August 23, 1979; *L'Orient-Le-Jour*, August 23, 1979, p. 2. "Jamil Muhanna," *Al-Rayya*, August 25, 1979.

155. *Al-'Amal*, August 28, 1979, p. 5.

156. 112 of these workers were from Dar'a, 58 from Dayr al-Zur, 20 from al-Hasaka Governorate, and 30 from elsewhere. "Hawl Awda' al-'Ummal."

157. 600 of these workers were reportedly from Dar'a region, 200 from al-Hasaka, 150 from Deir al-Zur, and rest from elsewhere. Ibid.

158. Al-Hamadi, "Arba' Sanawat,"

159. "Hawl Awda' al-'Ummal."

160. *Al-Anwar*, February 26, 1985. As *The Daily Star* reported on April 4, 1984: "Foreign labor has replaced Lebanese as the back-bone of Lebanon's unskilled and semi-skilled work force."

161. *Al-Anwar*, February 26, 1985.

162. Isma'il, *Al-'Ummala al-Ajnabiyya*, pp. 12, 42–44.

163. Idem. *Al-Anwar*, February 26, 1985.

164. See, for example, a 1984 essay by an important economist titled "Reconstruction, Investment and Economic Growth," arguing that open borders promoted economic growth. Saidi, *Challenges of Reconstruction*, pp. 190–191. Or, unsurprisingly, The League of Syrian Workers blamed the currency slide not on foreign labor but on speculative mafias. *Al-Nahar*, July 5, 1987.

165. Isma'il, "*Al-'Ummala al-Ajnabiyya*," pp. 43–44.

166. *Al-Anwar*, February 26, 1985.

167. Dib, *Al-Yawmiyyat*, p. 377.

168. *Al-Nahar*, August 3, 1985; Dib, *Al-Yawmiyyat*, p. 393.

169. Dib, *Al-Yawmiyyat*, p. 393.

170. Reported in *Al-Safir* on November 29, 1985. Dib, *Al-Yawmiyyat*, p. 591.

171. *Al-Safir*, August 28, 1986.

172. Hanna Butros, interview, August 11, 2004.

173. Joseph, interview, August 19, 2004.

174. Ibid.

175. He became head waiter after six months. Ibid.

176. Abed and Ibrahim, interview, August 9, 2005.

Chapter 4

1. Jani Nasrallah, "Al-'Ummal al-Suriyyun fi Lubnan: ba'su 'al-'alaqat al-akhawiyya [Syrian Workers in Lebanon: The Wretched of the 'Brotherly Relations']," *Al-Nahar*, December 16, 2000.

2. Scarlett Haddad, "Qui a peur de la main-d'oeuvre syrienne au Liban? [Who's Afraid of Syrian Labor in Lebanon?]," *L'Orient-Le Jour*, June 13, 1994.

3. Samir Kassir, "A Polity in an Uncertain Regional Environment," in *Lebanon in Limbo*, pp. 87–106, p. 89.

4. Cited in Ghayth Armanazi, "Syrian Foreign Policy at the Crossroads," in *Syria and Lebanon*, pp. 112–119, p. 115.

5. Fida Nasrallah, "The Treaty of Brotherhood, Co-operation and Co-ordination: An Assessment," in *State and Society in Syria and Lebanon*, pp. 103–111, p. 107.

6. Cited in Sawayd, *Al-Mas'ala al-Lubnaniyya*, p. 283.

7. Ibid., p. 279.

8. Ibid., p. 282.

9. See Johnson, *All Honourable Men*.

10. Abed and Ibrahim, August 9, 2005.

11. For the costs of war, see Ministry of Social Affairs—United Nations Development Programme, *Mapping of Living Conditions in Lebanon: An Analysis of the Housing and Population Data Base* (Beirut: MOSA-UNDP, 1998), p. 39.

12. Najem, *Lebanon's Renaissance*, p. 84; Nahad Khalil Dimashqiyya, *Al-Takammul al-Sina'i al-Suriy al-Lubnani: al-Imkaniyyat wa-l-Furus [Syro-Lebanese Industrial Integration: Possibilities and Opportunities]* (Beirut: Markaz Dirasat al-Wahda al-'Arabiyya, 2002), pp. 21ff, 417.

13. Saidi, *Challenges of Reconstruction*, p. 369.

14. For "extended collusion" between Syrian and Lebanese elites, see Kassir, "Uncertain Regional Environment," pp. 87, 100–102.

15. Saidi, *Challenges of Reconstruction*, pp. 241, 245–246, 298.

16. Nasr, "The New Social Map," pp. 150–152.

17. Cited in Tom Pierre Najem, *Lebanon's Renaissance: The Political Economy of Reconstruction* (Durham: Ithaca Press, 2000), p. 49.

18. Ali Moussa Khalil, "European Business Interests in Lebanon: An Assessment of EU Private Foreign Direct Investment in the Reconstruction Era." Unpublished Ph.D. thesis, University of Durham, Centre for Middle Eastern and Islamic Studies, 2000), p. 203. Fiscal policy was regressive in distributional terms. See Abdallah Dah, Ghassan Dibeh, and Wassim Shahin, *The Distributional Impact of Taxes in Lebanon: Analysis and Policy Implications* (Beirut: The Lebanese Center for Policy Studies, 1999), p. 44.

19. Sawayd, *Al-Mas'ala al-Lubnaniyya*, pp. 109–136, 116–119, 121, 127, 130–131. For a developed account of the construction of Syrian nationalism itself in terms of references to ancient texts, see Stéphane Valter, *La construction nationale Syrienne: Légitimation de la nature communautaire du pouvoir par le discours historique* (Paris: CNRS Éditions, 2002).

20. Antoun, conversation, February 21, 2004.

21. Joseph Abu Khalil, *Lubnan wa Suriyya: Mushaqqat al-Akhuwwa [Syria and Lebanon: The Broken Brotherhood]* (Beirut: Shirkat al-Matbu'at li-l-Tawzi'a wa

al-Nashr, 1991), pp. 7–12. Such accommodationism harked back to the more inclusive nationalism of Michel Chiha. It echoed Kamal Salibi's formula penned after a year of bloody fighting, the last sentence in his book: "Only in an Arab world where the bond of Arabism remains significant can a country like Lebanon retain its special importance." Salibi, *Crossroads to Civil War*, p. 162.

22. Saidi, *Challenges of Reconstruction*, pp. 325, 352, 357.

23. *Al-Diyar*, January 26, 1998; *Al-Diyar*, February 2, 1998.

24. *Al-Diyar*, February 2, 1998.

25. *Al-Diyar*, January 26, 1998; *Al-Diyar*, February 2, 1998.

26. Ibid. Others argued that economic problems in Lebanon did not stem from excessive immigration, but from the political economy of reconstruction. Albert Dagher, "Al-Quwa Al-'Amila wa-l-Namu fi Lubnan: Al-Waqi'a wa-l-Afaq Al-Mustaqbaliyya," in *Linking Economic Growth and Social Development in Lebanon* (Beirut: United Nations Development Programme, 2000), pp. 85–99, pp. 91–93, 95–96.

27. Ghalib Abu Muslih, "Shufiniyya Lubnaniyya Iqtisadiyya Ma'adiyya li-l-Suriy [Lebanese Economic Chauvinism Is Inimical to Syria]," *Al-Naqad*, April 23, 2001, p. 53; Sawayd, *Al-Mas'ala al-Lubnaniyya*, p. 130.

28. Khalil, "European Business Interests in Lebanon," pp. 279, 290.

29. The agreement was signed by Abdullah Al-Amin, the Lebanese Labor Minister, and 'Ali Khalil, his Syrian counterpart, on October 18, 1994. For a copy, see *Al-'Alaqat al-Lubnaniyya al-Suriyya*, pp. 371–373.

30. Khalil, "European Business Interests in Lebanon," p. 264. The business community was also to complain that there were too many jobs reserved for Lebanese, and that it was too difficult and costly to get work permits for foreigners. Ibid., pp. 265–267.

31. One author maintains that Lebanon—the source does not say who exactly—requested that "Syrian laborers were prevented from benefiting from Lebanese social security." Simone Ghazi Tinaoui, "An Analysis of the Syrian-Lebanese Economic Cooperation Agreements," *The Beirut Review* 8 (Fall 1994), pp. 97–112, p. 108.

32. "Al-Siniora: 'Ummal Suriyya fi Lubnan 150 Alfan [Al-Siniora: 150 Thousand Syrian Workers in Lebanon]," *Al-Mustaqbal*, November 17, 2000.

33. Najem, *Lebanon's Renaissance*, p. 228.

34. My own sources for this point are conversations and interviews: Mas'ud Daher, interview, March 1, 2004; Berengère, interview, March 1, 2004; Fatima Almana, conversation, March 2, 2004; Raghid El-Solh, Conversation, March 2, 2004. Political Affairs Officer at ESCWA.

35. Antoun, interview, February 21, 2004.

36. Gary C. Gambill, "Lebanese Farmers and the Syrian Occupation," *Middle East Intelligence Bulletin* 5, 10 (October 2003), www.meib.org/articles/0131o.htm..

37. Nada Oweijane Khoury, "L'Immigration au Liban: Aspects socio-économiques et incidences identitaires." Unpublished doctoral thesis, 3 vols., Lebanese University, Institute of Social Sciences, Section II, Rabieh, and Université Réné Descartes, Paris V, 2001, Vol. 1, p. 128.

38. Talal, conversation, September 8, 2003.

39. Jo Farah, interview, August 12, 2004.

40. Gary Gambill, *Middle East Intelligence Bulletin* 2, 4 (April 2000), http://www.meib.org/articles/000412.htm.

41. "Al-Siniora"; Bassam al-Hashim,"Al-Ittifaqat al-Ijtima'iya wa In'akasatuha al-Dimughrafiyya fi al-'Alaqat al-Lubnaniyya—al-Suriyya: Muhawila Taqwimiyya [Social Agreements and Their Demographic Effects in Syrian-Lebanese Relations: An Attempted Evaluation]," in *Al-'Alaqat al-Lubnaniyya al-Suriyya: Muhawila Taqwimiyya [Syrian-Lebanese Relations: An Attempted Evaluation]* (Beirut, Antiliyas: Al-Haraka Al-Thaqafiyya, 2001), pp. 110–148.

42. See Muhammad al-Hijayri, "Dahaya wa Sunna'?![Victims and Makers?!]", *Al-Nahar*, [Supplement], December 16, 2000; see also "Bassam al-Hashim Ruddan 'ala al-Hariri [Bassam al-Hashim Replies to al-Hariri]," *Al-Nahar*, November 24, 2000.

43. Khoury, "L'Immigration au Liban," Vol. 1, p. 58.

44. Ibid., pp. 11–19.

45. Ibid., p. 73.

46. In Khoury's study these margins of error left an initial balance of 1,462,591 Syrians in Lebanon. But this figure had to be tweaked because 10 percent of Syrians—a proportion that comes with no explicit justification at all—come with families, whose average size is 4.3. This accounts for 266,435 entries that must be removed from the grand total to give 1,196,246 active, working Syrians. However, this, in turn, is an underestimate because it forgets the clandestine Syrian workers, estimated (on what basis is unknown) to be 340,585, taking the total to 1,850,000 Syrians. Ibid., pp. 75–76, 85–88.

47. Syrian residents were estimated at 32,436 in 1995; Syrian tourists and visitors, shoppers, students, and the like were meant to account for 354,462 entries in 1995. The Haut Conseil Libano-Syrien, *Méthodologie de la lecture statistique* (Beirut/Damascus: Statistics Directorate, Center of Research, April 29, 1998). See also a report on the study in *Al-Hayat*, June 28, 1998. For an attempted rebuttal by Michel Murqus, see *Al-Nahar*, July 3, 1998. See also John Chalcraft, "Syrian Workers in Lebanon and the Role of the State: Political Economy and Popular Aspirations," in *Migration et politique au Moyen-Orient*, edited by François De Bel-Air (Beirut: Institut Français du Proche Orient, 2006), pp. 81–104.

48. Khoury's sample of 150 Syrian workers, for example, made an average of 6.67 trips to Syria per year. Khoury, "L'Immigration au Liban," Vol. 1, p. 145.

49. The economist Albert Dagher quotes Ziyad Majed's estimate of 450,000 Syrian workers at their peak in 1996, and quotes the Syrian labor minister's estimate that numbers had fallen to 225,000 by 2000. Dagher, *"Al-Quwa al-'Amila,"* p. 89. The U.N.'s estimate was that there were 200,000 Syrians in the country in 1992, and that this rose to 450,000 by the end of 1995. UNDP, *A Profile of Sustainable Human Development in Lebanon* (Beirut: UNDP, 1997), p. 75. Salim Nasr estimated that numbers fell from 600,000–700,000 in the mid-1990s at the peak of reconstruction to a low of about 250,000 in the year 2000. Nasr, "The New Social Map," p. 147. Picard estimated that Syrians numbered 600,000 at their peak and fell to 400,000 in the later 1990s. Picard, "Les Syriens," p. 98. See also Picard, *Shattered Country*, p. 195. See also economists Kamal Hamdan, Marwan Iskandar, and Ghassan 'Ayyash quoted in *al-Safir*, April 19, 2005. A Syrian study cited in *Al-Watan al-'Arabi*, the methodology of which I have not seen, estimated there to be 450,000 workers in Lebanon during the 1990s. "Tataraji' 5 Marat fi 5 Sanawat [Remittances Falling 5 Times Over in 5 Years]," in *Al-Watan al-'Arabi*, May 12, 2000. A study put together by a Syrian team in 2000 estimated numbers at 333,000. Cited in an article by Dhu-l-Fiqar Qubaysi, in *Al-Kifah Al-'Arabi*, June 13, 2000.

50. Cited in Khoury, "L'Immigration au Liban," Vol. 1, p. 196.

51. This was an "exhaustive census" of industrial and commercial businesses of all sizes during May and June 1997. The census also sampled 20,432 Lebanese households. Lebanese Republic, *Conditions de Vie des Ménages en 1997*, Études Statistiques No. 9 (Beirut: Administration Centrale de Statistique, 1998), pp. 3, 12.

52. Lebanese Republic, *Conditions de Vie des Ménages*, pp. 19, 25, 37.

53. The resident, permanent workforce in Lebanon was estimated at 1,362,232 in 1997. Lebanese Republic, *Conditions de Vie des Ménages*, pp. 19, 25, 37. See also Lebanese Republic, *La Population active en 1997*, Études Statistiques No. 12 (Beirut: Administration Centrale Statistique, 1998), p. 11. General Security entry and exit statistics for Syrians grow rapidly from about 623,000 entries in 1991 to a peak of just over 2 million in 1995, overtaking the peak entry rates of the early 1970s in 1994. Khoury, "L'Immigration au Liban," Vol. 2, pp. 190–196.

54. See Sabin 'Awais, "Taqallas al-'Ummala al-Suriyya fi al-Wirash [Fall in Syrian Labor on Construction Sites]," *Al-Nahar*, January 31, 2000; Ghayth Armanazi, senior Syrian diplomat, lecture delivered at School of Oriental and African Studies, University of London, October 26, 2004.

55. Youssef Courbage, "Evolution démographique et attitudes politique en Syrie" in *Population* (Paris: INED), 49th Year, May–June 1994, pp. 725–750, pp. 734, 743.

56. Abu-Aianah, *Al-Sukkan fi-l-Watan*, p. 230.

57. Winckler, *Demographic Developments*, p. 91.

58. For processes driving women into the agricultural labor force, see Martini et al., "Towards a Feminization of Agricultural Labor."

59. Hanna Butros, interview, August 11, 2004.

60. Roger Awwad, interview, August 11, 2004.

61. Roger's studies were completed late because he had to sit re-takes.

62. Al-Hajj Ali, interview, August 10, 2006; Radwan, interview, July 23, 2004.

63. Ibrahim, interview, July 23, 2004.

64. During the 1990s, al-Hajj Ali, used remittances to buy some land near Tal 'Aran, east of Aleppo, along with housing plots for three of his nine sons.

65. 'Abd al-Qadir, interview, July 23, 2004.

66. Omar, interview, August 5, 2005.

67. Ibid.

68. Khalil, "European Business Interests in Lebanon," p. 221. For a complete list, see Najem, *Lebanon's Renaissance.*

69. Najem, *Lebanon's Renaissance*, p. 147.

70. Dagher, "Al-Quwa al-'Amila," p. 89; Saidi, *Challenges of Reconstruction,* p. 363.

71. Kvaerner also employed 30 Britons in strategic and managerial roles, and 200 Lebanese engineers and administrative staff. Khalil, "European Business Interests in Lebanon," pp. 217–221.

72. 'Awais, "Taqallas al-'Ummala al-Suriyya."

73. Khoury, "L'Immigration au Liban," Vol. 1, p. 131.

74. Ibid., p. 134.

75. Ibid., Vol. 3, p. 144.

76. Ibid., Vol. 1, p. 132. I interviewed a taxi-driver from Aleppo making $15 a day. Ali, conversation, February 29, 2004.

77. For the details, see Al-Jumhuriyya al-Lubnaniyya [The Lebanese Republic], *Tasnif al-Mihan fi Lubnan [Classification of Occupations in Lebanon],* 2 Vols (Beirut: Al-Mu'assasa al-Wataniyya li-l-Istikhdam [National Employment Institute], 2005). This publication adopts the nine occupational group ILO employment classification based on skill similarities as developed from 1949 and last modified in 1988. See Eivind Hoffman, "International Statistical Comparisons of Occupational and Social Structures: Problems, Possibilities and the Role of ISCO-88," Paper prepared for *Symposium on Measuring Demographic Variables in International Perspective*, September 30–October 1, 1999, Cologne, Germany, http://www.ilo.org/public/english/bureau/stat/download/iscopres.pdf, accessed June 15, 2007.

78. Nabih Berri's companies, such as Kassioun, the road building company, did the same. Mas'ud Daher, conversation, March 1, 2004.

79. Cf. Nasr, "The New Social Map," p. 146.

80. Khoury, "L'Immigration au Liban," Vol. 1, p. 66.

81. Ibid., p. 64.

82. Cf. UNDP, *Sustainable Human Development*, p. 76.

83. Khoury, "L'Immigration au Liban," Vol. 1, p. 66.

84. Mona Fawaz, conversation, February 26, 2004.

85. Khoury, "L'Immigration au Liban," Vol. 1, p. 66.

86. Mona Harb, conversation, February 26, 2004.

87. Yahya Sadowski, conversation, February 17, 2004.

88. Maher al-Yamani, interview, February 24, 2004.

89. Khoury, "L'Immigration au Liban," Vol. 1, pp. 202–206. See also, UNDP, *Sustainable Human Development*, p. 77; Khalil, "European Business Interests in Lebanon," p. 219.

90. Sami Harb, interview, March 9, 2004.

91. Abu Subhi, interview, March 12, 2004.

92. "The foreigner is paid less, he costs less and works more. Moreover, he is not absent, he does not require a work contract or end of service indemnity etc." Khoury, "L'Immigration au Liban," Vol. 1, pp. 205–206.

93. Michael Young, interview, February 26, 2004.

94. Fadi Bardawil, "Behind the Sewing Machines: A Case Study of Migrant Labor in Lebanon." Unpublished term paper written for Professor Ray Jureidini, American University in Beirut, 2000.

95. Ahmad, conversation, February 18, 2004; Sunni taxi-driver from Beirut. also skilled electrician.

96. 'Abed and Ibrahim, interview, August 9, 2005.

97. Fatima al-Mana, conversation, March 2, 2004.

98. Omar, interview, August 5, 2005.

99. Mikhail 'Awwad, *Al-Diyar*, January 26, 1998.

100. Ray Jureidini, "Migrant Workers and Xenophobia in the Middle East," in *Identities, Conflict and Cohesion*, Programme Paper 2 (Geneva: United Nations Research Institute for Social Development, 2003).

101. See Giovanni Bochi, "The Production of Difference: Sociality, Work and Mobility in a Community of Syrian Dom between Lebanon and Syria," Ph.D. thesis, London School of Economics and Political Science, 2007.

102. Davis, *Late Victorian Holocausts*, p. 35.

103. For a systematic review of transnational discourses and institutions reducing "migrants . . . to a factor of production," see Beaugé, *Le migrant et son double*, pp. 29–65.

104. For example, Nasser H. Saidi is a published economist who taught at the University of Chicago and was Vice-Governor of the Central Bank of Lebanon and Minister of Economy and Trade in the 1990s.

105. Ibrahim, interview, July 23, 2004.

106. Abu Subhi, interview, March 12, 2004; Abd al-Qadir, interview, July 23, 2004.

107. The line of "absolute" or "miserable" poverty in Lebanon for a male breadwinner was defined by the U.N. at $300 per month, putting many Syrians at or below this line. Dagher, *"Al-Quwa al-'Amila,"* p. 89.

108. 'Abd al-Qadir, interview, August 3, 2005.

109. Muhammad, interview, July 31, 2004.

110. Radwan, interview, July 23, 2004. Radwan's friend Armange, however, said, "I can't do just anything. I can't work like Ibrahim [who also worked long hours]. He wakes up at 1 a.m. That's more than my body can take!" Armange, interview, August 5, 2004.

111. Khoury, "L'Immigration au Liban," Vol. 1, p. 130.

112. Adib Mahrus, interview, March 9, 2004; Radwan, interview, July 23, 2004.

113. Adib Mahrus, interview, March 9, 2004.

114. Ibid.

115. Khayat, conversation, March 6, 2004.

116. Adib Mahrus, interview, March 9, 2004.

117. Armange, interview, August 5, 2004.

118. Ibid. Armange worked for seven months without a contract and without insurance in radiography in Hammana Hospital. He was paid half-wages, he said, $400 a month. He explained that when the official from the social security or the ministry of health came to inspect the premises, he would hide or pretend to be a patient in order not to be discovered. Armange, interview, August 5, 2004.

119. Abu Subhi, interview, March 12, 2004.

120. 'Abed, interview, February 22, 2004.

121. Adib Mahrus, interview, March 9, 2004.

122. Mona Fawaz, conversation, February 26, 2004.

123. Radwan, interview, July 23, 2004.

124. Franck Mermier, conversation, February 25, 2004. Ray Jureidini's work suggests that such attitudes were not that unusual.

125. Khayat, March 6, 2004.

126. 'Abd al-Qadir, interview, July 23, 2004. In my presence, Abu Subhi called one of his delivery boys a good for nothing animal for not being able to find a delivery address. 'Abd al-Qadir tried subtly to soothe his employer, saying that the boy was inexperienced.

127. 'Abd al-Qadir, interview, July 23, 2004.

128. Ibid.

129. Ibid.

130. Ayman, interview, July 31, 2004.

131. Ibid.

132. Ibrahim, interview, July 23, 2004.

133. Radwan, interview, July 23, 27, 2004.

134. Khoury, "L'Immigration au Liban," Vol. 1, p. 353.

135. Muhammad, interview, July 31, 2004.

136. For example, a CD vendor I met on Hamra, Muhammad from Dar'a, February 29, 2004.

137. Armange, interview, August 5, 2004.

138. Mona Harb, conversation, February 26, 2004; Jim Quilty, conversation, March 5, 2004.

139. Radwan, interview, July 23, 2004. Syrians are OK, unlike the Palestinians, because they have a home to go to. Building consultant, Lebanese Christian, conversation, February 12, 2004.

140. Armange, interview, August 5, 2004. A variant on this narrative comes in which migrants tell you that they have "no opinions" about Lebanon, and that they are just in Lebanon for work and nothing else.

141. Jo Farah, interview, August 12, 2004.

142. Salim al-Dahash, interview, March 11, 2004.

143. Jo Farah, interview, August 12, 2004.

144. Omar, interview, August 5, 2005.

145. Michael Burawoy, *Manufacturing Consent: Changes in the Labor Process under Monopoly Capitalism* (Chicago: University of Chicago Press, 1982).

146. Radwan, interview, July 23, 2004.

147. Taxi-driver, conversation, February 22, 2004.

148. Syrian taxi-driver from Damascus, conversation, March 14, 2004.

149. Radwan, interview, July 23, 2004.

150. Ibid.

151. Ibid.

152. Salim al-Dahash, interview, March 11, 2004.

153. Radwan, interview, July 23, 2004.

154. Ibid.

155. Ibid.

156. Ibid.

157. Abu Yusuf, interview, August 10, 2004.

158. Radwan, interview, July 23, 2004.

159. This is why, he noted with a smile, "the security agencies will already know everything about you and your research."

160. Armange, Radwan, and Nazir, interview, August 23, 2004. A number of others explained Lebanese antagonism as stemming from Syrian military control. Talal, conversation, July 28, 2003.

161. Radwan and Nazir, interview, August 27, 2004.

162. Nazir, interview, August 27, 2004.

163. 'Abd al-Qadir, interview, August 3, 2005.

164. Armange, interview, August 5, 2004.

165. Radwan, interview, July 23, 2004.

166. Armange, interview, August 5, 2004. Compare these findings to Nada Oweijane's unlikely claim that Syrian workers comport themselves as if they were at home. "For them," she writes, "Lebanon is the paradise of the Middle East." Khoury, "L'Immigration au Liban," Vol. 1, p. 347.

Chapter 5

1. The phrase is from Weber, *Protestant Ethic*, pp. 180–183.

2. Khoury, "L'Immigration au Liban," Vol. 1, pp. 121, 126, 136–137.

3. Murqus estimated Syrian remittances to be much higher. Michel Murqus, "Al-'Ummal al-Ajanib yahawwilun 4.2 miliyarat dular [Foreign Workers Remit $4.2 Billion]," *Al-Nahar*, January 3, 1998. Picard estimated remittances at $500 million a year. Picard, *Lebanon: A Shattered Country*, p. 193; Dagher's estimate was between $700 million and $1 billion. "Al-Quwa al-'Amila," p. 89; and a Syrian study estimated $2 billion in 1995 and $470 million in 1999. "Tataraji' 5 Marat fi 5 Sanawat [Remittances] Falling 5 Times Over in 5 Years]," in *Al-Watan al-'Arabi*, May 12, 2000. On Kamal Dib's assumptions 200,000 workers (with families in Syria) would remit $312 million a year and 700,000 workers would remit $1.092 billion a year. See "Khurafat 'Sirqat' al-'Amal min al-Lubnani [The Myth of the 'Theft' of Business from the Lebanese]," *Al-Nahar*, October 9, 1999. For Syrian workforce estimates, see Winckler, *Demographic Developments*, p. 143.

4. See, for example, Khalil, "European Business Interests in Lebanon," pp. 199–201, 207, 210–211, 212.

5. Dib, "Khurafat 'Sirqat' al-'Amal."

6. Omar, interview, August 5, 2005.

7. Jo Farah, interview, August 12, 2004.

8. Ray Jureidini, conversation, February 17, 2004.

9. Radwan, interview, July 23, 2004.

10. Omar, interview, August 5, 2005.

11. Armange, interview, August 5, 2004.

12. Ibid.

13. 'Abed, interview, February 22, 2004.

14. Adib Mahrus, interview, March 9, 2004.

15. This was not idle boasting, but factually correct. Abu Subhi told me this himself when I asked him about where the idea for the shop came from well before I met Ibrahim or Nazir.

16. Armange, Radwan, and Nazir, interview, August 23, 2004.

17. Joseph, interview, August 10, 2004.

18. Armange, interview, August 5, 2004.

19. Armange, Radwan, and Nazir, interview, August 23, 2004.

20. Jo Farah, interview, August 12, 2004.

21. Radwan and Nazir, interview, August 27, 2004.

22. 'Abed and Ibrahim, interview, August 9, 2005.

23. Many serious commentators accept the thesis that there was some competition with foreign labor, but tend to understate its importance. See, for example, Dagher, "Al-Quwa al-'Amila," pp. 88–89, or, UNDP, *Sustainable Human Development*, p. 77. The unreliable and uninformative unemployment statistics are not always as useful in this debate as their frequent deployment might imply.

24. Nasr, "The New Social Map," p. 152.

25. Ibid. Those defined as below the "satisfaction threshold" by the United Nations make up more than one-third of the population (35.2 percent), more than a million individuals. UNDP, *Mapping of Living Conditions*, p. 22.

26. Waged workers in industry, for example, totaled 114,002; in construction, 77,615 persons; in commerce, 120,840; in hotels and restaurants, 24,707; and in transport and communications, 28,351. Lebanese Republic, *La Population Active*, p. 64.

27. These earnings were often supplemented earnings, it should be pointed out by secondary activities of one kind or another. Lebanese Republic, *Conditions de Vie*, pp. 62–63.

28. Ibid., p. 44.

29. Lebanese Republic, *La Population Active*, pp. 13, 91.

30. Salim Nasr, "The New Social Map," p. 143. See also Abdallah Dah and Hussein Hejazi, *Tawzi'a al-Dakhl, Namat al-Anfaq wa Zahirat al-Faqr fi Lubnan [The Distribution of Income, Consumption Patterns and Poverty in Lebanon]* (Beirut: The Lebanese Center for Policy Studies, n.d.); Adnan Fahs, *Tabaqat al-Mujtama' fi al-Lubnan: qabl al-harb, ithna' al-harb, ba'd al-harb [Social Classes in Lebanon: Before the War, During the War and After the War]* (n.p.: n.p, 2003).

31. Lebanese Republic, *Conditions de Vie*, pp. 19, 25, 37. Such workers, nonetheless, scraping by close to the poverty line on an average of $379 per month, hardly conformed to the Lebanese stereotype of ease and education.

32. Almost all the "heads of deprived households" worked in these jobs. UNDP, *Mapping of Living Conditions*, p. 21.

33. Lebanese Republic, *Conditions de Vie*, p. 42. For average earnings in the different sectors, see p. 217.

34. Employers of more than one worker in this sector earned $818 per month.

35. Roy, conversation, February 18, 2004.

36. For a reported dispute between Syrian and Lebanese vendors, see *L'Orient Le Jour*, June 13, 1994.

37. Lebanese Republic, *La Population Active*, pp. 96–97.

38. Employers of more than one worker in this category earned $708 per month on average.

39. Mona Harb, conversation, February 26, 2004.

40. Maher al-Yamani, interview, February 24, 2004.

41. Ibid.

42. Ahmad, conversation, February 18, 2004.

43. Employers of more than one worker in this sector earned $778 per month on average.

44. Mona Harb, conversation, February 26, 2004.

45. Hussein, conversation, February 15, 2004.

46. Lebanese Republic, *La Population Active*, pp. 96–97.

47. Yamut, *Al-Iqtisad al-Lubnani*, p. 70.

48. *L'Orient-Le Jour*, June 13, 1994.

49. Khoury, "L'Immigration au Liban," Vol. 1, pp. 185–188.

50. An ex-fighter and intellectual, who although trained as a doctor, was unable to practice because of Lebanese restrictions, and had perforce worked in many kinds of low-income jobs all over Lebanon.

51. Ali Safa, *Al-Liwa*, January 6, 1990.

52. Carol Samaha, "Foreign Labor Competes with Lebanese Labor in the Absence of Official Protection," *Al-Anwar*, January 14, 1993. See also *Al-Liwa*, June 30, 1994.

53. *Al-Siyasa Al-Kuwaitiyya*, December 16, 1992.

54. Suleiman Kattani, *Lubnan 'ala Nazif Khawasirihi* (Beirut: Dar al-Sadiq, n.d. [1970s]), pp. 26–27.

55. Ali Safa, *Al-Liwa*, January 6, 1990.

56. Carol Samaha, "Foreign Labor."

57. *Al-Nahar*, August 4, 1997. Of the other four key problems cited by Sfeir—the Israeli occupation, the Palestinian presence, the existence of 40,000 Syrian troops crushing democracy, and emigration—the latter two were also bound up with the issue of Syrian labor, ratcheting up the political sensitivity of the issue.

58. Khoury, "L'Immigration au Liban," Vol. 1, pp. 210–237.

59. *Al-Nahar*, January 3, 1998.

60. Khoury, "L'Immigration au Liban," Vol. 1, pp. 210–237.

61. Muhammad Zabib, "Ghazwat al-'Ummala al-Ajnabiyya fi Lubnan [Invasion of Foreign Labor in Lebanon]," *Al-Usbu'a Al-'Arabi*, August 14, 1995.

62. *Al-Nahar*, January 3, 1998.

63. Ibid.

64. Zabib, "Invasion,"

65. Ibid.

66. In the 1990s, economic reconstruction dominated debate in Lebanon like no other issue. Najem, *Lebanon's Renaissance*, p. 2.

67. For an account of Syrian heavy-handedness in Lebanon, see Johnson, *All Honorable Men*, pp. 237–249.

68. Najem, *Lebanon's Renaissance*, pp. 59, 81.

69. Ibid., pp. 142, 227.

70. Khalil, "European Business Interests in Lebanon," pp. 1, 242, 252.

71. Ibid., p. 206.

72. *Al-Nahar*, July 24, 1995; see also Michel Murqus, *Al-Nahar*, January 3, 1998, and Michel Murqus, "Al-Ihtimam bi-l-'Ummala al-Suriyya [The Interest in Syrian Labor]," *Al-Nahar*, July 2, 1998.

73. Zabib, "Invasion."

74. Khoury, "L'Immigration au Liban"; Bassam al-Hashim, "Al-Ittifaqat al-Ijtima'iyya."

75. Khoury, "L'Immigration au Liban," Vol. 1, pp. 11–19, 238–253.

76. The term colonization was also used by others. For example, Habib C. Malik, *Between Damascus and Jerusalem: Lebanon and the Middle East Peace* (Washington DC: The Washington Institute for Near East Policy, 1997), p. 42.

77. Khoury, "L'Immigration au Liban," Vol. 1, pp. 383, 386.

78. Ibid., pp. 11–19, 44, 259, 260–261, 265, 347.

79. Ibid., p. 379.

80. Ibid., p. 180.

81. For example, Muhammad Ali Al-Atassi, "'Adad al-'Ummal al-Suriyyin fi Lubnan [The Number of Syrian Workers in Lebanon]," *Al-Hayat*, April 18, 2001.

82. Picard, "Les Syriens," p. 99.

83. These questions are mentioned by Muhammad al-Hujayri, "Dahaya wa Sunna'?! [Victims and Makers?!]," *Al-Nahar*, Supplement, December 16, 2000.

84. Fatima Almana, conversation, March 2, 2004.

85. Mas'ud Daher, interview, March 1, 2004.

86. Picard, "Les Syriens," p. 99.

87. Ibid., pp. 96–97.

88. UNDP, *Sustainable Human Development*, p. 78.

89. Joseph, conversation, February 19, 2004.

90. Thanks to Rita Yazigi for providing these jokes.

91. These points became quickly evident. See, for example, "Tataraji' 5 Marat."

92. This return was even reported in the *Jerusalem Post*. David Rudge, "Hundreds of Syrian Workers Leaving Lebanon," *Jerusalem Post*, June 12, 2000.

93. This point was made to me by Ray Jureidini, conversation, February 17, 2004.

94. "Al-Tayyar al-Watani Da'a al-'Ummal ila al-Tamarrud 'ala al-Ihtilal [The National Movement Calls on the Workers to Resist the Occupation]," *Al-Nahar*, May 11, 2000. "'Awniyun Yabi'aun 'Khudar Lubnaniyya': Man yahmiy min al-munafisa ghayr al-mashru'a [Aounists Sell 'Lebanese Vegetables': Who Can Protect Us against Illegal Competition?]," *Al-Diyar*, May 12, 2000.

95. This was the position of Samah Idriss, leftist intellectual, writer, and editor of the important political and literary magazine, *Al-Adab*. (Samah Idriss, conversation,

February 20, 2004). Al-Hujayri,"Dahaya wa Sunna'?!; Nasrallah, "Ba'su 'al-'Alaqat al-Akhuwiyya."

96. "Quwat al-Amn Darabathum wa Ahanat al-Sahafiyyin wa Awqafat 10 min-hum li'annahum 'bi-la Rukhsa [Security Forces Beat Them, Abused the Journalists and Arrested 10 of Them Because They Were without a Permit]," *Al-Nahar*, July 10, 2000; "'Maktab al-Tansiq' Ayyad Majlis al-Mutarina wa Shajab 'Istifzaz al-'Ummal al-Suriyyin li-Lubnaniyyin [Coordination Office Supports the Bishops' Council and Condems the Incitement of Lebanese by the Syrian Workers]," *Al-Nahar*, July 12, 2000.

97. "Al-Ba'i' Lubnani al-Qama' Aydan [The Lebanese Vendor and Oppression]," *Al-Najwa*, July 17, 2000.

98. "Lubnan fi Nakba [Catastrophe in Lebanon]," *Al-Nahar*, August 22, 2000. Or Jani Nasrallah uses the term occupation in "Ba'su 'al-'Alaqat al-Akhuwiyya."

99. So ran a headline in *Al-Nahar*, November 16, 2000.

100. "Al-Hariri: Ila al-Bahr aw Isra'il [Al-Hariri: To the Sea to to Israel]," *Al-Kifah al-'Arabi*, November 17, 2000; "Muhadithat Dimashq Turakkiz 'ala al-Mutalib al-Lubnaniyya [Damascus Talks Focus on Lebanese Demands]," *Al-Safir*, November 17, 2000.

101. Siniora's claim came in November 2000. See, for example, Nasri Khouri's remarks about employers in December 2000 in "Nasri Khouri: al-'Ummal al-Suriyyin 150 Alfan [Nasri Khouri: The Syrian Workers 150 Thousand]," *Al-Nahar*, December 5, 2000.

102. "CFIL Launches Attacks Against Syrian Workers," *Middle East Intelligence Bulletin* 2, 4 (April 2000) www.meib.org/articles/0004_12.htm.

103. *Al-Safir*, September 26, 2000.

104. On May 6, 1999, a bomb was thrown on a garage containing Syrian workers in Hazemiyya. On December 24, 1998, the network had thrown a bomb near a Syrian military position in Hadath. One author claimed that Syrian vegetable shops were attacked by Palestinians in Ain al-Hilwa camp toward the end of 1999. Both labor competition and the bitter legacy of the 1980s "War of the Camps," which pitted Syrian-backed Amal against the Palestinians, were likely important factors. Shawqi Khalifa, *Lubnan bayn al-Jiyubulitik al-Isra'iliyya wa al-Dimughrafiyya al-Filistiniyya [Lebanon between Israeli Geopolitics and Palestinian Demography]* (Kisrawan: Dakkash, 2002), p. 158.

105. Reported in "Syrian Workers in Lebanon: The Other Occupation," *Middle East Intelligence Bulletin*, Feb. 2001.

106. "Musalihun yahajimun 'Ummalan Suriyyin [Gunmen Attack Syrian Workers]," *Al-Sharq al-Awsat*, April 7, 2001.

107. "CFIL Launches Attacks Against Syrian Workers," *Middle East Intelligence Bulletin* 2, 4 (April 2000), www.meib.org/articles/0004_12.htm.

108. Omar Nashabe, conversation, February 18, 2004.

109. "Ma'sa Tasna' Ukhra [One Misery Creates Another]," *Al-Safir*, July 13, 2000.

110. " 'Istifzaz al-'Ummal al-Suriyyin," *Al-Nahar*, July 12, 2000.

111. For example, "Ma'sa Tasna' Ukhra." Or see Trad Hamadeh's strictures against Lebanese 'racism' and discrimination towards Syrian workers, " 'An Dawr al-Muslimin al-Shi'a fi Lubnan [On the Role of the Shi'a Muslims in Lebanon]," *Al-Nahar*, April 22, 2005, p. 19.

112. Hamad, conversation, February 25, 2004.

113. Damascus claimed that there were 36 dead and 250 injured. *Al-Hayat*, July 19, 2005. The Lebanese daily *Al-Safir* reported on two deaths resulting directly from Lebanese aggression, and more than a dozen attacks in an investigation published on April 19, 2005.

114. Omar, interview, August 5, 2005.

115. Ibid.

116. Ibid.

117. 'Abd al-Qadir, interview, August 3, 2005.

118. See, for example, *Al-Nahar*, March 23, 2005.

119. Dhu-l-Fiqar Qubaysi, writing in *Al-Kifah Al-'Arabi*, June 13, 2000.

120. Ray Jureidini, conversation, February 17, 2004.

121. Khoury, "L'Immigration au Liban," Vol. 1, p. 112.

122. The average cost of school, per year, per household, in Lebanon was estimated in the 1990s to be $1,437. Lebanese Republic, *Conditions de Vie*, pp. 56–57.

123. Batatu argued that it was "justifiable to infer that . . . the chief sources of the government's tax revenue were the foreign trade and customs fees and, to a greater extent, the tax on the profits of public enterprises, private corporations, and independent individual businessmen, artisans, and professionals." Batatu, *Syria's Peasantry*, p. 63.

124. Courbage, "Evolution démographique," p. 746.

125. Mike Davis, *Planet of Slums* (London: Verso, 2006). Volker Perthes, *The Political Economy of Syria under Asad* (London: I. B. Tauris, 1995), p. 203.

126. Khayriyya, conversation, August 10, 2006.

127. Radwan, interview, July 23, 2004.

128. 'Abd al-Qadir, interview, July 23, 2004.

129. 'Abd al-Qadir, interview, August 3, 2005.

130. Ibid.

131. Ibid.

132. 'Abed and Ibrahim, interview, August 9, 2005.

133. Roger Awwad, interview, August 11, 2004.

134. Omar, interview, August 5, 2005.

135. Adib Mahrus, interview, March 9, 2004.

136. Roger Awwad, interview, August 11, 2004.

137. 'Abd al-Qadir, interview, August 3, 2005.

138. Men also felt the strain of being without their wives. 'Abd al-Qadir said, "Right now my wife is in Syria, I have to keep washing my clothes, making myself food. It's too much work besides the shop. When she is here it is a lot easier, I have clean clothes every day, and hot water and food when I come back home."

139. 'Abed and Ibrahim, interview, August 9, 2005.

140. 'Abd al-Qadir, interview, August 3, 2005.

141. Omar, interview, August 5, 2005.

142. Muhammad, interview, July 31, 2004.

143. This formulation is conceptualized and discussed in relation to Zionism in Glenn Bowman, "'Migrant Labour': Constructing Homeland in the Exilic Imagination," *Anthropological Theory* 2, 4 (2002), pp. 447–468.

144. Roger Awwad, interview, August 11, 2004.

145. Khoury, "L'Immigration au Liban," Vol. 1, p. 353.

Conclusion

1. Weber, *Protestant Ethic*, pp. 180–183.

2. In Japan, for example, Thai girls who thought they were going to be waitresses ended up being bought and sold by brothel-owners who forced them to undertake sex-work to pay off the "debt" incurred by their "purchase." See Anderson, *Labour Exchange*.

3. Offe, *Disorganized Capitalism*, p. 17.

4. As Frederick Cooper has argued, "open markets" are not a static package. The specific institutional and historical configuration of the "open market" varies by time and place, and is not heading in a distinct and clear direction. Frederick Cooper, *Colonialism in Question: Theory, Knowledge, History* (Berkeley: University of California Press, 2005), p. 236. Cooper maintained that we should avoid the generalization that we are now in a world dominated by the "all-determining discipline of the world market." Instead, "the reconfiguration of capital across space unleashes a politics of borders and border-crossings rather than a regime of borderlessness" (p. 237).

5. "The colonial difference is the space where *local* histories inventing and implementing global designs meet *local* histories, the space in which global designs have to be adapted, adopted, rejected, integrated, or ignored." Walter D. Mignolo, *Local Histories/Global Designs: Coloniality, Subaltern Knowledges and Border Thinking* (Princeton: Princeton University Press, 2000), p. ix.

6. Cited in Seteney Shami, "Mobility, Modernity and Misery: Population Displacement and Resettlement in the Middle East," in *Displacement and Resettlement*, pp. 1–10, p. 1.

7. Extended hegemony is a state of unfreedom in the sense meant by Hannah Arendt, where she writes, "Man cannot be free if he does not know that he is subject to

necessity, because his freedom is always won in his never wholly successful attempts to liberate himself from necessity." Hannah Arendt, *The Human Condition* (Chicago: University of Chicago Press, 1958), p. 121.

8. Bauman, *Wasted Lives*, pp. 5, 19, 39.

9. See John Chalcraft and Yaseen Noorani, eds., *Counterhegemony in the Colony and Postcolony* (Houndmills: Palgrave Macmillan, 2007).

10. Goethe, *Elective Affinities*, p. 56.

BIBLIOGRAPHY

Works of Reference, Government/UN Reports, and Publications

Administration Centrale de la Statistique (ACS). *L'Enquête par sondage sur la population active du Liban, novembre 1970.* Beirut: Ministry of Planning, 1972.

———. *Evolution de la structure des importations par genre d'utilisation 1964–1995.* Beirut: Etudes Statistiques No. 2, March 1996.

———. *La ville de Beyrouth. Résultats du recensement des immeubles et des établissements.* Beirut: Etudes Statistiques No. 9, République Libanaise, 1996.

———. *Conditions de vie des ménages en 1997.* Beirut: Etudes Statistiques No. 9, République Libanaise, 1998.

———. *La population active en 1997.* Beirut: Etudes Statistiques No. 12, République Libanaise, 1998.

———. *Budget des ménages en 1997.* 2 vols. Beirut: Etudes Statistiques No. 13, February 1999.

———. *Evolution de la structure des importations par genre d'utilisation pour les années 1996–1997–1998.* Beirut: Etudes Statistiques No. 14, August, 1999.

———. *Les permis de construire au Liban entre 1994 et 1997.* Beirut: Etudes Statistiques No. 15, December 1999.

Al-'Alaqat al-Lubnaniyya al-Suriyya 1943–1985: Waqa'i', Bibliyughrafiyya wa Watha'iq [Lebanese-Syrian Relations: Events, Bibliography and Documents], 2 Vols. Antiliyas: *Markaz al-Tawthiq wa-l-Buhuth al-Lubnani,* 1986.

Bechtel International and Dar Al-Handasah (Consultants). *Recovery Planning for the Reconstruction and Development of Lebanon, Working Paper 1: Overview of Lebanon,* August 1991.

Council for Development and Reconstruction. *Recovery Planning for the Reconstruction of Lebanon, Damage Assessment Report,* August 1992.

Dib, Yussuf, ed. *Al-Yawmiyyat al-Lubnaniyya 1985 [Lebanese Daily Events 1985]*. Beirut: Shirkat al-Fahrasat li-l-Intaj al-Thaqafi, 1986.

Economist Intelligence Unit. *Lebanon: Country Profile 2003*. London: Economist Intelligence Unit, 2003.

Etude Annuelle sur L'Economie Libanaise de L'Année 1968. Beirut: Bureau des documentations Libanaises et Arabe, 1969.

Etude Annuelle sur L'Economie Libanaise de L'Année 1970. Beirut: Bureau des documentations Libanaises et Arabe, 1971.

Etude Annuelle sur L'Economie Libanaise de L'Année 1972. Beirut: Bureau des documentations Libanaises et Arabe, 1973.

Fawaz, Mona, and Isabelle Peillen. *Reporting on Slums in Beirut for the Global Report on Human Settlements 2003*. Beirut: UN-Habitat, 2002.

Haddad, Antoine. *Poverty in Lebanon*. Beirut, UN-ESCWA, 1996.

Hameed, K. "Manpower and Employment Planning in Iraq and Syrian Arab Republic," in ECWA *Studies on Development Problems in Countries of Western Asia, 1975*. New York: ECWA, 1977, pp. 22–44.

'Issa, Najib. *Economic Reform and Reconstruction in Lebanon,* Amman: ESCWA, 1993. In Arabic.

Al-Jumhuriyya al-Lubnaniyya. *Al-Majmu'a al-Ihsa'iyya al-Lubnaniyya li-'am 1963 [Lebanese Statistical Totals for 1963]*. Beirut: Wizarat al-Tasmim al-'Am [Ministry of Planning], n.d.

———. *Al-Majmu'a al-Ihsa'iyya al-Lubnaniyya li-'am 1973 [Lebanese Statistical Totals for 1973]*. Beirut: Wizarat al-Tasmim al-'Am [Ministry of Planning], n.d.

———. *Tasnif al-Mihan fi Lubnan [Classification of Occupations in Lebanon]*, 2 Vols. Beirut: Al-Mu'assasa al-Wataniyya li-l-Istikhdam [National Employment Institute], 2005.

Khalidi-Beyhum, R. *Poverty Reduction Policies in Jordan and Lebanon: An Overview*. New York: UN-ESCWA, 1999.

Lebanese Center for Policy Studies. *A Study of the Needs and Opportunities for Skilled Workers in Lebanon*. Beirut: Prepared for The Near East Foundation by LCPS in cooperation with Amideast, January 1993.

Ministry of Social Affairs—United Nations Development Programme. *Mapping of Living Conditions in Lebanon: An Analysis of the Housing and Population Data Base*. Beirut: MOSA-UNDP, 1998.

Ministry of Social Affairs—United Nations Population Fund. *Analytical Studies of Population and Housing Survey*, 6 Vols. Beirut: MOSA-UNFPA, 2000.

Mission-IRFED-Liban. *Besoins et possibilités de développement du Liban*. Beirut: Ministère du Plan, 1960–61.

———. *Besoins et possibilités de développement du Liban*. Beirut: n. p., 1963.

Mouvement Social. *Recensement des Habitations et des Résidents dans les bidonvilles de Beyrouth et de sa banlieue*. Beirut: Ministry of Public Works (General Directorate of Urbanism), 1971.

Nashif, Antwan, and Khalil al-Hindi. *Al-'Alaqat al-Lubnaniyya al-Suriyya: Al-Jawanib al-Qanuniyya wa-l-Iqtisadiyya wa-l-Ijtima'iyya [Lebanese-Syrian Relations: Legal, Economic and Social Dimensions]*. Tripoli: Al-Mu'assasa al-Haditha li-l-Kitab, 1998.

Nouhad, Baroudi. *Horizon 2000: A Synopsis*. Beirut: Council for Development and Reconstruction, September 1995.

United Nations Development Programme. *A Profile of Sustainable Human Development in Lebanon*. Beirut: UNDP, 1997.

Unpublished Papers and Dissertations

Bardawil, Fadi. "Behind the Sewing Machines: A Case Study of Migrant Labor in Lebanon." Unpublished term paper written for Professor Ray Jureidini, American University in Beirut, 2000.

Bochi, Giovanni. "The Production of Difference: Sociality, Work and Mobility in a Community of Syrian Dom between Lebanon and Syria." Ph.D. thesis, London School of Economics and Political Science, 2007.

Gaspard, Toufic. "The Transfer Economy." Paper presented at the *Workshop on the Political Economy of Lebanon*, Center of Arabic and Middle East Studies and the Department of Economics, American University of Beirut, March 22, 2004.

Ghosn, Rania W. "Syrian Elites Practices and Representations of Beirut: The Intimate Nearness of Difference." Unpublished MSc dissertation, University College London, 2003.

Hoffman, Eivind. "International Statistical Comparisons of Occupational and Social Structures: Problems, Possibilities and the Role of ISCO-88." Paper prepared for *Symposium on Measuring Demographic Variables in International Perspective*, 30 September–1 October 1999, Cologne, Germany. http://www.ilo.org/public/english/bureau/stat/download/iscopres.pdf, accessed 15 June 2007.

Isma'il, Amal. "Al-'Ummala al-Ajnabiyya fi Lubnan (Halat al-'Ummal al-Srilankiyya) khilal al-Fitra 1982–1986 [Foreign Labour in Lebanon and the Condition of Sri Lankan Workers, 1982–1986]." Unpublished MA thesis. Beirut, Lebanese University, Institute of Social Sciences, Branch 1, 1987.

Jureidini, Ray, and Nayla Moukarbel. *Contract Slavery: The Case of Female Sri Lankan Domestic Labour in Lebanon*. Paper presented to workshop on Domestic Service and Mobility, The International Institute of Social History, Amsterdam, 5–7 February, 2001.

Khalil, Ali Moussa. "European Business Interests in Lebanon: An Assessment of EU Private Foreign Direct Investment in the Reconstruction Era." University of

Durham, Centre for Middle Eastern and Islamic Studies, unpublished Ph.D. thesis, 2000.

Khoury, Nada Oweijane. "L'Immigration au Liban: Aspects Socio-économiques et Incidences Identitaires." 3 Vols. Lebanese University, Institute of Social Sciences, Section II (Rabieh, Lebanon) and Université Rene Descartes, Paris V, doctoral thesis, 2001.

Labaki, Boutros. "Lebanese Emigration after the Taief Agreement, 1990–2000." Paper for Conference at Center for Migration Studies, Lebanese American University, Beirut, 28–29 June, 2001.

Lavelle, Pat. "The 'Other Occupation' or the Other? The Rights and Prospects of Syrian Workers in a Changing Lebanon." University of Virginia School of Law, Masters Independent Study Project with Professor Hurwitz, Spring 2005.

Martini, M. A. "An Analysis of Female Wage Labour in Northwest Syria in the Context of Agricultural Intensification." Reading University, UK, unpublished Ph.D. thesis, 1999.

Moussa, Bassam. "Is There a Way Out? The Case of a Migrant Syrian Household Looking for Assimilation." Unpublished term paper written for Professor Mona Fawaz, AUB, 2003.

Picard, Elizabeth. "Managing Identities Among Expatriate Businessmen Across the Syrian Lebanese Boundary." Unpublished paper, Middle East Studies Association of America (Annual Meeting) 2004.

Stefflbauer, Nakima Barbero. "An Analysis of Syrian-Lebanese Informal Trade: 1943–1993." Unpublished Ph.D. dissertation, Harvard University, 1999.

Traboulsi, Fawwaz. "The Lebanese System Revisited." Paper presented to the conference *The Lebanese System: A Critical Reassessment*. Center for Behavioral Research and the Chiha Foundation, American University of Beirut, 18–19 May, 2001.

List of Newspapers and Magazines Consulted

Al-Afkar (Beirut, weekly)
Al-'Amal
Al-Anwar
Al-Ba'th
Le Commerce du Levant
The Daily Star (Beirut, daily)
Al-Diyar (daily)
L'Économie des pays arabes (Beirut, monthly)
Al-Hayat
Al-Ishtiraki (Damascus, weekly)
Jerusalem Post
Al-Kabass (Kuwait)

Al-Khalij (Sharja, daily)
Al-Kifah Al-'Arabi
Al-Liwa
Magazine (Beirut, weekly)
Al-Massira (Beirut, weekly)
Al-Muharrar (Lebanon, daily)
Al-Mustaqbal
Al-Nahar
Al-Najwa
Al-Naqqad
L'Orient-Le-Jour (Beirut, daily)
Al-Ra'i al-'Am
Al-Rayya
Al-Safir
Al-Sayyad
Al-Sharq
Al-Sharq Al-Awsat
Al-Siyasa Al-Kuwaitiyya
Al-Aswaq al-Tijariyya
Al-Tariq
Tishrin
Al-Usbu'a Al-'Arabi
Wall Street Journal
Al-Watan al-'Arabi

List of Recorded Interviews

'Abd al-Qadir, 23 July, 2004, 3 August 2005
'Abed, 9, 30, 31 August 2005
Abu Subhi, 12 March 2004
Adib Mahrus, 9, 10 March 2004
Armange, 5 August 2004
Ayman, 31 July 2004
Hanna Awwad, 11 August 2004
Hanna Butros, 11 August 2004
Ibrahim (from Beirut), 9 August 2005
Ibrahim (from Aleppo), 23 July 2004
Jo Farah, 12 August 2004
Joseph, 10 August 2004
Omar, 5, 23, 29 August 2005
Muhammad, 31 July 2004

Nazir, 23 August 2004

Radwan, 23 July 2004, 27 July 2004

Rita Yazigi, 13 March 2004

Roger Awwad, 11 August 2004

Tony Elias, 12 August 2004

Trad Hamadeh, 20 August 2005

Articles

Abdelali-Martini, Malika, Patricia Goldey, Gwyn E. Jones, and Elizabeth Bailey. "Towards a Feminization of Agricultural Labour in Northwest Syria." *Journal of Peasant Studies*, vol. 30, no. 2 (January 2003), pp. 71–94.

Anon. "Working Conditions in Handicrafts and Modern Industry in Syria." *International Labour Review*, vol. 29, no. 3 (March 1934), pp. 407–411.

———. "Conditions of Work in Syria and the Lebanon under French Mandate." *International Labour Review*, vol 39, no. 4 (April 1939), pp. 513–526.

Abi Farah, Anis. "Commentary on Wage and Income Policy." *Aba'ad.*, no. 2 (November 1994). [In Arabic]

Abu-Iziddin, F., and George Hakim. "A Contribution to the Study of Labour Conditions in the Lebanon." *International Labour Review* (November 1933), pp. 673–682.

Abu-Lughod, Janet. "Recent Migrations in the Arab World," in *Arab Society: Social Science Perspectives*, edited by Saad Eddin Ibrahim and Nicholas S. Hopkins (Cairo: American University in Cairo Press, 1985), pp. 177–188.

Acuña, Rodolfo. *Occupied America: A History of Chicanos* (4th ed.). New York: Longman, 2000.

Arnold, Fred, and Nasra M. Shah. "Asian Labor Migration to the Middle East," *International Migration Review*, vol. 18, no. 2 (Summer 1984): 294–318.

Birks, J., Sinclair, C., and Seccombe, I. "Labour Migration in the Arab Gulf States: Patterns, Trends and Prospects." *International Migration*, vol. 26, no. 3 (1988), pp. 267–286.

Bourgey, André. "La Guerre et ses conséquences géographiques au Liban." *Annales de Géographies*, no. 521, 94th year (1985), pp. 1–37.

Bourgey, André, and J. Pharès. "Les bidonvilles de l'agglomération de Beyrouth." *Revue de géographie de Lyon*, vol 48, no. 2 (1973), pp. 107–139.

Bowman, Glenn. "'Migrant Labour': Constructing Homeland in the Exilic Imagination." *Anthropological Theory*, vol. 2, no. 4 (2002), pp. 447–468.

Brass, Tom, and Harry Bernstein. "Introduction: Proletarianisation and Deproletarianisation on the Colonial Plantation." *Journal of Peasant Studies*, vol. 19, no. 3–4 (April/July 1992), pp. 1–40.

Burawoy, Michael. "The Functions and Reproduction of Migrant Labor: Comparative

Material from Southern Africa and the United States." *The American Journal of Sociology*, vol. 81, no. 5 (March 1976), pp. 1050–1087.

Chalcraft, John. "Syrian Workers in Lebanon and the Role of the State: Political Economy and Popular Aspirations," in *Migration et politique au Moyen-Orient*, edited by Françoise De Bel-Air. Beirut: Institut Français du Proche Orient, 2006, pp. 81–104.

Chiswick, Barry R. "The Effect of Americanization on the Earnings of Foreign-Born Men." *Journal of Political Economy*, vol. 86, no.5 (October 1978), pp. 897–921.

Choucri, Nazli. "Migration in the Middle East: Transformation and Change." *Middle East Review*, vol. 16, no. 2 (Winter 1983/84), pp. 16–27.

Corm, Georges. "Ruptures et continuités dans la pensée et les politiques de développment et de reconstruction au Liban depuis l'indépendance." *Proche Orient, Etudes Economiques*. Beirut: University of Saint Joseph, November 1994.

Courbage, Youssef. "Evolution démographique et attitudes politique en Syrie," *Population*, Paris: INED, 49th Year, no. 3 (May–June 1994), pp. 725–750.

Dagher, Albert. "Al-Quwa Al-'Amila wa-l-Namu fi Lubnan: Al-Waqi'a wa-l-Afaq Al-Mustaqbaliyya," in *Linking Economic Growth and Social Development in Lebanon*. Beirut: United Nations Development Programme, 2000, pp. 85–99.

Deek, Wissam. "Studying a Camp, Sabra and Chatila" *Proceedings 2nd FEA Student Conference*, edited by Ibrahim N. Hajj and Samer M. Abdallah. American University of Beirut Press, 2003, pp. 85–88.

Frangié, Samir. "Les relations libano-syriennes: un compromis est-il possible?" *Travaux et Jours*, vol. 69 (Spring 2002), pp. 47–60.

Gambill, Gary C. "Lebanese Farmers and the Syrian Occupation." *Middle East Intelligence Bulletin*, vol 5, no. 10 (October 2003). http://www.meib.org/articles/0131o_htm.

Gates, Carolyn L. "Laissez-faire, Outward-orientation, and Regional Economic Disintegration: A Case Study of the Dissolution of the Syro-Lebanese Customs Union," in *State and Society in Syria and Lebanon*, edited by Yussuf M. Choueiri. Exeter: University of Exeter Press, 1993, pp. 74–83.

Gualtieri, S. M. "Gendering the Chain Migration Thesis: Women and Syrian Transatlantic Migration," *Comparative Studies of South Asia, African and the Middle East*, vol. 24, no. 1 (2004), pp. 69–80.

Gibert, André, and Maurice Fevret. "La Djezireh Syrienne et son Réveil Economique." *Revue de Géographie de Lyon*, vol. 28 (1953), pp. 1–15.

Hamdan, Kamal. "Les Libanais face à la crise économique et sociale: étendue et limites des processus d'adaptation." *Maghreb-Machrek*, vol. 125 (July–September 1989), pp. 19–39.

———. "Wage and Income Policy." *Aba'ad*, no. 2 (November 1994). [In Arabic]

Hannoyer, Jean. "Le Monde Rural Avant les Réformes," in *La Syrie D'Aujourd'hui*, edited by André Raymond. Paris: Centre National de la Recherche Scientifique, 1980, pp. 273–295.

Harik, Iliya F. "The Impact of the Domestic Market on Rural-Urban Relations in the Middle East," in *Rural Politics and Social Change in the Middle East*, edited by Richard Antoun and Iliya Harik. Bloomington: Indiana University Press, 1972, pp. 337–363.

Hashim, Bassam al-. "Vers une identité tout autre." *Universalia* (French Yearly, Paris). "La politique les connaissances la culture en 1997" (1998), pp. 218–222.

———."Al-Ittifaqat al-Ijtima'iya wa In'akasatuha al-Dimughrafiyya fi al-'Alaqat al-Lubnaniyya–al-Suriyya: Muhawila Taqwimiyya [Social Agreements and their Demographic Effects in Syrian-Lebanese Relations: An Attempted Evaluation]," in *Al-'Alaqat al-Lubnaniyya al-Suriyya: Muhawila Taqwimiyya [Syrian-Lebanese Relations: An Attempted Evaluation]*. Beirut, Antiliyas: Al-Haraka Al-Thaqafiyya, 2001), pp. 110–148.

Hawwa, Huda. "Linkages and Constraints of the Syrian Economy," in *State and Society in Syria and Lebanon*, edited by Yussuf M. Choueiri. Exeter: University of Exeter Press, 1993, pp. 84–102

Jureidini, Ray. *Women Migrant Domestic Workers in Lebanon*, International Migration Papers, No. 48. Geneva: International Labour Organization, 2002.

———. "Migrant Workers and Xenophobia in the Middle East." Programme Paper 2 on Identities, Conflict and Cohesion. Geneva: United Nations Research Institute for Social Development, 2003.

———. "Middle East Guestworkers," in *Global Migration in the Twentieth Century: An Encyclopedia*, edited by Matthew Gibney and Randall Hanssen. Oxford: ABC-CLIO, forthcoming.

Kanovsky, E. "The Economic Aftermath of the Six Day War: UAR, Jordan and Syria." *The Middle East Journal*, vol. 22, no. 3 (Summer 1968), pp. 278–296.

Kasparian, Robert. *Note Sur la répartition des revenus au Liban*. Beirut, 1974.

Kasparian, Robert, and A. Beaudoin. *La population déplacée au Liban 1975–1987*. Beirut: Saint Joseph University, Quebec: Laval, February 1992.

Kassir, Samir. "A Polity in an Uncertain Regional Environment," in *Lebanon in Limbo: Postwar Society and State in an Uncertain Regional Environment*, edited by Theodor Hanf and Nawaf Salam. Baden-Baden: Nomos Verlagsgesellschaft, 2003, pp. 87–106.

Khafaji, 'Isam Al-. "Hamishun fi-l-Mudun Al-'Arabiyya [Marginals in Arab Cities]." *Jidal* [Scholarly Journal] 4 issues (1993) published in Damascus.

Khalaf, Samir. "The Background and Causes of Lebanese/Syrian Immigration to the United States before World War I," in *Crossing the Waters: Arabic-Speaking Immigrants to the United States Before 1940*, edited by Eric J. Hoogland. Washington DC: Smithsonian Institution Press, 1987.

Klat, Paul. "Labour Movement in Syria and Lebanon." *Political Affairs*, vol 3 ((June 1948), pp. 75–76.

——. "Labour Legislation in Lebanon." *Middle East Economic Papers* (1959), pp. 69–81.

Klich, Ignacio. "*Criollos* and Arabic Speakers in Argentina: An Uneasy *Pas de Deux*, 1888–1914," in *The Lebanese in the World: A Century of Emigration*, edited by Albert Hourani and Nadim Shehadi. London: I. B. Tauris, 1992, pp. 243–284.

Labaki, Butros. "L'émigration depuis la fin des guerres a l'intérieur du Liban (1990–1998)." *Travaux et Jours*, New Series no. 61 (Spring 1998), pp. 81–142.

Leybourne, Marina, Ronald Jaubert, and Richard N. Tutwiler. *Changes in Migration and Feeding Patterns Among Semi-Nomadic Pastoralists in Northern Syria*. Network Paper, Pastoral Development Network, Overseas Development Institute, 1993.

Maila, Joseph. "La République de Taëf 13 ans après." *Travaux et Jours*, vol. 69 (Spring 2002), pp. 61–76.

Makinwa-Adebusoye, Paulina, "The West African Migration System," in *International Migration Systems: A Global Approach*, edited by Mary M. Kritz, Lin Lean Lim, and Hania Zlotnik. Oxford: Clarendon Press, 1992, pp. 63–79.

Marshall, Dawn I. "International Migration as Circulation: Haitian Movement to the Bahamas," in *Circulation in Third World Countries*, edited by R. Mansell Prothero and Murray Chapman. London: Routledge & Kegan Paul, 1985, pp. 226–240.

McMurray, D. "Recent Trends in Middle Eastern Migration." *Middle East Report*, vol. 211 (1999), pp. 16–19.

Metral, Françoise. "State and Peasants in Syria: A Local View of a Government Irrigation Project," in *Arab Society: Social Science Perspectives*, edited by Saad Eddin Ibrahim and Nicholas S. Hopkins. Cairo: American University Press, 1985.

Milenkovic, G. *Estimating Poverty Lines for West Beirut*. Beirut: American University in Beirut, December 1987.

Nasr, Salim. "Morphologie sociale de la banlieue-est de Beyrouth." *Maghreb-Machrek*, no. 73 (July–September 1976), pp. 78–88.

——. "The Crisis of Lebanese Capitalism." *MERIP Reports*, no. 73 (1978), pp. 3–13.

——. "Les formes de regroupement traditionnel (familles, confessions, communautés régionales) dans la société de Beyrouth," in *L'Espace social de la ville arabe*, edited by Dominique Chevallier. Paris: Editions Maisonneuve et Larose, 1979, pp. 145–199.

——. "Beyrouth et le conflit libanais, restructuration de l'espace urbain," in *Politiques urbaines dans le Monde Arabe: Maghreb, Proche Orient*, edited by F. Metral. Lyon: Maison de l'Orient, 1984. Sindbad, 1985.

——. "Guerre, migrations vers le Golfe et nouveaux investissements immobiliers dans le Grand Beyrouth," in *Migrations et changements sociaux dans l'Orient Arabe*, edited by CERMOC. Beirut, 1985, pp. 309–330.

———. "The New Social Map," in *Lebanon in Limbo: Postwar Society and State in an Uncertain Regional Environment*, edited by Theodor Hanf and Nawaf Salam. Baden-Baden: Nomos Verlagsgesellschaft, 2003, pp. 143–158.

Picard, Elizabeth. "Les Syriens, l'envers du décor," in *Beyrouth: La Brûlure des Rêves*, edited by Jade Tabet. Paris: Editions Autrement, 2001, pp. 92–102.

"Projet de loi réglementant le travail des étrangers au Liban." *L'Économie des pays arabes*, vol. 18, no. 211 (August 1975), pp. 51–54.

Prothero, R. Mansell. "Foreign Migrant Labour for South Africa." *International Migration Review*, vol. VIII, no. 3 (Fall 1974), pp. 383–394.

Salem, Adib. "Poor grow poorer." *The Lebanon Report*, vol. 3, no. 9 (1992).

Samman, Mouna Liliane. "Aperçu sur les mouvements migratoires récents de la population en Syrie." *Revue de Géographie de Lyon*, vol. 53, no. 3 (1978), pp. 211–228.

Sassen-Koob, Saskia. "The New Labor Demand in Global Cities," in *Cities in Transformation: Class, Capital, and the State*, edited by Michael Peter Smith. Beverly Hills: Sage Publications, 1984.

Shah, N. "Arab Labour Migration: A Review of Trends and Issues." *International Migration Quarterly Review*, vol. XXXII, no. 1 (1994), pp. 3–28.

Shami, Seteney. "Mobility, Modernity and Misery: Population Displacement and Resettlement in the Middle East," in *Population Displacement and Resettlement: Development and Conflict in the Middle East*, edited by Seteney Shami. New York: Center for Migration Studies, 1994, pp. 1–10.

Sirhan, Bassem. "Palestinian Refugee Camp Life in Lebanon." *Journal of Palestine Studies*, vol. 4, no. 2 (Winter 1975), pp. 91–107.

Soltau, Irene C. "Social Responsibility in the Lebanon." *Royal Institute of International Affairs*, vol. 25, no. 3 (July 1949), pp. 307–317.

Tinaoui, Simone Ghazi. "An Analysis of the Syrian-Lebanese Economic Cooperation Agreements." *The Beirut Review*, no. 8 (Fall 1994), pp. 97–112.

Traboulsi, Fawwaz. "Al-Takwin al-Tabaqi li-l-Sulta Ba'd Al-Harb [The Class Composition of Political Power in the Post War Period]." *Ab'ad*. Beirut: The Lebanese Centre for Policy Studies, no. 6 (May), pp. 79–92.

Trendle, Giles. "Lebanon: End of the Nightmare?" *The Middle East* (September 1991), 10.

Wallerstein, Immanuel. "The Construction of Peoplehood: Racism, Nationalism, Ethnicity," in *Race, Nation, Class*, edited by Etienne Balibar and Immanuel Wallerstein. New York: Verso, 1991.

Whiteford, Scott, and Richard N. Adams. "Migration, Ethnicity, and Adaptation: Bolivian Migrant Workers in Northwest Argentina," in *Migration and Urbanization: Models and Adaptive Strategies*, edited by Brian M. du Toit and Helen I. Safa. The Hague: Mouton Publishers, 1975, pp. 179–199.

Widmer, Robert. "Population," in *Economic Organization of Syria*, edited by Sa'id B. Himadeh. Beirut: American University of Beirut Press, 1936.

Zolberg, Aristide R. "Response: Working-Class Dissolution." *International Journal of Labor and Working-Class History*, vol. 47 (Spring 1995), pp. 28–38.

Books

Abu-Aianah, Fathi Muhammad. *Al-Sukkan fi-l-Watan al-'Arabi: Dirasat Giyu-dimughrafiyya [Population in the Arab World: Geodemographic Studies].* Alexandria: Dar al-Ma'rifa al-Jama'iyya, 1994.

Abu Khalil, Joseph. *Lubnan wa Suriyya: Mushaqqat al-Akhuwwa [Syria and Lebanon: The Broken Brotherhood].* Beirut: Shirkat al-Matbu'at li-l-Tawzi'a wa al-Nashr, 1991.

Adnan, Etel. *Sitt Marie Rose: A Novel.* 1st published in 1978, trans. by Georgina Kleege. Sausalito, CA: The Post-Apollo Press, 1982.

Ahzab al-Haraka al-Wataniyya al-Lubnaniyya, *Al-Muhajjarun: Dahaya al-Mukhatat al-In'azali [Forced Migrants: Victims of Isolationist Plans].* Beirut: Lajnat al-Wataniyya li-l-Muhajjarin, n.d. [c.1980].

Akarlı, Engin. *The Long Peace: Ottoman Lebanon, 1861–1920.* Berkeley: University of California Press, 1993.

Al-'Alaqat al-Lubnaniyya al-Suriyya: Muhawila Taqwimiyya [Lebanese-Syrian Relations: An Attempted Estimation]. Beirut, Antiliyas: Al-Haraka Al-Thaqafiyya, 2001.

Amin, Samir, ed. *Modern Migrations in Western Africa.* Oxford: Oxford University Press, 1974.

Anderson, Bridget. *Labour Exchange: Patterns of Migration in Asia.* London: Catholic Institute for International Relations, 1997.

———. *Doing the Dirty Work? The Global Politics of Domestic Labour.* London: Zed Books, 2000.

Arendt, Hannah. *The Human Condition.* Chicago: University of Chicago Press, 1958.

Averitt, Robert T. *The Dual Economy.* New York: Norton, 1968.

Avi-Ran, Reuven. *The Syrian Involvement in Lebanon since 1975.* Boulder, CO: Westview Press, 1991.

Banna, Ali al-. *Al-Intaj al-Zira'I fi Lubnan 1958–1968 [Agricultural Production in Lebanon, 1958–1968].* Beirut: Beirut Arab University, 1970.

Basch, Linda, Nina Glick Schiller, and Cristina Szanton Blanc. *Nations Unbound: Transnational Projects, Postcolonial Predicaments, and Deterritorialized Nation-States.* Amsterdam: Overseas Publishers Association, 1994.

Batatu, Hanna. *Syria's Peasantry, the Descendants of Its Lesser Rural Notables, and Their Politics.* Princeton: Princeton University Press, 1999.

Bauman, Zygmunt. *Wasted Lives: Modernity and its Outcasts.* Cambridge: Polity Press, 2004.

Beaugé, Gilbert, and Alain Roussillon. *Le Migrant et son double: migrations et unité arabe.* Preface by Bruno Etienne. Paris: Publisud, 1988.

Becker, Gary. *The Economics of Discrimination*. Chicago: University of Chicago Press, 1957.

Beirut Chamber of Commerce and Industry. *In'akasat al-Ahdath 'ala al-Yad al-'Amila fi Beirut [Effects of the Civil War on Labor Power in Beirut]*. Beirut: n.d.

Bhabha, Homi K. *Nation and Narration*. London: Routledge, 1990.

Bhadra, Gautam, Gyan Prakash, and Susie Tham eds. *Subaltern Studies X: Writings on South Asian History and Society*. Oxford: Oxford University Press, 1999.

Biqa'i, Qasim al-Haymani al-. *Dalil al-Muhajirin [Guide for Migrants]*. Havana, Cuba: Monte Street 103, 1931.

Birks, J., and Sinclair, C. *International Migration and Development in the Arab Region*. Geneva: International Labour Office, 1980.

Borjas, George J. *Friends or Strangers: The Impact of Immigrants on the US Economy*. New York: Basic Books, 1990.

Bourgey, André. *Industrialisation et changements sociaux dans l'Orient arabe*. Lyon: Editions du Centre d'Etudes et de recherches sur le Moyen-Orient contemporain, Lyon University Press, 1982.

Breman, Jan. *Of Peasants, Migrants and Paupers: Rural Labour Circulation and Capitalist Production in West India*. Delhi: Oxford University Press, 1985.

Burawoy, Michael. *Manufacturing Consent: Changes in the Labor Process under Monopoly Capitalism*. Chicago: University of Chicago Press, 1982.

Buwari, Elias al-. *Ta'rikh al-Haraka al-'Ummaliyya wa-l-Niqabiyya fi Lubnan [History of the Labour and Union Movement in Lebanon]*. 3 vols. Beirut: Dar al-Farabi, 1986–87.

Calavita, Kitty. *Inside the State: The Bracero Program, Immigration, and the INS*. New York: Routledge, 1992.

Castles, Stephen, and Godula Kosack. *Immigrant Workers and Class Structure in Western Europe* (2nd ed.). First published in 1973. Oxford: Oxford University Press, 1985.

Castles, Stephen, and Mark J. Miller. *The Age of Migration: International Population Movements in the Modern World* (3rd ed.). Houndmills: Palgrave Macmillan, 2003.

Cermoc [collective project]. *Migrations et changements sociaux dans l'Orient arabe*. Beirut: Cermoc, 1985.

Chalcraft, John. *The Striking Cabbies of Cairo and Other Stories: Crafts and Guilds in Egypt, 1863–1914*. Albany: State University of New York Press, 2004.

Chalcraft, John, and Yaseen Noorani, eds. *Counterhegemony in the Colony and Postcolony*. Houndmills: Palgrave Macmillan, 2007.

Chami, Joseph. *Le Mémorial du Liban, Tome I: Du Mont-Liban à L'Indépendence 1861–1943*. Beirut: Chemaly & Chemaly, 2002.

———. *Le Mémorial du Liban, Tome II: le Mandat Béchara el Khoury 1943–1952*. Beirut: Chemaly & Chemaly, 2002.

———. *Le Mémorial du Liban, Tome III: le Mandat Camille Chamoun 1952–1958.* Beirut: Chemaly & Chemaly, 2002.

———. *Le Mémorial du Liban, Tome IV: le Mandat Fouad Chéhab 1958–1964.* Beirut: Chemaly & Chemaly, 2002.

Chang, Grace. *Disposable Domestics: Immigrant Women Workers in the Global Economy.* Foreword by Mimi Abramovitz. Cambridge, MA: South End Press, 2000.

Cheng, Lucie, and Edna Bonacich, eds. *Labor Immigration under Capitalism: Asian Workers in the United States before World War II.* Berkeley: University of California Press, 1984.

Chevallier, Dominique. *La société du mont Liban à l'époque de la Révolution industrielle en Europe.* Paris: Librairie orientaliste Paul Geuthner, 1971.

———. *Villes et travail en Syrie: du XIXe au XXe siècle.* Paris: G.-P. Maisonneuve & Larose, 1982.

Choueiri, Yussuf M. ed. *State and Society in Syria and Lebanon.* Exeter: University of Exeter Press, 1993.

Choy, Catherine Ceniza. *Empire of Care: Nursing and Migration in Filipino American History.* Durham: Duke University Press, 2005.

Chreitah, Moh. Bourhan. *L'Economie Syrienne et les relations économiques et douanières de la Syrie aves les voisons arabes.* Doctoral thesis, University of Fribourg, Switzerland, 1958.

Cinel, Dino. *The National Integration of Italian Return Migration, 1870–1929.* Cambridge: Cambridge University Press, 1991.

Cohen, Robin. *The New Helots: Migrants in the International Division of Labour.* Aldeshot: Avebury, 1987.

Collinson, Sarah. *Europe and International Migration.* London: Pinter Publishers, 1993.

Cooper, Frederick. *Colonialism in Question: Theory, Knowledge, History.* Berkeley: University of California Press, 2005.

Courbage, Youssef, and Philippe Fargues. *La Situation démographique au Liban: II Analyse des données.* Beirut: Publications de l'Université Libanaise, 1984.

Dah, Abdallah, Ghassan Dibeh, and Wassim Shahin. *The Distributional Impact of Taxes in Lebanon: Analysis and Policy Implications.* Beirut: The Lebanese Center for Policy Studies, 1999.

Dah, Abdallah, and Hussein Hejazi, *Tawzi'a al-Dakhl, Namat al-Anfaq wa Zahirat al-Faqr fi Lubnan [The Distribution of Income, Consumption Patterns and Poverty in Lebanon].* Beirut: The Lebanese Centre for Policy Studies, n.d.

Daher, Mas'ud. *Ta'rikh Lubnan al-Ijtima'i, 1914–1926 [The Social History of Lebanon, 1914–1926].* Beirut: Dar al-Farabi, 1974.

———. *Al-Hijra al-Lubnaniyya ila Misr: Hijrat al-Shawwam [Lebanese Emigration to Egypt: Migration of 'Syrians'].* Beirut: Lebanese University, 1986.

Davis, Mike. *Late Victorian Holocausts: El Niño Famines and the Making of the Third World*. London: Verso, 2002.

———. *Planet of Slums*. London: Verso, 2006.

Dawisha, Adeed I. *Syria and the Lebanese Crisis*. London: Macmillan Press, 1980.

de Haan, Arjan. *Unsettled Settlers: Migrant Workers and Industrial Capitalism in Calcutta*. Calcutta: K P Bagchi & Co., 1994.

De Bel Air, Françoise. *Migration et politique au Moyen-Orient*. Beirut: Institut Français du Proche-Orient, 2006.

Dowty, Alan. *Closed Borders: The Contemporary Assault on Freedom of Movement*. New Haven: Yale University Press, 1987.

Dib, Kamal. *Warlords and Merchants: The Lebanese Business and Political Establishment*. Reading: Ithaca, 2004.

Dimashqiyya, Nahad Khalil. *Al-Takammul Al-Sinaʿi Al-Suriy–Al-Lubnani: Al-Imkaniyyat wa-l-Furus [Syro-Lebanese Industrial Integration: Possibilities and Opportunities]*. Beirut: Markaz Dirasat Al-Wahda Al-ʿArabiyya, 2002.

Dubar, Claude, and Salim Nasr, *Les classes sociales au Liban*. Paris: Presses de la Fondation Nationale des Sciences Politiques, 1976.

Eley, Geoff. *A Crooked Line: From Cultural History to the History of Society*. Ann Arbor: The University of Michigan Press, 2005.

Engels, Friedrich. *Anti-Dühring: Herr Eugen Dührings's Revolution in Science*. New York: International Publishers, 1939.

Fadil, Abd al-. *Intiqal al-ʿUmmala al-ʿArabiyya: al-Mushakil, al-Athar, al-Siyasat [Movement of Arab Labour: Problems, Effects and Politics]*. Beirut: Centre for Arab Unity Studies, 1983.

Faghali, Kamal. *Al-Tahjir fi Lubnan: Astratijiyya al-ʿAwada wa Al-Inmaʾ [Migration in Lebanon: Return Strategy and Development]*. Beirut: Lebanese Center for Policy Studies, 1997.

Fahs, Adnan. *Tabaqat al-Mujtamaʿ fi al-Lubnan: qabl al-harb, ithnaʾ al-harb, baʿd al-harb [Social Classes in Lebanon: Before the War, During the War and After the War]*. N.p.: n.p, 2003.

Fisk, Robert. *Pity the Nation: Lebanon at War*. Oxford: Oxford University Press, 1990.

Freeman, Gary P. *Immigrant Labor and Racial Conflict in Industrial Societies: The French and British Experience, 1945–1975*. Princeton: Princeton University Press, 1979.

Gardner, Katy. *Global Migrants, Local Lives: Travel and Transformation in Rural Bangladesh*. Oxford: Clarendon Press, 1995.

Gaspard, Toufic K. *A Political Economy of Lebanon, 1948–2000: The Limits of Laissez-Faire*. Leiden: Brill, 2004.

Gates, Carolyn L. *The Merchant Republic of Lebanon: Rise of an Open Economy*. Oxford: Centre for Lebanese Studies (in association with I. B. Tauris), 1998.

Gelvin, James L. *Divided Loyalties: Nationalism and Mass Politics in Syria at the Close of Empire* (Berkeley: University of California Press, 1999).

Gilsenan, Michael. *Lords of the Lebanese Marches: Violence and Narrative in an Arab Society*. Berkeley: University of California Press, 1996.

Glenn, Evelyn Nakano. *Issei, Nisei, Warbride: Three Generations of Japanese American Women in Domestic Service*. Philadelphia: Temple University Press, 1986.

Glick, Clarence E. *Sojourners and Settlers: Chinese Migrants in Hawaii*. Honolulu: University Press of Hawaii, 1980.

Goethe, Johann Wolfgang von. *Elective Affinities*. First published in 1809, trans. by R. J. Hollingdale. London: Penguin, 1971.

Gonzalez, Gilbert G., and Raul A. Fernandez. *A Century of Chicano History: Empire, Nations and Migration*. New York: Routledge, 2003.

Gordon, David M., Richard Edwards, and Michael Reich, eds. *Segmented Work, Divided Workers: The Historical Transformation of Labor in the United States*. Cambridge: Cambridge University Press, 1982.

Gordon, Milton M. *Assimilation in American Life: The Role of Race, Religion and National Origin*. New York: Oxford University Press, 1964.

Grossberg, Lawrence, Cary Nelson, and Paula A. Treichler, eds. *Cultural Studies*. New York: Routledge, 1992.

Guha, Ranajit, ed. *Subaltern Studies II: Writings on South Asian History and Society*. Delhi: Oxford University Press, 1983.

——. *Subaltern Studies III: Writings on South Asian History and Society*. Delhi: Oxford University Press, 1984.

Hamdan, Kamal. *Al-Azma al-Lubnaniyya: al-Tawa'if al-Diniyya, al-Tabaqat al-Ijtima 'iyya wa-l-Huwiyya al-Wataniyya [The Lebanese Crisis: Religious Confessions, Social Classes and National Identity]*. Beirut: Dar al-Farabi, 1998.

Hamidé, Abdul-Rahman. *La région d'Alep: Etude de géographie rurale*. Paris: Université de Paris, 1959.

Hanf, Theodor. *Coexistence in Wartime Lebanon: Decline of a State and Rise of a Nation*. Trans. by John Richardson. London: I. B.Tauris, 1993.

Hanf, Theodor, and Nawaf Salam, eds. *Lebanon in Limbo: Postwar Society and State in an Uncertain Regional Environment*. Baden-Baden: Nomos Verlagsgesellschaft, 2003.

Hanna, Abdullah. *Al-Haraka Al-'Ummaliyya fi Suriya wa Lubnan, 1900–1945 [The Labor Movement in Syrian and Lebanon]*. Damascus, 1973.

——. *Dayr Attiyya: al-Ta'rikh wa-l-'Umran [Dayr Attiyya: History and Civilization]*. Damascus: Institut Français d'études Arabes à Damas (IFEAD), 2002.

——. *Al-Fallahun wa Mallak al-Ard fi Suriyya al-Qarn al-'Ashrin [Peasants and Landowners in Twentieth Century Syria]*. Beirut: Dar al-Tali'a, 2003.

Harfouche, Jamal Karam. *Social Structure of Low-Income Families in Lebanon*. Beirut: n.p. 1965.

Harris, Nigel. *Thinking the Unthinkable: The Immigration Myth Exposed*. London: I. B. Tauris, 2001.

Hilal, Jubran. *Dhikriyyat al-Niqabi [Memoirs of a Trade Unionist]*, foreword by Abdullah Hanna. Stockholm: Al-Yanabia, 2005.

Himadeh, Sa'id B., ed. *Economic Organization of Syria*. Beirut: American University of Beirut Press, 1936.

Hinnebusch, Raymond A. *Peasants and Bureaucracy in Ba'thist Syria: The Political Economy of Rural Development*. San Francisco: Westview Press, 1989.

History Task Force. *Labor Migration under Capitalism: The Puerto Rican Experience*. New York: Monthly Review Press, 1979.

Hoerder, Dirk, and Inge Blank, eds. *Roots of the Transplanted: Volume One, Late 19th Century East Central and Southeastern Europe*. New York: Columbia University Press, 1994.

Hondagneu-Sotelo, Pierrette. *Gendered Transitions: Mexican Experiences of Immigration*. Berkeley: University of California Press, 1994.

Hooglund, Eric J. *Crossing the Waters: Arabic-Speaking Immigrants to the United States Before 1940*. Washington DC: Smithsonian Institution Press, 1987.

Hourani, Albert, and Nadim Shehadi, eds. *The Lebanese in the World: A Century of Emigration*. London: I. B. Tauris, 1992.

Ignatiev, Noel. *How the Irish Became White*. New York: Routledge, 1995.

'Issa, Ghassan Ahmad. *Al-'Alaqat al-Lubnaniyya-Al-Suriyya [Syrian-Lebanese Relations]*. Beirut: Shirkat al-Matbu'at li-l-Tawzi' wa-l-Nashr, 2007.

'Issa, Najib. *Al-Quwa Al-'Amila wa Siyasat Al-'Ummala fi Lubnan [Labor Power and the Politics of the Labor Movement in Lebanon]*. Beirut: Lebanese Center for Policy Studies, 1996.

Johnson, Michael. *All Honourable Men: The Social Origins of War in Lebanon* London: I. B. Tauris, 2002.

Jurdi, 'Isam al-. *24 Nisan 1997: Muhattat Al-Inqisam fi Al-Ittihad Al-'Ummaliy Al-'Am [24 April 1997 and the Division of the General Confederation of Workers]*. Beirut: Lebanese Center for Policy Studies, 1998.

Kabaniy, Jacques, et al. *'Amilat fi Lubnan [Female Workers in Lebanon]*. N.p.: Tajammu' Al-Nisa' Al-Dimukrati, n.d.

Kapiszewski, Andrzej. *Native Arab Population and Foreign Workers in the Gulf States*. Kraków: TAiWPN Universitas, 1999.

Kassir, Samir. *'Askar 'ala Man? Lubnan al-Jumhuriyya al-Mafquda [Soldier for Whom? Lebanon the Lost Republic]*. Beirut: Dar al-Nahar, 2004.

———. *Dimuqratiyyat Suriyya wa Istiqlal Lubnan: al-Bahth 'an Rabi'a Dimashq [Syrian Democracy and the Independence of Lebanon: Searching for the Damascus Spring]*. Beirut: Al-Nahar, 2004.

Kattani, Suleiman. *Lubnan 'ala Nazif Khawasirihi*. Beirut: Dar al-Sadiq, n.d. [1970s].

Khalifa, Shawqi. *Lubnan bayn al-Jiyubulitik al-Isra'iliyya wa al-Dimughrafiyya al-Filistiniyya [Lebanon between Israeli Geopolitics and Palestinian Demography]*. Kisrawan: Dakkash, 2002.

Khater, Akram Fouad. *Inventing Home: Emigration, Gender, and the Middle Class in Lebanon, 1870–1920*. Berkeley: University of California Press, 2001.

Khoury, Philip S. *Urban Notables and Arab Nationalism: The Politics of Damascus 1860–1920*. Cambridge: Cambridge University Press, 1983.

———. *Syria and the French Mandate: The Politics of Arab Nationalism, 1920–45*. London: I. B.Tauris, 1987.

Kienle, Eberhard, ed. *Contemporary Syria: Liberalization between Cold War and Cold Peace*. London: British Academic Press, 1994.

———. *Politics from Above, Politics from Below: The Middle East in the Age of Economic Reform*. London: Saqi, 2003.

Korm, George. *Al-I'mar wa-l-Maslaha al-'Amma: fi iqtisad ma ba'd al-harb wa-siyasatahu [Reconstruction and the Public Interest: Economy and its politics after the war]*. Beirut: Dar al-Jadid, 1996.

Kritz, Mary M., Lin Lean Lim, and Hania Zlotnik, eds. *International Migration Systems: A Global Approach*. Oxford: Clarendon Press, 1992.

Kubat, Daniel, ed. *The Politics of Return: International Return Migration in Europe*. Rome: Centro Studi Emigrazione, 1983.

Latron, André. *La Vie Rurale en Syrie et au Liban*. Beirut: Institut Français de Damas, 1936.

Lawless, Richard, ed. *The Middle Eastern Village: Changing Economic and Social Relations*. London: Croom Helm, 1987.

Lewis, Norman N. *Nomads and Settlers in Syria and Jordan, 1800–1980*. Cambridge: Cambridge University Press, 1987.

Linder, Marc. *Migrant Workers and Minimum Wages: Regulating the Exploitation of Agricultural Labor in the United States*. Boulder, CO: Westview Press, 1992.

Longuenesse, Elisabeth, Gilbert Beaugé, and Michel Nancy. *Communautés villageoises et migrations de main-d'oeuvre au Moyen-Orient*. Beirut: Cermoc, 1986.

Longva, Ahn Nga. *Walls Built on Sand: Migration, Exclusion and Society in Kuwait*. Boulder, CO: Westview Press, 1997.

Luxemburg, Rosa. *Accumulation of Capital*, published in German 1913, trans. by Agnes Schwarzschild. London: Routledge, 2003.

Makdisi, Samir. *The Lessons of Lebanon: The Economics of War and Development*. London: I. B. Tauris, 2004.

Makdisi, Ussama. *The Culture of Sectarianism: Community, History, and Violence in Nineteenth-Century Ottoman Lebanon*. Berkeley: University of California Press, 2000.

Malik, Habib C. *Between Damascus and Jerusalem: Lebanon and the Middle East Peace*. Washington DC: The Washington Institute for Near East Policy, 1997.

Mardorossian, Carine M. *Reclaiming Difference: Caribbean Women Rewrite Postcolonialism*. Charlottesville: University of Virginia Press, 2005.

Marx, Karl. *Capital*, Vol. 1, introduction by Ernest Mandel, trans. by Ben Fowkes, first edition published in 1976 with Pelican Books. London: Penguin, 1990.

Meillassoux, Claude. *Maidens, Meal and Money: Capitalism and the Domestic Community*, first published in French, 1975. Cambridge: Cambridge University Press, 1981.

Meyer, Günter. *Ländliche lebens- und wirtschaftsformen Syriens im Wandel [Changing Forms of Social and Economic Life in Rural Syria]*. Erlangen: Selbstverlag de Fränkischen Geographischen Gesellschaft in Kommission bei Palm und Enke, 1984.

Mignolo, Walter D. *Local Histories/Global Designs: Coloniality, Subaltern Knowledges and Border Thinking*. Princeton: Princeton University Press, 2000.

Miller, Kerby A. *Emigrants and Exiles: Ireland and the Irish Exodus to North America*. New York: Oxford University Press, 1985.

Mintz, Sidney W. *Sweetness and Power: The Place of Sugar in Modern History*, first published in 1985. New York: Penguin, 1986.

Mitchell, Timothy. *Rule of Experts: Egypt, Techno-Politics, Modernity*. Berkeley: University of California Press, 2002.

Mundy, Martha, and Richard Saumarez Smith. *Governing Property, Making the Modern State: Law, Administration and Production in Ottoman Syria*. London: I. B. Tauris, 2007.

Naff, Alixa. *Becoming American: The Early Arab Immigrant Experience*. Carbondale: Southern Illinois University Press, 1985.

Najem, Tom Pierre. *Lebanon's Renaissance: The Political Economy of Reconstruction*. Durham Middle East Monographs Series. Reading: Ithaca Press, 2000.

Nasr, Salim, and Theodor Hanf, eds. *Urban Crisis and Social Movement: Arab and European Perspectives*. Beirut: The Euro-Arab Research Group, 1984.

Nicholls, Theo, ed. *Capital and Labour: Studies in the Capitalist Labour Process*. Glasgow: Fontana, 1980.

Nugent, Daniel, ed. *Rural Revolt in Mexico: U.S. Intervention and the Domain of Subaltern Politics*, expanded edition, foreword by William C. Roseberry. Durham: Duke University Press, 1998.

Offe, Claus. *Disorganized Capitalism: Contemporary Transformations of Work and Politics*. Oxford: Polity Press, 1985.

Ong, Paul, Edna Bonacich, and Lucie Cheng, eds. *The New Asian Immigration in Los Angeles and Global Restructuring*. Philadelphia: Temple University Press, 1994.

Ong, Aihwa. *Flexible Citizenship: The Cultural Logics of Transnationality*. Durham: Duke University Press, 1999.

Palmer, Robin, and Neil Parsons, eds. *The Roots of Rural Poverty in Central and Southern Africa*. London: Heinemann, 1977.

Pappé, Ilan. *The Modern Middle East*. London: Routledge, 2005.

Parnwell, Mike. *Population Movements and the Third World*. London: Routledge, 1993.

Pateman, Carole. *The Sexual Contract*. Cambridge: Cambridge University Press, 1988.

Perthes, Volker. *The Political Economy of Syria under Asad*. London: I. B. Tauris, 1995.

Petran, Tabitha. *Syria: A Modern History*. London: Ernest Benn Ltd., 1972.

Petras, Elizabeth McLean. *Jamaican Labor Migration: White Capital and Black Labor, 1850–1930*. Boulder, CO: Westview Press, 1988.

Picard, Elizabeth. *Lebanon: A Shattered Country*, revised edition, trans. by Franklin Philip. New York: Holmes and Meier, 2002.

Piore, Michael J. *Birds of Passage: Migrant Labor and Industrial Societies*. Cambridge: Cambridge University Press, 1979.

Polanyi, Karl. *The Great Transformation: The Political and Economic Origins of Our Time*, first published in 1944. Boston: Beacon Press, 2001.

Portes, Alejandro, ed. *The Economic Sociology of Immigration: Essays on Networks, Ethnicity, and Entrepreneurship*. New York: Russell Sage Foundation, 1995.

Potts, Lydia. *The World Labour Market: A History of Migration*, published in German 1988, trans. by Terry Bond. London: Zed Books, 1990.

Putnam, Lara. *The Company They Kept: Migrants and the Politics of Gender in Caribbean Costa Rica, 1870–1960*. Chapel Hill: University of North Carolina, 2002.

Rabo, Annika. *Change on the Euphrates: Villagers, Townsmen and Employees in North East Syria*. Stockholm: Studies in Social Anthropology, n.p., 1986.

Rajan, Kaushik Sunder. *Biocapital: The Constitution of Postgenomic Life*. Durham and London: Duke University Press, 2006.

Reilly, James A. *A Small Town in Syria: Ottoman Hama in the Eighteenth and Nineteenth Centuries*. Oxford: Peter Lang, 2002.

Resnick, Stephen A., and Richard D. Wolff. *New Departures in Marxian Theory*. London: Routledge, 2006.

Sadr, Al-Imam al-Sayyid Musa al-. *Hawarat Sahifa (2) al-Wahda wa-l-Tahrir [Dialogues with the Press (2) Unity and Liberation]*. Bir Hassan, Beirut: Imam al-Sadr Centre for Study and Research, 2000.

Sahlins, Marshall. *Stone Age Economics*, first published in 1972. London: Routledge, 2004.

Saidi, Nasser H. *Growth, Destruction and the Challenges of Reconstruction: Macroeconomic Essays on Lebanon*. Beirut: The Lebanese Center for Policy Studies, 1999.

Sales, M. E. *International Migration Project, Country Case Study: Syrian Arab Republic*. Durham: Durham University, Department of Economics, 1978.

Saliba, Najib E. "Emigration from Syria," in *Arabs in the New World: Studies on Arab-American Communities*, edited by Sameer Y. Abraham and Nabeel Abraham. Detroit: Wayne State University Press, 1983.

Sassen, Saskia. *The Mobility of Labor and Capital: A Study in International Investment and Labor Flow*. Cambridge: Cambridge University Press, 1988.

———. *Guests and Aliens*. New York: The New Press, 1999.

Sawayd, Yasin. *Al-Masa'la al-Lubnaniyya: naqd wa tahlil [The Lebanese Question: Critique and Analysis]*. Beirut: al-Shirka al-'Alimiyya li-l-Kitab, 1998.

Seale, Patrick. *Asad of Syria: The Struggle for the Middle East*. London: I. B. Tauris, 1988.

Seikaly, May. *Haifa: Transformation of an Arab Society, 1918–1939*. London: I. B. Tauris, 2002.

Shafir, Gershon. *Land, Labor and the Origins of the the Israeli-Palestinian Conflict, 1882–1914*. Cambridge, Cambridge University Press, 1989.

Shalhub, Tanawwas Wadi'a. *al-Salamat al-Sina'iyya wa Bi'at al-'Amal fi al-Sina'a Al-Lubnaniyya [Industrial Safety and the Work Environment in Lebanese Industry]*. Beirut: Lebanese Center for Policy Studies, 1998.

Shami, Ali. *Tatawwur al-Tabqa al-'Amila al-Lubnaniyya fi Ra'smaliyya al-Lubnaniyya al-Mu'asira [The Development of the Lebanese Working Class in Contemporary Lebanese Capitalism]*. Beirut: Dar al-Farabi, 1981.

Shami, Seteney, ed. *Population Displacement and Resettlement: Development and Conflict in the Middle East*. New York: Center for Migration Studies, 1994.

Sharara, Waddah. *Al-Salm al-Ahali al-Barid: Lubnan al-Mujtami' wa-l-Dawla, 1964–1967 [The Cold Peace: Lebanon, State and Society, 1964–1967]*. 2 vols. Tripoli (Libya): Ma'had Al-Anma' Al-'Arabi, 1980.

Smith, Adam. *The Wealth of Nations*, edited by Edwin Cannan. Chicago: University of Chicago Press, 1976.

Swanson, Jon C. *Emigration and Economic Development: The Case of the Yemen Arab Republic*. Boulder, CO: Westview Press, 1979.

Sweet, Louise E. *Tell Toqaan: A Syrian Village*. Anthropological Papers No. 14. Ann Arbor: University of Michigan, 1960.

Taymumi, Al-Hadi Al-. *Al-Mughayyibun fi Tarikh Tunis al-Ijtima'i [The Invisible Men of the Social History of Tunis]*. Tunis: Bayt al-Hikma, Ministry of Culture, 1999.

Thoumin, Richard. *Géographie Humaine de la Syrie Centrale*. Paris: Libraire Ernest Leroux, 1936.

Traboulsi, Fawwaz. *Silat bi-la-Wasl: Michel Chicha wa-l-aydiyulujiyya al-Lubnaniyya*. Beirut: Riad Rayess Books, 1999.

Traboulsi, Fawwaz. *A History of Modern Lebanon*. London: Pluto Press, 2007.

Valter, Stéphane. *La construction nationale syrienne: Légitimation de la nature communautaire du pouvoir par le discours historique*. Paris: CNRS Éditions, 2002.

Van Dam, Nikolaos. *The Struggle for Power in Syria: Politics and Society under Asad and the Ba'th Party*. London: I. B.Tauris, 1979.

Van Hear, Nicholas. *New Diasporas: The Mass Exodus, Dispersal and Regrouping of Migrant Communities*. London: UCL Press, 1998.

Weber, Max. *The Protestant Ethic and the Spirit of Capitalism*, first published in 1930, trans. by Talcott Parsons. London: Routledge, 1992.

Weulersse, Jacques. *Paysans de Syrie et du Proche-Orient*. N.p.: Gallimard, 1946.

Williams, Richard. *Hierarchical Structures and Social Value: The Creation of Black and Irish Identities in the United States*. Cambridge: Cambridge University Press, 1990.

Wilson, Francis. *Labour in the South African Gold Mines (1911–1969)*. Cambridge: Cambridge University Press, 1972.

Wilson, Rob, and Wimal Dissanayake, eds., *Global Local: Cultural Production and the Transnational Imaginary*. Durham: Duke University Press, 1996.

Winckler, Onn. *Demographic Developments and Population Policies in Ba'thist Syria*. Brighton, UK: Sussex Academic Press, 1999.

Wolf, Eric R. *Europe and the People without History*, illustrations by Noel L. Diaz, first published in 1982. Berkeley: University of California Press, 1997.

Yamut, Abdulhadi. *Al-Iqtisad al-Lubnani wa Afaq al-Sharq Awsatiyya wa-l-'Awlima [The Lebanese Economy, the Middle East and Globalization]*. Lebanon: Al-Shirka al-'Ilmiyya li-l-Kitab, 2005.

Yashu'i, Iyli. *Al-Qita' Al-Sina'i fi Lubnan: Al-Waqi'a wa Al-Siyasat Al-Mustaqbiliyya [The Industrial Sector in Lebanon: Reality and the Politics of the Future]*. Beirut: Lebanese Center for Policy Studies, 1996.

Young, Michael. *Migrant Workers in Lebanon*. Beirut: Lebanese NGO Forum, 2000.

INDEX

Tripoli, 56, 124, 130, 156, 190, 197; Syrian
    workers in, 93; violence between sects
    in, 110
Tueni, Gibran, 199
Turkey, 27
Turkmen, 26

Uneven incorporation, 28–29
Unintended consequences, 11–12, 47–49
United Arab Republic of Syria and Egypt,
    1958–1961, 69, 77
United Nations in Beirut (ESCWA), 135
United Nations Security Council Resolution
    1559 of 2004, 202
United States, 8, 17, 18, 21, 25, 42, 44, 53, 54,
    157; adds Syria to "axis of evil," 201;
    allows Syria some control in Lebanon,
    136; cooling of relationship with
    Syria, 197; and Hafez al-Asad, 137, 139;
    hegemony of, after World War II, 53;
    invasion and occupation of Iraq, 205;
    as place where economists trained, 161;
    restrictions on immigration, 49
United States Marines, 78
Unsettled circulation between Syria and
    Lebanon, 20
Unsettlement, prolonged, 20–23
Unsettlement in Lebanon, 206–212
Uruguay, 49

Venezuela, 53
Violence and killings, 109–112
Violence in Lebanon, 201–204
Voluntary labor migrants, 24
Voluntary labor migration, 134

"Voluntary" migration, 222
Voluntary migrants, 15

War of words, 192–197; the economy, 193–195;
    numbers, 195–197
Wata Mussaitbé, 56
Weber, Max, 6, 11
Welfare mothers, 18
West Africa, 15, 53
West Beirut, 115, 123, 127–129
Weulersse, Jacques, 29–30, 31, 35, 46
Widmer, Robert, 25, 26, 37, 38, 40
Wilson, Francis, 3
Winckler, Onn, 94, 95
Women: Alawi workers, 84; labor controlled
    by men, 220; and *maquila* programs, 8;
    and Mexican migration, 21, 22; role in
    household economy, 90, 99–100, 207;
    Syrian migrants, 17, 21–22, 46
Work permits, 73–75, 118, 142, 145, 225; held
    by Asian workers, 95–96
World economic disarticulation, 49

Yabroud, 26
Yamani, Maher al-, 191
"Yellow peril," 1
Yusuf, Abu, 59–60

Zabib, Muhammad, 193, 194
Zahleh, 201
Zahrahy, 200
Zgorta, 27
Zolberg, Aristide R., 16